ADVERTISING

TOWER

JAPANESE MODERNISM

AND MODERNITY

IN THE 1920s

Harvard East Asian Monographs, 260

ADVERTISING

TOWER

JAPANESE MODERNISM
AND MODERNITY
IN THE 1920s

WILLIAM GARDNER

Published by the Harvard University Asia Center
and distributed by Harvard University Press
Cambridge (Massachusetts) and London 2006

Printed in the United States of America

The Harvard University Asia Center publishes a monograph series and, in coordination with the Fairbank Center for East Asian Research, the Korea Institute, the Reischauer Institute of Japanese Studies, and other faculties and institutes, administers research projects designed to further scholarly understanding of China, Japan, Vietnam, Korea, and other Asian countries. The Center also sponsors projects addressing multidisciplinary and regional issues in Asia.

Library of Congress Cataloging-in-Publication Data
    Advertising tower : Japanese modernism and modernity in the 1920s / William O. Gardner.
       p. cm.
Includes bibliographical references and index.
    isbn 0–674–02129–0 (cloth : alk. paper)
    1. Japanese literature—Taisho period, 1912–1926—History and criticism. 2. Modernism (Literature)--Japan. 3. Hagiwara, Kyojiro, 1899–1938. 4. Hayashi, Fumiko, 1904–1951. I. Title.
    pl726.63.m577g37 2006
    895.6'09112--dc22

                                      2006000332

Index by Jake Kawatski

♾ Printed on acid-free paper

Last figure below indicates year of this printing
16 15 14 13 12 11 10 09 08 07 06

ACKNOWLEDGMENTS

I am grateful to many people for their support and assistance during the years I was preparing this book. First of all, I would like to thank my dissertation advisor, Professor Makoto Ueda, for his guidance, for the example of his teaching and writing, and for encouraging my interest in Japanese modernism. Also, I sincerely appreciate the instruction and mentoring offered by my other professors at Stanford, especially the extraordinary ongoing support and friendship of Thomas Hare. Other faculty to whom I owe debts of instruction and research guidance include Jeffrey Schnapp, Susan Matisoff, Haun Saussy, Marjorie Perloff, and James Reichert. I would also like to thank a number of talented scholars who provided invaluable research advice and encouragement: Gennifer Weisenfeld, John Treat, Miryam Sas, Miriam Silverberg, Yasushi Ishii, Yoshio Abe, Walter K. Lew, Atsuko Sakaki, and Anne Soon Choi. Many of these scholars generously read sections of the manuscript and provided essential criticisms and guidance, for which I am very grateful. Any errors of fact or judgment in the book are my responsibility alone.

While doing research at the University of Tokyo, I was fortunate to benefit from the stimulating guidance of Professors Toshiko Ellis and Yōichi Komori. Both were remarkably generous with their time despite many other demands, and each of them was instrumental to the development of my research and analysis. For financial support during various stages of my research and writing, I am grateful to the Fulbright Foundation, the Freeman Foundation, Stanford

University, Middlebury College, and Swarthmore College. In addition, I would like to give my sincere thanks for the two anonymous readers for the Harvard University Asia Center, who offered many insightful and helpful criticisms on the manuscript, and to Ann Klefstad and Cheryl Tucker and the rest of the editorial staff of the Asia Center Publications Program.

For igniting my interest in Japanese literature, I am grateful to my undergraduate teachers at Columbia University, in particular Professors Paul Anderer, Amy Heinrich, and Donald Keene. Finally, I would like to thank my fellow graduate students at Stanford University and my colleagues at Middlebury and Swarthmore Colleges, whose friendship has made been so important to important to me during the years I have been at work on the book. This book is dedicated with love and gratitude to my parents and sister.

W.G.

CONTENTS

ADVERTISING

TOWER

JAPANESE MODERNISM
AND MODERNITY
IN THE 1920s

INTRODUCTION

This book will examine some of the responses of Japanese authors to the transformation of the Japanese city in the early decades of the twentieth century. In particular, it will observe the themes and formal strategies of the modernist literature that flourished in the 1920s, focusing on the work of Hagiwara Kyōjirō (1899–1938) and Hayashi Fumiko (1903–51). I argue that modernist literature developed in part as a response to the development of mass media and a new conception of the "masses" in interwar Japan, and show how modernist works present new constructions of individual subjectivity amid the social and technological changes that provided the ground for the appearance of mass media. Hagiwara Kyōjirō's conception of the poem and the poet transformed into an electric-radio "advertising tower" offers an emblem for the aesthetic tensions and multiple discourses of technology, media, urbanism, commerce, and propaganda that were circulating through the urban environment of the 1920s.

The proliferation of advertising messages invoked by Hagiwara's advertising tower, while gradual, was surely one of the most pervasive aspects of the transformation of the Japanese urban environment in the early decades of the twentieth century. Newspaper advertisements serve as one barometer of the growing scale of the advertising industry: increasing in step with the expanding circulation of newspapers themselves, the total yearly number of newspaper advertisements increased nearly sevenfold over the course of the

Taishō era (1912–26).[1] During the same period, posters and hand-bills proliferated in the urban landscape. On a December morning in 1925, a newspaper reporter reported receiving 25 different handbills in an hour's walk from Shinbashi to Kyōbashi in downtown Tokyo, advertising a diverse array of goods, shops, and attractions, including Western-style clothing, furniture, and sweet shops, charity organizations, phonograph recordings, plays, films, and a mysterious category of "strange cards" (*fushigi no kādo*), perhaps advertising demimonde services not fit for mention in the newspaper.[2] Advertising messages circulated on trains and buses and spread across the ephemera of city life, appearing on matchbook covers, business cards, and train tickets.

From the turn of the century, the architecture of storefronts in Tokyo had been transformed to include show windows, and by the 1920s some of the most innovative artists of the day were employed in creating window displays for prominent retail establishments such as Mitsukoshi department store or Maruzen bookstore.[3] Giant shop signs incorporating product advertisements spread across the city's commercial districts, and with the electrification of the city, a variety of illuminated advertising displays and shop signs vied for public attention. An advertising signboard employing roughly 1,000 electric light bulbs was erected in Tokyo's Asakusa Rokku entertainment district as early as 1903, while neon signs began to appear widely in the late 1920s, becoming an integral part of the architecture of new urban entertainments such as the cafés and dance halls that mushroomed across Tokyo after the Great Kanto Earthquake of 1923.[4]

The advertising industry was steadily professionalized and internationalized over the first three decades of the century, and innovative advertisers and entrepreneurs experimented with a variety of media to fill the stores, streets, and skies with their messages. "Sandwich men" walked the streets wearing signboards, *chindonya* bands announced sales as they paraded through the city, while stylish "mannequin girls" modeled clothes and promoted goods in stores.[5] Large companies such as Kirin Beer assembled brigades of advertising automobiles, and took to the air with airplane leaflet drops and "ad balloons," tethered hot air balloons that hoisted huge banners over the city streets.[6]

The activities of advertisers, and the new entertainment culture and patterns of consumption that they promoted, helped to define a new urban aesthetic. In a 1929 article on commercial building design for a landmark twenty-four-volume book set on the commercial arts, Mitsukoshi department store's chief designer, Hamada Masaji, offered a paradigmatic summation of this aesthetic. Drawing on terms in wide circulation in the 1920s, Hamada described the city as possessing a "phenomenological beauty" (*genshōbi*), consisting of "jazz, light, complexity, change, display windows, shop signs, marches, speed—a complex symphony of every tempo."[7]

The spread of advertising was not limited to capitalist enterprises, however: political parties, workers' organizations, and political and social interest groups of various stripes also vied to spread their messages across the city's public spaces. Government bureaucrats, alarmed by the spread of consumer culture and new urban entertainments, launched their own massive propaganda campaigns in the 1920s to promote "diligence and thrift." During the 1930s, as Japan became absorbed in wars for imperial power on the Asian continent, government ministries carried out increasingly vigorous propaganda campaigns to promote their colonial efforts and encourage patriotic sentiment.[8]

How would literature, a cultural field dominated by written language as mediated by the print industry, respond to this environment, increasingly saturated by the words and ever-changing signs of advertising and political propaganda? At the height of his collaboration with the avant-garde Mavo artists' group, many of whom were active in both commercial design and leftist propaganda, poet Hagiwara Kyōjirō ventured one extreme reply. In two works from the mid-1920s, Hagiwara imagined both the poet and the poem morphing into an "advertising tower" (*kōkokutō*), suggesting that the mode of poetic literature would necessarily transform itself to survive in an age of new technologies that were circulating words as advertising and propaganda. In a satirical sketch for the *MAVO* journal of a robotlike assemblage festooned with advertising messages, Hagiwara imbedded the apocalyptic message, "All forms of poetic literature are destroyed—now they will be replaced by the electric-radio advertising tower!!" (see Fig. 1).[9]

Author Hayashi Fumiko offered one perspective on the psycho-

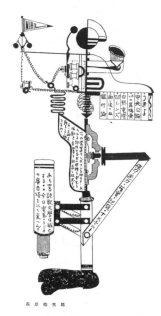

森 原 恭 次 郎

FIG. 1: Hagiwara Kyōjirō, untitled sketch, originally published in
MAVO, no. 5 (June 1925): 31. Reprinted in Hagiwara Kyōjirō,
Shikei senkoku, reprint edition (Tokyo: Nihon kindai bungakukan,
1972), as an unpaginated insert.

logical aspects of life as a writer in this advertising-saturated environment. In the postscript to the sequel of her bestselling novel *Hōrōki*,
Hayashi wrote of the disconcerting experience of seeing the words
"Hayashi Fumiko" written on advertising posters for magazines,
prompting her to wonder "just who this Hayashi Fumiko could
be." She identified an experience of alienation between an interior
self and the authorial self circulating in the marketplace of linguistic
signs. Moreover, she introduced this experience as a symptom of a
more pervasive condition of schizophrenia experienced while living
in an urban environment dominated by an advertising imperative.
"My way of living today," she wrote, "is like chopping myself into
pieces and throwing myself in every direction, like an advertisement."[10]

The works of Hagiwara and Hayashi provide two vantage points
on the cultural landscape in which writers were forced to reexamine
the very nature of literature in the 1920s. As urban Japan was being

transformed by ever more aggressive commercial strategies, works of literature were increasingly perceived as commodities. Indeed, as consumer items, literary books and magazines were subject to some of the largest and most innovative advertising campaigns of their day. The perception of the advancing commercialization of literature produced a strong reaction among some writers and critics who sought to define and defend "pure literature." As this defense of "pure literature" was taking shape, other writers organized a movement for "Proletarian Literature," inveighing against both the capitalist commoditization of literature and the hermetic ideals of literary purists, arguing instead for the role of cultural activity in transforming the people's political consciousness, and agitating for workers' rights and socialist revolution. This book will examine the ways in which modernist writers apprehended the changing nature of the Japanese urban landscape, the nature of the literary work, and the experience of the individual in the tumultuous interwar period, amid the competing aesthetic and political conceptions of advocates of "pure literature," "popular literature," and "Proletarian Literature."

IN EXAMINING ACCOUNTS of the social changes in Japan between the two world wars, among the themes that stand out most prominently are the Great Kanto Earthquake as both symbol and catalyst of Japan's urban transformation, the idea of "Taishō Democracy" (*Taishō demokurashii*) used to index the period's political and social liberalization, and the employment of the terms "modern" (*modan*) and "modern life" to describe the new lifestyles and cultural forms emerging in the interwar years. While each of these themes and frameworks has its limitations as a descriptive or interpretive tool, each serves to highlight different aspects of the social, political, and material transformations to which writers and artists of the period responded.

For many observers, the anxieties and utopic possibilities of the age were captured in a single event: the destruction of Tokyo in the Great Kanto Earthquake of 1923 and its subsequent reconstruction. This disaster devastated much of the Tokyo-Yokohama region, the massive quake and its subsequent raging fires leveling most of central Tokyo and leaving over 100,000 dead. Underlying social tensions in the capital city were painfully revealed in the chaos immediately following the quake, when police murdered numerous prominent dissidents and labor organizers, and bands of vigilantes lynched thousands of Koreans, Chinese, and suspected communists. In the wake of the disaster, numerous commentators compared the shock of the event, and the social and political chaos that followed it, with the upheaval and trauma recently experienced by Europeans in the Great War. Tokyo's residents were exposed to the unfamiliarity of life in temporary structures, and witnessed the appearance of a new cityscape and infrastructure above the ashes and rubble. Diverse groups of Tokyoites participated in the city's reconstruction, including the artists' groups who painted the temporary buildings with expressionistic designs and submitted competing plans for the new city. While some writers mourned the loss of the old city, others praised the spirit of creative improvisation that replaced it. In the journalism of the day and in many personal narratives afterwards, this chance event became an emblem of the destruction of the old order and the herald of a new era of innovation.[11]

The Great Kanto Earthquake has powerful appeal as a narrative event inaugurating a new era. However, the earthquake could more accurately be seen as accelerating changes already under way in such fields as architecture, transportation, and media enterprises, including the print industry. In political terms, the aftermath of the earthquake was only one of a series of periodic crises when the ongoing confrontation between the state and dissidents became particularly acute—a series of crises that would include the High Treason Trial of 1910–11, in which twelve anarchists and socialists were executed for their alleged participation in a plot to assassinate the emperor, and the massive roundup of Communist Party activists and other dissidents in 1927 under the newly inaugurated Peace Preservation Law.

Despite such periodic crises, postwar historians have memorialized the 1910s and 1920s as the heyday of Taishō Democracy, an interval of relative political liberalization marked by diverse popular movements, the rise of party politics, and the passage of the Universal Manhood Suffrage Act in 1925. Critics have pointed out the limitations and deep-seated contradictions of this "democracy"—contradictions epitomized by the passage, in the same Diet session as the Suffrage Act, of the Peace Preservation Law, giving authorities sweeping powers to crack down on thought offenders deemed to threaten the emperor-centered "national polity" (*kokutai*). Among the intelligentsia, the late 1920s are characterized less by an embrace of the possibilities of democratic political participation than a despair of the possibilities of working within the current political and economic system, and an advocacy of direct worker action and socialist revolution, leading to a confrontation between communist activists and authorities prepared to enforce the Peace Preservation Law. Nevertheless, the interwar years do mark the emergence of diverse groups of activists from across the political spectrum, including political parties, labor unions, tenant farmers' groups, women's organizations, outcast groups, and neighborhood organizations. Amid these various pluralities, ideologues of several orientations imagined the emergence of even wider social groupings: "the crowds" (*gunshū*), "the people" (*minshū*), "the masses" (*taishū*), and "national subjects" (*kokumin*). While the term "Taishō Democracy" may be misleading in describing the diverse political developments of the interwar years, it lingers as a convenient if somewhat timeworn sign pointing toward the emergence of these contesting social and political groups, of which advocates of liberal democracy were but one part.[12]

More recently, Japanese cultural historians have employed the term *modan* (modern) to describe the culture of the 1920s. In doing so, they have revived a word that was central to metropolitan Japan's self-perception in the post-earthquake era. Inaugurated by sweeping changes in urban design and architecture, transportation, communications, and entertainment media; punctuated by bold new fashions in clothing, makeup, and gesture—new ways of being in the city were described as "modern life" (expressed with the loan words *modan raifu* or with the Sino-Japanese gloss *kindai seikatsu*). Modern life's youngest and most fashionable practitioners were lampooned, excoriated, and praised under the labels of *modan gāru* (modern girl) and *modan boi* (modern boy). A school of urban ethnologists documented the transformations of urban life, identifying their discipline as *kōgengaku,* or modernology, on the analogy of *kōkogaku,* or archaeology. Finally, an innovative generation of writers coming on the scene in this decade were identified by critic

Hirabayashi Hatsunosuke as "modernists" and described by Ōya Sōichi as being on the *sentan* or "cutting edge" of "modern life."[13]

Without any pretense of restricting Japan's experience of modernity to one decade, we can confirm the importance of the 1920s as the time when many of the hallmarks of modernity—urbanization, the experience of simultaneity, the proliferation of new media, the transformation of gender roles—occupied the center of national attention, and a diverse range of public voices vied to represent and define this modernity. The rapidly expanding world of print journalism, the diversifying realm of literary production, and rival media such as film and popular music were themselves important aspects of this modernity as well as the chief venues for the representation and contestation of "modern life." The present study takes up the critical challenge, first essayed by Ōya and Hirabayashi, of probing the relationship between the modernist literatures that made a vivid appearance in the 1920s, and the rapidly transforming experience of urban life during the same period. In other words, it explores the relationship between Japanese modernism and Japanese modernity.

THIS EXAMINATION OF Japanese modernism will focus on the positions taken by modernist writers with regard to two interconnected but often conflicting phenomena: individual subjectivity and mass society. The delineation of individual subjectivity has been widely recognized as a cornerstone of Western philosophical and literary modernity. It has also been a crucial register for the self-constitution of Japanese modernity following the Meiji Restoration of 1868, as well as a recurring locus of anxiety in relation to the paradigmatically modern West, with its putative realization of the modern individual subject. Hence the approaches to individual subjectivity taken by modernist writers in the 1920s are part of a larger continuum of positions in regard to a problematic of individualism and subjectivity, which is roughly co-terminal with "modern" (post-Restoration) Japan.[14]

By contrast, the second of these phenomena, that of mass society, is more strongly associated with the 1920s in particular. While hopes and anxieties regarding "the people" (*minshū*) and "the crowds" (*gunshū*) are an integral part of the discourse associated with the movement toward "Taishō Democracy" inaugurated in the previous decade, the full articulation of a concept of "the masses" (*taishū*) can be persuasively traced to the mid-1920s. As Chapter 1 will outline, this concept of "the masses" was made possible by a major leap in the technology and diffusion of mass media, including the expansion of the print, film, and recorded music industries, and the appearance of the new medium of radio. Japanese modernist and avant-garde literature, I will argue, must be read as an active response to the possibilities and threats of these new media and the "masses," which they helped to constitute. Literary modernists contested the future of mass media and mass society with other voices in the public sphere—including competing literary and political groups—and with the Japanese state itself. Indeed, a recognition of the state as the key antagonist in the struggle over cultural production and reception was a primary basis for the strong connection between literary modernism / avant-garde and political anarchism.

Amid the diversity of Japanese avant-garde and modernist movements in the 1920s, I have chosen to focus on two writers whose works bring the questions of individual subjectivity and mass society into particularly high relief: the avant-garde poet Hagiwara Kyōjirō, and the poet and prose writer Hayashi Fumiko. In the mid-1920s these two writers shared the same milieu of cafés and cheap lodgings in the Hongō section of Tokyo, where aspiring writers and artists mixed with left-wing activists and theoreticians. They shared the same outlets for their works in the coterie journals associated with the artistic avant-garde and the political left. Yet their writings, while displaying many thematic and stylistic commonalities, ultimately reveal two distinct views of Japanese modernity.

Hagiwara Kyōjirō's first poetry collection, *Shikei senkoku* (*Death Sentence*, 1925), was the product of his collaboration with the Mavo group, a collective of avant-garde visual artists formed in June 1923, a few months before the Great Kanto Earthquake. *Shikei senkoku* featured poems of striking visual immediacy, employing characters of different sizes and orientations (to be read in multiple directions), combined with non-character elements such as dots, circles, triangles, lines, bars, and arrows: a visual style closely related to the "words-in-liberty" of the Italian Futurists and the "ferro-concrete poems" of Russian Futurist Vasily Kemensky. These strongly visual poems are integrated with the work of Mavo members: the linocut prints of

Okada Tatsuo and ten others, and photographs of the sketches, collages, assemblages, and architectural projects of nine artists including Okada, Hagiwara himself, Yanase Masamu, Ōura Shūzō, Mavo leader Murayama Tomoyoshi, and (non-Mavoist) Vladimir Tatlin, father of the Russian Constructivist movement. In its arrangement of printed characters and its incorporation of collage elements, Hagiwara's collection reflects a heightened awareness of the materiality of the poetic text and its mediation in print culture, an acute consciousness of media shared by many modernist writers and artists of the 1920s.

Construction (*kōsei*) was a key term for Murayama, Okada, and Hagiwara, and the alternating architectural and theatrical disposition of characters on the page, together with the integration of textual and nontextual visual material, distinguish *Shikei senkoku* as a landmark in the Mavo group's project of collective construction. Yet this poetry collection, with its distinctly anarchist political overtones, cannot be said to foreground the utilitarian aspects of the Constructivist movement. Rather, the collection can be taken as a provocation to its readers to imagine new constructions of subjectivity, untried possibilities of the artwork, and subversive political attitudes. Like many of the Mavo works, it exemplifies what Murayama called "Constructivism as an elementary slap in the face . . . Constructivism as Dada."[15]

In Chapters 3 and 6, I trace Hagiwara's career from his contributions to the Mavo group's urban avant-garde, through his intense involvement with the anarchist cause, his turn toward agrarianism, and his eventual endorsement of Japanese Imperialism. Throughout this varied trajectory, Hagiwara's intertwined conceptions of individual subjectivity and mass society prove central to both his avant-garde poetics and his confrontation with historical modernity. A reading of Hagiwara thus compels equal attention to the aesthetic and political valences of his work. This reading will be conducted in parallel with an examination of the early work of Hayashi Fumiko, who at the start of her career shared the same bohemian Tokyo milieu, and many of the same thematic concerns, as Hagiwara and the Mavoists.

Although she later became famous for her prose narratives, in the mid-1920s Hayashi was an obscure poet loosely associated with the anarchists and avant-garde poets who frequented the Café Lebanon in Hongō; her poems appeared, for example, in the fifth and sixth issues of the *MAVO* journal, co-edited by Murayama, Okada, and Hagiwara. Her first novel, *Hōrōki* (*Diary of a Vagabond*), was constructed out of her poems and of the diaries she kept during this period (Hagiwara and associates appear as characters), together with telegrams, shopping lists, fragments of popular songs, and other textual "found objects." Segments of *Hōrōki* appeared from October 1928 through September 1930 in the feminist journal *Nyonin geijutsu*. When the novel was published in book form in July 1930, it was an immediate best seller, prompting the publication of a sequel, *Zoku hōrōki*, in November of the same year, and propelling Hayashi on a career path very different from that of her fellow poets of the Café Lebanon.

Hayashi's reworking of her diaries, poems, and other textual materials is a work of construction closely akin to the work of the Mavo group and other avant-garde and modernist artists. In her presentation of "diary" entries and in her employment of montage techniques, Hayashi accentuates leaps, gaps, and often disorienting shifts in the work's narrative structure and temporal/spatial reference. This produces the effect of foregrounding the elements of *speed* and *tempo*, which—associated with such new urban phenomena as assembly lines, subways, motor cars, motion pictures, telephones, and radio communication—became key words in the 1920s discourse of modernity.[16]

Furthermore, her thematic material, which centers on such basics of urban survival as the search for work, food, and lodging, together with her inclusion of shopping lists, songs, and other "reality fragments" (to borrow Adorno's phrase), points toward the contemporary avant-garde impulse to connect art with everyday life. Indeed "everyday life" (*seikatsu*),[17] like "construction," "tempo," and "speed," became a watchword of the Japanese avant-garde, as the following passage from a newspaper column by Hagiwara Kyōjirō illustrates:

The fast tempo of our society. Our revolving lives. Machinelike speed. Luminescent ebullience, heat, lateral movement, vertical movement. The multileveled, three-dimensional form that spreads out from the many facets of our daily life, rivaling the greatest artworks, effecting a fusion of craft and nature unimagined even by artists. We mustn't overlook the importance of this everyday life.[18]

In reconstituting her diary, poems, and found texts into a kaleidoscopic portrait of a young female protagonist, Hayashi Fumiko presented her readers with a unique perspective on the construction of "everyday life" in modern Japan. The intertextual references to popular songs, plays, and movies in Hayashi's work suggest an understanding of everyday life as the interface between individual subjectivity and a highly mediated environment, in which the individual self is shaped in part by mass-media representations. As I argue in Chapters 4 and 5, Hayashi's *Hōrōki* presents us with both a personal history of one individual's subject-formation and a national history of the development of a mass society. This perspective on the interwoven construction of the individual subject and a new mass society makes *Hōrōki* a particularly valuable text for illuminating the Japanese experience of modernity.

Despite the importance of metropolitan concerns to modernist writing, it should be noted that like the vast majority of Japanese modernist and avant-garde writers in the interwar period, Hagiwara and Hayashi were not Tokyo natives, but provincial immigrants. Unlike the majority of modernists, however, Hagiwara and Hayashi did not repress their provincial origins, but instead made the issue of the relationship between the metropole and the provinces central to their work. Thus an engagement with these two writers' works compels the reader to confront not only urban modernity, but urban modernity's Other, the countryside. Indeed, while the issue is central to both writers, Hagiwara and Hayashi reveal quite different perspectives on the relationship between metropole and province. Moreover, given the imperialist nature of the Japanese nation-state in the post–Meiji Restoration era, the complex dialectic between metropole and province within the Japanese archipelago is further complicated by the Japanese metropole's relation to colonial and semicolonial territories throughout East Asia and the Pacific. The relationship between Japanese *naichi*, or "home territories," and *gaichi*, or colonial "outer territories," is of vital importance to the development of Japanese modernity, and of Japanese modernist and avant-garde literature as one constituent element of this moder nity. A broader consideration of the global situation of Japanese modernism in the age of imperialism will precede my close analysis of works by Hagiwara and Hayashi.

BEFORE PROCEEDING WITH this analysis, however, we might first step back to ask whether "Japanese modernism" and "Japanese modernity" are plausible terms within the contemporary historical field. It is no accident that Euro-American histories have for a long time largely ignored Japanese modernist and avant-garde movements (particularly the prewar variety) or dismissed them as shallow and short-lived imitations of Western artistic trends. This dismissal, which is far from being an "objective" value judgment, has been predetermined by an interpretive system in which truly authentic "modernism" and "modernity" can have occurred only in the West. Moreover, this Euro-American judgment is a mirror-reversed reflection and confirmation of the similar disavowal of Japanese modernism as inauthentic in Japanese nationalist discourse of the 1930s and 1940s.

Rather than being simply a temporal or descriptive term, the concept of "modernity" is intractably rooted in the historical self-recognition and self-realization of the West. As critic Takeuchi Yoshimi suggested as early as 1948, it is only through the encounter with the non-West, troped as the premodern, that the modern West has been able to fully realize its modernity and constitute itself as a historical subject. According to Takeuchi's analysis, the process of self-transformation, self-expansion, and liberation, first experienced in overcoming feudalism, served both to define Europe for itself and to ensure that this self-recognition could be sustained only through a constant overcoming of limits. This "fundamental self-extensiveness" found its expression through an invasive movement into the Orient. Thus, in the Orient's political, economic, and cultural resistance to Europe, Takeuchi finds the elements that will bring "World History to a greater degree of completion," both by providing the resistance that will allow self-extensive Europe to realize itself and through the fact that, in order to resist Europe, the Orient was itself compelled to "Europeanize":[19]

Through resistance, the Orient modernized itself. The history of resistance is the history of modernization; there was no path to modernization except through resistance. Europe recognized its own victory in the process by which the Orient was enfolded into World History through its resistance. This was conceived of as cultural, racial, or productive superiority. The Orient recognized its defeat through the same process. Defeat is the result of resistance; there is no defeat without resistance.[20]

Even in describing the Orient's resistance to the West, Takeuchi encounters familiar tropes of adoption and defeat. Historian Naoki Sakai expands on Takeuchi's thesis as follows:

As is amply shown by the fact that the Orient had to modernize and adopt things from the West in order to resist it, the modernization of the Orient attests to an advance or success for the West, and, therefore, it is always Westernization or Europeanization. So it necessarily appears that, even in its resistance, the Orient is subjugated to the mode of representation dominated by the West. And its attempt to resist the West is doomed to fail; the Orient cannot occupy the position of a subject. Is it possible, then, to define the Orient as that which can never be a subject?[21]

Even in Japan's effort to "resist" Western domination through the "self-extension" of its Asian imperialism, historians have frequently resorted to the concept of mimesis.[22] Such mimesis, however, has seldom been conceived of as a single moment of realization, but rather a process that, like Zeno's runner, never quite reaches its object.

In other words, the mimetic processes of non-Western modernities have typically been emplotted on what Dipesh Chakrabarty of the *Subaltern Studies* collective has referred to as a "transition narrative." The "transition narrative" of "modernization" has had the dual effect of further reifying the West as the site of seamless and fully realized modernity (Chakrabarty's "hyperreal 'Europe'") and of ensuring that modernity in the non-West will be regarded as deficient—what Chakrabarty identifies in the South Asian case as "the tendency to read Indian history in terms of a lack, an absence, or an incompleteness that translates into 'inadequacy.'"[23]

One might argue, however, that Japan has often been regarded as the exception to this rule of non-Western inadequacy—as the one case of successful "modernization," which has thus demanded an interpretive apparatus to explain its exceptional status. Such views of Japanese exceptionalism typically downplay the "dark valley" of

Japan's war years as an aberration between its prewar industrial-democratic tutelage and its postwar prosperity. Yet even those readings that would regard Japan as a successful modernizer still derive all their categories for this appraisal from the Western experience of modernity; the mimetic framework for understanding the Japanese historical experience is unchanged.

In reviewing the critiques of Takeuchi, Sakai, and Chakrabarty, I do not intend to argue that it is feasible to abandon the notion of modernity in discussing Japan. As Takeuchi makes clear, from the viewpoint of "World History" Japan has been enmeshed in modernity from the very geopolitical encounter that discursively produced the West, the Orient, and ultimately the modern nation-state of Japan. Since at least the turn of the century and the canonical foundations of "modern Japanese literature" in the texts of Sōseki and Ōgai, Japanese intellectuals have recognized the condition of Japanese modernity precisely in the unequal but inescapable embrace of modernity as a historical concept as well as a lived experience. During the height of the war years, the historical dilemma of modernity would be explicitly addressed in such philosophical forums as the *Chūō kōron* roundtables on "The World-Historical Standpoint and Japan" (1941–42), and the 1942 symposium on "Overcoming Modernity."

The present study, however, will focus on the 1920s as the moment when the concept of modernity was thrown open to a wider public discourse. This is the moment when a diverse range of voices in the public sphere articulated their experience of modernity through representations of "everyday life." Journalists, critics, filmmakers, advertisers, songwriters, visual artists, as well as writers of prose fiction, drama, and poetry, all competed to fill a seemingly urgent demand to represent contemporary urban modernity. The development of new communications media and mass journalism not only served as the forum for this public discourse, but were central to the experience of modernity itself in producing an ever-accelerating sensorium of global simultaneity, and in encouraging a new social imaginary (the masses). While the nature and orientation of Japanese modernity were the subject of public debate in this decade, however, the role of state censorship and political surveillance in limiting and attempting to dictate the terms of this debate should not be ignored. By reprising some of the voices of Japanese modernism and observing their relationship to the new forms of media and state power, I hope to explore how modernity was experienced and contested from within the Japanese public sphere, and thus offer a perspective removed as far as possible from that of mimetic analysis.

Contemplating the vicissitudes of the term "modernity" also sheds light on the fortunes of the more specific movements of Japanese "modernism" and "avant-garde." The writers associated with these movements have too often been placed within their own transition narratives, which have inevitably led to a disparaging of the "inadequacy" of their efforts in measuring up to European or American products; of their misapprehension of their supposed mimetic models; or of the misguided nature and colonial inauthenticity of their very efforts to produce new types of art and literature. An extreme example of such a viewpoint can be found in Dennis Keene's description of the early Japanese avant-garde in his *Yokomitsu Ri'ichi: Modernist*, the first book-length work to address Japanese modernist literature in English.

It is with this kind of literature [the work of Hirato Renkichi and Hagiwara Kyōjirō] that charges of imitation start to sound reasonable. The attempts to write "space cubist poems" look as preposterous as the attempts of Japanese poets in recent years to write "concrete" poems with typewriters when set against a thousand-year-old tradition of calligraphy which had established the poem as a visual object in a way totally impossible in the West. For these writers their image of writing and the writer is Westernized in the sense that they have a picture of what these things mean in the West, and it is to that picture they wish to conform. "Imitation" is thus not really the appropriate word here, since there is not sufficient acquaintance with the originals. An abstracted image sways them as they write, and since it must be an up-to-date image, it never has time to establish itself in any depth. The motive force comes from images, ideas, abstractions, rather than from actual words. Since this motive force is thus inevitably superficial, it either produces works of no value or, for a writer who does manage to write comparatively well, it has no real importance for his work as such.[24]

Despite its obvious tone of condescension, Keene's critique here is suggestive to the extent that it describes a tendency for Western writing to be abstracted into an object of mimetic desire. Yet this critique surely ignores the extent to which (colonial) performance and misprision are a part of any creative act. The more fundamental problem of Keene's approach, however, is the facile movement by which Japanese modernist literature, assumed to be fundamentally imitative, is compared with the authentic European original—a movement predestined to uncover the inadequacy of the imitation (which, as Keene puts it, begins to resemble "a parody written by a schoolboy").[25] In thus infantilizing the writers of this literature, his critique prevents them, to paraphrase Sakai, from occupying the position of a subject. Moreover, this comparativism blinds itself to the ways in which these works respond, not to European modernism, but to their situation within the contemporary Japanese literary sphere and, in broader terms, within their own cultural, technological, and historical moment (which, incidentally, had rendered the "thousand-year-old tradition of calligraphy" largely irrecoverable, if not irrelevant, for modern Japanese poetry).

In this study I will analyze Japanese modernism as an active response to developments within Japanese modernity, and not as a phenomenon motivated by the influence or imitation of Western literary movements. As Japanese modernity itself is not a closed phenomenon but is constituted through international economic, political, intellectual, and bodily exchanges, I will also examine the complex positions that modernist and avant-garde writers claimed in relationship to both European cultural hegemony and Japan's imperialist projection in East Asia. I hope that my explorations, then, will lead to a different conclusion from that of Dennis Keene, who writes, "The poems of Hirato Renkichi and Hagiwara Kyōjirō are connected to nothing and for this reason seem so empty."[26]

1 / MEDIA AND MODERNISM

Situation

The 1920s witnessed a major remapping of the Japanese literary terrain, accompanying this era's wider social and technological transformations. As the decade began, the prose literary establishment, referred to as the *bundan*, had been dominated by post-Naturalist personal narratives, which would be newly theorized and debated in this decade as the "I-novel," while the poetry world, known as the *shidan*, was split between poets loosely identified as the "Aesthetic School" (*geijutsu-ha*), many of whom were strongly influenced by French Symbolism, and the newly ascendant People's Poets, (*minshūshi-ha*), who favored more plainspoken poems addressing social issues. By the end of the decade, however, three major groups of writers had emerged to challenge the authority of the established circles of Japanese literary production. An eclectic group of modernist and avant-garde writers denounced and in some cases usurped the authority of the existing *bundan* and *shidan*; the socialist and communist writers of so-called Proletarian Literature (*puroretaria bungaku*) promoted alternative organs, aesthetic standards, and ideological bases for the production and reception of literature; and the writers of "popular literature" (*taishū bungaku*) invented and reinvented popular genres and sought new legitimacy for their works as they exploited new media and modes of distribution. A revitalized feminist literary and social movement had also emerged, with rival allegiances to each of the above camps.[1]

The changes in the literary terrain in the 1920s were not merely the passing of fashions or a remapping of power relationships within the literary establishment. Rather, they were intimately connected with the development of a new urban culture. The literary world reorganized itself on the basis of significant demographic changes, such as burgeoning urbanization and growth in literacy, as well as technological ones. Within the media of print, photography, film, and radio broadcasting, technological changes embodied the larger principles of speed and mechanization that were taken to be crucial aspects of global modernity. Hence the organs of these media, beginning with the publishing houses and newspaper offices, themselves became symbolic sites, key figures in the self-representation of Japanese urban modernity.[2]

By the early 1920s, Japanese literature was both a self-regulating system and, increasingly, a commercially viable aspect of mass culture, dominated by the Tokyo metropole. Already by the turn of the century, after such tentative beginnings as Futabatei Shimei's *Ukigumo* (*Floating Clouds*, 1888–90) and the *Shintaishi shō* (*Selection of New-Style Poetry*, 1882), the "modern novel" and "modern poetry" were firmly established in Japan, modeled to a large degree on their Western counterparts and self-consciously divorced from earlier forms of Japanese literature. While it also encompassed a number of countercurrents (such as the Ken'yūsha), the "modern novel," dominated by the Naturalists and their I-novelist successors, was established with its own stylistic conventions—increasingly universal and transparent standards that had their ideological roots in the idea of a unification of writing and speech, or *genbun itchi*. The speech that this writing alleged to represent was that of upper-middle-class educated males of Tokyo. By the early 1920s, Japanese poetry was dominated by the colloquial free verse, or *kōgojiyūshi*, of the People's Poets, who also claimed an oral basis for their writing.[3]

The hierarchical system of prose writers referred to as the *bundan* (which might be translated as the "literary world," "literary circles," or the "literary establishment") was an imagined community governed by the editors and senior writers of major literary journals. The institutions collectively referred to as the *bundan*, almost exclusively based in Tokyo, were another aspect of the metropole's domination of modern Japanese literature.[4] In the mid- and late 1920s, the most powerful literary journal in the *bundan* was *Bungei shunjū* (*Literary Seasons*), founded in January 1923 by Kikuchi Kan.[5] Conversely, the most visible "modernist" camp was the Shinkankaku-ha, or New Perception School—a group of young writers, led by Yokomitsu Riichi and Kawabata Yasunari, who broke away from *Bungei shunjū* in 1924 to form their own journal, *Bungei jidai* (*Literary Age*), while still maintaining some ties with *Bungei shunjū* and consolidating positions of power within the *bundan*.

The Japanese poetry world, though it operated on a smaller scale, was also governed by centralizing institutions perceived as the *shidan* (the *haidan*, or haiku world, and *kadan*, or tanka world, were for the most part separate entities). In the early 1920s, the *shidan* was led by the association Shiwakai (Poetry Discussion Association, founded in 1917), which published the monthly journal *Nihon shijin* (*Japanese Poets*) and the yearly anthology *Nihon shishū* (*Anthology of Japanese Poetry*). The work of such avant-garde poets as Hagiwara Kyōjirō can be read, in part, as a rebellion against the norms of *Nihon shijin*, which was dominated by poets of the People's Poetry orientation.[6]

In a parallel fashion, the Japanese art world was referred to as the *gadan* and, by the 1920s, had its own journals, such as *Mizue* (*Water Colors*), *Atorie* (*Atelier*), and *Chūō bijutsu* (*Central Arts*), and its own regulating institutions, such as the semi-governmental Imperial Academy of Fine Arts Exhibition (Teikoku Bijutsuin Tenrankai, or Teiten) and the independent Nikakai's Nikaten exhibition. The emerging artistic avant-garde, represented by such groups as Action, Mavo, and Sanka, must be read against this background.

Of course, it is easy to overstate the monolithic nature of such centralizing factors as the *bundan* and the standardization of literary language initiated by *genbun itchi:* no literary language can be completely insulated from heterogeneity, nor can any social system, real or imagined, exercise complete control over the anarchic tendencies of readers and writers. At any rate, by the mid-1920s, there were a number of new forces, both centripetal and centrifugal, at work on the Japanese literary scene. The two most significant of these changes were the growth of mass media and the concomitant discovery of the "masses." Both of these phenomena had a major impact on the development of Japanese modernism.

Among the many effects of the Great Kanto Earthquake was the paralysis of the Japanese publishing industry, which, with the partial exception of the newspaper industry, was heavily concentrated in Tokyo, especially in those "low city" areas most strongly affected by the quake.[7] According to the Japanese Publishing Association's statistics, the post-earthquake fires razed 82 percent of printing establishments and 92 percent of binding workshops in Tokyo.[8] While this disaster dealt the Japanese publishing industry a major setback, its ultimate effect was to stimulate the adoption of new technology and usher in a rapid period of expansion, thanks in large part to an infusion of capital from the Kansai region. The disruption and renewal due to the earthquake also stimulated a reorganization of the *bundan*, with many pre-quake literary journals discontinued and a wave of new journals established after the disaster.[9]

In the newspaper industry, a new scale of mass production had already been initiated prior to the earthquake, following the introduction of such technology as the Japanese-language monotype in 1920 and high-speed rotary presses in 1921.[10] The Osaka-based newspapers were among the most aggressive in the adoption of new technology and marketing techniques, and their hand was only strengthened by the earthquake. Despite the quake, the expansion in the newspaper industry in the early 1920s was phenomenal: from 1920 to 1924, the *Ōsaka mainichi shinbun* increased its circulation from 600,000 to 1,100,000; the *Tōkyō nichi nichi shinbun,* one of only three Tokyo newspaper facilities left standing after the quake, nearly doubled its circulation from 370,000 to 710,000.[11] The new era of newspaper publishing encouraged the centripetal trend toward linguistic standardization: in January 1924, for example, following a report by the Education Ministry urging character reduction and simplification, an association of seven major newspaper companies agreed to limit the number of Chinese (*kanji*) characters employed to 2,113.[12]

Expansion in the magazine industry was no less impressive. The Kōdansha publishing company's *Kingu* (*King*) magazine, mostly featuring morally edifying adventure stories, created a sensation in 1925 by selling 750,000 copies in its first issue. This feat was achieved through an aggressive advertising campaign employing a wide range of advertising media: newspaper advertisements, posters, handbills, signboards, ad-balloons, *chindonya* (parading musical advertising bands), *kamishibai* (traveling picture-story shows), sales canvassing, and large-scale nationwide mailings (approximately 325,000 sealed letters and 1,850,000 postcards).[13]

New technology and advertising techniques also helped to propel growth in the book-publishing industry. Following the earthquake, the development of a new type of binding machine enabled books to be mass-produced for a substantially lower price.[14] Such mass-produced and mass-marketed books made their dramatic debut in 1926, with competing series of books available on a subscription basis, each selling for one yen—thus giving rise to the nickname *enpon* (one-yen books). The first of these series was Kaizōsha's *Gendai nihon bungaku zenshū (Complete Collection of Modern Japanese Literature)*, followed by Shinchōsha's *Sekai bungaku zenshū (Complete Collection of World Literature)* in 1927. Many of the same advertising techniques used to promote *Kingu* magazine were also mobilized to sell the *enpon*. The advertising copy for Kaizōsha's *Gendai nihon bungaku zenshū* suggests the grand scale of the publisher's plans, as well as the ongoing formations of class-based and national identity that the publisher attempted to manipulate in its favor:

We let you read great books for a low price! With this slogan, our company has carried out a great revolution in the world of publishing, liberating the art of the privileged class (*tokken kaikyū no geijutsu*) for the entire populace (*zenminshū*). One subscription for each home! A life without art is like a desolate, wild moor. Why is it that our countrymen, who can boast of the great Meiji literature to the entire world, do not accomplish its national popularization (*zenminshūka*), as the English have done with Shakespeare? To this end, our company has gone forth with our bold plans for one million subscriptions and awaits the readership of every household in the nation![15]

In addition to their application of new marketing techniques, the *enpon* book series played a key role in the consolidation of normative generic ideas about literature. Kaizōsha's series represented a discrete, commoditized, and seemingly authoritative canon of modern Japanese literature. The publisher Shinchōsha soon answered with a canon of Western literature translated into "standard modern Japanese," while Heibonsha offered a segregated canon of popular literature, the *Gendai taishū bungaku zenshū (Complete Works of*

Contemporary Popular Literature). Thus "Japanese literature," dominated by texts in the *genbun itchi* style, became a new standardized commodity that could be displayed on the bookshelf of any Japanese consumer.[16]

Print, however, was by no means the only media to experience growth in the mid-1920s. The photo magazine, a new combination of print and high-quality photographic reproduction, made its Japanese debut with the *Asahi gurafu* (*Asahi Graph*) in 1923, in a special issue devoted to documentation of the Great Kanto Earthquake. Interest in photography, and photo/print media, steadily increased throughout the 1920s and 1930s, due in part to the introduction of more portable and affordable camera equipment. Cinema, meanwhile, had established firm roots in Japanese popular culture from the turn of the century. Domestic film production underwent significant growth and transformation throughout the Taishō period (1911–26), with Hollywood production techniques and technological innovations serving as important catalysts to continued reformation of the domestic industry, even as film imports served as an important window on foreign culture for elite and working-class audiences alike.[17] By 1926, the Japanese Filmmakers' Association reported yearly ticket sales of over 150 million—more than double the national population of 60 million.[18] By the early 1930s, talkies were establishing their hegemony over silent film, and television was already on the global media horizon.[19]

The most dramatic media development in the 1920s, however, was the introduction of radio in 1925. Much as in the case of film, the import, domestic manufacture, and distribution of phonograph records had been an important and steadily growing part of the Japanese cultural sphere since the turn of the century.[20] The introduction of radio, however, was correctly viewed as a phenomenon of a different order and was greeted with tremendous enthusiasm by the journalistic and business communities, as well as a significant portion of the populace.[21]

Perhaps the most interested, and certainly the most powerful, party in the early development of radio was the Japanese government. In 1926, the government engineered the merger of the Tokyo, Osaka, and Nagoya public broadcasting corporations into the national Nippon hōsō kyōkai (Japan Broadcasting Corporation, or NHK), which maintained a monopoly on radio broadcasts until 1951. The government enforced a strict policy of "guidance and control" over broadcast content; this content featured the relay of such national events as the Taishō emperor's funeral in 1927 and the Shōwa emperor's enthronement in 1928.[22] Government-controlled radio was also a powerful force for linguistic standardization in Japan, explicitly taking the speech of "the educated class of the Imperial Capital" as its broadcasting standard.[23]

The new media age dawning in the 1920s required the producers of cultural products not only to redefine their own roles and self-images but also to reconceptualize the multiple recipients of their products. As the new technology of radio beamed its messages across vast spaces and the products of the printing, music recording, and film industries reached more consumers than ever before, the diverse recipients of these mass-media products were for the first time conceptualized as a "mass." The terms of this conceptualization were of major consequence to Japanese literature and culture.

The concept of "mass" in Japan has its own complex history and prehistory, in which the term *taishū*, which appropriates the characters of the Buddhist term *daishu*, was a relative latecomer. This history is complicated by the fact that the three terms most directly related to the concept of "mass"—*gunshū, minshū, and taishū*—each developed in a transnational intertextual matrix, which involved the translation of political and literary discourse of Western countries, even as it responded to and shaped events in Japan.[24] It is clear, however, that in the period just before and after the Great War, during the early phase of so-called Taishō Democracy, there was a growing awareness of "the crowds" (*gunshū*) as a potentially threatening political and cultural force—a usage that reflected growing urbanization and industrialization, as well as the outbreak of violent urban protests such as the Hibiya Riot of 1905 and the rice riots of 1918.[25] During the same period, the term *minshū* achieved prominence during the movement to enfranchise "the people" (*minshū*) within the nation-state: this movement toward democratization (*minshūshugi*) finally culminated in the realization of universal manhood suffrage in 1925.

It was around this same year, the year of the first radio broadcasts, the year of *Kingu* magazine (and of Hagiwara Kyōjirō's *Shikei senkoku*), that a new term, *taishū*, articulated a different type of social imaginary. Among the first recorded applications of the term was in the field of literature: Ikeda Chōsuke, the editor of Hakubunkan's *Kōdan zasshi*, is credited with coining the term *taishū bungaku* (mass/popular literature) for advertising copy in 1924.[26] Over the next few years, writers such as Shirai Kyōji and Naoki Sanjūgo championed *taishū bungaku* (also referred to as *taishū bungei*), seeking to redefine and legitimize such traditionally "popular" or *tsūzoku* genres as historical fiction, as well as to establish alliances with writers in relatively new genres, such as the mystery writer Edogawa Ranpo. Shirai, Naoki, and associates formed the Twenty-First Club (Nijū-ichinichi-kai) in 1925 and began publishing a coterie journal, *Taishū bungei*, in January of the following year; meanwhile Shirai was editing a series of *enpon*, *Gendai taishū bungaku zenshū* (*Complete Works of Contemporary Popular Literature*), which began publication in May 1927.

The expanding audiences for fiction aggressively targeted by the publishing industry in the 1920s were composed of a patchwork of different reading constituencies, including literate members of the industrial laboring class; the new middle class of urban salarymen, government functionaries, and educators; women with increasing levels of education and participation in the workforce; students; rural educators; and remnants of the older urban townsman culture of shopkeepers and small business proprietors.[27] However, as significant as the diversity of these audiences is the fact that they were increasingly conceptualized as a single bloc, and that the audience for literature was generally perceived to be passing from a limited intelligentsia to a more broadly based audience, which was referred to however imprecisely by the term *taishū*.

The terms *taishū* (mass) and *taishūka* (massification) were also important for the Proletarian Literature movement, which represented another of the most significant developments in Japanese literature of the 1920s. This movement, with its roots in the pre-earthquake socialist journal *Tane maku hito* (*The Sower*, 1921–23), achieved a higher level of organization and prominence with the publication of a new journal, *Bungei sensen* (*Literary Front*, 1924–), and the establishment of the Nihon Puroretaria Bungei Renmei (Japan Proletarian Literary Federation) in 1925. The Proletarian

Literary Movement persisted through tumultuous years of governmental repression and factional infighting before being effectively crushed by the massive arrests of leftist activists beginning in 1927 and the public apostasy of jailed Communist Party leaders in 1933.[28] When proletarian writers and critics such as Sano Kasami argued for *bungeiPno taishūka* (the massification of literature), the term *taishū*, now associated more firmly with the proletarian class, invoked a different intellectual matrix than when it was employed by Shirai Kyōji.[29] Nevertheless, both "popular" and "Proletarian" writers, as well as public officials, were involved in the project of imagining a new type of recipient of the media message—a huge but still largely undefined social group who could be imagined as a passive block of consumers, as subjects ready for a new level of integration into the Japanese state, or as a potential collective agent for revolution.

The term *taishū* enters Hagiwara Kyōjirō's critical vocabulary in 1926, with an article promoting the idea of a "stadium-like, outdoor-like, advertising-like" literature.[30] While he did not use the term *taishū* in his earlier writings, the concept of the urban crowd (*gunshū*) and an acute awareness of the media transformation that would help to create "the masses" are central aspects of Hagiwara's *Shikei senkoku* from the previous year. Indeed, the question of the appeal to the masses—in a sense shared closely with the Proletarian writers—is crucial for Hagiwara and the Mavo artists. Similarly, although Hayashi Fumiko avoids the term *taishū*, the forms of technologically mediated popular culture associated with "the masses," and the constructions of class that underlie the term, are central concerns of Hayashi's *Hōrōki*.

AVANT-GARDE AND MODERNIST writing can be seen in part as a mode of resistance against the centralizing and standardizing forces in the literary world. At the same time, writers associated with modernism and the avant-garde sought to exploit the possibilities of new media and to intervene in the ongoing reappraisal of the nature of the artwork, its production, and its consumption. The literary journal *Bungei shijō* (*The Art Market*) provides one interesting example of the iconoclastic and eclectic spirit emerging to contest both the authority of the *bundan* and state-imposed constraints on literature in the mid-1920s. Edited by Umehara Hokumei and Kaneko Yōbun (soon to be joined on the masthead by Mavo leader Murayama Tomoyoshi), the first issue of *Bungei shijō* featured an Expressionistic cover and a manifesto denouncing an "art world" that has been too long "mesmerized" by names and labels. With a particular solicitude toward the emerging avant-garde, it urged contributions from all camps, including "Dada, which is in fresh supply, Expressionism, Shinkankaku-ha, Conte, Proletarian Literature, [and] *Shinjinsei-ha* (New Life School)."[31] *Bungei shijō*'s tongue-in-cheek manifesto acknowledged the status of the work of art as a commodity and attacked the ideology of the artwork's purity or autonomy from commercial concerns:

For a long time, superstition regarding art (*geijutsu*) has persisted. While in reality art is treated as a commodity and is evaluated by the abacus, there are many people in our world who still overestimate art, thinking it is the one thing that transcends money. *Bungei shijō* was born to destroy this superstition and pursue art as a commodity to its ultimate extreme. . . .[32]

Other manifestations of *Bungei shijō*'s iconoclasm included the transcript of a mock trial of *bundan* leader Kikuchi Kan in the first issue and a carnivalesque auction of writers' manuscripts on the streets of Kyōbashi.[33] The *Bungei shijō* editors thus called attention to the commercial context for the production of literary art, while mocking the pretensions of the literary establishment and publishing literature that tested the Japanese government's restraints on political and sexual public discourse.[34]

Another aspect of the modernist and avant-garde resistance toward literary standardization and centralization was a skepticism or overt hostility to *genbun itchi*, the standard form of modern prose that alleged to "unify" spoken and written languages. *Shinkankaku-ha* leader Yokomitsu Riichi, while staking an important position in the Tokyo *bundan* himself, made the shift away from *genbun itchi* an explicit part of his poetics: rejecting the ideology of "writing as one speaks" attributed to the Naturalists (as well as such contemporary writers as Sasaki Mosaku, Murō Saisei, and Takii Kōsaku), Yokomitsu argued for "writing as one writes." "As long as literature is destined to use letters (*moji*)," Yokomitsu declared, "it should be 'written as one writes' rather than 'written as one speaks.' How else can we explore the real value of letters?"[35]

Hayashi Fumiko's *Hōrōki* (discussed in Chapters 4 and 5) provides a radical example of the break with standard *genbun itchi* prose: her work foregrounds every type of linguistic hybridity, including regional dialect, colloquialisms, vulgarisms, and onomatopoeia excluded from the standardized "speech" model of *genbun itchi* prose, as well as verse forms, classical verb endings, and other aspects of "written" Japanese also excluded from the *genbun itchi* mode. As I will argue in Chapter 3, the extreme visuality of Hagiwara Kyōjirō's *Shikei senkoku* offered its own compelling challenge to orally based models of poetry and poetic subjectivity.

Sites: Cafés/Journals

One important strategy of the avant-garde movement was to cross from private spaces to public ones: to go outside the private or institutional spaces traditionally assigned to the production and reception of art—the study, the studio, the gallery—and take work, literally, to the streets.[36] Yet avant-garde writers and artists also established midway points between the study and the streets, semi-public spaces to pursue their individual aims in a collective context. Two such *topoi*, one "real" and one "virtual," were the café and the coterie magazine, or *dōjin zasshi*.

The development of a café culture was one of the most prominent iconographic features of social modernity (*modan*) in the 1920s.[37] Yet within this heading there were many subcategories, including the elegant and expensive cafés of the Ginza, the many cafés in which sexually charged social contact with the waitresses was the primary draw for customers (the most dominant type in media representations of café culture), and more humbly appointed cafés in which drinking and disputing, primarily by young males, were the main forms of entertainment. Among this last type of café was the Café Lebanon in Hongō's Sakana-chō, located above the Nantendō Bookstore (and often referred to as the Nantendō). This was the gathering place of a group of anarchists and avant-garde poets; it is here that the biographies of Hagiwara Kyōjirō and Hayashi Fumiko overlap.[38]

The Café Lebanon was located at the top of Dōzaka and Dangozaka, on the high ground in Hongō, a hilly area of northeast Tokyo, site of Tokyo Imperial University, and where many writers and aca-

demics had their homes. While Hongō had its high-culture associations, it was also a student neighborhood, and in the depressed economic conditions of the 1920s, it was a place where unemployed and
underemployed young people (including Hagiwara and Hayashi)
could find housing (*geshuku*) for low rents and flexible terms.[39]

Hongō's complex associations of "high" culture and unruly
youth subculture were compressed into the Café Lebanon. In his
postwar autobiographical novel *Hanayaka na shikeiha* (*The Mag-
nificent Death Sentence School*), former Shinkankaku-ha writer Kon
Tōkō offers a satirical description of this café:

> The next day, I visited Nantendō's "Café Lebanon," known as the fore-
> most Valhalla of Hongō. This café had become a den of anarchists, who
> nearly every night gave bloom to the flowers of contestation, engaging in
> fights with anyone outside their clique who ventured in. At one time, the
> Café Paris, run by two sisters in Hongō Sanchōme, also had a reputation
> for fights, and even the young toughs of Kanda and Asakusa would stay
> out of the way of its rowdy students. But the anarchists of the Café Leba-
> non exuded the romantic scent of a leftist activist minority. Compared
> with the rest of the young delinquents in Tokyo, who were mostly an
> uncultured and feeble-minded lot, the gang in Café Lebanon was positively
> highbrow.[40]

The semi-violent atmosphere that hovered over the Café Lebanon lent a certain mystique, and sometimes an air of intimidation,
to the activities of Hagiwara and his associates. Yet, aside from this
youthful romanticism, which makes an easy target for Kon Tōkō's
satire, the Café Lebanon served as an important meeting-ground for
such figures as anarchist leaders Ōsugi Sakae and Ishikawa Sanshirō;
Tsuji Jun, translator of Max Stirner's *Der Einzige und sein Eigenthum*
(*The Ego and His Own*);[41] poet and self-proclaimed Dadaist Takahashi Shinkichi; feminist and socialist writer Hirabayashi Taiko; as
well as Hayashi and Hagiwara.

The social rifts and connections established through a type of
public performance in such spaces as the Café Lebanon were articulated in a different way through the coterie journal, or *dōjin zasshi*.
Aka to kuro (*Red and Black*), widely considered the first avant-garde
poetry journal in Japan, was founded in January 1923 by *dōjin* Okamoto Jun, Tsuboi Shigeji, Kawasaki Chōtarō, and Hagiwara Kyōjirō.
The example of *Aka to kuro* helped to stimulate the appearance of

other avant-garde coterie journals both in and outside of Tokyo.[42] After an interval of disruption due to the September earthquake, there was an explosion of Japanese-language experimental art and literary journals in 1924: *GE.GJMGJGAM.PRRR.GJMGEM* in June; *MAVO* in July; *Damu damu* (*Dum dum*), and *Bungei jidai* in September; and *A*, founded in Dairen (Dalian), Manchuria, in November. By the summer of 1926, the magazine *Bungei shijō* could publish a list of "nationwide coterie journals" with 194 entries.[43]

Damu damu, published out of the Nantendō bookstore, was an expansion and reorientation of the *Aka to kuro* project.[44] Running over 130 pages and featuring twelve *dōjin* (including Hagiwara, Okamoto Jun, Tsuboi Shigeji, Ono Tōzaburō, Takahashi Shinkichi, Hashizume Ken, and Hayashi Masao), the journal was as ambitious as it was short-lived: September 1924 was its first and only issue. The publication of this journal, together with the enthusiastic reception that greeted Hagiwara's *Shikei senkoku*, mark the brief peak of cultural visibility for the anarchist and Dadaist strains of interwar literature.

Of course, just as writers (such as *Bungei jidai*'s Kon Tōkō) would make forays outside their established haunts to "alien" urban territory (such as the Café Lebanon), avant-garde and modernist writers would also contribute to other writers' *dōjin zasshi*, as well as to mainstream newspapers and journals. Hayashi Fumiko's early career provides an extreme example of such mobility: she contributed poetry and prose to the Proletarian journal *Bungei sensen*; to avant-garde publications such as *MAVO*, *Nihiru* (*Nihil*), and *Sekai shijin* (*World Poet*); and later to the feminist journal *Nyonin geijutsu* (*Women's Arts*), where the first installations of *Hōrōki* appeared; she also produced the littlest of little magazines with Tomotani Shizue, *Futari* (*Two People*).[45]

Her first poetry collection, *Aouma o mitari* (*I Saw a Pale Horse*), published in 1929, garnered support from both *Nyonin geijutsu* and the Café Lebanon group: a feature piece on the collection appeared in the August 1929 issue of *Nyonin geijutsu* with reviews by such peers as Hirabayashi Taiko and Enchi Fumiko; meanwhile, Café Lebanon regulars Tsuji Jun and Ishikawa Sanshirō contributed prefaces to the collection. A passage from *Hōrōki*, a loosely autobiographical novel constructed in part out of Hayashi's diaries, gives an idea of the urban and literary environments in which she established herself:

June Xth

Today was the day that Isori, the friend of the man I broke up with, moved into the eight-mat room next door. It made me feel uneasy, sensing that that man was somehow up to something.—On my way to the dining hall, I bought a stick of incense and offered it to the Jizō Bodhisattva. Back home, I washed my hair, and feeling refreshed, paid a visit to Shizue's boarding house on Dangozaka. I was full of energy as I climbed the hill, thinking that our poetry pamphlet *Futari* should be ready. . . . In the evening, we went to pick up the pamphlet at the printer's. It was only eight pages long, but was as fresh as a newly plucked fruit. On the way home, we stopped by Nantendō, and passed out a copy to everyone. I'd like to keep working and keep this pamphlet going for a long time. Tapping on my coffee-drinking shoulder, Tsuji loosened his headband and lavished praise on the pamphlet. "You've come out with something really good. Keep it up!" Leaving a smile for lofty Tsuji Jun's drunken figure, Shizue and I left the café in a jubilant mood.

June Xth

The group from *Tane maku hito* are now coming out with a magazine called *Bungei sensen*, so I sent them "Jokō no utaeru" (The Factory Girl's Song), a poem about the factory where I worked painting celluloid toys. Today the Miyako newspaper printed a poem I wrote to my ex-lover. I should stop writing this type of poem. It's ridiculous. I want to study harder and write better poetry. In the evening I went to a café in Ginza called the Shōgetsu, because they were having an exhibition of *Don* poetry. My sloppy characters were right there in the front. I met with Mr. Hashizume.[46]

Hayashi's mention of the *Don* poetry exhibition[47] points to one example of the visual experimentation that characterized the 1920s poetry scene. *Aka to kuro* suspended publication for nine months following the Great Kanto Earthquake. When it reappeared for a final issue in June 1924, it bore the title *Aka to kuro gōgai* (*Red and Black Extra Number*), as if to acknowledge the extraordinary circumstances behind its discontinuation. In the following month, a group of *dōjin zasshi* centering on *Aka to kuro* organized an exhibition of poetry (displayed in the manner of paintings), to be presented in a number of cafés throughout the city (including Hongō, Kagurazaka, and the Ginza), beginning with the Café Lebanon. This exhibition was imitated by other journals in other sites, as the passage from *Hōrōki* referring to an exhibit organized by the poet Don Zakkii (Miyakozaki Tomoo), suggests. The original Café Lebanon exhibition was disrupted, however, when police confiscated the poems on charges of "corruption of public morals" and "disruption of public stability and order."[48]

Aka to kuro's presentation of poetry on the walls of cafés had an important precedent a few months before (October 1923), when the Mavo group of artists mounted a traveling exhibition of their works in over twenty cafés and restaurants throughout the city, beginning with the Mavoists' own favored haunt, Café Suzuran. This was the Mavo group's first major activity following the earthquake and reflected the renewed importance of cafés and restaurants (whether in buildings spared from the fires or in improvised "barracks") as places of refuge and communication in the wake of the disaster.[49]

Like the Mavo group's other post-quake activities, such as barracks decoration and the exhibition of architectural plans, this series of exhibitions demonstrates the Mavo group's effort to move outside the spaces and modes of presentation traditionally assigned to the artwork and to actively participate in the construction of a new Tokyo following the earthquake. Similarly, the *Aka to kuro* exhibition challenged not only the traditional modes of presentation of the poem but the borderline separating poetry and visual art and the place of that "artwork" in society.

The proliferation of *dōjin zasshi* and the lively intellectual exchange in such spaces as the Café Lebanon suggests the continued importance of social allegiances among writers, which have played a vital role in the production of Japanese literature throughout the modern period. Yet the proliferation of *dōjin zasshi* also represents an important counterforce to the centralizing power of the *bundan*, which threatened to only increase with the growing scope and commercial viability of the publishing industry. Thus, for example, when *Bungei shijō* magazine serialized a "Dictionary of Common Publishing Terms for Amateur Publishers," it reflected an interest in alternative publishing venues among the

Japanese intelligentsia, as well as the political-cultural agenda of the *Bungei shijō* editors to undermine the central authority of the *bundan* (and perhaps also to encourage methods to circumvent state censorship).[50]

Modernism and Avant-Garde

In his book *The Concept of Modernism*, Astradur Eysteinsson tries to establish where a critical consensus can be found regarding this concept and notes the many contradictions regarding the idea of modernism in Western literature. "There is a rapidly spreading agreement that 'modernism' is a legitimate concept broadly signifying a paradigmatic shift, a major revolt beginning in the mid- and late nineteenth century, against the prevalent literary and aesthetic traditions of the Western world," he writes. "But this is as far as we can assume a critical and theoretical consensus to go. Beyond this point we face strikingly variable and often seemingly irreconcilable theories concerning the nature of the revolt."[51] Typically, even the broadest, most consensual definition Eysteinsson is able to provide begs the question of the meaning, or even the possibility, of modernism arising in a place such as Japan, by tying its meaning to the traditions and anti-traditions of the "Western world." Nevertheless, Japanese modernism did not develop as a strictly nationalist revolt against "prevalent literary and aesthetic traditions of the Western world"; nor was it merely an unreflexive copy of Western modernism. Rather, as my preceding discussion of Japanese modernism in relation to the *bundan* and *genbun itchi* should indicate, Japanese modernism, while certainly influenced by Western avant-gardes, developed and attained meaning in relation to domestic practices and institutions that, although also partly appropriated from the West, had already established their own shape and trajectory in Japan.

Unlike Proletarian Literature or "popular literature" (*taishū bungaku*), which emerged as relatively clearly defined camps with their own champions and theorists in the literary world of the 1920s and '30s, the terms "modernism" and "modernist" (*modanizumu, modanisuto*) and avant-garde (*aban gyarudo, zen'ei*) have only retrospectively been widely applied to a cluster of literary texts and authors from this period.[52] As outlined above, writers at the time were typically associated with coterie journals or groupings of writers associated with a particular journal, such as the *Shi to shiron* (*Poetry and Poetics*) group in poetry, or in prose the Shinkankaku-ha group associated with *Bungei jidai*.[53] While the identification of specific authors and artists as modernist or avant-garde has largely been a retrospective critical process, a number of terms closely related to the concept of modernism were in frequent use by authors, artists, and critics of the 1920s. These include *modan* (modern) and *sentan* (leading edge or pointed edge). In the following paragraphs, I will examine the use of these terms in Japanese discourse and make a few preliminary observations regarding modernist and avant-garde strategies in the work of Hayashi Fumiko and Hagiwara Kyōjirō, bearing in mind, *pace* Eysteinsson, that the formidable breadth and contested nature of the modernist "revolt" would counsel that any such observations remain provisional.

Hagiwara Kyōjirō, Mavo, and the Avant-Garde

Crucial to modernism is conscious innovation, the sense of being on the leading edge in cultural activity, and this consciousness reaches its ultimate point in the rhetoric of the avant-garde. Thus, as suggested by Matei Calinescu, we can see the avant-garde as constituting a radical front within a broader modernist movement, in "dramatizing certain constitutive elements of the nature of modernity and making them into a revolutionary ethos."[54] The Japanese word *zen'ei*, now used frequently as a translation for "avant-garde," was not very widely used by artists or authors in the prewar period, except by some authors affiliated with the Proletarian Literature movement. However, another term bearing a close relationship to "avant-garde" was commonly employed: *sentan*, which, depending on the kanji characters used, could be literally translated as either "leading edge" or "pointed edge." The term *sentan* was used in several key statements by artists and critics of the 1920s, including the founding manifesto of the Mavo group, which employed the kanji for "pointed edge," translated below as "spearpoint":

We are standing at the spearpoint (*sentan*). And we will surely always stand at the spearpoint. We are not enchained. We are radicals. We will carry out a revolution. We will advance. We will create. We will cease- lessly affirm, and ceaselessly deny. We are alive in every sense of the word, incomparably.[55]

This statement brashly expresses several important elements found in expressions of Japanese artists in the mid-1920s: an imagination of revolution; a strong will toward artistic and personal freedom; a related emphasis on either the daily life of the artist, or in this case, the artist's very life force; and a rhetoric embracing the seeming opposites of creation/destruction or affirmation/negation. Further- more, the manifesto locates this fusion of affirmation and denial in "ceaseless" time, creating a paradoxically compressed and extended temporality resembling what Calinescu refers to as modern artists' "utopia of a radiant instant of invention that can suppress time by repeating itself endlessly."[56] The manifesto's use of the term *sentan*, too, conflates a spatial description ("standing at the spearpoint") with an implied temporal position at the brink of a revolution. This compression and conflation of time and space is typical of avant- garde rhetoric, including the term "avant-garde" itself, which origi- nally referred to the forward disposition of troops on a battlefield, but came to imply a temporal state of being at the leading edge of the present in its passage to futurity.

Some of the most characteristic expressions of the avant-garde— collages, assemblages, Dada poetry, and certain forms of avant- garde theater—enact a similar compression and conflation of time and space.[57] In collage, artifacts from different places and historical moments are transposed into a single pictorial field. For example, in Mavo artist Murayama Tomoyoshi's 1925 mixed-media assemblage "Konsutorukuchion" ("Construction," presently in the collection of the National Museum of Modern Art, Tokyo), the upper right hand consists of a collage of photos clipped from the pages of a German illustrated newspaper, including modern factories, office buildings, automobiles, power, telephone or telegraph lines, radio towers, women's fashion photographs, a military review, a battleship, and the famous Potala Palace in the Tibetan capital of Lhasa.[58] While the collage consists largely of iconographic imagery of technological, militarist, and consumerist aspects of modern life (and also points to the roles of photography and print media in the construction of that life), the juxtaposition of the many images of modern Germany with a prominently placed image of a Tibetan palace sets up a compressed and provocative tension between disparate points in time (premodern/modern) and space (East/West), with the palace's walls curiously echoing the forms of modern factories and office buildings pictured elsewhere in the collage.

The examples of collage and assemblage also point to the avant-garde tendency to assault the "organic" integrity of the picture-surface and, ultimately, to rupture the frame of the work of art.[59] The breaking of the frame can be enacted quite literally, such as in Murayama's "Konsutorukuchion," in which a piece of wood projects at a right angle across the rectangular frame of the artwork, or more figuratively, as in the case of Russian Constructivist Vladimir Tatlin's corner reliefs of 1915, which not only transgressed the boundaries between pictorial and sculptural work, but problematized the exhibition space of the gallery as well. The avant-garde artwork or performance does not entail the total elimination of frame conditions, but rather is to be found in the ecstatic moment in which, through an act of transgression, the existing frame becomes fully visible.

The success of the Mavo group's activities in both "breaking the frame" and "making the frame visible" are confirmed by the suggestive remarks of critic Kawaji Ryūkō upon viewing the first Sanka exhibition of May 1925, combining the works of members of the Mavo and Action artists' groups, many of which were "constructivist" mixed-media assemblages:

We face ourselves when we look at paintings within a frame. That is to say, we and the frame both go out in our best clothes to see and be seen. But to make this relationship more intimate, think about a form where you yourself become embedded into the painting, or a condition where the painting is absorbed into you. [Sanka's] plastic art . . . jumps out of the frame and seizes us. We think of plastic art as a real object in the same way as we view a utensil on the table or part of a wall, or part of a column supporting a room. In other words, we look at it as a real thing that relates to and exists in our everyday lives. It is not simply expression. In a word, it has an organic relationship to daily life. No, rather, it is an art that possesses a part of daily life. This is probably the intention of the constructivists. Making art real (*geijutsu no jissaika*) and transforming it into daily life (*seikatsuka*), is the result of this abstract, machine-like art.

The result of this new art, Kawaji concludes, is a utilitarian understanding of art as "a material object necessary to daily life." This new understanding of art simultaneously leads to an awareness of, and dissatisfaction with, the previous framing of artwork, whether a hanging scroll in an alcove (*tokonoma*), or "the oil paintings that are gently hung in frames on the wall." [60]

From an early point, the Mavo group's activities of "breaking the frame" went beyond the individual artwork, extending to the "productive and distributive apparatus" and the "ideas of art that prevail at any given time and determine the reception of works," which, in Peter Bürger's formulation, serve to define "art as institution."[61] On August 28, 1923, Murayama Tomoyoshi, leader of the Mavo group, planned a "moving exhibition" to welcome works that had been rejected from the state-sponsored Nika Exhibition in Ueno Park, as a protest against the selection committee's alleged bias against new and experimental works. The young artist Sumiya Iwane, who had submitted his painting "Kōjō ni okeru ai no nikki" ("Diary of Love in a Factory") under the pseudonym Iwanov Sumiyavich, then withdrew his work from the exhibition, claiming it had only been accepted because of the foreign-sounding signature. Adding his work to Murayama's counterexhibition, Sumiya/Sumiyavich climbed to the roof of the exhibition hall and hoisted the Mavo flag. Meanwhile, another Mavo member, Takamizawa Michinao, shouted and threw rocks at him, breaking an exhibition hall window in the process.

After the young artist scrambled down from the roof, the "moving exhibition" began, as the Mavo members paraded their works on a course to Shinbashi station, accompanied by a *chindonya* band. This procession was broken up midway by the police, who briefly detained Murayama. The day's events succeeded in generating publicity for the newly formed Mavo group, attracting coverage in the *Tōkyō asahi, Tōkyō nichi nichi,* and *Yomiuri* newspapers.[62]

This episode provides a vivid example of the tendency of avant-garde artists to dramatize the breaking of frame conditions—in this case, the exhibition space and selection and distribution apparatus for visual art. The Mavo performance itself unfolded in such a way as to emphasize the artists' acts of boundary transgression: Takamizawa's antithetical act of shouting and throwing rocks at Sumiya/Sumiyavich, whether committed in genuine anger or in a spirit of play, dramatized the transgressive nature of his target's roof-climb. Similarly the arrest of Murayama (who had publicized the parade route prior to the event) served as a confirmation of the group's position outside the frame of legitimate artistic activity and highlighted the role of state authority in demarcating the acceptable bounds of artistic expression.

The Mavoists' carnivalesque brush with the forces of political authority during their "moving exhibition" prefigured more serious confrontations to come. The potential of avant-garde artists to be viewed as threats to social order and persecuted accordingly was confirmed in the aftermath of the Great Kanto Earthquake, which occurred just four days after the Mavo group's "moving exhibition." Mavo artist and socialist activist Yanase Masamu was among those "dangerous elements" rounded up and physically abused (beaten and pierced with bayonets) by military police immediately following the quake, while anarchist Ōsugi Sakae, whose writings had inspired many radical young writers and artists, was killed in police detention.[63]

Hagiwara Kyōjirō formally joined the Mavo group in 1925, and the poetry collection *Shikei senkoku*, a product of his collaboration with the Mavo group, reveals the numerous thematic concerns and formal strategies that were shared between the poet and his fellow Mavoists. The collage or assemblage aesthetic of many Mavo artworks is paralleled in the poems of *Shikei senkoku*, which feature expressive deployment of printed characters in various orientations and sizes, together with elements such as bars and arrows. These textual and para-textual elements are tightly interposed with other design elements, including numerous linoleum prints contributed by various Mavo members, and inserted photographs of Mavoists' artworks. In his postscript to the collection, Hagiwara's primary artistic collaborator, Okada Tatsuo, reveals their plan to introduce rags, sticks, wire, and other foreign material into the binding, thereby pursuing the collage aesthetic even further and disrupting the collection's "frame," the form of the book itself. This plan was apparently aborted, however, because of the difficulty of mass-producing such a work.[64]

It is evident from such episodes as the police confiscation of the works exhibited in the *Aka to kuro* poetry exhibition and the banning of issue number 4 of the *MAVO* magazine that state censorship was a significant frame condition for Japanese art and literature. In the year of the earthquake, 893 publications were banned on charges of "disruption of public stability and order" and 1,442 banned for "corruption of public morals."[65] Moreover, a combination of self-censorship, in-house censorship, and partial state censorship was pervasive, often taking the form of *fuseji*, literally "hiding characters," typically black dots— ● ● ● ● ● ● ● ●—used to conceal a word, phrase, sentence, or passage that the editors anticipated would lead to problems with state censors.[66]

In Hagiwara Kyōjirō's poetry *fuseji* cease to be an exclusive tool of censorship and are transformed into a prominent poetic device. *Fuseji* are employed toward a variety of poetic means, in differing contexts: they may used as abstract elements of the poetry's visual texture; they may verge on the visually mimetic, seeming to represent heads, bullets, electric buttons, automobiles, or explosions; or they may be used, as in the general practice of *fuseji*, in place of an (often reconstructable) obscene or politically forbidden word or phrase. Often, the border between these various uses becomes obscure, leading to an unusual sense of destabilization or indeterminacy in Hagiwara's work. Thus, by employing a visual poetic device that on first glance would seem little different from his Italian and Russian Futurist predecessors, Hagiwara performs an act of frame-braking—or rather the transgressive making-visible of frame conditions, which addresses the political situation of the Japanese literary work in a very specific way.

The Japanese avant-garde's emphasis on transgression of frame conditions, on critiquing the institutions of production and reception of art, and on attempting to reintegrate art within a "praxis of life" would seem very much in line with Peter Bürger's theory of the avant-garde as the autocritique of art, which seeks to negate the autonomy of art in bourgeois society by the sublation of art into the praxis of life. While this theory may be persuasive in *describing* many of the activities of the Japanese avant-garde, its theoretical basis in the autonomy of bourgeois art from life praxis is highly problematic even in the European context—seeming to suggest, for instance, that the work of art can be divorced from the commercial relations that distinguish bourgeois "life praxis."

Even granting the Kantian concept of autonomy that Bürger outlines in his work, it is clear at the least that the Japanese art world did not enjoy "autonomy" from state censorship. Nor had the art institutions that Bürger takes for granted, such as bourgeois patronage, developed in Japan as they had in Europe. Rather, the Mavo activities (including those of Hagiwara) should be read as an intervention—a dramatic reorientation of the "bourgeois" work of art in a chaotic situation in which bourgeois social systems, totalitarian institutions, and a new type of mass society were emerging simultaneously.

Hayashi Fumiko and Modernism

While *modanizumu* (modernism) was only occasionally used to refer to literature in 1920s Japan, both the terms *modan* (modern) and *modanizumu* were in frequent use to describe the broader technological and social transformations of the time. As such, the Japanese usage of *modan* bears a close relationship to Maud Lavin's description of the term *Modernismus* as used in Weimar Germany. Lavin notes that *Modernismus* could refer to an art movement such as Expressionism, but it could also refer more broadly to "the culture of contemporary life and the experience of technology, electricity, urbanism, speed, mass media, and consumerism."[67] In the Japanese context, several important critical statements combined the concept of modernism with the concept of the avant-garde as expressed in the term *sentan*, suggesting that Japanese modernism, both as a literary movement and as a manifestation of the "culture of contemporary life," was at the vanguard (*sentan*) of contemporary society.

Much of the early criticism related to modernism in Japan was written by Marxist critics, who typically used the base-and-superstructure model to define and explain the phenomena of modernism and modernity. In such an analysis, the base of modern Japanese society is industrial capitalism, which finds its superstructural expression in the fast-changing phenomena of urban consumer culture. "Modernism," as expressed in both urban life-styles and the arts and literature that explore such lifestyles, appears to have revolutionary potential through its development of social and artistic innovations. However, a true revolution can only come not in the superstructure but in a revolution of the industrial base of society from capitalism to communism. In his well-known essay "Modan sō to modan sō" ("Modern Social Strata and Modern Mores"), Ōya Sōichi states that "'Modern' (*modan*) means the vanguard (*sentan*) of the age." "And yet," he declares, "that vanguard is not a genuine productive vanguard but the tip of petty consumerism."[68]

Hirabayashi Hatsunosuke makes the base-and-superstructure model more explicit in his essay "Shihonshugi no sentanteki shisō urutora modanizumu" ("Ultra-modernism, the Vanguard Philosophy of Capitalism"), where he connects "modernism" with certain strains of contemporary literary production:

Japanese modernists are still sentimentalists, like medieval lyric poets. The modernity reflected in their eyes is hairdressing, skirts, and movie actresses. It is the hit parade, department store mannequins, *gin bura* [cruising the Ginza], and "*chic* boys" and "girls." In a word, it is flapper modernism. The true roots and bases of modernity are modern industry, financial capital, factories, and trading floors. Japanese modernists tremble before these like the leaves of a tree.[69]

While ostensibly analyzing Japanese modernity in terms of base and superstructure, Hirabayashi subtly injects the element of gender into his theory of modernity: the consumer culture introduced as the superstructure of Japanese capitalism is dominated by images of femininity, contrasted with the base elements that are implicitly masculinized. Indeed, a female gendering of *modan*, demonstrated here by Hirabayashi's description of a "flapper modernism," associated with "hairdressing, skirts, and movie actresses," pervades the Japanese discourse of the 1920s. The same tendency to associate the term *modan* with an often negative gender stereotype is seen in the word's most frequent usage, as part of the compound *modan gāru* (modern girl).[70] In his "Hyaku pāsento moga" ("One Hundred Percent Modern Girl"), for example, Ōya Sōichi sketches the modern girl as a fiendish mix of shallow consumerism and manipulative sexuality, and then counters this stereotype with an idealized picture of a female socialist activist, who is the true "modern girl."[71]

In exploring Japan's developing urban culture through the eyes of a female protagonist, Hayashi Fumiko's *Hōrōki* pursues a dialogue with the contemporary constructions of *modan* (modernity/modernism) offered in the popular press and elaborated by contemporary critics. While she plays upon many of the same assumptions and popular journalistic images as Ōya and Hirabayashi, Hayashi complicates the reifications of class and gender that occur in their representations. In *Hōrōki*, she introduces a female protagonist who is both a consumer and a producer of culture. The "modern girl" (the word occurs only in ironic contexts in Hayashi's work), objectified in the male-dominated discourse on modernity, becomes a subject in Hayashi's text, a subject who is alternately a viewer/participant of the modern consumer spectacle on the Ginza, a factory laborer, a café waitress, and a writer.

Nevertheless, Hirabayashi's idea of the "lyrical poetry" of modernism, which is implicitly contrasted with the "prose" of modernity, does have a certain resonance with Hayashi's work. The dialectical impulse which informs Hayashi's use of montage frequently leads her to contrast idealistic, utopian, or sentimental ideological constructions (such as self-fulfillment, free love, and socialist revolution) with more "realistic" accounts of the disappointments, humiliations, and practical struggles of daily life. Often this dialectical movement occurs in a shift from lyric poetry—modern Japanese popular song and poetry (including Hayashi's own)—to the prose of the narrator/protagonist's diary entries. This contrast, however, does not take the form of the strict bifurcation that Hirabayashi proposes, but of a complex, multivalent, and often ironic dialogue.

While a temporally limited and spatially intensified practice of collage typifies the works of the avant-garde, Hayashi's work is distinguished by the cinematic practice of montage. Although these two practices are closely related, in montage the element of time is emphasized over that of space.[72] While the experience of time in montage is defamiliarized and displaced from linear narration, the reintroduction of the temporal element in collage nevertheless allows for a greater engagement with history, which is often compressed or negated in the most aggressive avant-garde works.

In his essay "The Age of the World Picture" ("Die Zeit des Welt-bildes"), Martin Heidegger suggests that the very act of viewing "the modern" and "the world" as a "picture" serves to define what he describes as the fallen state of modernity.[73] While Heidegger writes of this mode of viewing as pervading modernity in general, we might posit that the novel, as a quintessential product of European modernity, is particularly invested in the process Heidegger identi-fies as enframing "the modern world picture." As a modernist novel that hybridizes the novel's form with diverse narrative and lyrical elements, Hayashi Fumiko's *Hōrōki* confounds expectations of lin-ear narrative or spatial contiguity established in the canonical forms of the eighteenth- and nineteenth-century European novel. Yet her novel nevertheless offers a persistent sounding-out of prevail-ing tropes of "the modern" in the contexts of personal and national history. In contrast to the avant-garde project of making the frame visible through transgression, we can observe a contrary impulse to reframe modernity in Hayashi's *Hōrōki*. My reading of *Hōrōki* in Chapters 3 and 4 will aim to reinstall Hayashi's montage practice and her act of "enframing modernity" within a critical view.

Like most observers, I do not perceive a clear and fast division between modernism and the avant-garde, but rather see them as different modalities within the same general project. We can view modernist and avant-garde artists as active subjects in the process of defining and orienting Japanese modernity. Toward this end, mod-ernist and avant-garde artists consciously employed heterogeneous materials: in the case of literature, they championed linguistic het-erogeneity and constructedness over previous speech-centered mod-els of linguistic naturalness. In provisionally distinguishing between modernism and the avant-garde in terms of their formal concerns and strategies, I have tried to elucidate their characteristic attitudes to time and space. The avant-garde work of art tends to be spatial, paratactic, and synchronic—a sudden utopian moment of present-ness opening on the future, it finds its characteristic form in the collage. The broader category of modernism embraces works with these avant-garde tendencies as well as works oriented toward tem-poral, hypotactic, and diachronic expression.

I have suggested that the avant-garde work enacts an ecstatic moment of "breaking the frame," which serves to collapse the distance between "art" and "daily life," and to both clarify and critique the artwork's frame conditions. These frame conditions include the productive and distributive apparatuses of the artwork, where state guidance and censorship played a significant role in the case of inter-war Japan. The modernist work of art, on the other hand, could offer a reopening to history while remaining skeptical of established narrative strategies, thus cautiously situating itself within a more pervasive project of enframing the "modern world picture." The following chapters will examine these avant-garde and modernist strategies in the works of Hagiwara Kyōjirō, Hayashi Fumiko, and other writers, as they offer their own representations of Japanese modernity.

2 / LANGUAGE AT THE LIMITS
The Global Situation of Japanese Modernism

My aim throughout this book is to explore the relationship between the development of Japanese modernist and avant-garde literature in the 1920s and 1930s and the historical experience of modernity in the same decades. In the chapters that follow, I will discuss the literary activities of Hagiwara Kyōjirō and Hayashi Fumiko primarily in the context of domestic cultural, social, and political developments. The specificities of the cultural situation in which Hagiwara and Hayashi produced their works illuminate these works' status as responses to Japanese modernity, rather than as imitations or local variants of a modernism assumed to have found its original and true form in the West.

Nevertheless, it is clear that the modernity to which writers such as Hagiwara and Hayashi responded was deeply imprinted by Japan's encounter with a globally hegemonic West, an encounter that occasioned an extensive overhaul of Japanese culture and society following the Meiji Restoration of 1868. That modern Japanese literature also took shape as part of this encounter with the West and is a product of a complex process of translation, adaptation, and resistance to Western literary and intellectual concepts is a truism whose nuances have been explored in numerous literary studies.[1] The modernist literature of the 1920s and 1930s arose as a part of literary culture that was keenly aware of literary developments in Europe and America, as well as the broader cultural and social developments of which such literatures were a part, and modernist writers frequently related their own literary positions to these international developments. Moreover, as Hagiwara Kyōjirō's enigmatic final poems on "Asia" and Hayashi Fumiko's extensive regional travels and experience as a war reporter on the continent testify, Japanese modernists situated themselves not only with reference to Europe but also to the Asia-Pacific borders of the expanding Japanese empire.

In her discussion of Japanese modernist and postmodernist writers, the literary scholar Toshiko Ellis notes the imperative for modernist writers coming of age in the 1920s and 1930s to define their positions in global cultural terms. "They had to define themselves not only against contemporary Japan and its modern institutions," she writes, "but also against the traditional Japan which persisted on various levels of people's lives, and furthermore, against the West, which was the source of their inspiration as well as a threat to their cultural identity."[2] This complex process of staking positions apposite to domestic and global cultural developments was simultaneously a process of adopting a political stance: even an explicitly apolitical position would be perceived in political terms by critics on both the right and left in the politically charged atmosphere of Japan circa 1930. The political choices available to the Japanese people were themselves often figured in global terms, with the United States and the Soviet Union offering contrasting examples of the cultural and political possibilities of capitalism and communism respectively, while Europe and Asia offered a range of intermediate positions and counterpositions for cultural and political affiliation.

Thus we can see that "the West," while sometimes functioning discursively as a large and vaguely defined entity opposed to "the East" or to Japan, was at other times differentiated into a number of contesting political and cultural models that writers could use to articulate their own artistic and political goals. Hence to individual writers the West was not necessarily perceived as a monolithic "source of inspiration" or as a hegemonic "threat to cultural identity," but could function quite flexibly in enabling writers to stake their positions within the Japanese cultural and political spheres. Nevertheless, despite writers' flexible and strategic citation of European or American models, such citational practices cannot be completely divorced from the modern historical experience of

Western imperialist pressure and Japanese nationalist self-fashioning, in which some degree of anxiety regarding the West as both a source and a threat was conjoined with the anxieties and opportunities of Japan's own emerging role as a colonial power. Thus, in examining Japanese modernism, it is necessary to develop a critical viewpoint that acknowledges the individual agency and complexity of writers' citational practices, while at the same time remaining cognizant of the historic and geopolitical situation in which those citations occurred.

In this chapter, I will explore some of the rhetorical uses that Japanese modernist writers made of the West and their strategic, sometimes utopian, and sometimes ironical views of the West and its influence. In addition, I will consider the vital role of Japan's colonial and semicolonial territories in constituting and contesting Japanese modernism, a role that has often been overlooked in literary studies. This glimpse at the geopolitical articulations of Japanese modernism, while necessarily schematic and incomplete, should suggest the deep interdependency of the *naichi,* or "home territories" of the Japanese archipelago, and the *gaichi,* or "outer territories" in the sphere of Japan's colonial and semicolonial influence. This sketch of the geopolitical situation of Japanese modernism will also frame my analysis of Hagiwara Kyōjirō and Hayashi Fumiko with a consideration of works by writers outside their immediate circle of literary associates, including the poets Haruyama Yukio, Anzai Fuyue, and Yi Sang.

Strategies of Citation

The complexities of the modern Japanese apprehension of Western literature are closely tied to the wide-ranging and sometimes contradictory reforms of the Meiji political leaders and their successors. In response to the threat of Western imperialism, the Meiji government encouraged the study and emulation of multiple facets of European and American technological, political, social, and economic organization, while simultaneously endeavoring to fashion a modern Japanese nation-state and assert a unique national identity centered on the imperial institution. During the Meiji period, the reform of language and artistic representation seen as a significant aspect of this process of nation building, and the discourse on reform of language and literature reflected the larger intellectual climate of intensive reference to European and American models and the simultaneous imperative for national self-assertion.

As Dennis Washburn outlines in *The Dilemma of the Modern in Japanese Fiction*, Meiji writers' foremost concerns were the establishment of a national literary canon to more clearly define the modern in relationship to the traditional; the reformation of the Japanese language, including but not limited to the pursuit of the unification of written and spoken languages (*genbun itchi*); and the creation of a new form of literary realism that would reflect and embody modern experience.[3] This strong impulse toward reform and linguistic and literary renewal was inherited by successive generations of Japanese writers, even as their artistic programs, and the political context for their reforms, differed.

We can thus observe a modern paradigm emerging from the Meiji period onward, characterized by the need for constant reform and renewal in the realms of language and literature, which was viewed by many authors as a vital component of social and political reform. Operating under this paradigm of literary innovation, writers consistently cited the authority of Western authors and literary schools. Such citation might make use of the European critical vocabulary, as in the case of Naturalism in Meiji prose writing, or it might involve the citation of a more eclectic intellectual constellation of Western "influences" in response to specific rhetorical exigencies, as in the case of the Taishō-period "People's Poets" (*minshūshi-ha*), whose references included Walt Whitman, Edward Carpenter, Leo Tolstoy, and Romain Rolland. Thus the strong imperative toward artistic innovation and renewal, the active reference to current European literary and artistic trends, and the conviction that literary innovations could have a strong social impact were not new to Japanese modernist and avant-garde literature of the 1920s, but were extensions of a dominant literary paradigm established by the literary reformers of the Meiji era.

Translation of works of Western literature has played a key role in this pattern of self-positioning through citation, and the importance of translation is nowhere more salient than in the creation and development of the new form of "modern poetry" (*shi*). At the onset of Japanese literary contact with the West, translators held existing verse forms, such as haiku, tanka, and kanshi (poetry in Chinese) to be inadequate to translate the long stanzas, novel meters, and unfamiliar themes of European verse, and experimented with new verse forms as means of conveying these elements.[4] The creators of the seminal poetry collection *Shintaishi shō* (*A Selection of New-Style Poetry*, 1882) deployed these newly invented verse forms not only for use in translation but also as the basis of their own original poetry. This "new-style poetry" (*shintaishi*) was successfully parlayed into the dominant mode of modern poetry, eventually referred to simply as *shi*, which coexisted as a literary mode independent from haiku, tanka, and kanshi.[5]

As the didactic verses of the *Shintaishi shō* on such themes as evolution and human liberty testify, this simultaneous project of translation and generic invention was carried out with a specific political and aesthetic agenda in the domestic sphere. Moreover, the patriotic and military themes of several of the created poems underscore the close relationship between the movement for a new literature and fast-evolving Japanese nationalism, while the intent to forge a poetry out of the "existing plain and everyday words of our fellow countrymen" (*waga hōjin no jūrai heijō no go*) expressed in Yatabe Ryōkichi's preface to the collection foreshadows the coming *genbun itchi* movement that would stress the role of a literature based on the vernacular in creating a modern, national language-community.[6] The influence of the *genbun itchi* prose movement would in turn be reflected in the further development of modern poetry away from the metrical employment of regular groups of five and seven syllables, and toward the so-called *kōgojiyūshi* (colloquial free verse) around the year 1907.[7]

Even after Japanese poets had thoroughly assimilated "new-style poetry," translations of European poetry continued to play a major role as catalyst in the creation of new poetic styles and political-aesthetic stances for successive generations of Japanese poets. Ueda Bin's collection of Symbolist poems *Kaichōon* (*Sound of the Tide*, 1905) and Horiguchi Daigaku's collection of translations from post-Symbolist poets *Gekka no ichigun* (*A Gathering Under the Moon*, 1925) were especially significant not only for the high quality of their translations but for the keen attention they received from young poets seeking to establish new styles in Japanese verse. Later, the journal *Shi to shiron* (*Poetry and Poetics*, 1928–1932) and its successor journal *Bungaku* (*Literature*, 1932–1933) played a central role in the translation and critical introduction of Surrealism and other currents of French modernism, as well as the English-language modernism of such figures as James Joyce and T. S. Eliot, helping to reinforce the strong association between Japanese modernist poetry and the enterprise of translation from European languages.

In the context of this complex process of citation and self-positioning, it would thus be a mistake to consider the transmission of Western literature independently of the artistic and political agendas of the agents of this transmission, who often were creative artists themselves. Similarly, the critical trope that would speak of the "influence" of the works thus introduced must be questioned, since the word "influence" engenders a syntactical relationship that allots a passive, receptive role on the part of the author who is "influenced" by a previously existing works or authors. This model fails to adequately capture the active agency of the "recipient" of the influence, not only in apprehending the literary or artistic "source" but also in redeploying the "source" as part of an individual artistic stance that responds to a specific local aesthetic and political context.

While traditional studies of influence tend to focus on linear genealogies, in fact the nature of the "influence" of European culture in Japan in the early twentieth century was multilayered and occurred across many media simultaneously. The avant-garde movement of the 1920s was an expressly interdisciplinary enterprise, and works in various media from several artistic centers contributed to the Japanese interpretation of international modernist and avant-garde movements. German Expressionist film, together with French Impressionist film and film criticism, drew the keen attention of writers and visual artists as well as filmmakers, while the theater community in Japan displayed a concerted interest in German Expressionist drama. In the visual arts a steady attention to post-Impressionist Parisian artistic practice was supplemented by information on Italian Futurism, German Expressionism, and Russian Futurism and Constructivism purveyed by such figures as Kanbara Tai and Murayama Tomoyoshi, both of whom were active critics and creative writers as well as visual artists.[8]

Moreover, as will be explored throughout the current study, modernist and avant-garde literary and artistic movements were introduced and reconstituted in Japan as part of a wider series of debates on the nature of daily life in the context of the transformation of the urban environment, the development of communications technologies, and changes in social mores, as well as philosophical and political debates over such subjects as individualism and collective action. Modernism, in other words, was not perceived simply as a literary or artistic movement, but was integral to a larger discourse about the nature and orientation of Japanese modernity.

Given the multifaceted discourse on modernity and the diverse forms of mediation of cultural contact with Europe and America, the operation of Western "influence" on Japanese modernism is thus more complex than has sometimes been acknowledged. It is true that Japanese modernist and avant-garde writers of the 1920s established their positions in part through a familiar pattern of citation of European literary and artistic movements, whether through their activities as translators and critics or through an act of symbolic affiliation with a European avant-garde movement, such as Hirato Renkichi's promulgation of the "Japanese Futurist Manifesto Movement" in 1921, Takahashi Shinkichi's self-proclamation as a Dadaist in his maiden poetry collection *Dadaisto Shinkichi no shi* (*The Poems of Dadaist Shinkichi*, 1923), or the emergence of a group of self-identifying Surrealist poets in the late 1920s.[9] Nevertheless, after an initial rhetorical positioning through such acts of affiliation, most Japanese avant-gardes were eager to establish their creative independence from any subordination to a foreign literary ideology. Thus Hirato progressed from his advocacy of Futurism to an attempt to propagate his own school of "analogisime," while Takahashi developed a highly individual interpretation of Dadaism in relationship to Zen Buddhism.[10] After an awareness of European avant-garde movements was established in Japan in the early 1920s, many aspiring modernists and avant-gardes, such as the artists and poets affiliated with the Mavo group or the prose Shinkankaku-ha writers, were able to establish their literary and artistic positions through a more eclectic citation and manipulation of European sources in relation to the domestic situation, without proposing any affiliation with a specific foreign avant-garde movement.

While most progressive artists and writers paid keen attention to developments of European modernism, the Japanese apprehension of Western culture in this period is further complicated by the emergence of America and the Soviet Union as powerful cultural models.[11] The perception and reception of each of these cultural models was multivalent, with the still young Soviet Union hailed or excoriated by commentators across the political spectrum. America, offering a dramatic countermodel to Soviet communism, was associated with Taylorist technological efficiency on the one hand and decadent Hollywood popular culture on the other.[12]

One powerful expression of the perception of rival Soviet and American models and their application in the Japanese context is Mavo leader Murayama Tomoyoshi's essay "Kōsei-ha ni kan suru ikkōsatsu: keisei geijutsu no han'i ni okeru" ("A Thought on Constructivism: With Respect to the Scope of the Plastic Arts)," published in the journal *Atorie* (*Atelier*) in August 1925. While Murayama played an instrumental role in the introduction of Constructivism in Japan, in this essay he expresses doubts about its applicability to Japan's domestic situation, and argues instead for the adoption of a subversive Americanism as a form of "neo-Dada."[13] In serving as the antithesis to gestures of support for Constructivism, Murayama's call for Americanism exemplifies his dialectical strategy of "conscious Constructivism."[14]

Constructivism is a communist art. However, while it is a socialist art, it is not a revolutionary art. It is a constructive art; it is not an art for destruction or struggle. . . . Therefore, in a place like contemporary Japan that is in the midst of an age of destruction and class struggle, Constructivism will only come and go as surface fashion. Like so much colored soda water.

Most of so-called Constructivism in Japan cannot help but be a bonbon, a display window in a department store, a piece of candy.

In such a Japan, Constructivism must pass as quickly as possible. The medicine needed for today's Japan is Americanism.[15]

While Murayama advocates "Americanism" here, he also acknowledges that Americanism can have multiple meanings, and clarifies the type of Americanism that would serve his strategic purposes:

Americanism is also in high gear in today's Russia. But this mustn't be misunderstood. Americanism in Russia (in other words, to be fresh, to be vivid, to be a fish, to be a dog, and science! science! science! speed! purity! in other words, Constructivism) is a way of restoring health. It is hygiene. It is economics. It is a sanitarium for the people. They need first of all to wash away many years of hardship at this sanitarium, so that they can depart for the hardships of the future.

The Americanism needed in Japan is the opposite of this. It is a laxative, a vaccination, a symptom aggravator, morphine, laughing gas.

Unless you're Christ, you can't be a virgin and liberate the yellow woman.

Neo-Dadaism in this context. A parade of cripples, bunglers, and imbeciles!

In Japan today, we need neo-Dadaism to prepare the way for Constructivism![16]

In addition to offering a provocative geopolitical context for the activities of the Mavo artists' group under Murayama's leadership, Murayama's polemic points to the inadequacy of the model of "influence" as a passive transmission from a source (Constructivism or American popular culture) to a receiver (Murayama or the Japanese avant-garde). Instead, Murayama demonstrates here how foreign "influence" could be employed consciously and strategically to address the cultural and political situation in Japan; or rather, an "America" or "Soviet Union" could be invented for this purpose. Moreover, this passage illustrates Murayama's strong social concern, couched in terms that take the nation-state as the basic unit of social analysis, as well as his underlying conviction that art can have a strongly transformative social and political impact. Despite their subversive radicalism in Murayama's hands, these are all critical parameters that connect Murayama with his Meiji reformist predecessors.

The Character in Question

For Japanese poets, written language itself offered a series of strategic choices that could express political as well as stylistic positions. Scrutiny of modernist and avant-garde poetry from the 1920s and 1930s reveals a particular attention to the visual effects of poetic language as mediated by the printing process. In particular, poets focused on the various distinct orthographies in use in modern written Japanese: kanji, or Chinese characters; hiragana, a syllabary used for the phonetic representation of the Japanese language; katakana, a syllabary parallel to hiragana, often used for the transcription of words of foreign origin; and romaji, the Roman or Latin alphabet. While no strict correspondence between use of these orthographies and a political or cultural affiliation should be assumed, poets did make use of each of these distinct orthographic registers to establish their individual poetic voices and, in so doing, to claim political and aesthetic positions, or to comment upon the very nature of the choices and positions available to them. In bringing increased scrutiny to the written aspect of poetry and the heterogeneous components of the Japanese language that its contrastive written registers reveal, the work of modernist writers also subtly undermined the hegemony of the ideal of *genbun itchi*, which had proposed a transparent written language based on oral foundations that would serve as a standard national language.

One of Hagiwara Kyōjirō's most provocative literary statements on the nature of modern poetic language is his "Aruhabetto ni tai suru sengen" ("Manifesto on the Alphabet"), which is situated as the penultimate poem of his first poetry collection, *Shikei senkoku* (*Death Sentence*, 1925). (See appendix for translation from this collection.) On the most immediate level, at least, "Manifesto on the Alphabet" extols the ability of written language to convey the psychological sensations of a modern subject. The poem proposes a classification of the roman alphabet into "shapes" that accompany three different internal states: those shapes that accompany "feelings of oppression and foreboding," shapes that accompany "an exaggerated sensation of speed," and shapes that accompany "clear sounds and harmonious affectionate music." Hagiwara thus divides the interior experience of the modern subject into three areas, reproducing three major tropes within the discourse of modernity, and proceeding to give further examples of these tropes, in what amounts to a list of romantic and modernist literary clichés.

However, the most intriguing aspect of the poem is that each of these three modern tropes and lists of illustrative examples are ascribed to the semiotic powers of certain alphabetic letters.[17] For example, the letters or "shapes" "B, D, Gj, M, U, V, W, Z" are said to correspond to "feelings of oppression and foreboding." illustrated by such items as "a northerner's language," "the sound of freight cars and wagons climbing a grade," "the sound of water mains beneath the city," "your different feelings when suffering an insult," "psychological effects accompanying venereal disease," "the sound a suicide enjoys," "the taste in a stomach patient's mouth," and "the sky in a factory zone."

Finally, the poem ends in the hortatory section of the "manifesto," with the declaration that "we shall use the shapes classified above, and all the musical ● painterly sensations of the alphabet, as elements in constructing our own interiors!"[18] This declaration is not unlike Hagiwara's other statements of his artistic philosophy, asserting the reciprocity between the construction of the poetic text and the construction of the self.[19] Thus, a literalist reading of the text would treat it as a manifesto in the form of a poem, a relatively straightforward declaration of Hagiwara's poetic program.

However, a number of internal dissonances within the structure of the "Manifesto" suggest that it is rather a poem in the form of a manifesto—in fact a satire of a manifesto that comments on the situation of modernist poetry in Japan with a subversive humor. As the poem continues, the illustrative lists for the three modern tropes become progressively diverse and arbitrary. The final category, "clear sounds and harmonious affectionate music," is illustrated with such incongruous examples as "a pen running over a blank sheet of paper," "the cheeks and arms and legs of your lover," "the music of the harvest," "intellectual restraint and growth," "sound waves," "radio," "virgin beauty," "the tranquility of a laboratory," "katakana," "the speed of an automobile or a stagecoach," "orange soda," and "young madam." (These qualities, in turn, are associated with the shapes C, F, H, L, N, S, T, and Y.)

The ultimate paradox of this manifesto is that while it holds up the expressive value of the "shapes" of the Roman alphabet, the poem itself, including all the examples of the emotional correspondences to these "shapes," is written in Japanese, consisting of a relatively normative mixture of hiragana, kanji, and katakana. The only examples of romaji or alphabetic characters are in the list of "shapes" at the end of each section. (This paradox is intensified by the fact that "katakana" is given as one of the examples of "clear sounds and harmonious affectionate music" expressed by the last series of alphabetic "shapes.") Thus the poem offers itself as an extreme and paradoxical case of "translation"—indeed, it appears for a moment as if it were itself a translation of a lost Italian Futurist manifesto.

In his study of the modernist poet Nishiwaki Junzaburō, Hosea Hirata argues that the process of translation fundamentally defines modernism in Japan. This consciousness of translation at the heart of Japanese modernism is accompanied, in Hirata's analysis, by a mixture of anxiety and desire concerning the "origins" of translation. "The authentic origin remains a powerful source of seduction," he writes, "the final paradise, waiting for our naked entry—we, moderns, who may one day finally discard the robes of translation."[20] While Hirata's thesis might present an overly sweeping view of the impulses and dilemmas of Japanese modernist poetry, it does offer insight into the problematic addressed in Hagiwara's poem. If the West and Western literature are to be taken as the "origin" of modern Japanese poetry, then Hagiwara's "manifesto" could be seen as a utopian call to recapture these origins and rebuild Japanese poets' subjectivity out of the raw materials (the alphabetic characters) of this originary terrain.

As such, the manifesto calls to mind a number of utopian moments in modern Japanese cultural history, most immediately Hirato Renkichi's proclamation of the "Japanese Futurist Manifesto Movement" on the streets of Hibiya in 1921. The leaflet that Hirato distributed to passersby, itself a type of synthesis and "translation" of several of Italian Futurist founder F. T. Marinetti's manifestos, was devoted to ecstatic praise of the dynamic beauty of the city and its machines, as well as a denunciation of existing cultural institutions. It also contained the following lines to convey a technical program for Futurist poetry:

We, who favor momentary fulfillment, are much indebted to Marinetti, who loves the bewitching movements of the cinematograph. We strive to employ onomatopoeia, mathematical symbols, and every organic method to participate in the ultimate truth of creation. To the greatest extent possible, we will destroy the conventions of writing and grammar, in particular sweeping away the corpses of adjectives and adverbs, and, using the infinitives of verbs, advance into heretofore unclaimed territory.[21]

Hirato's "manifesto movement" thus enacted a paradigmatic rhetorical gesture in proposing to open "unclaimed" territory through the infusion of a linguistic strategy heavily "indebted to Marinetti" (*Marinettei ni ou tokoro ooki*) into the Japanese cultural context. For Hirato's contemporaries, the significance of Hirato's manifesto was not necessarily in the words of the manifesto themselves—the work of the Italian Futurists was already familiar to many Japanese intellectuals—but rather in the novel action of distributing his poetic pamphlets in a public space. By linking poetry with a type of public action, in moving the locus of literary activity, in the language of the day, from the study to the streets, Hirato's "manifesto movement" had a markedly utopian public import, to the extent that this action was remembered by many of Hirato's contemporary poets as an epochal event.[22]

Beyond its immediate association with this earlier moment of utopian poetic agitation, in its fixation on the transformative power of the "shapes" of the Western alphabet, Hagiwara's "Manifesto on the Alphabet" recalls a history of ambitious language reforms since the Meiji Restoration, including culture minister Mori Arinori's proposal in 1873 to replace Japanese with English as the national language of Japan.[23] Alternatively, the poem could be seen as a transposition of the utopian universalism of Christianity and Marxism, each of which offered their own orthodox scriptures and emancipatory formulas for the masses of Japan.[24] Or, it could be seen to anticipate the works of later Japanese modernists whose formalist and surrealist experiments often were carried out in a utopian, "pure" world of occidental imagery.

At the same time as it invokes utopian Japanese efforts to transform society through the reform of language, Hagiwara's poem is a surprising inversion of Western exoticist, utopian fantasies of foreign writing systems, specifically "pictographic" or "ideogrammatic" writing systems such as Egyptian hieroglyphics and Chinese characters that were taken to be pictorial representations of the objects, actions, or qualities indexed by the characters.[25] In contrast to the perceived alienation of phonetic writing systems in their arbitrary relation to the world of material objects, many European and American thinkers have posited hieroglyphics and Chinese characters as having an intimate, pre-lapsarian relationship to the things that they name. Such a conception, whereby, in the words of nineteenth-century French sinologist Jean Pierre Abel-Rémusat, the characters of Chinese would "present to the eye not the sterile and conventional signs of pronunciation but the things themselves," was to have a lasting impact on English-language modernism through the work of Ernest Fenollosa and Ezra Pound and was also reflected in the modernist interest in "ideogrammatic" writing systems in other national contexts.[26] Hagiwara's poem turns these persistent orientalist/modernist conceptions of the mystical or energizing aspects of foreign "ideogrammatic" written language on their head, proposing a "hieroglyphic" and utopian dimension to the roman alphabet.

Hagiwara's poem, then, could be seen either as an extreme example of the modern Japanese paradigm of national reform through citation of Western sources, or as an ironic travesty of this paradigm through an inversion of Western orientalism. Given the dissonances and obvious clichés embedded in Hagiwara's poetic lists, we could conclude that his poem simultaneously holds out the utopian possibilities of (foreign) language and mocks them. With its paradoxical form, "A Manifesto on the Alphabet" is ultimately an absurdist text that resonates with the calls for a subversive "neo-Dada" issued by both Hagiwara and his Mavo colleague Murayama.

Pure Poetry and the European Ideal

Regardless of Hagiwara's satirical foray, in the years following the publication of *Shikei senkoku*, numerous modernist poets delved quite seriously into the pursuit of creating a utopian realm of "pure poetry," in part through the aid of language and imagery that pointed toward modern Japanese poetry's "origins" in the West and away from the experience of the everyday embedded in the quotidian language and material culture of Japan. The words of Nishiwaki Junzaburō, in the preface to the 1927 poetry anthology *Fukuiku taru kafu yo* (*O Fragrant Firemen*), point to this new impulse to separate the poetic realm from the realm of the everyday: "Poems construct a vacuous desert inside the brain and, by beating down all sensations, sentiments, and ideas connected to the experience of reality, are one method by which to squeeze the brain purely. Here is pure poetry."[27] This emphasis on a poetic "purity" disassociated from "reality" must be read as part of Nishiwaki's complex and ironic poetics informed by his study of European metaphysical, Symbolist, and Surrealist poetry and poetic theory. Nevertheless, on its most basic surface level, it serves as a stark contrast with the calls for a new poetic engagement with "daily life" earlier issued by Hagiwara Kyōjirō and his peers.[28]

The impulse toward poetic purity articulated by Nishiwaki was shared by a group of poets affiliated with the journal *Shi to shiron* (*Poetry and Poetics*), whose contributors included poets associated with the nascent Japanese Surrealist movement as well as what was identified at the time as poetic formalism. Founded in 1928 by a coterie including Kondō Azuma, Anzai Fuyue, Kitagawa Fuyuhiko, Take-naka Iku, Kanbara Tai, Iijima Tadashi, Takiguchi Takeshi, Miyoshi Tatsuji, Ueda Toshio, Toyama Usaburō, and general editor Haruyama Yukio, the journal also featured contributions from prominent modernist poets outside this coterie, most notably Nishiwaki Junzaburō and Kitasono Katsue. While the works of such a large group of poets will necessarily be diverse, the poems of editor Haruyama Yukio provide some index to the poetic concerns and strategies of several *Shi to shiron* affiliates during this period.

Haruyama's poems provide numerous examples of the tendency among modernist poets in the late 1920s to move away from a treatment of daily life in Japan, in part through recourse to language and imagery associated with Europe. The following verse, a section of the series "ALBUM" from the 1929 poetry collection *Shokubutsu no danmen* (*Cross-section of a Plant*), captures something of Haruyama's style and motivic tendencies from this period, although it is not representative of his boldest formal experiments:

> The roofs of the churches
> Line up beside the cactus flowers
>> A banana-colored zeppelin
>> Clinching a pipe in its mouth
> The scent of bread
> Strolls out from the balcony
>> A bottle and
>> A guitar and
>> A salad and
>> What's that?
> Shabby clouds
>> Are playing in
>>> The soiled corset[29]

Although the setting of this poem is unidentified, it has a strongly Western flavor, created by its repeated reference to material objects associated with European or American culture: the churches, cactus flowers, zeppelin, pipe, bread, balcony, [wine] bottle, guitar, salad, and corset. The poem has a particularly close relationship to European painting traditions: it begins with a description of a landscape or cityscape, focusing in on a balcony, and momentarily presenting the "still-life" of bottle, guitar, and salad. The ambiguity of its spatial relationships and the lightly humorous defamiliarizing effect of its metaphors remind us of the cubists' appropriation and distortion of the European landscape and still-life traditions.

The vaguely European or "Western" atmosphere of the original poem is amplified by its use throughout of only kanji and katakana—katakana is used not only to transcribe European-derived words such as "bread" (*pan*) and "salad" (*sarada*), but also to represent words and parts of speech with Japanese-language origins that would typically be written in hiragana. This is a technique used not infrequently by Haruyama and other *Shi to shiron* poets, not necessarily to serve as index to the poem's degree of "Westernization," but arguably to give a striking visual counterpoint to the more normative use of hiragana, particularly in the case of a poem or verse in a series, as in the verse above.

Nevertheless, the successful effect of this use of katakana as visual counterpoint cannot be wholly removed from katakana's modern association with Western discourse. With fewer strokes than most kanji and a more angular writing style than hiragana, katakana is the form of Japanese writing that might be said to bear the greatest physical resemblance to the Roman alphabet in its technologically mediated, printed form. The "clarity" and "angularity" of katakana, together with its use for the phonetic transcription of Western discourse, gives it an overdetermined relationship to cultural values associated with the West, such as materialism, rationalism, and the ideal of progress. This overdetermined quality is brought to the fore by the inclusion of "katakana" in Hagiwara's list of items exemplifying "clear sounds and harmonious affectionate music" in his "Manifesto on the Alphabet." Through its employment of katakana, Haruyama's poem could be said to speak with a vaguely European "accent."

In her superb, imaginative study *Fault Lines: Cultural Memory and Japanese Surrealism*, Miryam Sas takes a singularly nuanced view of the relationship between Japanese Surrealist poets and European literature, emphasizing the agency of Japanese poets in using the West for their own purposes as an "ideal space":

Surrealist practice in Japan can be seen to reframe the narrative of Japanese modernization as an imposition of values from a hegemonic West. The operation performed here is closer to the nature of a chance, or the functioning of a Surrealist image: a resonant and "true" juxtaposition. Here the "West" becomes a space that transcends its "real" position and begins to function as an ideal space, a place that provides material for the Japanese writers' poetic encounters, as well as a screen upon which their fantasies may be projected.[30]

Regardless of Sas's salutary move away from a simplistic narrative of Western cultural hegemony, we should not lose sight of the global situation of interlocking imperial pressures in which Surrealist poets' citation of Europe was more than "chance," but had complex cultural precedents and political overtones. In immediate political terms, the "high collar" associations of the ideal (Western European) West conjured in Surrealist and formalist modernist poetry carried manifestly bourgeois class implications at a time when the "Proletarian" literary movement was reaching the peak of its power within Japanese literary circles despite governmental repression, while the modernists' Europe-facing stance also distinguished them from the cultural nationalism that was re-emerging as an increasingly powerful force in the late 1920s and early 1930s.

Beyond such immediate political considerations, however, the use of the West as an "ideal space" functioned as a strategy for achieving ambitious poetic aims for several Japanese modernists, who consciously employed European language, iconography, and literary style to break with the rhythms, imagery, and graphic appearance of previous Japanese poetry. As Hosea Hirata observes, Nishiwaki Junzaburō could subtly defamiliarize both Japanese and Western literary traditions, as he purloined European literary texts and subjected them to idiosyncratic processes of transposition and translation.[31] In the cases of Haruyama Yukio and especially Kitasono Katsue, "high collar" European imagery could be overprogrammed to the extent where it transcended immediate referential value and even self-parody and aspired to function as an abstract field of linguistic play. Yet while such abstracted linguistic play with occidentalist signifiers might be one way of striving for poetic "purity," this "purity" could never be completely separated from the historical relationship in which Japan had looked to Europe as the source of "civilization and enlightenment" from the Meiji Restoration on.

Anzai Fuyue and Japan's Colonial Periphery

Given the Europhilic bent of so many of its contributors, it might be surprising to note that three of the eleven original coterie members of *Shi to shiron* (Anzai Fuyue, Kitagawa Fuyuhiko, and Takiguchi Takeshi) had previously been associated with a journal, entitled *A*, edited not in Tokyo, Yokohama, or Paris, but in Dalian, Manchuria, a port city that anchored Japan's commercial and territorial claims in northeastern China.[32] As an important precursor to *Shi to shiron*, the journal *A* played an instrumental role in the establishment of a new phase of Japanese modernism marked by a more formalist, aestheticist, and theoretically oriented approach to poetry, in contrast to the Futurist and Dadaist-inspired work of Hagiwara, Hirato Renkichi, Kanbara Tai, and Takahashi Shinkichi in the early and mid-1920s.

One of the poetic forms championed by the members of *A*, the *tanshi* or short poem, could be seen as a remediation of the Japanese lyric tradition of haiku and tanka, which was recuperated in part through a citation of the "influence" of French post-Symbolist poets who had themselves been inspired by translations of Japanese haiku and tanka.[33] In addition to this triangulated engagement with both European modernism and the Japanese lyric tradition, the work of the *A* coterie is also distinguished by its thematic attention to the Japanese imperial enterprise in East Asia—a thematic concern that found expression through a distinctive approach to the issues of graphic design and orthography that were a persistent focus of Japanese modernist poetry.

Writing in 1925, *A* co-founder Kitagawa Fuyuhiko outlined the sort of poetry he and his associates were striving to create, in a polemic against the poetic techniques favored by Hagiwara Kyōjirō in his collection from the same year, *Shikei senkoku:*

We should reject the abuse of printing techniques in poetry. By abuse of printing techniques, I mean making certain printed characters excessively large, printing others upside down or on their side, using mathematical signs or other symbols, and recklessly employing the arrangement of printed characters as an expressive method.

The abuse of printing techniques in poetry kills the poem's spiritual sense, and defiles the poem's impression. It does not increase the poetic effect the slightest bit.

Techniques such as those used by Kyōjirō are unconvincing and incomplete. If printing techniques are so precious, then surely one should carry through with the graphic arrangement of characters until it forms a pictorial poem. However, since Guillaume Apollinaire's collection "Calligrammes," from about the year 1916, this has already proven to be a splendid failure.[34]

In addition to its hasty dismissal of Apollinaire (betraying either a precocious critical self-confidence or, in Harold Bloom's terms, a high degree of anxiety about European "influence"), Kitagawa's critique is notable for the appearance of such terms as "spiritual" and "defile[ment]" (implying its opposite, "purity,") that had been consciously excluded from Hagiwara's poetics as expressed in the preface to *Shikei senkoku,* which advocated the disorderly interpenetration of the poetic text, the poet's subjectivity and corporeality, and the chaotic life of the modern city.[35] Nevertheless, it is also important to note the continuities between Hagiwara's and Kitagawa's poetics: when Kitagawa proposes an alternative to "the abuse of printing technique," his alternative also shows a strong consciousness of the printed page—a consciousness of modern poetry as a physical artifact enabled by a specific technological process, which both exploits and draws attention to the resources of that printed medium:

The most effective printing technique is the use of "blank" [space]. This corresponds with that excellent method of achieving visual effect in which the painter skillfully uses the ground of the canvas. . . . With regard to the use of blank space, I believe that Anzai Fuyue's "Townscape and Civilization Ranged in File," from the third issue of *A,* is certainly a success.[36]

Anzai Fuyue's poem cited by Kitagawa indeed employs a literal "blank" space of roughly ten lines between the main sections of the poem. The author drew further attention to this space in the poem's original journal publication by framing the entire poem with linear borders. Anzai's poem, moreover, provides as sure a guide to the new modernist poetic concerns emerging in the mid-1920s as does Kitagawa's polemic.

TOWNSCAPE AND CIVILIZATION RANGED IN FILE

The photography studio that advanced civilization into the future is wearing with age amidst the scenery.

(At this toffee-colored crossroads, "municipal reform" has already arrived.)[37]

Thematically, this poem typifies Anzai's ironic sensibility, applied to the question of historical consciousness. The photography studio, a site for a commercial technology representative of the modern material culture propagated by Western imperialism and adopted by Meiji reformers under the ideology of advancing "civilization," has already become a dated artifact, to be supplanted by a new wave of "municipal reform."

As a representative *tanshi* (short poem), this poem shares with other *tanshi* of the period a dual strategy of simultaneously referencing and distancing itself from the Japanese haiku tradition. In this case, the poem's link to haiku, aside from its relative brevity, is its two-part structure of topic and comment, identified by Kawamoto Kōji as the root and superimposed section of the haiku.[38] In contrast to haiku, where this two-part structure is created by purely syntactical means such as the use of a *kireji*, or "cutting-word," Anzai's poem emphasizes the gap between the two parts of the poem by means of the spatial gap or "blank" between the two lines, as pointed out by Kitagawa.

A similar strategy of referencing and distancing from haiku is manifested in Anzai's now-canonical short poem "Spring":

SPRING

A single butterfly crossed over the Tartar Strait.[39]

Here the Japanese lyric tradition is invoked by the seasonal reference—the explicit statement of season in the poem's title, as well as
the lexeme of the butterfly, which has a well-established place in the
haiku canon as a *kigo*, or season-word, related to spring.[40] The single
line of the poem, however, differs strongly from haiku not only in
its syllabic pattern but also in its lack of a syntactical break, employing a single, straightforwardly arranged statement of subject, object,
and predicate.

The chief interest of this poem is the contrast between the
words "butterfly," rendered with the hiragana てふてふ (*tefutefu*,
pronounced *chōchō* in modern Japanese), and "Tartar Strait," rendered with the kanji 韃靼海峡 (*dattan kaikyō*). The use of the
exotic, multi-stroke Chinese toponym "Tartar Strait" is typical of
Anzai's poetic practice: the toponym refers to the strait between
Sakhalin and the Asian mainland (stretching north from Manchuria)
and is derived from a Chinese word for northern nomadic tribes.[41]
Numerous commentators on this poem have pointed to a poetically
effective correspondence between signifier and signified in these
contrasting phrases, with the simple, curvilinear hiragana conveying the frailty and fluttering motion of the lone butterfly, while the
dense and infrequently encountered kanji for *dattan kaikyō* convey
a sense of rugged, vast, and inhospitable terrain.[42] This contrast in
orthography brings us closer to the quality at the heart of Anzai's
distinctive poetic voice—the manipulation and balance of exotic,
contrastive lexical elements. This lexical strategy is inseparable from
Anzai's thematic exploration of continental exoticism, which is tied
in turn to his own personal experience in Japan's colonial territory
in Manchuria.[43]

This careful balance of poetic vocabulary and contrastive
orthographical elements is exemplified in another of Anzai's short
poems:

LATE SPRING

The streets are moaning with the cauchemar of fever
pagoda

How do we get out to under there?

Each of the three lines that form the body of this poem highlights a different orthography: the first line uses two conspicuous
multi-stroked Chinese compounds, which would normally be read
gaiku and *byōnetsu* but are glossed with furigana (phonetic characters attached to a Chinese character to indicate the reading) with the
more colloquial *machi* (town streets) and *netsu* (fever), followed by
the rather literary predicate *unasarete iru* (to cry out in sleep while
having a nightmare), also incorporating a dense, multi-stroke kanji
character. The second line is English written in romaji or alphabetic
letters, and the final line is a thoroughly colloquial phrase primarily
in hiragana, employing only two relatively inconspicuous kanji.

The first line of "Late Spring" evokes dense streets in a city
caught in an epidemic. The "pagoda" of the second line suggests
that it is an East Asian city, and although the exact location is not
given, we might imagine it is Chinese, given the recurrence of continental settings in Anzai's poetry and the contemporary trope of
China as the "sick man of Asia," a trope as prevalent in Japan as it
was in the West.[44] Ironically, the most identifiably "oriental" element
in the poem, the pagoda, is written in romaji. This orthographic
juxtaposition raises several questions. Is the speaker of the third line
attempting to reach the pagoda by consulting an English-language
map? Or does the viewer so strongly identify with orientalist modes
of viewing and signification that this "traditional" building is associated with a Western signifier? Is the speaker seeking out a religious
complex as a sanctuary from the epidemic? To offer prayers for the
victims? Or is he blithely ignoring the epidemic as he searches for
the pagoda on a tourist excursion?

Anzai frequently relies on an adoption of an orientalist persona
to achieve his idiosyncratic poetic of modernist irony. This strategy is most fully realized in the lengthy prose poems of his third
poetry collection, published in 1933, such as "Ikaru kawa,"[45] which
tells of a railway surveying crew lost in a sandstorm in the Gobi
Desert, or "Gisō yōkan," which describes the results of an archeological survey of the eponymous lost city in the Sinkiang region of
Central Asia, whose name is not to be found "in the most detailed
maps stored in the any of the royal libraries of the earth."[46] In the
poem "Shōbai-gataki" the poet likens himself to his former school-
mate, an antique dealer who is in search of "curios" in China; again

the word "curio" appears symptomatically in romaji.[47] Later in his career, Anzai returned to the archeological metaphor, and described his role as a poet as an "excavator of dead words." Thus the orientalist persona appears in the several guises of surveyor, archeologist, linguist, corrupt colonial administrator, tourist, curio collector, and armchair traveler.[48]

Anzai's orientalist persona calls to mind the important role played by many Japanese literati in the prewar and wartime periods in constructing an imaginative map or image of Japan's colonies and Asian neighbors in the eyes of the Japanese reading public. This mapping or image-making was achieved through works of fiction or poetry set in these territories, or, more often, by travel journals, essays, and speaking tours based on their experiences abroad. A great number of the most prominent Japanese writers produced such travel accounts of Taiwan, Korea, Manchuria, Inner Mongolia, and China, including Natsume Sōseki, Tanizaki Junichirō, Yosano Akiko, Akutagawa Ryūnosuke, Yokomitsu Riichi, and Hayashi Fumiko, to name only a few of the most prominent examples.[49]

As literary scholar Shu-mei Shih has argued, such tours and travel literature provided the means by which Japanese modernity and cultural superiority could be confirmed by the fervent reception of cultural celebrities in the colonies, while simultaneously Japanese identity and modernity could be reaffirmed as resembling and yet differing from the colonial other.[50] This "resemblance" was often couched in terms of Japan's shared premodern cultural heritage with her East Asian neighbors, while the "difference" was figured most broadly in terms of Japan's achievement of modernity and the comparative political, cultural, and material "backwardness" of her neighbors. Thus travel literature could be seen as a sort of mirror that preserved the difference between self (metropolitan Japanese) and mirror-object (colonial subject), and in which the gaze primarily served the function of narcissistic self-regard—a point to which I will return in my analysis of poems by Anzai Fuyue and Yi Sang.

The close relationship to the Japanese colonies and "informal empire" in Asia is particularly striking in the case of Japanese modernist poetry, as a number of prominent poets either lived in the Asian periphery of Japan or spent extended periods of time there.[51] In addition to Anzai, Kitagawa, and their associates, we can cite the examples of Kusano Shinpei, who began his poetic career in the Chinese province of Guangzhou, and Kaneko Mitsuharu, who spent much of the 1920s and 1930s traveling in Southeast Asia and China as well as Europe. The title of the journal *A,* co-founded by Anzai, Kitagawa, and two associates in 1924, is emblematic of the close relationship between Japanese modernism and the *gaichi* or colonial periphery. This journal title employs the first character, 亞 (*a*) in the Chinese-character transcription of the European-derived geographical term "Asia" (Chinese *yaxiya,* Japanese *ajia*).[52]

As this title suggests, "Asia" represented an alternative point of identification for modern poets, an alternative from the opposition between "Japan" and "the West" (albeit an ironic one, since the word "Asia" itself is of European provenance). This alternative point of identification was exploited in part to contravene the over-determined, anxious relationship between Japan and "the West" as the "source" of Japanese modernism and modernity. On the colonial periphery, Japanese modernists could play a heroic role as representatives of Japanese modernity and broaden their poetics through their exploration of a variety of linguistic elements and chronotypes tied to historical traces on the Asian continent, all the while circumventing a Japanese poetic tradition that they viewed as exhausted. This strategy of identification with "Asia" applies as much to Kitagawa's poetic career, which in many respects was more critical and resistive to the Japanese imperialist project, as to that of Anzai, whose aestheticist orientalism was more clearly complicit with Japanese imperialism.[53]

More so than the utopian modernism of Haruyama, which strives for poetic purity through a manipulation of signs associated with the West, Anzai's ironic modernism exploits an awareness of the complex, overlapping character of language in a geopolitical realm marked by interpenetrating forms of imperialism. Anzai's poetic language cleverly manipulates the marks of Japan's double colonial situation—put simply, the historical incursion of Western cultural and geopolitical power onto Japan, and the simultaneous projection of Japanese culture and power in Asia and the Pacific. In the face of this polyglot colonial situation, Anzai's poetic language reveals the inadequacies of standard modern Japanese—represented in prose by the *genbun itchi* orthodoxy and in poetry by the plainspoken language of the People's Poets who briefly held sway in Japanese poetic circles before the advent of 1920s modernism. Thus Anzai's modernist project of expanding the poetic possibilities of the Japanese language can be seen as coextensive with the process of absorbing or digesting the new realities of Japan's position as colonial power and providing an image of self and other in the age of Japanese imperialism—albeit an ironical and often disturbing one.

"Abnormal Reversible Reaction": The Poetry of Yi Sang

In sketching a picture of the geopolitical situation of Japanese modernism, we should also take note of the relationship between Japanese modernism and the modernisms emerging elsewhere in East Asia at the same time. Modern Japanese writings and Japanese translations of Western literature were important sources for Chinese and Korean authors in the early twentieth century, and many of the pivotal writers in forging new Chinese and Korean literatures spent periods of study in Japan. This generalization could be applied quite broadly to writers of several different affiliations, but it is particularly salient in the case of writers whose works have been identified as modernist.[54] Thus not only can we not ignore the activities of Japanese writers in the neighboring territories of Asia, but we should also be mindful of the work of Chinese, Taiwanese, and Korean writers exposed to modern Japanese literary culture in our accounts of Japanese modernism. Without question, one of the most important and eloquent modernist voices to emerge within the historical Japanese empire is the Korean poet, essayist, and novelist Yi Sang. The following examination of Yi Sang's work in the context of Japanese modernism is not an attempt to appropriate the author from his established place in the genealogy of modern Korean literature, but to observe what has often been missing from a broader discussion of modern Japanese literature.[55]

Yi Sang (the pen name of Kim Hae-gyŏng, 1910–1937), is remembered primarily for his series of poems "Ogamdo" ("Crow's-Eye Views"), which created a *succès du scandale* in 1934 when published in the *Chosŏn chungang ilbo* (*Korea Central Daily*) newspaper and then discontinued due to vociferous reader objections, for his essays, and for his short fiction, especially the brilliant novel *Nalgae* (*Wings*), written in 1936. However, Yi Sang actually began his poetic career writing poetry in Japanese and continued to compose poetry in Japanese throughout his short writing career; many of the poems in his landmark Korean-language series "Crow's-Eye Views," in fact, are based on "originals" in Japanese. Yi Sang was reportedly an avid reader of the Japanese journal *Shi to shiron*, and his poems bear significant resemblances to the works of such Japanese modernists as Haruyama Yukio, Kitasono Katsue, and Kondō Azuma.[56]

Yi Sang's works are extremely multivalent, simultaneously resisting conventional modes of sense-making and opening themselves to a number of modes of analysis: cosmological, biographical, formalist, and psychosexual, to name only a few. One of the most significant avenues of analysis is to consider them as comments on the Korean colonial experience, and numerous critics have persuasively explored this approach, despite the fact that Yi Sang was not an anticolonial activist and distanced himself from doctrinaire forms of political expression.[57]

Yi Sang was born in 1910, the year of Japan's annexation of Korea, and received an elite education at Seoul's foremost technical institute. Although he obtained a coveted position as an architectural engineer for the Japanese Governor-General's Department of Public Works, he was forced to quit his post in 1933 due to health problems after contracting tuberculosis. Yi Sang's first poems were published in the architectural journal *Chōsen to kenchiku* (*Korea and Architecture*) during his period as an architectural engineer. After resigning his post, he continued to write while managing a series of cafés throughout Seoul, all of which proved to be financial failures. Consonant with his early career as an architectural engineer, many of the motifs in Yi Sang's Japanese-language poems are taken from design, optics, science, engineering, and mathematics, although his treatment of these motifs is divorced from the realism of scientific and mathematical laws—or at least from the certainties of Newtonian physics.[58] For example, the Japanese-language poem "Undō" ("Motion") creates a schematic sense of architectural space while placing the poetic subject in relation to a perplexing universe of space-time.

MOTION

> I climb up above the first floor above the second floor above the third
> floor to the roof garden and look south but nothing's there and look
> north but nothing's there so when I descend below the roof garden
> below the third floor below the second floor to the first floor the sun
> that rose in the east is sinking in the west rising in the east sinking in
> the west rising in the east sinking in the west rising in the east and right
> up in the middle of the sky so when I take out my watch and take a
> look it's stopped but the time is correct so rather than to say that the
> watch must be younger than myself it would surely be better to say
> that I must be older than the watch so I threw out the watch.[59]

Oddly, while the temporal-spatial scale of this poem is quite broad,
encompassing four floors, a roof garden, a rooftop panorama, the
cosmic dimensions of the sun's rise and fall, and seemingly even
the sudden passage of several days, the effect of the poem is not of
expansive space and time but of constriction and stagnancy. Running through a number of Yi Sang's poems we can observe the paradox of a multigenerational or even cosmic scale of time and space
reinforcing a sense of stagnancy or despair. This is especially the
case in the following three verses of his "Sen ni kan suru oboegaki
5" ("Notes Concerning Lines 5"), which employ the terms of Einstein's theory of relativity in the poetic expression of personal and
historical dilemmas:

> When you run away faster than a ray of light do you see light? You see
> light, in the vacuum of years passing you wed twice, do you wed three
> times? Oh run away faster than a ray of light!

> You who run away into the future and look at the past, running away
> into the past do you see the future? running away into the future is not
> the same as running away into the past, running away into the future
> *is* running away into the past. Oh you who grieve at the expansion of
> the universe, live in the past, escape into the future faster than a ray
> of light!

> [six stanzas omitted]

> Oh run away once one time, run away to the utmost, before you are
> born a second time, before you are *xx,* you hesitate to run away fast

from your fear of looking back from the future at the primordial past of the galaxies of galaxies of galaxies of your ancestors' ancestors' ancestors, you run away, running away fast you live in eternity, caress the past, from the past you live again in the past, oh innocence, innocence, never fulfilled eternal innocence![60]

In its expansive movement through space, "Notes Concerning Lines 5" paradoxically expresses a claustrophobic fear of space; in its expansive movement through time, it expresses a fear of stagnancy, of lack of progression. Through its reiteration of the theme of flight into the past or the future, the poem reinforces a sense of the impossibility or intolerability of inhabiting the present moment, and the dual temptations of a nostalgic escape into the past or a utopian preoccupation of the future. Moreover, in its intimations of anxiety regarding birth, marriage, and ancestral inheritance, the poem expresses not only a distrust of such nostalgia or futurist utopia, but an underlying fear of reproduction, that the present and future will be a meaningless repetition of the past. (This theme is taken up again in Yi Sang's Korean-language "Poem No. II" from "Crow's-Eye Views," which begins, "When my father dozes off beside me i become my father and also i become my father's father and even so while my father like my father is just my father why do i repeatedly my father's father's father's . . . .")[61]

While not foreclosing philosophical, biographical, or psychosexual readings with regard to Yi Sang's approach to the theme of time, we cannot neglect the sense in which these poems speak to the experience of colonialism—at the suggestion of another of Yi Sang's poems, we must connect "temporality" with "historicity."[62] In other words, the fear of stagnation, the fear that the present moment is an uncanny replica of past and future moments ("temporality"), is in part an expression of a national experience ("historicity") that has been wrenched out of the modern nationalist narrative of self-determination and historical progress by the violence of colonial domination.[63]

Similarly, we can note that the theme of constriction of space that is subtly coded through its inverse in these early poems becomes more dominant, and more desperate, in Yi Sang's later poetry and prose. For example, the theme of flight or escape introduced in "Notes Concerning Lines 5" reappears in the first of the "Crow's-

Eye Views" poems, where the "running away" is specified as a flight *into a dead-end alley*.[64] Later, settings of constricted space become important elements in Yi Sang's prose as well, such as in the novel *Wings,* where the protagonist lives a life largely constricted to a back room ("flight," the inverse of "constriction" in both senses of "escape" and "taking wing," becomes the central motif of the story's final scene).

Korean literary critic Choi Won-shik, alluding to both the author's pen name and his novella *Wings,* argues that Yi Sang's modernism itself is a "backroom modernism" reflecting the stifled space experienced by the subject population in a colonial city:

> Yi Sang's modernism, as his writing name "sang" (literally, box) suggests, is not a "modernism of the streets" but a pathetic "backroom modernism." The streets of colonized Seoul, caught in a dense net of taboo, are streets where the possibility of creative dynamism has been blocked at its source.[65]

While Choi's comments should not be taken to detract from Yi Sang's creative achievements, his remarks connecting the atmosphere of enclosure in his works with the situation of colonized Korea are incisive. The sense of frustration of creative energy in Yi Sang's works is equally expressed in the vectors of time (the stopped watch of "Motion") and space (the "canceling out" of contrary motion in the same poem's description of the ascent and descent of the flight of stairs). This paradoxical canceling out of motion in the poem "Motion" is but one instance of the pervasive rhetoric of cancellation in Yi Sang's poetry. For example, the poem "Notes Concerning Lines 1," which introduces many of the motifs of "Notes Concerning Lines 5," also relies extensively on the rhetoric of "canceling out," as seen in the following stanza:

> The regulation of speed etc for example if it is given that light can run away at the speed of 300000 kilometers per second then surely it is not the case that human invention cannot run away at the speed of 600000 kilometers per second. If this is multiplied several tens several hundred several thousand several ten thousand several hundred million several trillion times, couldn't people see the truth of the primordial past of several tens several hundred several thousand several ten thousand several hundred million several trillion years ago? shall we suppose that

this will constantly disintegrate? atoms are atoms are atoms are atoms, does the physiological effect vary? atoms are not atoms are not atoms are not atoms are not atoms, does radiation disintegrate? people are eternity to live in eternity is life-existence it is not living it is not existence it is light it is it is.[66]

The rhetoric of "canceling out" is seen here in the double negative of the phrase "it is not the case that human invention cannot run away at the speed of 600000 kilometers per second," or in the self-contradictory statement, "atoms are atoms are atoms are atoms, does the physiological effect vary? atoms are not atoms are not atoms are not atoms are not atoms."

Yi Sang's poetry, like much of the modernist poetry of the *Shi to shiron* group, employs graphic elements such as lines (vectors of motion), numerals, and geometric and mathematical symbols, together with words. What is remarkable about Yi Sang's work is the thoroughgoing consistency with which he treats these elements, each being equally prone to the rhetoric of "canceling out." This interchangeability of the mathematic and the syntactic under the rhetoric of cancellation is indicated in a phrase from another of Yi Sang's poems, "the nullification of numbers by means of the conjugation of the verb-endings of numbers."[67] Furthermore, we should note that this rhetoric of cancellation is closely related to the phenomena of mirror images that appear in many of Yi Sang's poems, and the concept of "reversibility" that is announced in the title of Yi Sang's first published Japanese poem, "Ijō na kagyaku hannō" ("Abnormal Reversible Reaction").[68]

The distinctive quality of Yi Sang's poetic use of the Japanese language is the effect of this language being manipulated as if it were a mathematical equation, although no more subject to the rules of logic than the actual mathematical equations within his poetry are prone to the rules of conventional arithmetic.[69] Perhaps it is this quality of dispassionate, mathematical manipulation of language that leads Japanese critic Kawamura Minato to argue for Yi Sang's unique position in the history of modern Japanese poetry, claiming that "Yi Sang's Japanese-language poetry is the realization of the never completely successful attempts of Japanese modern poets to free themselves from the bonds of Japanese lyricism and the rhythm and sensibility inherent in the Japanese language."[70]

Turning to Yi Sang's use of the orthographical elements of modern Japanese (kanji, hiragana, katakana, and romaji), we find his poetry again bears strong affinity to the *Shi to shiron* poets. Like such *Shi to shiron*–associated poets as Haruyama and Kitasono, Yi Sang employs scientific and technical vocabulary extensively in his poetry, encoded in katakana, romaji, and in kanji compound neologisms originating in the modern Japanese encounter with Western science.[71] Similarly, in several of his poems, Yi Sang employs the technique also seen in Haruyama's poetry, of using katakana to transcribe the Japanese-derived parts of speech that would more conventionally be written in hiragana.

Yi Sang's use of blocks of katakana text would seem to have a similar poetic function as Haruyama's: producing a striking, angular visual effect and loosely associating the poem with Western material, artistic, or scientific discourse. However, we can detect a subtle difference in the case of Yi Sang. For example, while both Western loan words and Japanese-derived parts of speech are transcribed in katakana in Haruyama's poem discussed above, in Yi Sang's poems such as "V no yūgi" ("The play of V") and "Hige" ("Beard"), hiragana is used for Western loan words and katakana for Japanese-derived speech: in other words, hiragana and katakana are completely reversed from their standard usage. Yi Sang's katakana poems, then, are a type of "mirror image" of standard modern Japanese orthography.

We should also note that in the modern period katakana is not used only to transcribe Western languages, but is also used to transcribe words and speech from other foreign languages, including languages of countries within the sphere of Japanese imperialist domination, such as Korean, setting them visually apart from native vocabulary transcribed in hiragana or the Sinitic linguistic heritage conveyed by kanji. This fact leads us to wonder: is the foreign "accent" imbedded in the use of katakana in Yi Sang's modernist poems a European accent or a Korean one? Could we not say that this katakana, the voice of "cosmopolitan" (European-oriented) formalist modernism in Haruyama's poetry, becomes re-ethnicized, differently inhabited, in its appropriation by a Korean poet?[72] From the narcissistic perspective of modern Japanese literary history, the "abnormal reversibility" of Yi Sang's poetry is the uncanny mirror image of a Japanese modernism that is already embroiled in the twinned geopolitical situations of Western and Japanese imperialism.[73]

However, while Yi Sang's poetry may hold an uncanny mirror up to Japanese modernism, it more saliently offers a complex and challenging reconfiguration of the dominant issues facing Korean nationalism in the early twentieth century. With their defamiliarizing approaches to written language in general and scientific discourse in particular, Yi Sang's poems hone in on two highly symbolic political registers for Korean nationalism. From the nineteenth century on, acquisition of scientific and technical expertise was seen by many progressive nationalists as central to establishing the basis for Korean independence. Furthermore, the movement to standardize and spread the Korean vernacular and to promote the han'gŭl script was another vital element of the nationalist cultural movement (*Munghwa undong*).[74] Yet while both of these fields were seen as crucial for Korean national independence, they were also intertwined with Japanese influence on the Korean peninsula: the promotion of scientific and technical knowledge (modern "civilization") was one aspect of the paternalistic ideology of Japanese imperialism, while major Korean-language reforms were inaugurated as part of the ambitious Kabo Reform movement (1894–1896) carried out under Japanese sponsorship, although modern standard Japanese was later propagated as the "national language" following colonial annexation in 1910.[75] Thus these two crucial registers of Korean nationalism, language and science, were, like other elements of Korean modernity as described by Shin and Robinson, "entwined with outside economic and political influence, and ultimately . . . evolved in a context of colonial domination."[76]

In its sophisticated and yet ultimately irrational employment of scientific, mathematical, and technical discourse, and in its viruslike exploration of the permeability and reversibility of Japanese and Korean languages, Yi Sang's poetry both appropriates and subverts the dominant paradigms of modernity that were contested between Korean nationalists and Japanese imperialists. Thus his work could be seen as a threat to orthodox visions of Korean nationalism, and yet it has also been recognized by many Korean intellectuals as an eloquent challenge to Japanese imperialism in its withering and absurdist presentation of the conditions of Korean modernity and subjectivity.[77]

Coda: Butterflies and Mirrors

I would like to conclude this excursus on the international situation of Japanese modernism with a comparison of three poems, one by Anzai Fuyue and two by Yi Sang, which share many motifs, even though it is unlikely that there is any direct influence or citation occurring between the texts. The first, "Dattan kaikyō to chō" ("Tartar Strait and Butterfly"), which appeared in Anzai Fuyue's 1943 poetry collection *Daigaku no rusu* (*Absence from University*), is a sort of fantasia based on images from Anzai's best-known short poem, "Haru" ("Spring"):

TARTAR STRAIT AND BUTTERFLY

Crossing my legs on the wooden chair, I put the gun muzzle to my nose. The smell of gunpowder sniffed by my pale brains led me toward a world of internal forms.

[two stanzas omitted]

Her eyes were shut in sleep. With a map hanging loose from the wall pressed against the side of her face. Slipping across her shoulder, the faded Tartar Strait flowed down like a shawl.
There was always a resentful fire in the flow of her gaze.
But I never paid it any mind.
Heedlessly, I gave her her lessons.
Trying to give her her lessons, I would strut around.
Trying to strut around, I would stand still. Seeing me like this, she would smile for the first time.
The smile suddenly enticed a bullet trajectory.
The bullet trajectory stitched her to the Strait.
In the next instant, her structure will undoubtedly disintegrate. The Strait will plummet and boom from the burrowed hole. How should one accommodate oneself amidst this flood?
I made my decision.
The sound of the safety releasing on the gun resembled the ticket-puncher in a country train station.
Aiming the gun, I marked her with exactitude.

At this moment, a single butterfly appeared, and silently covered the muzzle of the gun.[78]

"Tartar Strait and Butterfly" is a poem of colonial desire, enacted within the sort of sadomasochistic theater-space found in a number of Anzai's works. While a number of reading strategies could be productively applied to the poem, if we read it in terms of its potential as a colonial allegory, we can identify the colonizing subject in the "I" or masculine subject of the poem, the "tutor" to the feminized colonial subject or "pupil" (draped with a map of empire), who is the object of the "I"'s desiring gaze. With no true access to the "pupil"'s interiority beyond her resentful gaze and her smile, we could say that the pupil's gaze is actually a type of mirror of the gaze of the subject, reflecting his narcissistic desire to be desired. In terms of the colonial relationship, this is the desire of the colonizer or "tutor" to constitute himself as a subject through the mirror-eyes of the colonized, or "pupil."

The gaze of the colonialist subject is one of violence, as is acknowledged in the transformation of the "I"'s glance into a phallic "bullet trajectory." Yet in addition to being one of violence, the colonial gaze is also one of fear of the repressed vengeance of the subjugated. This fear is deferred in Anzai's poem by a magical intervention, the "poetry" of the poem's ending. We could read the butterfly that appears between the "tutor" and "pupil" as an expression of eroticism, the seeming consummation of the couple's desire. But it is also an aporia, an object that blocks vision between subject and object, a magical deferment of violence, fear and revenge, if only a temporary one.

With Anzai's fantasia in mind, we can observe the very different way that Yi Sang handles the shared motifs of the gaze, mirror, butterfly, and pistol, in two Korean-language poems from the series "Crow's-Eye Views," as translated by Walter K. Lew:

Poem No. X

In the tattered wallpaper I see a butterfly dying. Secret mouthpiece bearing endless traffic to and from the other world. One day in the mirror I see on my beard a butterfly dying. Wings collapsed in exhaustion the butterfly eats the meager dew that collects glistening from my exhaled breath. If I die while blocking the mouthpiece off with my palm the butterfly too as if starting up after resting shall fly away. Never do I let word of this leak out.

Poem No. XV

1

I'm in a mirrorless room. Naturally the I in the mirror has gone out. I'm trembling now in fear of the I in the mirror. Has the I in the mirror gone somewhere to plot what to do next to me?

2

Slept in a dank crime-cuddling bed. In my precision dream I was absent and an artificial leg crammed into an infantry boot soiled my dream's white page.

3

I secretly enter a room with a mirror. To free myself from the mirror. But with its gloomy face the I in the mirror definitely enters at the same time. The I in the mirror conveys to me that it's sorry. Because of him it's as if I've become a prison and because of me he too becomes a prison and is trembling.

4

Dream I am absent from. Mirror of mine in which my imposter makes no entrance. Impossible though it may be it is that which aspires to solitude for the good I. Finally I decided to proffer suicide to the I in the mirror. I shall show him a raisable window that doesn't even have a view. It is a window meant only for suicide. But he points out to me the fact that as long as I do not kill myself he too cannot kill himself. The I in the mirror is practically a phoenix.

5

I shield with my bulletproof metal where my heart is on the left side of my chest and aiming at the left side of my chest in the mirror fired a pistol. The round penetrated the left side of his chest but his heart is on the right side.

6

From the replica heart red ink spills. In my dream I arrived late and received capital punishment. The controller of my dreams is not I. To have blocked off from each other these two persons unable even to shake hands is a great crime.[79]

The relationship of desire and violence between subject and object—"tutor" and colonized "pupil"—seen in Anzai's poem has been internalized in Yi Sang's work into a tortured relationship of subject and subject, distributed onto the self and the double in the mirror. Several Korean critics have analyzed the split subject in Yi Sang's mirror poems in terms of the double consciousness of the colonial subject. As Walter K. Lew argues, however, it would be too simplistic to identify one of these mirror selves as the self that identifies with the colonialist, and the other as the self that resists colonialism.[80] Nevertheless, we can say that the mirror-space functions as a type of enclosure, which simultaneously splits the subject and alienates him from himself, with no outside world of potential action outside of the "box" enclosing self and double. To borrow the words of one of Yi Sang's Japanese poems, we can see this enclosing mirror-space as "a concave lens formed by the constriction and constriction of the system of subjectivity."[81]

The grammar of this mirror-space, too, is not an active grammar of subject and object, but an intransitive grammar of subject and subject, where the subject "cancels" himself through the dream of suicide. Furthermore, the mirror-space is another manifestation of the constriction of time and space, seen in Yi Sang's other poems to have an intimate relationship to the historicity of colonized Korea. Within this hall of mirrors, the butterfly in "Poem No. X" is no longer a symbol of eroticism, but rather the manifestation of a delicate, pathetic beauty of exhaustion and impermanence—the most fragile, doomed possibility of contact with another world. Furthermore, the bullet trajectory in Yi Sang's "Poem No. XV" is not the subject-object trajectory of colonial violence or sadomasochistic sexuality, but the subject-subject trajectory of suicidal self-cancellation.

Although they were almost certainly composed independently of any direct influence, Yi Sang's and Anzai's works are in a type of complex dialogue about the conditions of subjectivity in the Japanese empire. However, we should also keep in mind the limitations of the "dialogue" that the Korean poet Yi Sang maintained with Japanese modernism. Outside of the architectural journal *Chōsen to kenchiku*, Yi Sang never published his Japanese-language poems, or translations of his Korean poems, in the literary journals favored by his Japanese modernist peers. And, while Yi Sang did travel to Japan at the end of his life, this trip did not culminate in the recognition of Yi Sang's formidable literary talents within the Japanese literary community, but rather in a case of profound and tragic misrecognition.

Despite Yi Sang's professed admiration for the work of Haruyama Yukio, there is no indication that he tried to contact Haruyama or any other Japanese literary figures while in Tokyo. Perhaps at this stage in his career, when his Korean-language prose works were receiving significant attention in Korean literary circles, he had no desire to ingratiate himself with Japanese literati. Indeed, in his posthumously published essay "Tong'gyŏng" ("Tokyo"), he expresses nothing but disillusionment and disgust with the Imperial metropole.[82]

If Yi Sang held the metropole in contempt, he was to find himself an object of contempt as well. Several months after his arrival in Tokyo, the poet was arrested as a "disorderly Korean" (*futei senjin*) and incarcerated for five weeks, during which his tubercular health condition rapidly deteriorated. He died in Tokyo less than a month after his release. Yi Sang's fateful arrest on suspicions of political subversion is especially ironic given that, regardless of the political undercurrents in his literary works, he avoided a public political stance and was not considered in Korean intellectual circles to be among the writers actively opposing Japanese colonial rule.[83]

Yi Sang's "conversation" with Japanese modernism, then, flowed in only one direction during his lifetime. This one-way conversation reproduces the relationship between Japanese modernism and Europe, in which Japanese modernists were acutely aware of cultural events in Europe, but European artists and writers regarded Japanese culture almost exclusively in terms of its traditional and exotic elements.

Building on the earlier avant-garde work of such figures as Hagiwara Kyōjirō and Murayama Tomoyoshi, while distancing themselves from their activist political stances and disorderly poetics, *Shi to shiron* poets such as Haruyama Yukio pushed their poetry toward an idealized Europe and away from references to Japanese material culture and literary heritage, as part of a poetics that, in its most utopian moments, attempted to unhinge language from representation altogether. On another literary front, Anzai Fuyue reintegrated the languages on the physical and temporal borders of the Japanese empire into a new vocabulary of Japanese modernism, while ironically citing the orientalist system of knowledge that Japan was in the process of retrofitting to serve as the epistemological underpinnings of its own imperialism. Both Haruyama and Anzai, then, could be said to explore the limits of the Japanese language within a situation of overlapping Western and Japanese imperialist pressures.

In Yi Sang we find a writer in a colonized population, who in retrospect can be hailed as a brilliant interlocutor of Japanese modernism, but whose contemporary recognition as such was obscured by the prejudicial structures of colonialism, acting out the sadomasochistic theater of the apprehensive, violent "tutor" and the resentful "pupil." While Yi Sang's work has been of continuing significance to Korean literature, in relation to Japan his career could be said not to push the limits of Japanese modernism, but rather to reveal where those limits lie. On the one hand Yi Sang's work is indispensable to a consideration of Japanese modernism in its international context. Yet there is also something in Yi Sang's work—including his Japanese-language poems—that resists a too easy assimilation into the category of Japanese "national language" (*kokugo*) or a narrative of "modern Japanese literature" (*kindai nihon bungaku*). In this respect as in others, Yi Sang's work affirms the avant-garde function of revealing and problematizing the frame conditions for the production and reception of art.

3 / "ALL FORMS OF POETIC LITERATURE ARE DESTROYED"
Hagiwara Kyōjirō's *Shikei senkoku*

An urgent concern for the self has been one of the salient features of modern Japanese literature. Hagiwara Kyōjirō was one of several generations of Japanese intellectuals who endeavored both to realize the independence of the self from traditional social structures, and, conversely, to imagine possibilities in overcoming the atomization of the modern individual resulting from this very liberation. The vital importance of the self, redefined in Japanese discourse through the appropriation of successive waves of European thought, was accepted as a given in Hagiwara's intellectual and artistic milieu. "The significance of the new art," Hagiwara wrote in 1924, "is not to be found in any external decoration, nor is it to be found in changes in the external world, but comes only from the power of the self (*jiga no ken'i*)."[1]

Yet the concept of the "self" as it developed in the European philosophical and literary tradition is complex and contradictory, and the Japanese discourse of the self, emerging in dialogue with this multifaceted Western tradition as well as with local political and artistic exigencies, was also fluid and multilayered.[2] It would be a mistake, then, to imagine the "modern self" as a given (Western) ideal to be aspired to, achieved, or disavowed by Japanese intellectuals; rather, the "self," in the Japanese as in the European context, was always a variable term to be reworked, reconstructed, and repositioned. Hagiwara Kyōjirō's writings in particular reveal an acute awareness of the constructedness of the self, as well as a restless search for how the individual can be positioned within a broader social nexus.

The ideological bases of the self in Japanese literature can be traced back to Meiji-period attempts to promote the individual as a basis for autonomous political and economic action in society, based on the principles of Enlightenment and post-Enlightenment philosophy. The influential translations of such tracts as Samuel Smiles's *Self Help* and John Stuart Mill's *On Liberty* (translated in 1870 and 1871, respectively), as well as the heroic individualism depicted in early Meiji political novels, represent the first waves of a modern effort to reimagine the relationship between self and society outside a strict Confucian framework, which would place the individual in a series of relatively fixed hierarchical relationships. As Janet Walker has suggested, the emphasis on the self in Meiji literature can also be attributed to the influence of the protestant Christian ideal of an "inner life." This Christian influence was in turn deeply interconnected with Meiji political events, including the dissolution of the samurai class and the growth of the People's Rights Movement in the 1870s. An early involvement with Christianity formed a part of the biography of many Meiji and Taishō intellectuals, including Hagiwara Kyōjirō.[3]

At the turn of the century, the introduction of the philosophies of Nietzsche and (somewhat later) Max Stirner offered a critique of Christian and Enlightenment philosophies that nevertheless maintained, or even strengthened, the emphasis on individual subjectivity, which would no longer be subordinated to God or the State. At the same time as more radically egoistic visions of subjectivity were being introduced in the world of philosophy, the latter phase of Japanese Naturalism ushered in an intensive focus on individual subjectivity, as the thematics of literature were increasingly restricted to an examination of the private life and mental states of the individual. Intellectual historians such as H. D. Harootunian have suggested that this shift reflected a disillusionment within the intelligentsia regarding the possibilities of social action and socially oriented literature following the Meiji government's actions to stifle political dissent, including the suppression of the People's Rights Movement in the 1880s and the steady passage of legislation restricting the scope of political activity and speech, such as the Ordinance on Assembly and Political Societies of 1890 and the Peace Preservation Law of 1900. According to this analysis, the Japanese government's foreclosure of the possibilities of autonomous political action contributed to a shift from a literature that would explore the relationship between self and society in the service of social and political ideals, to one that would largely bracket social issues in favor of an intense examination of private issues, represented by the later phase of Japanese Naturalism and the burgeoning importance of the I-novel to the Tokyo *bundan*.[4] While the story of this shift to more inwardly directed literature remains a persuasive narrative, one should recall that the seemingly apolitical turn in Naturalist literature focused on aspects of the self—especially sexual drives—that disrupted social harmony and challenged the complacency of bourgeois life, suggesting that an investigation of the individual's private life could actually be the basis for an oblique public critique.

Regardless of the extent to which the inward turn of later Naturalism was truly a retreat from public concerns, by the Taishō period, rival political and artistic philosophies emerged to offer new perspectives and alternatives to the Naturalists' ostensible inward emphasis. The writers of the Shirakaba school championed broad humanistic values such as the elevation of art and the establishment of a just society, while generally eschewing direct political involvement in favor of an ethic of personal cultivation. Yet while the radius of the group's outward concern extended to encompass humanity as a whole, the individual was still at the center and origin of their conception of cultivation and transformation, as articulated by Shirakaba leader Mushakōji Saneatsu. Mushakōji offered a bold and influential affirmation of the group's ethos of self-cultivation, writing "What is of utmost importance is my Self (*jiga*), the development of my Self, the growth of my Self, the fulfillment of the life of my Self (*jiko*) in the true sense of the word. I chose writing for this purpose."[5]

In the world of poetry, the "People's Poets" (*minshūshi-ha*) of the early Taishō reached beyond the ethos of personal cultivation to advocate a socially engaged poetry reflecting the voices of the people, a call that resonated with the contemporary movement for social and political reform, beginning with the expansion of the voting franchise, advocated by such liberal spokesmen as Yoshino Sakuzō.

During this same period, moreover, communist and anarchist intel-lectuals emerged to challenge both the idealist humanism of the Shi-rakaba school and the liberalism of figures such as Yoshino, whose political philosophy was still reconciled to the bourgeois state and the imperial institution. Communism offered a cogent critique of individualism and a new construction of the self as part of an inter-national collective of the proletariat, while anarchism, particularly as formulated in the early writings of Ōsugi Sakae, offered by con-trast a renewed focus on the individual as the locus of radical social rebellion. In the words of Ōsugi biographer Thomas A. Stanley, Ōsugi's anarchism provided Japanese intellectuals with "a prescrip tion for social reform through the liberation of individual human energy."[6]

Ōsugi's vision of the self had a decisive impact on Hagiwara's generation of avant-garde artists and writers, albeit one that would have to compete with the collectivist vision of communism.[7] In a series of articles for the journal *Kindai shisō* in the years 1912–1914, Ōsugi described Japanese modernity as governed by what he called "the reality of subjugation" (*seifuku no jijitsu*). This reality, Ōsugi suggested, was limited neither to the subjugation of the proletariat to the capitalist class, nor even to the subjugation of the populace to an autocratic government, but could be traced back to Japanese feudal structures and beyond, to the relationship of master and slave and to the subjugation of one tribe to another in prehistoric times.[8] Ōsugi argued that this reality could be countered by liberation of individual life praxis, such that people "will not submit to author-ity above them, that the self (*jiga*) will rule the self."[9] Ōsugi termed this liberated life praxis "the extension-fulfillment of life" (*sei no kakujū*).

Ōsugi specifically linked this idea of life praxis to a revolution in the realm of artistic practice, arguing for a new conception of "dynamic beauty," which would combine with "the beauty of trea-son" and "the beauty of malice":

Rebellion against the reality of subjugation—the most effective action we can take to satisfy our tenacious demands for life—has indeed emerged. And a destructiveness has emerged against this reality, and all that impedes the extension-fulfillment of our lives.

And I who see the ultimate beauty of life in the extension-fulfillment of life, today see the ultimate beauty of life only in this rebellion and destruction. Today, when the reality of subjugation has reached its apex, harmoniousness is no longer beauty. Beauty is only in disorder. Harmoniousness is a lie. The truth is only in disorder.[10]

It could be argued that Ōsugi's political and aesthetic vision, itself a synthesis of an eclectic range of European sources, was more significant than any European movement or manifesto as an inspiration for the early Japanese literary and artistic avant-garde.[11]

The importance of Ōsugi's ideas of individual rebellion notwithstanding, the works of Hagiwara and his peers suggest that the concept of the self, and the related question of subjectivity as expressed in literary works, were entering a phase of renegotiation in the late Taishō period. An examination of the avant-garde literary journal *Damu damu* (*Dum dum*), for example, reveals a range of different approaches to self and subjectivity. In the magazine's opening manifesto, Hayashi Masao defends a "subjective" vision of art against the "objective" modes of realism, urging writers to "Expose your own mental images or subjectivity just as they are!"[12] On the other hand, Okamoto Jun warns against the solipsism of an overly subjective approach to literature, while also inveighing against the trends of contemporary "journalism" or mass media, which, he claims, are "rendering all forms of so-called cultural production commercial and superficial." At the junction of these two trends, Okamoto identifies what he calls "the fashion of melancholy" or the "commercialization of Hamlet," concluding somewhat cryptically that "the walled-in and ineffectual self must be freed by the explosion created by the instinctual self-scorn of art."[13]

Hagiwara Kyōjirō's late Taishō writings participate in this exploration of subjectivity and scrutiny of the relationship between self and society. Indeed, while Hagiwara inherited a politics of individual rebelliousness from Ōsugi, his literary writings increasingly complicate or reject the model of the autonomous individual found in Enlightenment thought or even the post-Romantic individualism that Ōsugi had developed from sources such as Nietzsche and Stirner. Threading through the writing of various points of Hagiwara's career, we can observe both a rhetoric of self-assertion, and a seemingly contradictory impulse toward the strategic concealment of the individual and the dispersal of individual subjectivity, reflecting an urge to connect to or even merge the self into broader social entities.

Reading, Writing, and Construction

Hagiwara published the poetry collection *Shikei senkoku* (*Death Sentence*) in October of 1925. It consists of 83 poems written between 1921 and the time of publication, and is divided into nine sections, from "Armored Coil," the first section, to "Raskolnikov," the last. Since the poems are presented in a rough chronological order, the reader can trace the formal and thematic evolution of Hagiwara's poetry during this period, from the earlier poems, with the strongest links to established modes of lyric poetry, to the later poems, which present more dispersed forms of subjectivity through a battery of formal experiments.[14]

Although *Shikei senkoku* was Hagiwara's first poetry collection, he was hardly an unknown poet when the collection appeared. Throughout the early 1920s, Hagiwara had achieved increasing visibility as a *dōjin* of the avant-garde journals *Aka to kuro*, *Damu damu*, and *MAVO*; his poems had also been published in such mainstream forums as *Nihon shijin* (*Japanese Poet*) and the annual *Nihon shishū* (*Anthology of Japanese Poetry*). The much-anticipated publication of *Shikei senkoku* was celebrated with an unprecedented three opening receptions in Tokyo, Kobe, and Toyohashi. The collection also received a whole section of reviews in *Nihon shijin* and warranted an enthusiastic two-part review by Futurist painter and poet Kanbara Tai in the *Yomiuri* newspaper.[15]

In the preface to *Shikei senkoku*, Hagiwara addresses an audience that can be expected to already know something of his work; his remarks suggest many of the ideas of reading and writing that underlie the work and its reception. He writes, "My poems are definitely not life (*seikatsu*) itself. They are no more than reflections of a few moments of this life. . . . Therefore, in order to know me, I would have you construct me out of the entire collection, rather than any single poem."[16] Hagiwara is addressing a literary context in which a close relationship is assumed to exist between the subjectivity expressed in the poem and the subjectivity of the poet. Indeed, his remarks imply that one purpose of reading is to know or understand the author.

Hagiwara does not challenge this basic paradigm of reading, but he does offer a significant revision in its mode of operation. In Hagiwara's formulation, no unmediated or mystical access between reader and author is suggested, nor is it suggested that "authorial intention" or biographical information be read into the text. Instead, the reader must construct (*kōsei suru*) the author out of the text. That such a construction will necessarily be artificial, provisional, and incomplete is evident from Hagiwara's remarks above, which are amplified in another section of *Shikei senkoku*'s prefatory material:

Our poetry is not the whole! It's only a part. The whole is infinite. The part only continues its accelerating revolutions. From the part, we must discover the meaning of the whole. Even so, ultimately we cannot arrive at completion. Only in incompletion can we find the endless, intense shape.[17]

While Hagiwara states that the poem itself is "definitely not life," we can perhaps use life (*seikatsu*) to name the whole of which poetry is a part. As critic Takahashi Shūichirō notes, the writing of a poem was not envisioned by Hagiwara as the completion of a single autonomous work of art, but rather as a methodology (*hōhōron*), an aspect of life praxis (*ikiru kōi*).[18] By inverting the formula in the *Shikei senkoku*'s preface, we can see Hagiwara's poems as moments in the author's construction of the self—as elements in the construction of the author's self-consciousness.[19]

The title of one of the poems in *Shikei senkoku* is suggestive in this regard: "Jikoku," literally, self-carving. This title hints that the poem is both a self-portrait and a painful, even masochistic, act of self-alteration.[20] This point becomes even more explicit in the afterword to Hagiwara's second poetry collection, *Danpen* (*Fragments*, 1931). With a striking turn of phrase, Hagiwara writes, "I can call each of these [poetic] fragments nails which I have pounded into my own body, in order to construct myself from today to tomorrow" (*kyō yori ashita e to jibun o kizukō to shite jibun no shintai ni uchikonde ita ippon ippon no kugi*).[21] Hagiwara's conception of the self is clearly not restricted to consciousness; it is equally concerned with the body. The poem or artwork is posited in an intimate recip-rocal relationship with this self; the act of writing is a construction of the mind/body totality.

Just as the poem is in an intimate reciprocal relation with the self, it is also in a vital medial position between self and society. In fact, Hagiwara's poetic theory offers a challenge to the dualism of self and society or private and public, which had been introduced with Enlightenment thought in Meiji Japan, and, according to Harootunian's analysis, reinforced in intellectual life by the Meiji government's legal restrictions on public activities.[22] Later in the essay quoted at the head of this chapter, Hagiwara writes:

Art is the product of the self (*jiga*), and the product of the self is indisput-able (*dokudan*). Yet when we analyze the self, we discover that all the ele-ments of society are fused together inside one's own tube. All the elements of society course through our blood vessels. Every possible kind of blood runs through our blood vessels and to our heart. The heart of the self flows into the heart of the society-self (*shakaiga*).[23]

Hagiwara's choice of metaphors here prepares the way for a deconstruction of the self/society duality. While dominant post-Meiji concepts of the self were founded on a clear boundary between the body and the outside environment, Hagiwara counters this conception with a view of the self as a physiological system that transcends the conventional bounds of the body. While the blood vessels lead in and out of the heart and permeate the body, they are also, in the lungs, part of a system of constant transactions with the "outside" environment (the exchange of oxygen and carbon diox-ide), ultimately effacing the distinction between inside and outside and replacing them with a series of interlacing physical and chemi-cal systems (the digestive system providing another such series of systems). Similarly, the tubular shape that Hagiwara uses to describe the self is open-ended and (depending on its material substance) pos-sibly reversible; what appears at first glance to be a solid, discrete shape upon further examination confounds the distinction between inside and outside.

Hagiwara's conception of the self as interfaced with and insepa-rable from society in this passage bears a striking affinity to the work of postwar American cybernetics researchers, who explored ways of understanding both machines and organisms as systems involved in the processing of information. Gregory Bateson, an anthropologist who was closely involved with early cybernetics research, summarizes the challenge that systems theory poses to the conventional boundaries of subjectivity in the following passages on human cognition: "The total self-corrective unit which processes information, or as I say 'thinks' 'acts' and 'decides' is a system whose boundaries do not at all coincide with the boundaries either of the body or of what is popularly called the 'self' or 'consciousness.'. . . The network is not bounded by the skin but includes all external pathways along which information can travel." "The 'self' is a false reification of an improperly delimited part of this much larger field of interlocking processes."[24] This conceptual link to cybernetics is especially interesting given Hagiwara's exploration of cyborglike subjectivities in the poem "Kōkokutō!" ("Advertising Tower!") and its related texts, as discussed below.

Hagiwara's physiological, proto-cybernetic view of the self and the environment, transplanted onto the relationship between "self" and "society," undermines a number of influential political and cultural constructions. On the one hand, this view problematizes the idea of an "autonomous individual" who would be the agent of political activity in Enlightenment philosophy. On the other hand, it precludes any recourse to the "self" as a place of refuge or retreat from "society." Even an attempt to bracket "society" in favor of an intense scrutiny on the "self" will, Hagiwara suggests, only reveal the viscera of society.

Commentator Amo Hisayoshi describes this unorthodox conception of self and environment as the "spring" that propels *Shikei senkoku*'s unusual imagery: "the internal is forcibly externalized, the external is forcibly internalized, and high-pressure images are tied together with a strange sense of amalgamation."[25] In *Shikei senkoku*, the "outside" that interpenetrates the self's "inside" is the city, the privileged site of Japanese modernity. Hagiwara's portraits of the modern city are always simultaneously self-portraits—a doubling effect that he executes with a keen sense of the strange, and the self-estranged.[26]

Despite the continued importance granted the notion of the self in Hagiwara's writings, the subjectivity of Hagiwara's poetry undergoes a surprising set of mutations. These mutations, in turn, are connected to the historical changes in the urban environment in which that self is placed—changes such as the destruction of the city by the Great Kanto Earthquake, the subsequent radicalization of the city's political culture, and the development of mass media. Hagiwara responds to these changes in society by offering new models of the self and the poem, such as futuristic machine, terrorist (or bomb), and advertising tower. These poetic constructions, then, are also constructions of Japanese modernity, offered in a historical moment when the nature and future of that modernity were the subject of heated disputes. My readings of these poems will explore Hagiwara's vision of modernity, and secondarily, as Hagiwara's preface suggests, comprise a limited readerly "construction" of the poet. While we may not ultimately be able to "know" Hagiwara Kyōjirō through such an exercise, a familiarity with the building blocks should provide us, at least, with a new perspective on the modernity that shaped his life, and which he aspired to shape.

The City and the Self

In January 1922, two years after welcoming Russian Futurist David Davidovich Burliuk to Japan, and one year after promulgating the "Japanese Futurist Manifesto Movement" on a street corner in Hibiya, journalist and poet Hirato Renkichi published the article "Watashi no miraishugi to jikkō" ("My Futurism and Practice") in the journal *Nihon shijin*. In this article, Hirato attempts to clarify his own vision of Futurism and to counter the perception that his is merely a derivative form of Russian or Italian Futurism, writing "while I receive stimuli from Marinetti and other Futurists, I am by no means subordinate to them."[27]

Invoking the notion of *seikatsu* (everyday life), which would continue to be a key term for the Japanese avant-garde, Hirato offers a view of Futurism as a mode of living, rather than a literary or theoretical construction. "My Futurism is not theory. It is only 'life' (*seikatsu*) at the moment of movement. It is nothing but realization."[28] In order to describe his approach to life (and to art), Hirato employs the term *chokujō*—translatable as frankness, impulsiveness, straightforwardness, or more literally, "direct emotion":

At this time, our little, *Passéiste* Japan, with the chattiness of its everyday life, its confusion, the futility and blindness of its cultural life (*bunka
seikatsu*) holds no surprises for us. At this time, it is no surprise that my
"direct emotion" would arise.

Direct emotion is my morality.

Direct emotion is my action.

Direct emotion is my art.

The Futurism of direct emotionalism is no different from the action of
a rapid steel machine, capable of causing fatal injury.[29]

Hirato Renkichi's Futurism had little chance for further development or execution. Seven months after these words were published, Hirato was dead of tuberculosis. During the last year or two
of his life, he had served as a mentor for Hagiwara Kyōjirō, who was
making periodic trips to Tokyo but had been unable to disentangle
himself from his familial obligations in rural Gunma Prefecture.[30]

A month after Hirato's death, Hagiwara wrote a tribute to his
mentor, describing him with the phrase "realist poet of fulfilled
life" (*seimei jūjitsu no genjitsu shijin*). This epithet implies Hirato's
lifespan (*seimei*) was now complete (*jūjitsu*), but it also carries an
echo of Ōsugi Sakae's "extension-fulfillment of life," suggesting a
link between Ōsugi's egoistic political ethic and Hirato's Futurism
of "life," "realization," and "direct emotion." The following month,
September 1922, as if to succeed his dead mentor as activist poet of
urban life, Hagiwara finally broke his ties to home and moved to
Tokyo.

Within the collection *Shikei senkoku*, the opening poem "Sōkō
danki" ("Armored Coil") presents Hagiwara's earliest vision of
the modern city (first published in March 1921), and the one with
the most direct links to Futurist representation.[31] In "Sōkō danki"
Hagiwara presents an image of a fantastic machine, neither loco-
motive nor tank nor factory, but suggesting simultaneously all of
these forms of industrial civilization. Much as Hirato's Futurism of
"direct emotionalism," expressed in the figure of a rapid and deadly
"steel machine," was opposed to the chattiness and futility of Japanese "cultural life," Hagiwara's "armored coil" is contrasted to the
finer things of *Passéist* "Female Civilization":[32]

Amid the leaping bustle of the modern city
I see a giant mechanical armored coil

Spouting out moody smoke
A charmless and dull-witted fellow

He gives out a military shout
Ignorant of the flavors, colors, and delicate textures
That give the city its high taste
He spouts out strong yellow smoke
Soiling the city, getting angry
Oppressing the fearful heart

He follows neither the bullet nor the heart of the crowd
Possessing the reddest, most barbarian heart
Tenaciously, indifferently
Resisting the throng's commercial world
A powerful, powerful emergence, toward chaos

Ah! That charmless fellow, shrugging his broad shoulders
At fine, oversensitive Female Civilization
Neither joy nor sadness
Appears on his ugly face[33]

The poem's final stanza reconfigures the image of "armored coil," which at first seemed to be a personification, or rather mechanized embodiment, of the industrial city under the poet's gaze: now the "armored coil" is revealed to be the poet himself.

Ah! Behold! Now, I am
A giant mechanical armored coil!
Amid the leaping bustle of the modern city[34]

"Sōkō danki" is thus the first of several instances in *Shikei senkoku* in which the poetic subject is fused with the modern mechanized city. Yet even as this fusion of subject and city will continue, the nature of this poetic subjectivity (and of the city itself) will change as the poems of the collection reflect progressively later moments of composition. The "I" (*ware*) of "Sōkō danki" "shouts" or "spouts" with a truculent indifference to his surroundings, much as the poet described in Hirato's manifesto expresses his emotion (*jō*) with an aggressive directness. The poetic subject must strive to be the equal of the bustling, dirty, and brutal modern city. Poetry, which in the past may have been counted as one of the elements of "high taste" attuned to the bourgeois city's "colors, flavors, and delicate textures," is now equated with the industrial city's "strong yellow smoke." Aside from these schematic contrasts, however, neither the poetic subject nor the modern city achieves a high degree of differentiation (this is no identifiable city or neighborhood); like the chimerical mechanism of the "armored spring" itself, the modern city/self in "Sōkō danki" is an amorphous compound of reaction (armor) and potentiality (spring/coil).

"Hibiya," published over three years after "Sōkō danki," presents a significantly different portrait of the modern city, as well as the subjectivity that inhabits this city. First of all, the poem invokes a specific topos: the neighborhood of Hibiya in central Tokyo. In contrast to the barbaric straightforwardness of the city as expressed in "armored coil," the city in "Hibiya" is depicted as a "refracted space" with "endless pitfalls and burials." While the poem describes the city's buildings, which soar "ever higher," it also mentions the "slaughter and exploitation and mauling" that occur in the "dark spaces between high buildings":

HIBIYA

Intense rectangles
      Chains and gunfire and intrigue
      Troops and gold and honors and fame
Higher higher higher higher higher   soaring higher
      The very center of the city———Hibiya

A refracted space
      Endless pitfalls and burials
      The graveyard of the new intellectual employees
Higher higher higher higher higher even higher even higher
      The dark spaces between high buildings
      Slaughter and exploitation and mauling

Higher higher higher higher higher higher higher
   higher higher higher higher higher higher higher
      Hibiya

He goes through————

He goes through————
    Pushing everything forward
He holds his own key in his hands
    A nihilistic laugh
    The stimulating dance of currency

He goes through————
One
One more one more ———— cemetery ———— towards the
    eternal burial
The final toast and dance
The center and summit
Higher higher higher higher higher higher a tower soaring ever
    higher

He goes through   **one man**

He goes through   **one man**

Hibiya[35]

By naming a specific district as the "very center of the city,"
Hagiwara gives the poem a specificity lacking in "Sōkō danki," and
invokes the multiple associations that a central district of a major
metropolis has built up over time. In choosing this district as the
"very center of the city" over other possible candidates (such as, for
example, Nihonbashi, the Imperial Palace, or the Ginza), Hagiwara
indicates his perception of the nature of the city, and indeed the
nature of Japanese modernity.

A center for government buildings, major hotels, and financial offices (where the growing white-collar class of "salaryman,"
or "new intellectual employees" worked), the "high-soaring" Hibiya district was the site of a building boom even prior to the
Great Kanto Earthquake, although Japanese building codes would
not permit skyscrapers like those found in New York or Chicago.[36] In his essay on Hagiwara's poem and urban space, Unno
Hiroshi describes the Hibiya district's geographical situation as
follows:

Hibiya is in the center of Kōjimachi, where all the buildings of the modern
state mechanism, such as the Diet and government offices, were crowded
together. To the east were the financial institutions of the Ginza, and the

entertainment streets of the Imperial Theater and the Imperial Hotel. While it was the center of Japan, laborers still milled about. . . . And to the north it bordered on the symbol of the imaginary nation—what Hagiwara Kyōjirō could not write about—the Imperial Palace.[37]

Hibiya also gave its name to Hibiya Park (*Hibiya kōen*), a major park covering the western portion of the district. Hibiya Park had its own share of associations: it was built on the site of a parade ground for the imperial army; after opening in 1903, the new park was soon appropriated by couples for their romantic encounters.[38] The park also became a favored site for labor rallies and political demonstrations. One of the first and most violent of these demonstrations was the Hibiya Riot of 1905, when a crowd of hundreds defied a police ban and assembled in Hibiya Park to protest, in the name of the Emperor, the terms of the Portsmouth Treaty ending the Russo-Japanese war. After clashes with police, angry crowds attacked or burned the offices of the *Kokumin shinbun*, streetcars, several government buildings, police headquarters, and many police boxes; the rioting ended two days later with seventeen dead, hundreds injured, and over two thousand arrested.[39]

The political drama inherent in Hibiya was provided by the situation of the Tokyo Metropolitan Police Headquarters (*keishichō*) just across from Hibiya Park, where "the masses" would gather for their rallies and demonstrations. The Police Headquarters was perhaps the most imposing of all the soaring towers and "intense rectangles" (*kyōretsu na shikaku*) of Hibiya—about 80 meters (262 feet) wide, 50 meters (164 feet) deep, and with an observation tower rising 30 meters (98 feet) high.[40] It was places like this that Hagiwara invoked with the line "Chains and gunfire and intrigue."

Who is the subject that inhabits *this* kind of city? Together with the refrain of "Higher higher higher higher . . ." (*takaku takaku takaku*), the poem repeats the phrases "He goes through" (*kare wa iku*) and "one man" (*hitori*). The identity of this one man, which remains a mystery, has generated numerous critical hypotheses.

Hibiya was the place chosen by Hirato Renkichi to distribute his fliers pronouncing his Japanese Futurist Manifesto Movement (*Nihon miraiha sengen undō*); the location thus carried with it, together with all its other associations, a symbolic status as the birthplace of avant-garde poetry in Japan. Especially given the fact that the poem was apparently composed on the first anniversary of Hirato's death, it is possible, as Komata Yūsuke suggests, to read "Hibiya" as a tribute to Hirato, and to see the person moving through the streets in Hagiwara's poem as a figure of the Futurist poet "of life at the moment of motion": a composite portrait of Hirato and Hagiwara himself.[41]

On the other hand, in light of the fusion of city and subject in poems such as "Sōkō danki," it is also feasible, as Unno Hiroshi suggests in his essay, to view the "one person" in "Hibiya" as an embodiment of Hibiya itself, or rather as an embodiment of the modern city as epitomized by Hibiya.[42] However, due to the emphasis on the man's solitude, his motion, his "nihilistic laugh," and his mysterious agency (holding the "key in his hands"), it is perhaps more appropriate to view this person as working against the telos of Hibiya, rather than fusing with it.

In the collection *Shikei senkoku*, this poem is placed at the head of a section of seven poems; the section as a whole is also entitled "Hibiya." The remaining six poems in the collection thematize, in various ways, a commitment to a radical political cause (anarchism being implied), or resignation to the use of violence for unstated political ends. In two of these poems, the poetic "I" declares: "The black target! / I love my cold pistol and cold-blooded intention!" and "Life can only be saved by the sword / Death cares not whether master or slave / My only goal / Is to fire my shot."[43] An attraction to martyrdom also permeates several poems. The second stanza of "Chinchaku to mukuchi no aki" ("Calm and Wordless Autumn"), for example, reads:

I have only one goal!
Angry will and angry blood!
Calm and wordless autumn!
The graveyard, even quieter, has endless void and earth
It's waiting for the day our corpses are lain down![44]

This stanza amplifies the more abstract lines of "Hibiya": "One / One more one more————cemetery————towards the eternal burial / The final toast and dance."

The placement of the poem "Jishin no hi ni" ("On the Day of the Earthquake") as the final poem of the "Hibiya" section would suggest a link between the Great Kanto Earthquake and the anarchist/terrorist's "cold-blooded intention." Indeed, many of those involved in the anarchist movement were radicalized by the violence and repression that followed the disaster. This violence included the lynching of thousands of Koreans and Chinese, the arrest of hundreds of political activists, the murder of ten labor leaders at the Kameido Police Station, and the death of Ōsugi Sakae, Itō Noe, and Ōsugi's nephew at the hands of the infamous military police lieutenant Amakasu Masahiko. In "Jishin no hi ni," originally published two months after the earthquake, the poetic narrator urges his fellows to absorb the life force of the victims, and, if not to seek revenge, then at least to rededicate themselves to the cause: "To whom shall we dedicate / The tumbled head, / The white bones, remaining from the fire, / The remaining life? / Lick the blood and blood, / Comrades!"[45]

In fact, a number of incidents of anarchist violence did follow the earthquake. The "Guillotine Society" (*Girochinsha*), a small anarcho-terrorist cell which had formed prior to the earthquake, carried out a number of unsuccessful attacks to avenge Ōsugi's death: an aborted shooting attack on Lieutenant Amakasu's younger brother, and two attacks on Fukuda Masatarō, the general in charge of the martial law imposed after the earthquake.[46] The most prominent "terrorist" reprisal in the post-quake period, however, was the so-called Tora no Mon Incident of December 1923. In this incident, Nanba Daisuke, the declassé son of an Imperial Diet member, used a homemade rifle to attack the Imperial Regent (the future Shōwa Emperor), who was passing by the Tora no Mon intersection en route from the Imperial Palace to the Diet. Nanba's shot shattered the window of the Regent's car, but the Regent himself was unharmed. Nanba was arrested, tried, and sentenced on November 13, 1924; the next day, newspapers throughout the country carried news that the death sentence (*shikei*) had been declared (*senkoku*)—a series of events which brought down a Japanese cabinet and riveted the attention of the entire nation.[47]

In addition to a probable reference to these events in the title of Hagiwara's collection, a number of the poems in *Shikei senkoku* offer literary parallels to such incidents of terrorist violence. Another poem in the Hibiya section, "Mudai" ("Untitled"), seems to depict a terrorist bombing attack on a moving vehicle. As printed in *Shikei senkoku*, "Mudai" offers a good example of Hagiwara's innovative poetic technique, with the three sections of the poem printed at 90-degree angles to each other and connected by thick black arrows in the upper right and upper left corners, suggesting the movement of an automobile around a city block. "Mudai" also features Hagiwara's expressive (or anti-expressive) use of *fuseji*, which delete portions of supposed conspiratorial information in the poem, thus destabilizing the process of signification in the text.

Damn!
    Around the corner
Turned an ash-colored car
As fast as a criminal

I turned
My nerves   like a spiral
Making my small eyes————harder
My body forward   as if bending down

Pressing down on my heart

        Go! At once
        To the third location
        The intersection
————————————————that ● ● ● ● ●
————————————————that ● ● ● ● ●
Chasing
        the cloud of yellow dust

Starving stomach
        That suddenly painful malice
Advance!
Ten times
        A hundred times
                faster than
The explosion's   drastic   rush
The streets where laughter and tears have dried

Run! Stinking of gunpowder
   Run

      Run

         Run

            Rage of instinctual flight
————————————————— that xxxxxx
————————————————— that xxxxxxxxxx

Despite the similarity between the events at Tora no Mon and the thematic material of this poem, "Mudai" was actually printed in its initial form in the third issue of *Aka to kuro* journal, six months before the Great Kanto Earthquake and eight months before Nanba's assassination attempt. This fact has led commentators to point out the literary as well as the historical intertexts for Hagiwara's depictions of anarcho-terrorist violence, particularly Aono Suekichi's influential translation of Boris Savinkov's novel *Kon'blednyi* (*The Pale Horse*).[48] In fact, the connection between poetry and terrorist violence was established even earlier, by the statement on the cover of the first issue of *Aka to kuro*, the journal that first brought Hagiwara, Tsuboi Shigeji, and Okamoto Jun to the attention of the Tokyo intelligentsia. This frequently quoted statement, later attributed to Tsuboi, read "What is a poem? Who is a poet? We discard all conceptions of the past, and fearlessly declare, 'The poem is a bomb! The poet is a black criminal lobbing this bomb against the hard walls and door of his prison!'"[49]

Returning to Hagiwara's poem "Hibiya," it is quite possible to see the unnamed moving figure in this poem as an incarnation of the anarchist/terrorist whose actions and psychological states are described in the other poems of the Hibiya section of *Shikei senkoku*. Indeed, while "Hibiya" was also composed before the Tora no Mon incident, these historical events superimposed themselves on Hagiwara's poem before *Shikei senkoku*'s publication in October 1925—the situation of Tora no Mon on the western edge of Hibiya adding one more layer to the complex geographical and historical associations upon which the poem played.[50]

A number of hypotheses, then, have been advanced to account for the "one man" who moves through Hagiwara's poem. This man may be an embodiment of the modern city, a symbol of Death (another Unno Hiroshi interpretation), a terrorist such as Nanba

Daisuke, a portrait of Hirato Renkichi, a self-portrait of Hagiwara, or a composite of some or all of these figures. Yet more important than confirming or denying any of these possibilities is the very fact that such a multiplicity of readings is possible. The "identity" of the "one man" in this poem is obscure and multiple. "Hibiya" thus marks a stage in the continual progression from a subjectivity defined by aggressive individual self-expression or "direct emotion" to one defined by multiplicity and strategic anonymity.

The urban subject in Hagiwara's poems mutates under the pressures of Japanese modernity—a modernity forged by rallies at Hibiya Park, the "stimulating dance of currency" in the neighboring Ginza, and the "intense rectangles" of the Metropolitan Police Headquarters. *Shikei senkoku* captures the shift from a poetics of presence to a poetics of absence, in which, as Hagiwara suggests in his preface, "from the part, we must discover the meaning of the whole." This absence is figured by the anonymous protagonist of "Hibiya," the *fuseji* of "Untitled," and, throughout, by the missing name of the Emperor.

Hagiwara and Mavo

Apart for its possible role in galvanizing or radicalizing Hagiwara's political vision, the Great Kanto Earthquake also served indirectly to bring Hagiwara closer to the Mavo group of artists. Immediately after the earthquake, a number of artists became active in designing and decorating the diverse temporary structures, called "barracks" (*barakku*), which sprouted up to replace the buildings leveled by earthquake and fire. The avant-garde rhetoric of joining art and daily life suddenly acquired a new relevance in the wake of this disaster, and a broad range of artists rallied around the slogan "from the atelier to the streets."[51]

The Mavo group was actually a relative latecomer to barrack decoration: the first and most prominent group involved in this project was the Barrack Decoration Company (Barakku Sōshokusha), founded by Waseda University architecture professor Kon Wajirō, Tokyo University professor Iwamoto Roku, design graduates of the Tokyo Art Academy, and members of the Action group of artists, led by Kanbara Tai. The Mavo group soon joined in the barrack decoration movement and extended their work to other architectural projects, including the design and decoration of permanent structures and the submission of plans and models for the Exhibition of Plans for the Reconstruction of the Imperial City (Teito Fukkō Sōan Tenrankai), a major design contest sponsored by the Citizen's Art Association (Kokumin Bijutsu Kyōkai).[52]

In April of 1924 Hagiwara Kyōjirō wrote an enthusiastic review of the various barrack decoration projects, specifically mentioning both Action and Mavo projects. While Hagiwara seems to have been acquainted with several Mavo members before this time,[53] this article is the first direct evidence of Hagiwara's interest in the group. In this review, Hagiwara contrasts the lively, colorful, and often eccentric designs of the barrack decoration artists with what he portrays as the dull and morose works of literary art in contemporary Japan:

Looking at the novels or plays of today's Japan, one grows impatient with their lack of freshness and originality—they generally read like second-rate novels in translation, or rely on the lifeless techniques of Naturalism. This is because they are indifferent to elements of color that are divorced from actual appearances, and they are insensitive to the internal consciousness of form. By opening oneself to form and color, one becomes more aware of the first-order elements of art, such as innovation and surprise. In this respect, the present-day artist has much to learn from the architectural methods and color-forms of the barrack streets.[54]

In addition to the freshness and dynamism of the barrack-street forms, Hagiwara was attracted by the activist spirit of the barrack decoration artists, which he contrasts with the melancholy and overly theoretical "empty talk" (*kūdan*) of contemporary poetry, fiction, and criticism.

Hagiwara's full-scale involvement with the Mavo group began the following year, when he joined the editorial staff of the *MAVO* magazine and began preparation of his first poetry collection with the collaboration of the Mavo artists. *MAVO* magazine had been inaugurated in July 1924, under the exclusive editorial control of Murayama Tomoyoshi. Over the first four issues, contributions to the magazine were mainly limited to Mavo members. Although these members were primarily visual artists, they wrote their own avant-garde poetry, theater scenarios, essays, translations, and other texts for the magazine, in addition to reproducing their visual artworks.

While the magazine had a great impact on contemporary writers and artists, the Mavo group and its magazine soon suffered a number of setbacks. The third issue of *MAVO* announced the withdrawal of a number of members who felt alienated by the increasing political radicalism of the group. This same issue (September 1924) was banned and confiscated by state censors, dealing the Mavo group a major financial blow. The fourth issue was greatly curtailed in size, and publication of the magazine was henceforth suspended due to financial problems and disarray within the group.[55]

In June 1925, the magazine was revived with two new editors, Okada Tatsuo and Hagiwara Kyōjirō, joining Murayama on the masthead. This issue (number 5) included for the first time literary contributions by a significant number of non-Mavoists, including Hayashi Fumiko, Onchi Terutake, Nomura Yoshiya, Hashimoto Renkichi (better known by the pen name Kitasono Katsue), Okamoto Jun, and Tsuboi Shigeji.[56] Editorial comments articulated the policy reversal from an exclusive *dōjin* format to a more open one: "From today, *MAVO* has no more *dōjin*. Everyone who has heard the word 'mavo' even once is a Mavoist." The editors' sometimes tongue-in-cheek remarks clarified the magazine's genre-crossing intent, as well as its ideological orientation, calling for contributions related to "theater, prose, painting, poetry, architecture, film, sports—anything. We solicit original works and criticism with the crushing force to overturn the authority of existing values, overconscious *isms*, and high-and-mighty power."[57]

Hagiwara referred to *MAVO* as "a training ground for new artists and new engineers,"[58] claiming that "*MAVO* is an engineer who puts into practice the intercourse and commonality of all things." Indeed, from its inception, the *MAVO* journal explored the possibilities of "intercourse" and "commonality" between different artistic genres. Moreover, the magazine served as a workshop in the techniques of mechanical reproduction, focusing both artist and viewer attention on the methods of hand and mechanical production and reproduction. Photographic reproductions (of Mavoists' paintings, collages, assemblages, architectural projects, and performances), linocuts or other types of prints, and even such physical objects as hair and firecrackers (on the cover of issue 3) were incorporated into the magazine; sheets of newspaper were recycled as pages of the magazine on which photographs, prints, or printed text were pasted in a type of integral collage practice.

The printed texts, especially the poems, expanded the experiments with expressive Japanese typography begun by such Futurist and Dadaist poets as Hirato Renkichi and Takahashi Shinkichi, typically employing arrows, lines, *fuseji*, and other geometrical symbols, in addition to alphabetic, numeric, syllabic, and ideographic characters of various sizes and orientations. In one visually striking example, Mavo member Takamizawa Michinao created a "poem" by freely applying the characters for "poison" (*doku*) and "sickness" (*yamai*) with a hand stamp to a portion of blank page (issue 4).

The Mavo members thus interrogated the relationship between hand production, which had been considered the basis of "art," and mechanical reproduction, which, as outlined in Chapter 1, was then expanding on a new mass scale within the realm of journalism and print media. As art historian Gennifer Weisenfeld argues, "editorially and philosophically, the magazine argued for a link between art and mass communication in modern society. The design techniques employed in the magazine asserted the connection between mass-circulated print media and artistic practice—between journalism and culture."[59]

In his book-length study of the Constructivist movement, Murayama Tomoyoshi outlined the international context for the Mavo group's exploration of print media:

One could say that print technology (*insatsujutsu*) has been given a new life by the Constructivists. Print technology, which had formerly been limited simply to the reproduction of images and text, has now come to possess its own unique value. The shape, size, and position of printed characters, the placement of lines, and so forth, have all become extremely important.[60]

At the same time the Mavo artists placed a greater focus on the technical aspects of the print medium, they also acknowledged that print was only one of several rapidly developing media. In the study of Constructivism quoted above, Murayama lists print technology as one of three spheres of the "mass production" and "mechanization" of art which were attracting the attention of contemporary artists, the other two being photography and film. Photography, when combined with print in the form of the photo magazine, was capable of exerting "tremendous power and influence," while film, he wrote, held a "limitless promise for tomorrow."[61]

The emergence of rival media encouraged artists and critics to view the print media, and written language itself, not as a given of culture but rather as a contingent historical phenomenon. In an article on the "technical revolution of literature and art" published in 1928, Hirabayashi Hatsunosuke examined established literary and artistic production alongside such new phenomena as radio drama, film drama, and mechanically produced and reproduced music, concluding that all of art was "on the eve of a great technological revolution." In this expanded context, Hirabayashi claims that "the foundations of literature as art are not built on an immovable rock as is widely thought, but are really quite unstable."[62] Reflecting on written language as a medium, he writes:

When we speak of "written language" (*moji*), this is not something that human beings have had since the beginning, when we evolved from a common ancestor to the apes. Since it was invented in a definite historical period, there is no guarantee that it has an immortal lifespan. If human beings discover a more convenient method, they may bid farewell to written language. At such a time, literature will be forced to undergo a technical metamorphosis.[63]

Several of the works that Hagiwara Kyōjirō produced for *MAVO* magazine, and the contemporaneous works collected in *Shikei senkoku*, pointedly comment on this changing media landscape. In keeping with the Mavo artists' proclivity to work outside their primary genres, Hagiwara published no poems in *MAVO* (although he was undoubtedly responsible for the large number of his associates' poems printed in the magazine). Instead of poems, Hagiwara published two essay/manifestoes, two collages, and one cartoonlike sketch.

This sketch, which was reprinted in *Shikei senkoku*, provides one instance of Hagiwara's imaginative engagement with new media.[64] The sketch features a strange anthropomorphic mechanical device, upon which are written various messages (Fig. 1, p. 4).[65] At the upper left, as if hoisted by a robotic 'hand,' is a banner reading "NIHIL" in roman letters. At the bottom right is a protuberance inscribed with key words (in Japanese) and symbols of mechanical civilization: "force-speed-certainty-symbol- + × ÷ = —O." In the center is a message that seems to describe the operation of the device: "Push a functioning button—every part will independently revolve, shine, swing, reverberate, emit sound, emit light. Oh, civilization! Give birth to a new spirit!" The most important clue to the identity and nature of the device, however, is written on the lower left: "All forms of poetic literature are destroyed—Now they will be replaced by the electric-radio advertising tower!!"

We can identify this strange device then, as an electric, radio, "advertising tower." Yet, the word *kōkokutō*, translated here as "advertising tower," encompasses a fairly wide range of semantic possibilities. The first part of this compound, *kōkoku*, or advertisement, is homophonous with the word for an official pronouncement, reminding us of the synonym *senden*, which can refer to either commercial advertising or political propaganda. The second part of the compound, "tō" or "towers" could signify a fairly small kiosk, a billboardlike construction or neon signpost, or a larger structure such as might be used for a broadcasting station. Hagiwara's tower, which emits light, sound, and radio waves, would seem to combine a number of these structural types.

The advertising, or propaganda, kiosk was a favored architectural genre of the Russian Constructivists, beginning with the "radio-orators," "radio-tribune," and "cinema-photo stands" designed by Gustav Klutsis in 1922.[66] If one defines propaganda as political advertising, then Tatlin's famous design for the Monument to the Third International (1919–1920), which included a broadcasting/propaganda center at its summit, could be considered the world's largest plan for an "advertising tower." As a pamphlet on the monument described, the uppermost revolving cylinder of this tower was to house "centers of an informational type: an information bureau, a newspaper, offices for public proclamations, pamphlets, and manifestoes—in short, all the various mass media for the international proletariat, in particular telegraph, projectors for a big screen located on the axes of a spherical section, and radio transmitters, whose masts rise above the monument."[67]

FIG. 2: Ōura Shūzō, *Kōkokutō* (Advertising Tower). Photograph of an architectural construction in *MAVO*, no. 2 (August 1924).

Issue 2 of *MAVO* magazine (August 1924) includes a photograph of an advertising kiosk (*kōkokutō*) designed by Mavoist Ōura Shūzō (see Fig. 2). This unusual building, with its rectangular first floor, high vaulted roof, and slender protruding tower, employs a somewhat different architectural idiom from the Russian kiosks. Its purpose is different too: rather than serving the state in the distribution of propaganda, Ōura's kiosk functions in a commercial context—its surface is covered with numerous advertisements for different types of Maruzen Ink, and a window in the kiosk seems designed for the sale of these commodities. While the kiosk's playful architectural forms could be cited as evidence of what Weisenfeld calls Mavo's "theatricalization" of urban space, its function serves as a reminder that many of the Mavo members' activities involved energetic participation in developing commercial practices, rather than an exclusively antagonistic stance toward capitalism.[68]

Hagiwara's attraction to the idea of the advertising tower was thus another point of convergence between his poetic interests and the projects of the artistic avant-garde. As a meaning-bearing site with the potential for quite different political and economic articulations, the advertising tower provides an ideal location to observe Hagiwara's own exploration of ideological themes. What, then, are the messages promoted or items for sale by Hagiwara's anthropomorphic "advertising tower," with its power to serve as midwife to the birth of civilization's "new spirit"? At the upper right of Hagiwara's sketch are a number of written messages that seem to be a display of sample advertisements. Yet the nature of these messages is quite diverse, a mixture of product names with other, less clearly identifiable signifiers: "Floating World / *Central Review* (*Chūō kōron*) / Hoshi Stomach Medicine / Incandescent Electric Lamps / Concave Lenses / Rain-Tears-Blood / Theories of Banking."

This strange list of divergent signifiers exemplifies the Mavo group's propensity to compress absurdly heterogeneous types of discourse into a single collage-like space. In this case, rather than offering a positive example of the propagandist's or advertiser-poet's "message," the display serves as a satirical comment on functions of media in a capitalist context to homogenize different types of information and experience as commodities. Thus the serious intellectual discourse of *Chūō kōron*, the possibly agitational "Theories of Banking," the vital fluids "Rain-Tears-Blood" (subjects of former "poetic literature"), and a product such as "Hoshi Stomach Medicine" are all commodities for sale in the new media age.

"Advertising Tower!"

Hagiwara's involvement with the idea of the advertising tower, however, did not stop at this sketch; nor did he stop writing poetry after serving notice of the destruction of "all forms of poetic literature." His poem "Kōkokutō!"[69] ("Advertising Tower!") is a centerpiece of the "Rasukōrinikofu" section of *Shikei senkoku*, the final and most aesthetically radical section of the collection. In this poem, the problems of literature and individual subjectivity in the age of mass media, which Hagiwara explored in a playful manner in his sketch, are given a more sustained and complex hearing. The collage aesthetic that informed Hagiwara's contributions to *MAVO* magazine is also evident in the poem "Kōkokutō!," which juxtaposes a number of different subjectivities and uses of language.

Both Hagiwara's poem and sketch suggest that the poet in a

new age must himself become an "advertising tower" in order for the poetic message to be seen or heard in the age of mass media. Man and machine fuse to produce a new type of subjectivity capable of "mass production" and "agitation," two phrases from the opening section of "Kōkokutō!" This first section, employing a complex arrangement of text and *fuseji*, contains a number of phrases that can be read as actions performed by the poet-cum-advertising tower subject: "discharges / exchanges / explodes / assaults / pivots / shocks / ejects / collapses / wails / overturns." Referring back to the sketch, we might see the *fuseji* that surround the central text of the opening section as representations of "functioning buttons" that will cause "every part" of the tower to "independently revolve, shine, swing, reverberate, emit sound, emit light."

Much of "Kōkokutō!" is composed of a lengthy middle section consisting entirely of brief sentences arranged in three rows of twenty-six lines each, achieving a strong visual effect but resisting any logical or narrative connection. Each row is composed of highly parallel sentence constructions with an identical number of characters. The syntax of the sentences is quite simple, the top row consisting of such sentences as "He laughs! / He cries! / He walks! / He rejoices! / He sleeps! / He eats! / He rages! / He runs!" etc.; the middle, upside-down, row formed of such sentences as "He is affirmation! / He is negation! / He is assertion! / He is a demand! / He is a wish! / He is a realist!" and so on; and the bottom row of such sentences as "She gives thanks to God! / She turns to bones! / She walks the path of thorns! / She withers with fatigue! / She keeps it a secret! / She is a fine wine! / She is the shade of death! / She is delicate!" and so on.

The gendered division of actions and qualities in these sentences form a grotesque parody of stereotypical representations of gender in literature, advertising, and other spheres of public discourse. The often-contradictory actions and qualities presented here eschew traditional models of poetic sense-making, such as narrative (*joji*) or the relation of personal sentiment (*jojō*). Instead, we can see these sentences as an example of the "discharge" or "mass production" of the poet who has been transformed into an "electric-radio advertising tower"—a vision of poetry in the age of mechanical reproduction. Indeed, the overdetermined, even parodic, quality of the gender stereotypes in these sentences underscores the stanza's mechanical quality, in which a gendered pronoun is yoked together with a predicate according to the rules of stereotyped discourse in an indefinite series.

This, however, is not the only type of poetic language in "Kōkokutō!" Between the opening section and the above section of parallel sentences, there is a section that seems much closer to traditional models of lyric poetry:

> The languid brains sing a song
> I'm listening to the noise of the water
> Everything is the ocean's sunless black abyss!
> With no beginning and no end!
> Each thing comes and passes!
> Life? Who has a clue?! The face of a hobby-horse!
> Ah, Pierrot!
> I can believe in neither freedom, nor God, nor mankind!
> Only, I find the utmost fissure in the Dadaists!
> You want to find a meaning?! Go ahead!
> All is but a series of affectations!
> I'm tired of this continual boredom! [Etc]

Here, the sentences seem to represent the "expression" of a consistent subjectivity represented by the pronoun *watakushi* ("I"). Furthermore, this "I" relates feelings of frustration, despair, and ennui that were commonly expressed by Taishō intellectuals and could easily be attributed to "Hagiwara" himself.[70] Yet given this stanza's placement in "Kōkokutō!," it is also possible to read the stanza as a parody of just such "poetic literature" in a media context in which, as Okamoto Jun suggested, even the modern-day Hamlets are commercialized. The opening line of this stanza, "The languid brains sing a song" (*monouge na zunō wa uta o utau*), drives a thin wedge between the "I" of the stanza and an "I" attributable to "Hagiwara," dramatizing the self-alienation of lyric poetry.

Toward the end of "Kōkokutō!" the reader is presented with yet another type of subjective expression. Here, the pronoun *watakushi* in the melancholy stanza above is replaced by the pronoun *ore*, typical of a rougher type of male speech:

In the road, on the streets, on the rooftops, in the rooms, the warehouses,

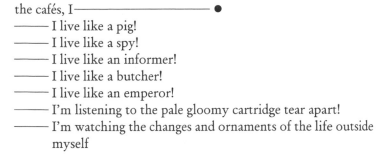

————— I live like a pig!
————— I live like a spy!
————— I live like an informer!
————— I live like a butcher!
————— I live like an emperor!
————— I'm listening to the pale gloomy cartridge tear apart!
————— I'm watching the changes and ornaments of the life outside myself

These lines represent a different sort of subjectivity from the lyrical "I" of the previously quoted stanza. This subjectivity, like the subjectivity outlined in the previous discussion of "Hibiya," is obscure, multiple, and treacherous. Here, the "I" explicitly denies any subjectivity based on "subjecthood": the "spy" and "informer," like the "traitor" of the opening section, are prepared to betray any allegiances to the nation-state, or even to counter-state organizations. Furthermore, this "I" will not accept any subjectivity subordinate to or predicated upon a transcendental signifier such as an "emperor"; rather, the "I" himself will live like an emperor.[71] Once again, at the head of this stanza, the *fuseji* appears as the mark of the censor, which has been appropriated into the code of poet/ terrorist.

Yet the poem is not allowed to come to rest even on this shadowy and multiple subjectivity. Deflating of the grandiose claims of the "I" who would live like a "butcher" or an "emperor," the final section of the poem gives a final ironic portrait of the poet-cum-advertising tower (words in italics in the translation below are in boldface katakana in the original):

————————————————Several bodily cavities and a bumpy
face and several round sticks and
        yellow and hair and *springs* and a *compass* and tendons
        and a *tapeworm* and socks and a calling card!
A dirty *shirt* with several *buttons* coming off and *pants* that
        look like I just changed—
                —that instrument called me!

This stanza, for the first time in "Kōkokutō!," places its focus on the body of the subject, rather than his "brains," actions, or political identities. While the conceit of a man-machine is carried into this final stanza, the robotic "self" portrayed here seems less a powerful product of modern technology (the "force-speed-certainty" cited in Hagiwara's sketch) than a makeshift and disarmingly mortal assemblage.

Eleven years after Hagiwara published "Kōkokutō!" in *Shikei senkoku*, and eight years after Hirabayashi Hatsunosuke issued his prognostications on the "technical revolution" of literature and art, Frankfurt School theorist Walter Benjamin published his influential essay "The Work of Art in the Age of Mechanical Reproduction."[72] In this essay, Benjamin advances his well-known thesis that the "aura" of the work of art, based on the "authenticity" of the original, withers in the age of mechanical reproduction.

Hagiwara's "Kōkokutō!" can be read as a response from the realm of literature to a new media situation marked by an intensification and extension of mechanical reproduction. While the relationship between poet and reader has long been mediated by printing technology, the poem in Japan nonetheless widely retained its own claim to "authenticity" in representing the emotive "voice" of the poet—an expressive poetics rooted in the earliest statements of poetics in the waka tradition and revived in various forms by modern poets.[73] The relationship between poetry and oral expression was further redefined and reinforced in Meiji and Taishō Japan by the incorporation of *genbun itchi* ideology in the creation of the "colloquial free-verse poem" (*kōgojiyūshi*), which was extended through the work of the People's Poets (*minshūshi-ha*). The deep-seated link between poetry and the expression of individual sentiment is also reflected in Hirato Renkichi's conception of a Futurism of "direct emotion," even while Hirato compares the effect of such a "direct emotion" to the mechanical "action of a rapid steel machine."

Hagiwara breaks down this auratic link between poetry and the individual voice by juxtaposing any number of poetic subjectivities or "I"'s, complicating any search for an originary or authentic poetic voice in the poem. Even the second stanza, which comes closest to presenting the "self-expression" of a lyrical "I," establishes an ironic distance from this "I" with its opening line, "The languid brains sing a song." Following this "lyric" stanza, the poem then launches into the lengthy and highly visual arrays of such lines as "He laughs! / He cries! / He walks! / He rejoices! / He sleeps! / He eats! / He rages! / He runs!" These lines, which could continue indefinitely until the depletion of all possible verbs and stereotyped phrases, seem more like the output from a linguistic machine than lyrical "self-expression."[74] The break from an oral-expressive poetics achieved in this section is further underscored by the regularity of the lines—attained by the identical number of printed characters in each line, rather than the number of spoken syllables conveyed by each—in other words, a regularity that is entirely visual rather than metrical or syllabic.[75]

Taking the idea of the advertising or propaganda tower in the abstract, we can say that such a tower has no "subjectivity" of its own beyond the messages which are posted on it, broadcasted through it, or generated inside it by a mechanical process. By placing the poem and poet in the position of advertising tower, Hagiwara seems to disavow the originary claims of poetic language to authenticity, and to offer the poem as an intersubjective site for the distribution, display, or reassemblage of messages that are as likely to be generated from the "outside" as the "inside." This reconception of the subject is reminiscent of Hagiwara's description of the artist's body as a tube fusing together "all elements of society," or as a cardiovascular system transporting the elements of society in and out of the "heart of the self."

With their imaginative combinations of body and text with the functions of a futuristic advertising tower, Hagiwara's sketch and poem suggest not so much a robot as a prototype of the cyborg, a hybrid of human and nonhuman that emerged from American cybernetics and biological research in the postwar period.[76] While the robot is associated primarily with mechanics and industrial production, the cyborg or "cybernetic organism" evokes a combination of the human with the technological processing and routing of information. Similarly, in Hagiwara's work, the cyborglike advertising tower functions as a node in the transfer of messages—the site of circulation where the "self" and "society-self" intermesh. Although it is a site of circulation and exchange, the advertising tower must adapt to the city's treacherous political environment through tactics of encryption and appropriation.

In the epilogue to "The Work of Art in the Age of Mechanical Reproduction," Benjamin suggests that the effect of the new age of mechanical reproduction is to efface the boundary between politics and art. In a memorable formula, he describes Fascism (which he links closely to Futurism) as the aestheticization of politics, and concludes that "Communism responds by politicizing art."[77] While Benjamin's symmetrical formula may be overly schematic even in the European context, it does provide an index to the political tensions underlying the mechanical transformation of art and communication in the opening decades of the twentieth century.

In May 1925, five months before the publication of *Shikei senkoku*, the Japanese legislature moved to foreclose the possibilities of the "politicization of art" or other forms of public discourse by passing the Peace Preservation Law (*Chian iji hō*), which strengthened existing thought control measures by stipulating imprisonment for anyone agitating for the abolition of private property or changes in the *kokutai* (the national polity headed by the emperor), or to anyone forming or joining an organization designed to attain these goals.[78] The new law, which was soon used to crack down on communists and anarchists, was passed in the same legislative session as the act for universal male suffrage. As Isoda Kōichi has suggested, the simultaneous passage of these bills was the legislative equivalent to the spatial disposition of Hibiya, in which the public space of Hibiya Park was placed under surveillance by the forbidding rectangles of the Police Headquarters.[79]

Hagiwara's "Kōkokutō!," while challenging the distinction between "art" and "politics," has no clear place on either side of Benjamin's symmetrical formula, neither a Futurist/Fascist aestheticization of politics nor a straightforward Communist politicization of art. Just as Hagiwara had portrayed the urban landscape of Hibiya as "a refracted space," the political expression in such poems as "Hibiya" and "Kōkokutō!" is likewise refracted, warped, and duplicitous. Thus the political self proclaimed in some sections of "Kōkokutō!" is that of a double agent: a "traitor," "spy," or "informer." Just as Hagiwara's poems incorporate the tools of censorship as technical elements, the political expression in his poetry dramatizes a situation in which the open politicization of art has been rendered treasonous. It is this "refracted" vision of city and subject that constitutes Hagiwara's most poignant representation of Japanese modernity.

4 / FRAMING MODERNITY IN HAYASHI FUMIKO'S *HŌRŌKI*

Hōrōki, or *Diary of a Vagabond*, was the first novel by Hayashi Fumiko, whose prolific writing career spanned the prewar, wartime, and postwar eras until her death in 1951. The novel was remarkable for its audacious use of language; its fast-paced, montage texture; and its compelling subject matter, which focused on the struggles of an independent young woman to find work, living space, and personal fulfillment in the rapidly changing urban environment of 1920s Tokyo. Based in part on journals that the author kept throughout the decade, the novel was first published in installments in the feminist literary journal *Nyonin geijutsu* from 1928 to 1930.[1] When published in book form as part of Kaizōsha's Shin'ei bungaku sōsho (Innovative Literature Series) in July 1930, it became an instant bestseller, lifting Hayashi out of poverty and obscurity.[2] The novel was quickly followed by a sequel, *Zoku hōrōki*, in October 1930. In the postwar period, Hayashi published a second sequel, or "part three," *'Hōrōki' daisanbu*, in the journal *Nihon shōsetsu* (1947).[3]

Throughout her novel, Hayashi keeps a keen eye on the role of modern media and incipient forms of mass culture in the subject formation of her protagonist. Yet while she shows how these mass-cultural forms helped to mold her protagonist's consciousness, she also asserts her protagonist's subjectivity as a cultural producer, as well as a perceptive and often cynical judge of her mass-mediated environment. Hayashi performs this destabilization of the cultural consumer/producer duality through a highly fluid and eclectic novelistic style, which itself defies the distinction between the rapidly consolidating categories of "popular literature" and "pure literature."

Hayashi offered the best description of her own work in the postscript-like final section of the novel's sequel, *Zoku hōrōki* (*Diary of a Vagabond Continued*), stating that the novel was an "admixture" or "adulteration" (*kyōzatsubutsu*), with "nothing pure in it."[4] In a work that features a particularly strong correspondence between the literary form of the text and the subjectivity of its protagonist, this self-avowed quality of the text as an "admixture" mirrors the protagonist/narrator's own declaration of personal identity as a "mongrel" (*chabo*) in the opening paragraphs of the work. While Hayashi appears to renounce her own work in this final section of *Zoku hōrōki* and deleted her self-identification as a mongrel in later editions of the text, it is precisely the novel's aggressively hybrid quality that links it with the works of contemporary modernist and avant-garde writers and marks its special significance in Japanese literary history.

Hōrōki, Modernism, and Montage

While Hayashi's works may have been for years "segregated and effectively stigmatized by their categorization as 'women's literature,'" as argued by Joan Ericson,[5] there has recently been a revival of interest in Hayashi, including a new appreciation of her contribution to the modernist movement of the 1920s and early 1930s. Commentators such as Unno Hiroshi and Watanabe Kazutami have noted the importance of Hayashi's depiction of the modern city of Tokyo, particularly the fresh perspectives of her female characters as they claim new freedoms of movement and expression in this rapidly transforming urban space.[6] Seiji Lippit, in his study *Topographies of Japanese Modernism,* has placed Hayashi's *Hōrōki* alongside the writings of Akutagawa Ryūnosuke, Yokomitsu Riichi, and Kawabata Yasunari among the key works of 1920s modernism that "record the internal, formal dismantling of the structures of the modern novel." This dismantling included the rejection of the conventions of narrative fiction and the language of *genbun itchi,* the form of written Japanese held to fuse written and spoken languages and established as the standard language of the modern novel at the turn of the century.[7]

As Lippit argues, the distinguishing formal quality of *Hōrōki* is its extreme fluidity: the novel constantly moves through multiple styles and genres of writing.[8] Hayashi's writing courses between prose journal entries and poetry, as well as regularly interspersed "reality fragments," such as songs heard or recalled, conversations overheard, or shopping lists drawn up by the protagonist. Within both her prose and her poetry, moreover, Hayashi juxtaposes the multiple languages of feminism, anarchism, *shishōsetu* (the I-novel), Proletarian Literature, fashionable modernism, the sentimentalism associated with the *katei shōsetsu* (domestic novel) and *shimpa* drama, and the classical tradition of *nikki bungaku*, or "diary literature," to name only a few. The diversity of language types in *Hōrōki* strongly evokes M. M. Bakhtin's theory of heteroglossia as the essential stylistic feature of the novel as a literary form, whereby "the novel can be defined as a diversity of social speech types . . . and a diversity of individual voices, artistically organized."[9] In particular, the aggressive challenge that *Hōrōki* presents to the unified style of *genbun itchi* demonstrates how the novel can orchestrate the unruly "centrifugal" forces of language into conflict with "centripetal" forces that, in Bakhtin's formulation, work to "unite and centralize verbal-ideological thought, creating within a heteroglot national language the firm, stable linguistic nucleus of an officially recognized literary language."[10]

Nevertheless, one should recall that Bakhtin's is a general theory of the novel, not one restricted to modernist or avant-garde works. Indeed, among generations of Japanese novelists, even those associated with the development of *genbun itchi*, we can find instances of diverse and contrastive language types being "artistically organized." What is truly distinctive about Hayashi's *Hōrōki* is not the coexistence of different language types—although it must be admitted that Hayashi takes this practice to the extreme—but the novel's unique temporality, which is fragmentary and fast-moving, juxtaposing language types and jumping and cutting between genres of writing and diagetic temporalities. This quality links *Hōrōki* with the techniques of montage, particularly cinematic montage, which was a focus of keen attention among modernist and avant-garde artists, writers, and filmmakers during the 1920s.[11]

For example, in the first section of the novel after the introduction, Hayashi narrates the first-person protagonist's movement through the city of Tokyo by train and on foot as she searches for work by day and returns to her Shinjuku lodgings at night. This section, entitled "Inbaifu to meshiya" (Prostitutes and mess halls), consists of four journal entries, each broken up by a temporal shift from day to night. The prose of these entries is further fragmented by the insertion of two poems, a tanka by Ishikawa Takuboku that begins the section, and one of Hayashi's own free-verse poems quoted in the second journal entry. Within sixteen pages of the generously spaced first edition, the scene changes twelve times, as the protagonist wanders from the home of a writer in the Hongō neighborhood where she's briefly employed as a maid, to a deserted "culture house" (*bunka jūtaku*) real estate development on the western edge of Tokyo, to a mess hall on Ōme Kaidō, an employment agency in Kanda, the Italian embassy in Kōjimachi, from there through the city on foot again to Hongō, and back again regularly to her rooming house in Shinjuku—a tour through the city's various socioeconomic and cultural strata as well as its geographic space.[12] The kaleidoscopic effect of this movement, marked by sudden jumps in the narrative flow and mediated by the urban technology of the electric streetcar, is remarkably similar to that of progressive cinematic montage, particularly the modernist genre of the city symphony, exemplified by such works as Walter Ruttman's 1928 film *Berlin, Symphony of a City* (1928).[13]

The modernist sensibility that Hayashi brought to her first novel, together with her facility in capturing (and sometimes mocking) a number of dialects of 1920s intellectual and novelistic discourse, can be understood in part on the basis of the personal ties that Hayashi established as an apprentice writer.[14] As discussed in Chapter 1, soon after she moved to Tokyo from her native Kyushu, Hayashi established close personal connections with the group of avant-garde artists and poets, many of whom were involved with the anarchist movement, who frequented the Café Lebanon in the Hongō neighborhood of Tokyo, including Tsuji Jun, Hagiwara Kyōjirō, "Dadaist" Takahashi Shinkichi, and Hirabayashi Taiko.

In addition to her ties to these young leftist writers, Hayashi also sought contact with more established literary and intellectual figures, including the anarchist Ōsugi Sakae and the veteran Naturalist writer Tokuda Shūsei, whose works, like Hayashi's, focus on the everyday life of people of the lower classes.[15] In the late 1920s she was to find another community of support among the writers associated with the feminist literary journal *Nyonin geijutsu,* where her novel *Hōrōki* was first serialized.[16] Although she later wrote that she was "constantly thinking about political movements and art" during this period, as she established herself as a writer she resolutely avoided identification with the "Proletarian Literature" movement or any other clearly delineated literary school or political ideology.[17] Nevertheless, Hayashi's challenging personal experiences growing up in Kyushu and establishing herself in Tokyo served as the themes for many of her narratives, while her exposure to writers affiliated with Naturalism, avant-garde poetry, anarchism, feminism, and Proletarian Literature formed the intellectual context for the incisive depiction of mass culture achieved in her first novel. Drawing on personal experiences of the provinces and the metropole, she constructs her own narrative of the birth of mass culture, suggesting that this culture was not simply modern and urban, but a product of the complex relationship between rural and urban, past and present.

Framing Modernity

I have cited the poems in Hagiwara's *Shikei senkoku,* with their explosion of traditional forms of poetic subjectivity and incorporation of heterogeneous typographic and visual elements, as an example of the avant-garde artwork's tendency to problematize and transgress aesthetic and political frame conditions. Hayashi Fumiko's *Hōrōki* shares with Hagiwara's work a foregrounding of linguistic heterogeneity, a problematization of authorial subjectivity, and an impulse to reconnect literary activity with daily life. When compared with contemporary examples of novelistic subjectivity, language, and organization, Hayashi's work can indeed be said to transgress, or at least to severely test, the frame conditions of the modern novel.

Yet, even as it is testing the aesthetic frame conditions of the novel, in a different and equally important sense Hayashi's work is engaged in an act of enframing—an attempt to represent, demarcate, and display Japanese modernity. In this regard, *Hōrōki* bears comparison with a number of contemporaneous projects that attempt to bring Japanese modernity within a new ethnographic and historical framework. One such noteworthy project is that of the professor of architecture Kon Wajirō, who in the mid-1920s founded a new discipline to study the practices of contemporary urban life, which he called modernology, or *kōgengaku*, on the analogy of archeology, or *kōkogaku*.[18] Another such project is that of Yanagita Kunio, who around the year 1930 turned his attention from interpreting the vanishing folklore and folklife of rural Japan to a historical consideration of Japanese modernity, as manifested in the everyday life of subjects in both rural and urban areas. This project culminated in the volume *Meiji Taishōshi: sesōhen* (*A History of the Meiji and Taishō Eras: Social Conditions*), published in 1931.[19]

Like the studies of Kon and Yanagita, Hayashi's *Hōrōki* exhibits a strong ethnographic impulse; the narrator's reminiscences and diary entries display an exacting attention to the details of material culture, the shifting modes and fashions of everyday life, and the local nuances of historical change. Cultural markers of various types—place names; song titles and fragments; reading lists; descriptions of food, clothing, and housing conditions; and the (often ironic) use of popular phrases and slang expressions—are enfolded into Hayashi's textual montage, not only for their utility in telling a personal narrative, but also, I believe, in order to construct a narrative of Japanese modernity.

In the present chapter, I will focus primarily on the first chapter of Hayashi's *Hōrōki*, which is entitled "Hōrōki izen," or "Before the Diary of a Vagabond." Unlike the main body of Hayashi's text, this introductory chapter does not consist of diary entries, but takes the form of an essay-memoir of the narrator's childhood. Whereas action in the main text takes place primarily in Tokyo, "Hōrōki izen" is set among a series of small towns and provincial cities in southwestern Japan. Historically, too, the cultural references of "Hōrōki izen" are not to the heyday of self-defined *modan* ("modern") Japan in the 1920s (the late Taishō and early Shōwa periods), but to an earlier, transitional period of Japanese modernity, the late Meiji and early Taishō periods. Finally, the prose style of "Hōrōki izen" also contrasts with the rest of the novel: while the practice of montage, including the incorporation of popular song texts, is conspicuous from the very first lines of this chapter, the prose as a whole is more consistent and subdued than the often fragmentary, unstable, and boisterous prose style employed in the subsequent chapters.

Historically, geographically, and stylistically, then, "Hōrōki izen" serves as a frame for the main portion of Hayashi's text. Thus her work, which, as I argue, is itself embroiled in the larger project of enframing modernity, is distinguished formally by the use of a prominent framing mechanism. This framing mechanism does more than simply contrast the urban with the rural, or the Meiji/Taishō with Shōwa culture. Rather, Hayashi's text points to the intimate relationship *between* rural and urban Japan, and *between* the novel's present and the recent past. It points to the cultural presence of the provinces in the metropolis (and vice versa), as well as to the persistence of the Meiji/Taishō elements in the Shōwa period, and conversely to the roots of the Shōwa in an earlier phase of Japanese modernity.

As critics such as Unno Hiroshi and Watanabe Kazutami have pointed out, *Hōrōki* is fundamentally an urban novel—indeed, one of the crucial urban novels of twentieth-century Japan.[20] Yet the frame mechanism outlined above establishes the novel not as a native urbanite's urban text, but as the experience of an immigrant to the city. This essential fact ties Hayashi's work to trends in Japanese urban development and also to patterns in the development of modernist literatures and the historical avant-garde throughout the world.

In his essay "The Metropolis and the Emergence of Modernism," Raymond Williams attempts to outline the "decisive links between the practices and ideas of the avant-garde movements of the twentieth century and the specific conditions of the twentieth-century metropolis."[21] Among the "specific conditions of the twentieth-century metropolis," Williams identifies the phenomenon of large-scale immigration to the city as crucial for the development of modernist and avant-garde subcultures:

The most important general element of the innovations in form is the fact of immigration to the metropolis, and it cannot be too often emphasized how many of the major innovators were, in this precise sense, immigrants. . . . Liberated or breaking from their national or provincial cultures, placed in quite new relations to those other native languages or native visual traditions, encountering meanwhile a novel and dynamic common environment from which many of the older forms were obviously distant, the artists and writers and thinkers of this phase found the only community available to them: a community of the medium; of their own practices.[22]

Although Williams's remarks are directed primarily to the cultural situation of interwar Europe, they resonate equally with Hayashi Fumiko's experience of immigration from Kyushu to Tokyo and her discovery of a "community of the medium" among the poets of the Café Lebanon.

One of the most acute cultural differences between the metropolis and the provinces was language: the language spoken by the narrator's parents and other *Hōrōki* characters from western Japan is a dialect very different from that spoken in Tokyo. Aside from direct quotations from such characters, however, Hayashi's novel is written not in dialect, but in the language of the metropole: a language disseminated in public schools throughout Japan as the language of the nation-state, and further spread by the print media, including modern literature; by popular song and stage drama emanating from the capital; and by the new medium of radio. The metropole's language is the language of power, and Hayashi, as an aspiring writer (and a member of the swelling national ranks of female secondary school graduates) exploited this power.[23]

The "standard Tokyo speech" of *Hōrōki*, however, is anything but standard. Rather, on the level of grammar, Hayashi employs a highly eccentric mix of the *genbun itchi* prose style, classical Japanese expressions and sentence endings, and informal sentence fragments. On the level of vocabulary, Hayashi's style is equally eclectic, incorporating slang, buzz words (*ryūkōgo*), vulgar expressions (*zokugo*), and a high proportion of onomatopoeia (*gitaigo/giongo*). These incongruities highlight the diversity of actual spoken languages (according to factors such as class and gender) even *within* the metropolis on the one hand, and the constructedness of *Hōrōki* as a written text on the other, inveighing against the transparency of the *genbun itchi* style of prose.

Raymond Williams also points to an experience of estrangement from language as a general feature of modernism, and one linked closely to the phenomenon of immigration:

Thus language was perceived quite differently [by the Modernists/avant-garde]. It was no longer, in the old sense, customary and naturalized, but in many ways arbitrary and conventional. To the immigrants especially, with their new second common language, language was more evident as a medium—a medium that could be shaped and reshaped—than as a social custom. Even within a native language, the new relationships of the metropolis, and the inescapable new uses in newspapers and advertising attuned to it, forced certain productive kinds of strangeness and distance: a new consciousness of conventions and thus of changeable, because now open, conventions.[24]

While Williams's remarks shed light on the experience and achievements of Hayashi and other "immigrant" modernists, his employment of the terms "customary and naturalized" versus "arbitrary and conventional" language fails to elaborate the political and cultural implications of the modernists' defamiliarization of specifically modern, *national* languages—in this case, standard modern spoken Japanese based on the Tokyo dialect—and the *genbun itchi* writing style held to reflect this spoken language. Benedict Anderson has argued in *Imagined Communities* for the importance of such semi-official, orally based languages to the formation of modern nation-states.[25] In deforming the language of the metropolis and disrupting the integrity of *genbun itchi* prose, Hayashi not only challenges the literary establishment, but also undermines a crucial register in which the modern nation-state establishes its hegemony. The challenge posed by her heterogeneous prose style corresponds with the "mongrel" personal identity that, as I discuss below, Hayashi posits for her protagonist from the opening lines of her novel.

A reading of Hayashi Fumiko's act of "enframing modernity," moreover, allows us to see beyond Williams's Manichaean opposition of "the imperial and capitalist metropolis," represented by Paris, London, Berlin, and New York, and "the deprived hinterlands, . . . [and] the poor world which has always been peripheral to the metropolitan systems."[26] Like most canonical narratives of modernism and modernity produced by European and American

observers, Williams's account fails to take into account the experience of modernity, or the potential development of modernisms,
in such developing metropoles as Buenos Aires, Cairo, Shanghai,
or Tokyo. Williams describes the European and North American
capitals as sites of a new "complexity and sophistication of social
relations," and further notes "not only the complexity but the
miscellaneity of the metropolis." This "complex and open milieu"
is contrasted with "the persistence of traditional social, cultural,
and intellectual forms in the provinces and in the less developed
countries."[27] The works of Japanese artists and writers in the 1920s,
however, suggest that cities such as Tokyo were equally possessed
of the heterogeneity, mobility, and "miscellaneity" that could foster the development of modernist art and literature.

Moreover, as Hayashi's "Hōrōki izen" makes clear, even "the
deprived hinterlands" of the Japanese backwaters were being incorporated into the economic and cultural matrix of "urban modernity" through the fast-developing forms of twentieth-century commerce and mass media. Thus the experience of "simultaneity" was
a defining modern phenomenon that linked not only the world
capitals (such as Tokyo and Berlin), but the capitals and the hinterlands (such as Tokyo and the provincial towns of Kyushu) as well.[28]
By enframing the main chapters of *Hōrōki* with the brief memoir
entitled "Hōrōki izen," Hayashi explores the reciprocity between
province and metropole, between Taishō and Shōwa, and between
early mass-culture eclecticism and avant-garde constructivism.

Peripheral Networks in "Hōrōki izen"

Hayashi begins her novel with the following lines:

When I was in a grammar school in Kita-Kyushu, this was one of the songs
I learned:

> Under the darkening autumn sky
> Traveling alone, distressed by lonely thoughts
> Yearning for my home town
> Missing Mother and Father

I was fated to be a vagabond.
I have no home town.

I am a crossbreed, a mongrel.

My father, from Iyo in Shikoku, was a peddler of cotton clothing.

My mother, from Sakurajima, near Kagoshima in Kyushu, was the daughter of a hot springs innkeeper.

After Mother was chased out of Kagoshima for marrying someone from another province, she and my father finally settled down in Shimonoseki in Bakan. And that was where I took my first breath.

Since my parents couldn't return to their birthplaces, the open road became my home town. And so, a born wanderer, I learned the song about "yearning for my home town" with a heavy heart.[29]

These opening lines, in which the narrator who has "no home town" declares herself "fated to be a vagabond," are perhaps the best-known lines in Hayashi's oeuvre. Yet readers familiar with later editions of the text may be startled to discover the subsequently deleted line "I am a crossbreed, a mongrel" (*watashi wa zasshu de chabo de aru*) in the original edition.[30] This line, like the declaration of being "fated to be vagabond," has both a literal and figurative implication. In the literal sense, it refers to her parents being from different provinces of Japan, one from present-day Ehime Prefecture and one from present-day Kagoshima Prefecture. That the narrator's parents would be chased out of Kagoshima because of this "mixed marriage," and that the narrator would consider herself a "crossbreed" (*zasshu*) or "mongrel" (*chabo*), points to the strong sense of regional identity that persisted in parts of Japan well into the twentieth century: an identification with the *kuni*, or local province, over the *kokka*, or modern nation-state. On the figurative level, the narrator's self-identification as a "mongrel" establishes a trope of hybridity or cultural impurity that, like the trope of the vagabond, resonates throughout the text.

As a "vagabond" bereft of a "home town," the narrator speaks not only for herself but for her parents and dozens of other characters living uprooted and marginal lives who are introduced throughout the text. The narrator's life as a wanderer begins in earnest at the age of eight, when her father, having settled in Shimonoseki, makes a small fortune selling clothes at auction in neighboring Wakamatsu, and takes a runaway geisha as a concubine. At this juncture, her mother leaves her father's house and sets out on the road, with the young protagonist in tow. Her mother also takes as companion another itinerant peddler, who becomes the narrator's stepfather, and the three wind their way through the provincial cities of Kyushu, living, by the narrator's account, "without a permanent home" in a series of "cheap lodging houses" (*kichinyado*).

In her biography of Hayashi Fumiko, writer Hirabayashi Taiko points to a whole class of such "vagabonds" who were alienated not only from a "pre-modern" regional identity but also from the organs of the "modern" nation-state:

At that time, in the cheap lodging houses (*kichinyado*) of western Japan, there were many such Japanese living outside of the nation-state. They neither obeyed the law, nor were they protected or interfered with by the law. They made their living through their freedom and panache, and through some degree of vice. . . .

Undoubtedly, all countries have such a class of people. But their alienation and rebelliousness is strongest in a so-called orderly society such as Japan—especially in the provincial areas where the sense of social cohesion still has a feudalistic tint. . . . At times, these [socially alienated] people do not even consider themselves Japanese.[31]

One can extrapolate from Hayashi's text the existence of a diaspora of such wanderers, alienated from both regional ties and national institutions, traveling through the towns of southwest Japan.[32] Yet while these traders and itinerant laborers may have been estranged from local communities and distrustful of state authority, their lives were by no means disconnected from national and international political, economic, and cultural developments. On the contrary, Hayashi's text suggests that the routes established by this itinerant population both followed and reinforced regional economic and cultural ties—ties that were both radial, connecting the province and metropole, and peripheral, connecting the provincial cities of western Japan and East Asia.

The names of the towns through which the narrator, her mother, and her stepfather travel are themselves an important part of the linguistic texture of "Hōrōki izen": Shimonoseki, Wakamatsu, Nagasaki, Sasebo, Kurume, Moji, Tobata, Orio, and Nōkata.[33] The name of each provincial region and city Hayashi mentions in her text carries its own historical and economic associations, and their usage in the text suggests a complex economic and social network, with historically contingent flow of people and goods.

For example, the Iyo region of Shikoku (present-day Ehime Prefecture), where the narrator's birth father comes from, was well known from the Edo period onward for its production of cotton goods centered in the town of Imabari. From the middle of the Meiji period, production of cotton goods shifted from hand to machine manufacture, and a variety of new weaves, such as muslin and imitation flannel (*men neru*), were introduced into everyday life. In the Meiji era, simplified clothes made from such mass-produced textiles were associated with the progressive "improvement of life" (*seikatsu kairyō, seikatsu kaizen*) and were called "improvement clothing" (*kairyōfuku*).[34] Hayashi places a reference to this fragment of linguistic and material history in her narrator's account of childhood:

It was in Nagasaki that I first had a legitimate place to play—the elementary school. I would set off to school near Nanking Ward every day from our room in the "Grain Shop Inn," wearing the "improvement clothes" that were popular back then.[35]

It was precisely this type of inexpensive, machine-manufactured cotton clothing that the narrator and her parents make a living at selling in the provincial towns of Kyushu. The narrator describes her participation in this business when the family moves to the coal mining town of Nōkata:

In July, we settled down in a place called the "Stables Inn" in Taishō Ward. My father and his gang would leave me behind in the inn, and Mother and I would borrow a cart, fill a wicker case with knitwear, socks, new muslin, waistbands, and such, and go hawking our goods to the mine or the ceramics workshop.[36]

New weaves and types of cotton clothing were significant not only for their impact on everyday material culture in twentieth-century Japan, but also for their central role in Japan's economic development. Cheap cotton cloth and clothing went from being import items in the early Meiji period to a staple export item by the turn of the century; by the Shōwa period, cotton goods were manufactured by Japanese-owned mills and factories in China. The large, volatile trade in raw cotton, yarn, cotton cloth, and cotton clothing inextricably linked the economies of Japan, China, India, Britain, and the United States.[37]

Many of the place names recorded in Hayashi's text—Shimono-seki, Moji, Tobata, and Wakamatsu in the Kita-kyūshū area, and Nagasaki and Sasebo in northwestern Kyushu—were port cities with roles in the East and South Asian cotton trade, as well as the international and domestic transportation of coal and industrial products from towns such as Kurume, Orio, and Nōkata. The live-lihoods of the narrator, her mother, father, and stepfather depend on this economic network, and their commercial activities, though marginal, are themselves a constituent part of it. In framing her tale of a woman's attempts to survive in the metropolis, then, Hayashi first sketches this network of peripheral relations, before shifting her descriptive axis to the radius of center and periphery.

The Shinjuku *kichinyado* (lodging house), one of the first places the narrator describes in the main section of *Hōrōki*, forms a link between Tokyo and the regional subculture of "vagabonds" who are introduced in the first chapter. At that time Shinjuku was on the expanding western edge of Tokyo and just beginning to grow into a major urban center. The liminal space of the Shinjuku *kichinyado*, with its shifting cast of prostitutes and other socially marginal fig-ures, is one indication of the presence of the periphery within the metropolis.

Later, as the narrator's living quarters move to communal bar girls' quarters on the second floor of cafés in Shinjuku and elsewhere, the tales of fellow waitresses woven into the narrative also point to the presence of the provinces in the new city. Indeed, the social and cultural periphery of Tokyo these women represent includes not only the domestic territories (*naichi*) such as the protagonist's home region of Kyushu, but the outer regions (*gaichi*) of Japan's colonial and semi-colonial territories. The waitress Yoshi, for exam-ple, comes to Tokyo by way of Sakhalin, Harbin (Manchuria), and Korea; Toshi also hails from the northern territories of Sakhalin and Hokkaido; Okimi was born in Tokyo but claims to have been kidnapped and sold to a geisha house in Manchuria before escaping back to Tokyo; Omiki is from Akita Prefecture; and other wait-resses come from Kagoshima, Kanazawa, and Chiba.

The diverse provenance of these waitresses, while exacerbated, no doubt, by their socially marginal profession, was by no means atypical of the metropolitan population as a whole. In the first two decades of the century, Tokyo was a rapidly expanding city of immigrants, its population increasing by over 60 percent in twenty years. According to official statistics, a full 40 percent of Tokyo residents in the year 1920 were born outside the city.[38]

Like the narrator of *Hōrōki*, such immigrants were both cut off from their rural or provincial roots, and largely excluded from the townsman culture of long-standing Tokyo residents, which was at any rate receding in the face of cultural and demographic change. In the 1920s, the new Tokyo residents were rewritten into the social imaginary as key constituents of "the masses" (*taishū*), a broad social stratum defined less by regional or class affiliation than by shared consumption of cultural products emanating from the metropolitan center. It is these uprooted subjects, experiencing their own losses of a "home town," who were increasingly the makers, as well as the consumers, of Tokyo's modern culture.

Hōrōki and the Dawn of Mass Culture

Although Hayashi employs a relatively subdued and essaylike prose style in "Hōrōki izen," she highlights the technique of montage in this as well as subsequent chapters, incorporating various found texts as her narrative unfolds in time. Indeed, as excerpted above, she begins her narrative with a quotation from the song "Ryoshū," or "Sorrow in Traveling," which became a fixture of Japanese schoolroom music texts after its composition in 1908.[39] Throughout "Hōroki izen," Hayashi focuses an exacting attention to the role played by songs of various genres in shaping the cultural environment of modern Japan; these songs, in turn, become an integral part of her montage text.

Titles of stories and novels encountered by the narrator, as well as poems and passages excerpted from works of literature, also form an important part of "Hōrōki izen" and subsequent chapters of the novel. In describing her own self-development, the narrator of "Hōrōki izen" catalogs the books she read as a child:

Before long, instead of going to grammar school, I was working in a millet cake factory in the Susaki district for a wage of twenty-three *sen* a day. At that time, I remember clearly that the rice I brought home in a bamboo basket cost eighteen *sen*.

At night, from the book-lenders' I would take home such books as *Ude no Kisaburo* [*Kisaburo the Arm*], *Yokogami yaburi no Fukushima Masanori* [*Headstrong Fukushima Masanori*], *Hototogisu* [*The Cuckoo*], *Nasanu naka* [*No Blood Relation*], *and Uzumaki* [*The Whirlpool*]."

What did I learn from tales like these? Like a sponge, my brain soaked up the heroism, sentimentalism, and indulgent daydreams of happy endings.

All around me, from morning to night, there was talk of money. My only aspiration was to become a "woman millionaire."[40]

In this passage, the narrator offers a portrait of her own intellectual development, not as a member of the intelligentsia, but as a member of the masses. It is noteworthy that most of the books cited in this passage had double lives as novels and as plays. One of them, *Kisaburo the Arm*, was based upon a character in a kabuki play. Three of the remaining four titles were so-called *katei shōsetsu*, or domestic novels, melodramatic stories centering on the travails of married women. These tales became part of the standard repertoire of the *shinpa* theater groups, a hybrid drama that combined modern plots with elements of kabuki drama, including *onnagata*, or male actors who specialized in female roles. With these titles, then, Hayashi invokes not only a certain literary genre, but an entire episode of early twentieth-century culture.[41]

It is noteworthy that Hayashi's writing itself was sometimes denigrated or dismissed as being overly sentimental. In this passage, her narrator offers a genealogy of her own sentimentality while at the same time establishing an ironic distance from it. Typically, she contrasts the dreaminess of such literature, and her own girlhood dreams of being a "woman millionaire," with the prosaic financial details of her salary at the millet cake factory and the price of a basket of rice.

Hayashi maintains this dual focus on popular culture and everyday life in provincial Japan in the next section. Here, her protagonist has moved to Nōkata, a town in the coal fields of northern Kyushu:

August.

On the scorching hot streets of Nōkata, billboards of Katyusha began to appear. They were pictures of a foreign girl at a train station, with a blanket wrapped around her head, pounding at a train window in the falling snow.

Before long, the Katyusha hairstyle, parted in the middle, was the new fashion.

> Ah, darling Katyusha, how sad this parting
> Shall we say a prayer to God above
> Before this shallow snow melts

This song brings back memories. This is a song I love.
"Katyusha's Song" instantly permeated this mining town.

A Russian woman's pure love—when I went to see the motion picture, I turned into a very romantic girl. I had never been to a theater before, except to see *naniwabushi* folk ballads. Now, I hid out and watched Katyusha's film day after day. I was completely entranced by Katyusha.

On the way to buy oil, in a square where white oleanders bloomed, I would play "Katyusha" and "miner" with the town children.

When we played "miner," the girls would pretend to push coal cars, and the boys would dig in the dirt while singing a mining song.[42]

Katyusha was the heroine of Tolstoy's novel *Resurrection* (translated into Japanese as *Fukkatsu*), which was adapted for the stage and performed by Shimamura Hōgetsu's *shingeki* (or Western-style) theater troupe Geijutsuza in 1914. The role of Katyusha was performed by Matsui Sumako, the first major actress of modern Japan, where theatrical traditions had been dominated by males playing both male and female roles. The play was a huge success, performed 444 times throughout Japan, Manchuria, and Vladivostok, from 1914 to 1919. During this period, Hōgetsu and Sumako were idolized by Japanese fans, with the hint of scandal from an extramarital love affair between the two only adding to their cultural cachet.[43] The play's success, as the passage from *Hōrōki* suggests, was clinched by the overwhelming popularity of its theme song, co-written by Hōgetsu and Sōma Gyofū and performed by Sumako.

The recording of Sumako singing "Katyusha's Song" became the first hit record on a truly national scale in Japan, selling an unprecedented 27,000 copies and saving the struggling Orient Record Company from bankruptcy.[44] The success of *Resurrection* also extended to the cinema, beginning with the release of a filmed version of the Geijutsuza performance. Shortly thereafter, the Nikkatsu film studio came out with its own highly successful version, entitled *Katyu-*

sha, which was quickly followed by two sequels. Interestingly, the Nikkatsu *Katyusha* was performed by *shinpa* actors, including the *onnagata* (or female impersonator) Tachibana Teijirō as Katyusha. In screenings of this silent film, however, female singers were brought in to perform the indispensable theme song.[45]

Hayashi's *Hōrōki,* then, captures a new form of modern popular culture at its very moment of inception. The simultaneous nation-wide rage for Katyusha, experienced firsthand by *Hōrōki*'s narrator, indicates the possibility of a mass culture based on the shared consumption of cultural commodities.[46] This, in turn, signals a new relationship between the provinces and the metropole, in which a cosmopolitan cultural product generated in Tokyo is available even to a little girl in a Kyushu mining town. Indeed, the strange juxtaposition of children's games described in Hayashi's passage—"Katyusha" and "miner"—suggests an uneven reciprocal relationship between province and metropole, where metropolitan cultural products are dispatched to the provinces, and raw materials from the provinces feed the metropole. Hayashi's text needs not mention that the mines in the Nōkata region were owned primarily by the Mitsui and Mitsubishi *zaibatsu* of Tokyo.

Hayashi's next citation of popular song refers to this labor situation in the Kyushu coal fields, and how labor strife affected peddlers such as the narrator's parents:

In October, there was a strike in the mine. The town was wrapped in an asphyxiating silence, and only the infuriated miners returning from the mine had any energy. "A strike—now that's hard times." I learned this kind of song too. Strikes were frequent, and the miners would quickly move on to another mine. All their accounts with the peddlers in town would be wiped out, and the goods lent out to miners would rarely be returned. Even so, peddlers would say that selling to miners was quick and easy work.[47]

Intriguingly, the "Song of the Strike" to which Hayashi alludes in this passage took its material not from a coal miners' or industrial workers' strike, but a walk-out of prostitutes in a red-light district. The complete second verse of this song is:

> I left the brothel, walking out of my job
> *Chorus:* And what happened then?

No place to go, picking up rags
> *Chorus:* A courtesan's strike
> Now that's hard times
> So they say

When this song was popularized in the years 1899 and 1900, prostitutes in Hakodate and Nagoya, who had been held by their brothels against their will, successfully sued for the right to leave their work (*jiyū haigyō*).[48] The song's lyrics highlight the social incongruities of this moment with the phrase "a courtesan's strike" (*ukareme no sutoraiki*), juxtaposing the time-honored language of the entertainment quarters with the language of the nascent labor movement. Prostitution, incidentally, was another important link between rural and urban Japan, with labor flowing from impoverished rural areas to urban brothels, and a network of procurers extending the economic reach of the cities into the provinces.

This muted allusion to social conflicts accompanying prostitution ties this paragraph to other passages in *Hōrōki* which thematize prostitution more directly, such as the description of a prostitute with a missing thumb whom the protagonist befriends elsewhere in "Hōrōki izen," or, later in the novel, the prostitutes who are rooming in the protagonist's Shinjuku flophouse.

While the protagonist takes a great variety of jobs in the course of the narrative, including that of a café waitress on the edge of a red-light district, the line between such jobs in the so-called water trade and literal prostitution is one that the protagonist refuses to cross, no matter how destitute she becomes. Yet the possibility, and at times the temptation, of falling into prostitution remains a constant undertone in *Hōrōki*—an undertone sounded even in this snippet of song from her childhood.

"One Hundred Faces"

The series of childhood remembrances designated as "Hōrōki izen" ends, and the series of journal entries that comprise the main text begins. When the journal opens, the protagonist has left the provinces and is attempting to make her own way in Tokyo. Despite the numerous, largely unsatisfying liaisons with men the narrator describes in her diary, her approach to life in the city remains one of fierce independence; she writes at one point that depending on a man for her meals was more insufferable than eating mud.[49]

Twenty years before, there would have been few employment alternatives for a penniless young woman from the provinces other than to work as a prostitute, as a domestic servant, or as a factory worker in the textile mills.[50] But a conspicuous element of 1920s urban Japanese modernity was the increasing number of women performing a wider variety of jobs in the work force.[51] In fact, the phrase *shokugyō fujin* or "working woman" first achieved currency in the early 1920s, making its way into the public imagination with songs such as Soeda Azenbō's "Shokugyō fujin no uta," or "Song of the Working Woman."

The verses of this song are sung from the point of view of various working women, including a typist, telephone operator, office worker, nurse, teacher, driver, housewife, model, and aviator:

> I am a typist, a typist in an office!
> > *Chorus:* A typist!
> Off to work! My spirit's always dancing
> A dancing spirit, bathed in light
> The letters I type away, one by one
> Exude a flavor that words can't express
> > *Chorus:* Oh, this feeling! Girls who depend on a man
> > Just can't understand.[52]

The jobs performed by the protagonist of *Hōrōki* are even more varied, although not always as fashionable. In different episodes of the narrative, she works as a nanny and a maid, a peddler of cotton goods on the streets of Tokyo, a worker in a factory that produces celluloid dolls, a waitress in *gyūdon* (beef and rice bowl) and sushi restaurants, a café waitress, a shop attendant, a pharmacist's assistant, an office worker, an advertising solicitor, and a journalist. She also applies for a job as a bus conductor but is rejected because of her poor eyesight, and toys with the idea of becoming an actress. Moreover, all this time the protagonist is determined to become a writer, and devotes much of her energy to trying to sell her poems, short stories, and children's stories to various newspaper and magazine publishers.[53]

The protagonist's employment history cuts across class boundaries, including jobs associated with pre-industrial, family-owned businesses; factory work and other manual labor; and white-collar jobs associated with the emerging service sectors of the urban economy. Yet perhaps because of the very instability of economic and class positions the protagonist occupies in the narrative, many readers seem to have identified the protagonist not as an upwardly mobile "working woman" but as a member of the underclass or "lumpen proletariat."[54] Indeed, poverty and a concern for obtaining the bare minimum of food and shelter are recurrent themes in *Hōrōki,* and it is not surprising that this emphasis on survival amid adversity resonated with contemporary readers. As the economy stalled repeatedly in the 1920s, even white-collar workers found themselves struggling to meet their living expenses. The situation was even more difficult for women workers, whose wages were far lower than those of men.[55] While Soeda Azenbō's song praises the coming of a bright new day for independent working women, the reality for women seeking employment in the new metropolis was more equivocal, and few could have documented the contradictions, ironies, and perils of the new women's job market more thoroughly than Hayashi Fumiko.

There is a protean quality to the narrator-protagonist of *Hōrōki*—as if she were determined to perform with her own body every possible role in the new metropolis. Appropriately, one of the chapter headings in the original edition of the novel is "Hyakumensō," or "One Hundred Faces."[56] The suddenness with which the protagonist moves from one role to the next can be considerably disorienting to the reader. In fact, one can identify a tension in the novel between the desire of the narrator-protagonist to present herself as a writer and the equally strong impulse to present herself as the anonymous and ubiquitous everywoman. This tension is related, I believe, to the developing concepts of "the masses" and "mass literature" in the 1920s.

Mass Literature and Mass Culture in *Hōrōki*

As we saw in Chapter 1, the concept of *taishū bungaku,* "mass literature" or "popular literature," developed in the mid-1920s, just as Hayashi Fumiko was beginning her career as a writer in Tokyo. Indeed, use of the word *taishū* to refer to "the masses" was a late Taishō period neologism. The term *taishū bungaku* encompassed both a new generic category and a new conception of audience. As a generic category, *taishū bungaku* bridged previously popular or "lowbrow" (*tsūzoku*) genres such as adventure stories and swash-buckling historical fiction with new genres associated with con-temporary urban settings, such as detective fiction. The concept of *taishū bungaku* also posited a new social imaginary, cutting across previous class or regional constructions: a social aggregation made possible by the spread of literacy and primary education, and by the nationwide dissemination of media products (including *taishū bun-gaku* itself) from the metropolis. Thus, for the writers and editors who helped to formulate this new literary category, "the masses" were conceived primarily as a market for their products.

No sooner had the concept of *taishū bungaku* been formulated than the opposing concept of *jun bungaku*, or "pure literature" also came to the fore. Advocates of *jun bungaku* upheld the value of liter-ature as individual self-expression rather than as a commodity aimed at a mass market. Ironically, one of the clearest articulations of the opposition of *jun bungaku* and *taishū bungaku* came from the devel-oping realm of mass media production itself, in the form of oppos-ing canons of modern Japanese literature marketed as series of one-yen books (*enpon*): the publishing house Kaizōsha's *Gendai nihon bungaku zenshū* (*Complete Collection of Modern Japanese Literature*, 1926–) and Heibonsha's *Gendai taishū bungaku zenshū* (*Complete Collection of Modern Popular Literature*, 1927–).

Soon after mainstream writers and editors developed the cat-egory of *taishū bungaku*, a debate emerged within the burgeoning camp of communist and socialist writers over the need to enact a "popularization" or "massification" (*taishūka*) of Proletarian Litera-ture.[57] In this case, however, the masses were envisioned not merely as a consumer market for a cultural product, but as a potential col-lective agent of revolutionary political change.

Hayashi's *Hōrōki* represents an unusual intervention into this discourse on mass culture. Her narrative captures certain key moments in the development of Japanese popular culture, and links her first-person protagonist's personal growth and cultural aware-ness to these developing cultural forms, such as the "domestic novel," and the song, advertising posters, and films associated with Katyu-sha and the *Resurrection* stage play. While the narrator establishes a certain ironic distance from these early forms of mass culture, her work simultaneously serves as an homage to them; indeed *Hōrōki*, which itself was to become a major popular success, seems to be constructing its own lineage as a mass-cultural artifact.

Generically, however, Hayashi's novel conforms to none of the formulas associated with *taishū bungaku*, "mass literature." Rather, insofar as this eccentric novel fits any established literary categories, it can be deemed a type of *shishōsetsu* or "I-novel," the prose genre most closely associated with *jun bungaku*, pure literature. The novel's prose style, with its mixture of colloquialisms and vulgar language with classicisms and literary language, also cuts across the usual distinctions between *taishū bungaku* and *jun bungaku*. Furthermore, while citations of popular culture are perhaps the most striking elements of the novel's montage texture, works of classical literature, such as the *Ise monogatari* (*Tales of Ise*), the *Sarashina Nikki* (*Sarashina Diary*), Saikaku's *Kōshoku ichidai onna* (*One Woman Who Loved Love*), or the haiku and travel narratives of Bashō, are equally parts of Hayashi's intertextual frame of reference.[58]

Hayashi's work thus confounds the distinction between *taishū bungaku* and *jun bungaku*, positing itself as neither pure, nor purely mass, literature. But the novel's unusual position with regard to the developing category of mass literature lies primarily within the character of the protagonist herself. Previous constructions of literary identity tacitly assumed a binary relationship, with the writer on one side and the masses on the other. In the case of *jun bungaku*, this binary relationship was one of pure opposition; in the case of *taishū bungaku*, it was the relationship between the creator of a cultural product and his or her market; in Proletarian Literature, it was the pedagogic relationship of a member of the "vanguard" (*zen'ei*) to the unawakened masses. In each case, it was a relationship between a strongly defined artistic subject on the one side, and an objectified mass on the other.

Hayashi, by contrast, attempts to construct her narrator's subjectivity on both sides of this divide. She narrates both the birth of a modern writer, and, atypically, the birth of a modern reader: her protagonist is both a producer and a consumer of culture, a writer and an urban everywoman. Although Hayashi's resistance to these rapidly solidifying categories is remarkable, the strain of challenging the binary relation of "the individual" and "the masses" is evident in the mercurial and fragmentary nature of her protagonist's subjectivity.

Given that an important narrative strand of *Hōrōki* is the story of Japanese mass culture itself, it is worth briefly inquiring into the nature of this culture as depicted in the novel. First of all, we can note that it is extremely heterogeneous or hybrid in terms of its sources and expressions. Among the cultural artifacts incorporated into Hayashi's montage narrative, we can identify no purely Japanese or Western culture, nor is there a clear distinction between traditional and modern. Especially in the early mass culture depicted in "Hōrōki izen," there is an extreme fluidity among different genres: novels, songs, different types of theater, and cinema are all combined and mutually reinforced in imaginative ways—what film historian J. L. Anderson identifies as the phenomenon of "commingled media."[59]

It is no surprise that when the narrator-protagonist moves to Tokyo, she expresses her enthusiasm for the neighborhood of Asakusa, the district that housed both an amusement park and a large concentration of movie theaters, review theaters, halls for storytelling, arcades, cafés, eateries, and other entertainment venues.[60] Asakusa was thus the site within the capital where precisely the sort of syncretic, genre-crossing mass entertainment identified as "commingled media" flourished. As the syncretic cultural space of Asakusa corresponds strongly with the "mongrel" subjectivity of Hayashi's protagonist and the "admixture" quality of her text, it seems almost inevitable that Asakusa scenes would be included as set pieces in *Hōrōki* and its sequels.

In his influential cultural study of Tokyo published in 1987, Yoshimi Shunya identifies four primary characteristics of prewar Asakusa as urban space: first, its syncretism: it is a space that "digests" every type of person and thing, without losing its own individuality. Next is its provisional nature: it is a "stage" that is never static or complete, but is always ready to adopt new characters or scenarios. The third trait is its fluidity: people and events in Asakusa are constantly shifting their roles and identities. Last, its communal and interactive nature is distinctive: a sense of common identity and purpose exists between members of the Asakusa crowds, or between stage performers and their audience.[61]

These four points can be applied not only to much of the popular culture described in *Hōrōki*, but arguably to the *Hōrōki* text itself, and indeed to the nature of its protagonist's subjectivity.[62] The syncretism of *Hōrōki* as a text is clear, as is the narrator's own declaration to be "a crossbreed," or "mongrel." Also striking is the provisional or incomplete nature of the text, which eschews chronological narrative and constantly embraces new scenarios (a nonlinear development that readily carries over into the novel's sequels). Similarly, the protagonist's subjectivity appears to be open, provisional, and constantly shifting.

Finally, although *Hōrōki* is no more intrinsically communal or interactive than any novel, the protagonist's unusual protean quality offers multiple points of identification for the novel's audience, which may help to account for its exceptional popularity. The stories of other women such as café waitresses and factory workers that are woven into the novel, as well as the communal bonds forged between these women in their shared work and living environments, also provide a communalistic counterpoint to the protagonist's otherwise strong individualism and dominating narrative voice.

If *Hōrōki* is partly an homage to new forms of media and "mass culture," then the entertainment industry has repaid the compliment: the novel has been repeatedly appropriated by various media with considerable popular success. One year after the novel's publication, a version of *Hōrōki* was performed by the most famous review theater troupe of the day, the Asakusa Casino Follies. In 1935, *Hōrōki* was adapted for film by the director Kimura Sotoji. The novel and its adaptations were suppressed during the war years, but *Hōrōki* reemerged as a cultural icon in the postwar period. Two more film adaptations were released in 1954 and 1962, the latter a highly regarded film directed by Naruse Mikio; the novel and its many adaptations also received considerable airplay on radio and television.[63] In addition, the actress Mori Mitsuko had great success as the protagonist of *Hōrōki* for the reconstituted Geijutsuza troupe's theater adaptation—a role she reprised over 1,200 times after her debut in the role in 1961.[64]

Nevertheless, the popular success of Hayashi's novel, and its subsequent appropriation into various mass media, should not be allowed to obscure the novel's significance as a critical representation of mass culture, and not simply an example of it. In her chapter "Hōrōki izen," Hayashi frames her exploration of urban modernity with a prelude that examines the reciprocal relationship between metropolitan and provincial Japan. Incorporating key events in the development of mass or commercial popular culture into her own personal narrative, she suggests the importance of this culture to her first-person protagonist's subject-formation, while maintaining an ironic distance that suggests that this cultural consumption does not preclude the possibility of critique. In particular, her account highlights the important role that gender played in the marketing of the new mass culture: how certain cultural products were designed to appeal to, and indeed to produce, a certain kind of romantic female subject. The narrator's attitude to this subject-formation is highly ambivalent: she acknowledges its power, yet asserts, through her ironic tone, her own degree of mastery over it.

In the subsequent chapters, Hayashi places this first-person subject within the urban masses, performing a kaleidoscopic variety of roles as both producer and consumer of material and cultural goods. With this multifaceted subjectivity, she poses her own challenge to the developing discourse on mass literature and mass culture, which tended to posit an active culture-producing intelligentsia on the one hand and a passive, objectified mass of culture consumers on the other.

Hayashi Fumiko's modernism is neither strictly of mass culture nor strictly opposed to it. Rather, as part of her project to reframe Japanese modernity, she documents the development of a new mass culture, while boisterously disrupting the boundaries that would separate individual from mass, producer from consumer, and high from low. Hayashi combines a culturally rooted sentimentalism with a new cynicism; her work is both an homage to the dawn of mass culture, and an attempt to build something new.

5 / *HŌRŌKI* AND THE MODERN GIRL

A new and contradictory Tokyo emerged from the 1923 earthquake: fast-paced, industrialized, consumeristic, sexually charged, and politically radicalized. Tokyo's print and visual media, themselves a vital part of this new urban culture, explored their city's transformations with a mixture of anxiety and fascination. The new self-consciousness of Japan's modernity was captured in such neologisms as "modern life" (*kindai seikatsu*), "modernology" (*kōgengaku*), "modern girl" (*modan gāru*), and "modern boy" (*modan boi*). Of all of the words and images called in to represent Japan's new urban culture, however, it was arguably the figure of the "modern girl" which generated the most media buzz and carried the greatest historical resonance, inviting new media representations and academic interpretations even to the present day.[1]

Modern Girls, "Red Love," and Mass Media

The prominence of the "modern girl" is emblematic of the tendency for interwar Japanese social and cultural modernity to be troped in the female gender. In particular, the "modern girl" was associated with those aspects of modernity related to consumer culture, to the contingent realm of fashion, and to the "superficial" aspects of Westernization or Americanization. The tendency to cast social and cultural modernity as female was demonstrated by conservative commentators who assailed Japan's modernization, as well as by Marxist critics such as Hirabayashi Hatsunosuke, who, in the essay quoted in the first chapter, associated the industrial base of modernity with masculinity and the superstructural elements of "flapper modernism," including the literary representations of Japanese modernists, with the female gender.[2]

In the series of essays collected as *Modan sō to modan sō* (*Modern Social Strata and Modern Mores*), Ōya Sōichi, another prominent critic with Marxist affiliations, articulated a similar view of Japanese modernism as a superstructural phenomenon, although his appraisal of this "modern culture" was largely negative, whereas Hirabayashi held out hope for modernism as a force for positive social change. In the title essay, Ōya gives his definition of "the modern," a concept with both social and literary valences:

"Modern" (*modan*) means the vanguard (*sentan*) of the age. And yet that vanguard is not a genuine productive vanguard but the tip of petty consumerism. A sharp, fine, brittle, weak tip. It is the keenly sharpened nerves of the age. It is the people's antenna, which perceives the new and the rare with the greatest acuity and passes it on to their contemporaries.[3]

In a later essay entitled "A Critique of Women Vanguards" (*Josei sentanjin hihan*), Ōya again uses the metaphor of radio transmitters and receivers—important new forms of media technology in 1920s Japan—to articulate his conception of the modern vanguard. Here, he connects this conception first with literature, and then with women:

Literature is the antenna of the age. It is the antenna that picks up the newest trends which are occurring in and outside the country and transmits them to the everyday people. . . .

Needless to say, in an age such as this, it is the people in the lead, the so-called "vanguard," who are the objects of the greatest interest and fascination, and the source of the greatest stimuli. This is especially the case when they are women, and when they are active in the fields of literature and thought.[4]

It seems that for Ōya, "modernity," "literature," and "women" are closely related, interlocking concepts, from which he would like to claim a space apart, a space of critical autonomy. In the same essay, Ōya elaborates on the modern qualities of women's literature, which he describes as being "sensation-based" or "perception-based" (*kankakuteki*), as well as "intellectual" (*richiteki*)—a seeming contradiction which he qualifies by describing this intellectuality as shallow and sensationalized. Most of all, however, Ōya stresses that women's literature, like Japan's modern culture, is completely artificial (*gikōteki*). Having made these sweeping generalizations, however, Ōya then concedes that a number of contemporary women writers fail to conform to his own stereotypes. At this point in the essay, his interlocking construction of "women," "literature," and "modernity" collapses, and he embarks on a subclassification of women writers, including Hayashi Fumiko, whom he places in the ranks of "women anarchist writers."[5]

The existence of active "Proletarian" women writers poses a particular challenge to Ōya's identification of women with the superficial "modern" vanguard as opposed to the "genuine productive vanguard." Ōya explores this contradiction more fully in a third essay from the volume, "One Hundred Percent Modern Girl" ("*Hyaku pāsento moga*"). Here, he contrasts a bob-haired, artificially made-up, consumeristic, parasitic, "sensation-based," superficially intellectual "modern girl" with two examples of self-sacrificing Marxist activists. The second of these activists so inspires Ōya's admiration that he names *her* the "one hundred percent modern girl."[6]

In her essay "The Modern Girl as Militant," cultural historian Miriam Silverberg suggests that Ōya's essay fits a wider pattern, in which cultural commentators of the 1920s were torn between depicting women as representative of Japan's developing consumer society on the one hand and as representative of the urban populace's newfound political engagement on the other. Thus, according to Silverberg, these essayists often "resorted to a twofold definition, determining that there were Modern Girls—and then there were *real* Modern Girls."[7]

Ironically, Silverberg's essay presents its own twofold definition of the modern girl. In the first portion of her essay, she discusses the modern girl as a "highly commodified" media construct: the subject of both sexually provocative light entertainment and of serious intellectual commentary, but ultimately an amalgamation of "confusions and fantasies about class, gender, and culture" created by the media itself.[8] In the second part of her essay, she attempts to go beyond this phantasmagoric image by contextualizing the pundits' discussion of the modern girl with the historical record of women's political and labor-oriented activism. "The Modern Girl is rescued from her free-floating and depoliticized state when her willful image is placed alongside the history of working, militant Japanese women," Silverberg writes. "Then the obsessive contouring of the Modern Girl as promiscuous and apolitical (and later, as apolitical and non-working) begins to emerge as a means of displacing the very real militancy of Japanese women."[9]

The impulse to separate the media image of the modern girl from the authentic historical experience of Japanese women, however, may obscure the extent to which lived reality and media image were intertwined. Another article by Hirabayashi Hatsunosuke suggests a different perspective: "Women in the Age of Collapsed Authority: The Social Roots of the Modern Girl's Appearance" ("Ken'i hōkaiki no fujin: modan gāru hassei no shakaiteki konkyo"). In this article, Hirabayashi claims that the advent of the modern girl was a characteristic of "the age of collapsed authority"—a collapse that found its physical parallel in "the utter destruction of things traditional near the Imperial Capital" in the Great Kanto Earthquake.[10] Specifically, Hirabayashi points to the withering of parental authority and the younger generation's lack of deference to their elders. In a society dominated by the principle of speed, he notes, paradigms of the older generation are soon overturned by those of the younger: "in a superior vehicle," he writes, "it's easy to outpace those in front of you, even if you get off to a later start."[11]

Hirabayashi cites the growing importance of mass media for the transmission of social values and cultural information: "What governs their [modern girls'] thoughts and morals is not their parents or their elders, but newspapers, magazines, books, films, theaters, and lecture halls."[12] He illustrates his thesis of "collapsed authority" with the disuse of arranged marriage, noting that for today's youth, "the opinions of their parents have almost no decisive power," and claiming that free (as opposed to arranged) marriage was already the established practice in contemporary Japan.[13]

As Hirabayashi's essay suggests, the media discourse on the modern girl should not be read merely as a reflection of the "reality" of women's changing lives; nor should it be read as a self-generating, self-referential "hyperreality" with little connection to those lives. Rather, insofar as we can imagine real women's lives behind their always-mediated historical representations, we can surmise that part of what was changing in these lives during the 1920s was the role of the mass media in the formation of their lifestyles and consciousness.

It is in this light that I would like to continue my reading of Hayashi Fumiko's *Hōrōki* and *Zoku hōrōki*. Hayashi's work is, in a sense, no more than one more prominent media representation of gender and modernity, serialized in the outspokenly feminist literary journal *Nyonin geijutsu* and reissued as a novel by the major publishing company Kaizōsha. Yet it offers a striking exploration of the relationship between the narrator's individual consciousness and various contemporary journalistic, literary, and mass-media representations of gender, containing within itself a whole range of contemporary discourse. Thus it can be seen to work in a slightly different fashion from most straightforward expositions on "the modern girl," or from novels less informed by the principles of montage.

Aside from discussions of women's changing appearance (hairstyles, clothes, makeup, physique), the two themes that dominate accounts of the modern girl are the rise of working women and the changing of sexual mores. Notably, these two themes—work and sexuality—also dominate Hayashi's *Hōrōki*. Moreover, the themes were deeply interconnected, both in Hayashi's novel and more broadly in discussions of the modern girl.

The proliferation of types of work open to women in the 1920s gave at least some women a greater chance for economic (and thus, potentially, sexual) independence, although most of these jobs were so undercompensated that even paying rent on a single woman's wages was a major obstacle.[14] The opening of new jobs in the service and white-collar sectors also encouraged the adoption of new forms of dress (including Western-style clothes) and lifestyle (such as the widespread use of commuter trains); these changing appearances and everyday practices alone gave some observers the impression of a lowering of sexual morals.[15]

The rise of marriages based on "love" (*ren'ai kekkon*) or "friendship" (*yūai kekkon*) rather than parental arrangement was another trend identified with the modern girl, as suggested by Hirabayashi's essay above. However, the new sexual mores associated with the modern girl did not stop at the boundaries of marriage. Accounts of the "modern girl," generally written from male perspectives, suggest that her clothes and behavior enacted a new eroticization of public spaces in urban Japan: at stake, in perception at least, was the question of women's chastity (*teisō*).[16]

In fact, countless articles in both general magazines and women's magazines throughout the 1920s were questioning established social and sexual practices and exploring new ones. In Japan as in other countries at the time, birth control was one of the new sexual practices undergoing public scrutiny. Despite the Japanese government's efforts to discourage discussion of birth control, including forbidding public mention of the "birth control movement" (*sanji seigen undō*), women's magazines continued to publish articles on the subject throughout the decade. Even the relatively conservative *Shufu no tomo*, for instance, provided coverage of American birth control advocate Margaret Sanger's visit to Japan in 1922. Many subsequent articles in women's magazines publicized the so-called *Ogino-hō* (or *Ogino-shiki*) rhythm method of birth control, based on research on ovulation and fertility published by Dr. Ogino Kyūsaku in 1924.[17]

While the dissemination of information on birth control was considered by the Japanese authorities at least to have a potentially corrosive effect on the marriage system, marriage also came under more direct attack by some of Japan's public intellectuals. After liberal commentators such as Kuriyagawa Hakuson argued for reform of marriage customs,[18] other voices soon emerged to advocate a more extreme course. Radical feminist Takamure Itsue, for example, urged not the reform of marriage but its abolition. This, she argued, should be accompanied by the abolition of the system of private property, the decentralization of political control, and the dispersal of population centers away from the metropolis; a new social system should emerge that permitted women's free expression of sexual and maternal love. With these goals before her, she gave her support to the Japanese anarchist movement as well as to feminists.[19]

Marxist and communist intellectuals, who increasingly outnumbered anarchists within the Japanese left, also made major contributions to the debates on gender, sexuality, and social construction. Marxist feminist pioneer Yamakawa Kikue, for example, campaigned vigorously for the restructuring of society on the basis of equality for men and women, while maintaining that gender issues must be addressed within a larger context of class analysis and struggle.[20] While Yamakawa concentrated primarily on the rights of women, especially women laborers, within the public sphere, others such as Proletarian Literature writer Hayashi Fusao expounded on the private matters of marriage and sexuality, drawing heavily on the work of Engels.[21]

While such *ren'ai ron*—reappraisals of gender, marriage, and sexuality—proliferated in the 1920s, it was the appearance of Bolshevik and diplomat Alexandra Kollontai's novella *Vasilisa Malygina*, translated as *Akai koi*, or *Red Love*, in 1927, which touched off the greatest sensation.[22] Together with two other stories published as *Ren'ai no michi* in 1928, *Akai koi* gave a fictional account of women's attempts to forge new structures of work, sexuality, and family in Soviet Russia. Based in part on the author's own experiences, these stories offered Japanese readers a rare glimpse of women's lives in the midst of revolution, as well as a look at alternative social structures that might develop in a post-revolutionary society. Thus Kollontai's writings were of great interest for Japanese intellectuals such as socialist feminist Hirabayashi Taiko, who reviewed the book for the Proletarian Literature journal *Bungei sensen*. Hirabayashi's review opens with a justification of socialists' interest in gender and sexuality:

We are not "explorers for love" (*ren'ai mosakusha*).

No matter whether people advocate new and free relations between the sexes, if they ignore the social structures that produce these relations, and are merely "exploring for love," their efforts will inevitably result in ultraromanticism (*ren'ai shijōshugi*). Today, if we think about new forms for love and have a deep interest in relations between the sexes, it is because we hope to find there a necessary clue for our future society, and thus gain a new confidence and a new resolve.[23]

If Hirabayashi's tone sounds defensive, this is partly because of the wider public reception of *Akai koi*, which tended to equate "Kollontai-ism" with unbridled free love.[24] The sensational aspects of *Akai koi* were amplified in the advertising copy that announced the book's publication (and helped to ensure its commercial success): "Red love! This is the flame of lust and love that fires the crucible of Red Russia. It is the battle cry which obliterates all narrow-minded and obstinate traditional morality. . . ."[25]

The issues of sexuality and the social construction of gender and labor roles were thus squarely before the public's eyes during Japan's most self-consciously modern decade. While there were a great variety of viewpoints concerning the desirable future construction of sexual relationships and gender roles, it was widely recognized that a restructuring of these roles and relationships was, for better or for worse, central to the definition of Japan's modernity in the 1920s and beyond. Hayashi Fumiko's *Hōrōki* and its sequels were in many ways an exploration of this new modern culture; it should come as no surprise that the issues of sexuality and gender should be front and center in these works too.

Here as elsewhere, Hayashi's form, a series of diary entries organized on the principle of montage, is essential to her presentation of the content. The two most conspicuous montagelike elements of Hayashi's narrative are her use of "cutting," which creates sudden gaps in the temporal and spatial texture of the work and produces the effects of speed and disorientation; and her incorporation of "found texts" such as poems, popular songs, shopping lists, and fragments of novels and treatises.

This use of montage construction can be related to the collages and three-dimensional constructions produced by Japanese avant-garde artists in the 1920s, as well as to the methods of cinematic montage that were being explored in Japanese film. Beginning in the 1920s, there was a tremendous interest among Japanese directors, film critics, and other intellectuals in the principles of montage, particularly in the work of Soviet directors, who were understood to exploit the principles of contrast and dialectical development, rather than the principles of continuity editing which dominated the Hollywood film codes. Montage was thus a primary focus of Japanese reception of international film in the 1920s, and Japanese film directors such as Kinugasa Teinosuke and Mizoguchi Kenji made montage a central feature of their own film language.[26]

Hayashi also relies heavily on the principle of contrast, often juxtaposing poetry and prose within her narrative, and exploiting both linguistic and thematic contrasts on many levels. She employs this contrastive montage technique to sound out differing ideas of gender, sexuality, and modernity. Weaving fragments of her personal life through her montage of diary entries, Hayashi's narrator outlines her relationships with a series of men—often articulated on a bohemian basis of "free love," but which seldom providing emotional or physical satisfaction. On the other hand, the narrator also describes the close relationships between working women—relationships that represent an underground economy of mutual support, love, and sexual desire.

The narration also sketches the erotically charged service economy that developed around the new institution of the café; this milieu is developed in relief against the *kuruwa*, or Japanese licensed quarters, which represents an older type of sexual service economy. Just as the café developed as part of a larger culture of "modern life" in the 1920s, the brothels of the licensed quarter were part of an older series of social and cultural constructions, which might be described as Edo-esque: this too constitutes one of the elements of *Hōrōki*'s montage. Finally, the novel presents an alternative vision of the heroine as a fully independent writer, a solitary figure free from romantic entanglements and sexual-economic exchange.

As discussed earlier, *Hōrōki* features a protean central character, who seems compelled to enact with her own body every possible role available to women in the new city. Hence the protagonist's identity could be conceived as a montage of various new roles related to love and work. Many of the identities with which the protagonist experiments can also be found among the most prominent media portrayals of girls and women in the 1920s. Juvenile delinquent, factory girl, café waitress, office worker, political radical, sexual rebel, writer—the "identities" the narrator tests in the course of the novel are precisely the subcategories that combined to form the contradictory media image of the "modern girl."[27] *Hōrōki* and *Zoku hōrōki* represent the complex interaction between the narrator's subjectivity and these languages of literature, journalism, and other mass media forms.

Hōrōki and *Zoku hōrōki:* Desire Liberated and Desire Commodified

One of the most striking aspects of *Hōrōki* and *Zoku hōrōki* is the focus on the most basic physiological needs and desires. In particular, the frequently destitute narrator directs a tremendous amount of attention to food, describing in detail the food she is able to purchase, and richly documenting her cravings for food beyond her economic grasp. Similarly, she is disarmingly honest about her feelings of sexual desire and frustration. Indeed, in the final chapter of *Hōrōki,* the narrator twice repeats the refrain "Hunger and sexual desire!" (*shokuyoku to seiyoku!*) as if to summarize all of her struggles thus far.

In the harsh urban environment of *Hōrōki,* the narrator must place herself on the labor market to fulfill her desire for food, and must "market" herself as an available single woman to seek fulfillment of her sexual desires. At one point, describing her desperate search for employment, she writes, "like a stray dog, I went from one café to another, searching for notices of openings for waitresses. I was simply in search of something to eat—more than anything, I wanted something solid in my stomach."[28] These words echo an earlier passage in the novel, in which the narrator describes her search for sexual companionship: "Selling my womanhood, looking for a buyer, again today I walked the beautiful city's pavement like a stray dog" (*utsukushii machi no hodō o kyō mo watashi wa, onna o katte kurenai ka, onna o urō . . . to noraiunu no yō ni hōkō shite mita*).[29]

In the above passage, the narrator is not literally selling her body as a prostitute, but using the metaphor of prostitution to describe her search for companionship. In the modern city, in which appeals to sexual desire are used every day to market all kinds of goods and services, it is no surprise that the rituals of courtship borrow the metaphors of commercial exchange. Nevertheless, this is an especially loaded choice of metaphors for the economically marginal narrator, who is but one step away from having to sell her body in order to obtain food. Throughout *Hōrōki* and *Zoku hōrōki,* the narrator will maintain a close scrutiny on the economic basics of the labor and sexual markets, seeking to maintain as much independence as possible as she drifts in and out of the gray area where these two markets intersect.

As the diary entries of *Hōrōki* and *Zoku hōrōki* accumulate, they outline the protagonist's relations with a number of men. Her most serious romantic attachments are to a penniless, tubercular, and abusive poet and to a middle-aged actor involved in the Proletarian theater movement, who is portrayed as hypocritical and unfaithful. Other encounters include those with Matsuda, a suitor whose attempts to ensnare the protagonist in a relationship of mutual dependence represent the threat of a complacent domesticity; Matsu, who offers her a thrilling ride in an automobile, only to sexually assault her on a deserted road; and Yoshida, an art student with whom she has a brief sexual encounter that proves physically but not emotionally satisfying.

Throughout the protagonist's attempts to construct relationships with men, she cannot achieve a balance of sexual and emotional fulfillment, nor can she balance these needs with her desire to maintain her hard-won economic and spiritual independence. Indeed, rather than gravitate toward relationships with the promise of stability, she seems drawn to obsessive and ill-fated affairs that only serve to destabilize her daily life. These obsessive and unfulfilling relationships serve the important narrative function of keeping the protagonist off-balance, of insuring her identity as a "wanderer."

Hōrōki, literally an "account of wandering," concentrates its narration on the portions of the protagonist's life where she spins in and out of Tokyo's orbit of love and work, often uprooting herself from her urban jobs and lodgings to make elliptical trips to the provinces before gravitating back to new jobs, lodgings, and relationships in the metropolis. Much of the substance of the romantic relationships themselves is cut out of the narrative, taking place in the substantial gaps between diary entries. Thus the reader must constantly read not only the actual diary entries but also the gaps between the diary entries to get a complete understanding of the novel's development.

As *Hōrōki* progresses, the protagonist's relations with men occur more and more frequently in a commercial context. For the protagonist of Hayashi's novel, the café is the primary location where the "labor market" and the "sexual market" intersect. In this, the fictional *Hōrōki* protagonist had plenty of real-life counterparts. By the mid- to late 1920s, cafés were one of the primary sites for women's work in urban Japan, absorbing wage-seeking young women from various class and regional backgrounds during a period of deepening economic recession.[30] Arguably, however, the café's cultural prominence superseded even its significant economic role in urban Japan.

As noted in the first chapter, the café was one of the primary sites for the self-reproduction of Japan's modernity: an indispensable scene for the public performance, as well as the literary and cinematic representation, of *kindai seikatsu*, "modern life."[31] The café, in which, typically, female waitresses (*jokyū*) served drinks to male customers in an erotically charged environment, was seen as the manifestation of a new form of culture in Japan, significantly different from previous sites of erotic and commercial interaction between men and women, such as the geisha house.[32]

By narrating the "daily life" of a café waitress in her novel, Hayashi thus took the subject-position of a figure who was already the focus of much media attention in contemporary Japan. She offered on the literary market an "inside account" of the life of this media figure; her novel can thus be seen to reproduce (in an Althusserian as well as a mimetic sense) the public fascination with the café and its female workers. Hayashi's reproduction, however, performs a significant reversal, wherein the objectified café waitress—the object of sexual desire and journalistic, literary, graphic, and cinematic representation—becomes the narrating subject, with the ability to represent her own desires.

It is the interest generated by this reversal, together with the general fascination with cafés and waitresses, which may account for much of the novel's initial commercial success. The critic Furuya Tsunatake, who was a twenty-two-year-old café patron when *Hōrōki* first appeared, presents his recollection of the novel's impact as follows:

In those days, the easiest way for boys like me to freely have contact with a young woman was to drink with a café waitress. I had already become a regular customer in a café. And I had a strong curiosity about the hidden life, that is, the private life, of the women who were working in places like that.

Throughout *Hōrōki*, the job which was described most often was that of café waitress. At that time, rather than reading it as a work of literature, I should say that I read it to get a glimpse at the side of life waitresses didn't show to their customers.[33]

The account the *Hōrōki* narrator gives of cafés and their customers is not a flattering one. While working in a setting that objectified and commercialized women's sexuality, the narrator, conversely, comes to see the male customers in the café as objectified and commercialized. "Every customer's face looked like a piece of merchandise," she writes, "every customer's face looked tired."[34] As the narrator's frustration with this setting of sexual objectification grows, so does her anarchic impulse to resist. Visiting in her fantasies some of the more outrageous public representations of women, she imagines crossing the border into complete criminality: "Life has become completely meaningless. Working at a place like this I grow wilder and wilder—I start wanting to become a shoplifter. I want to become a female mounted bandit. Or I want to become a whore."[35]

When faced with the thoroughgoing commercialization of sexuality in the café workplace, the narrator makes her most extreme statements of anarchic, "free" sexual impulses. For example, in the chapter "Nigori zake," a certain Mizuno, a hard-drinking college student and regular customer, is drinking and flirting with Hatsu-chan, one of the protagonist's co-workers. When the protagonist returns to the café from a trip to the public bathhouse, Mizuno claims to have caught a glimpse of her unclothed body by "mistakenly" going through the women's entrance at the bath. While Mizuno's peeping is certainly a violation of the protagonist's privacy, his sexual banter on the subject is arguably within the ground rules of the male-centered erotic space of the café. The narrator's anger at this incident, however, seems less due to Mizuno's original intrusion than at the falsity and hypocrisy of the flirtatious sexuality that is the norm of the café. The narrator records in her diary, "I felt like screaming, 'You want to see me naked? I'll strip down naked in the broad daylight!'"[36]

The tensions of the narrator's situation are encapsulated in one of Hayashi's poems, which is incorporated as a montage element in *Zoku hōrōki*.

> If you buy me ten shots of King of Kings
> Shall I toss you a kiss?
> Ah, a pitiful café waitress
>
> Outside the blue window, it's raining glass shards
> Beneath the lantern, everything turns to liquor
>
> Is "revolution" a wind that blows to the north?!
> I've poured out all the whisky.
> Above the glass on the table, I open my red lips
> And breathe fire

Shall I dance in my blue apron?
"The golden wedding" or "Caravan"—
What will tonight's program be?

Well now, there are three more glasses
Do I know what I'm doing, you ask
Sure, I'm okay
I'm a clever girl
I'm such a clever girl
To be lavishing my emotions without regret
On men like miserable pigs
As if tossing cut flowers
Is "revolution" a wind that blows to the north? . . .[37]

With this remarkable poem, Hayashi juxtaposes a number of conflicting languages of gender, sexuality, and politics that were a part of contemporary media representations. With such phrases as "blue window" and "red lips" Hayashi employs common markers of the erotic environment of the Japanese café. Moreover, with the last line of the first stanza, "Ah, a pitiful café waitress" (ō, *aware na kyūjijo yo*), Hayashi draws upon contemporary depictions of the café waitress as a pathetic figure. In this regard, her poem can be compared with the lyrics for the hit song "Jokyū no uta" ("The Café Waitress's Song") by Saijō Yaso, from the year 1930:[38]

[first verse]
I am a flower of the bar scene   blossoming at night
Red lipstick   gossamer sleeves
Floating, dancing   in the neon lights
But lonely when the drink wears off   petals of tears

[third verse]
Having their way with weak women   then throwing them aside
Those are the vain and empty   exploits of men
The woman loves him   but gives him up
A red blossom flowering   in the bitter floating world[39]

While Hayashi seems to quote from the repertory of similar depictions of waitresses as objects of pity, the differences between Hayashi's poem and Saijō's lyrics are soon apparent. By presenting the song's "I" as passive and thoroughly resigned, Saijō merely reproduces the image, and the ideology, of woman as victim. While

Hayashi also alludes to this image of woman as victim, at other moments in the poem she strikes a belligerent tone unimaginable in Saijō's song lyrics, denigrating the café patrons as "men like miserable pigs" (*tsumaranai buta no yō na otokotachi*).

Indeed, Hayashi juxtaposes phrases echoing the popular image of the victimized café waitress not only with a tone of belligerence, but with the language of revolution. It is the twice-repeated line "Is 'revolution' a wind that blows to the north?" (*Kakumei to wa hoppō ni fuku kaze ka*) which serves as the powerful, yet ultimately ambivalent, crux of the poem. With this refrain, Hayashi raises the possibility that revolution will overturn the oppressive situation in which the waitress labors. Perhaps the poem's "I" herself will be the agent of this change: the "I"'s red lips signal not only sexuality but violence, breathing fire: can a liberated "Red Love" be far away? With this refrain, then, Hayashi quotes from the language of leftist activism, which was an undeniable aspect of the 1920s media discourse, yet one that seems irreconcilable with the sentimentalism of Saijō's song lyrics.

Nevertheless, in Hayashi's poem, the possibility of violent change is raised as a question, not an assertion. The word "revolution" (*kakumei*) is not printed in Sino-Japanese kanji characters, which would clarify, fix, and naturalize its meaning, but in katakana, as if the poet is quoting a foreign language, or a suspicious term of intellectual argot. While the winds of revolution may blow to the north across Russia, it remains highly uncertain that there will be a change of weather in Japan. The power, and even the meaning, of the word "revolution" remain in doubt when considered against the pervasive commercialization of sexuality, and structural asymmetries of gender, with which the poem's "I" must contend as a café waitress. In the end, the poem leaves little room for optimism, as the "I"'s violence remains directed not toward overcoming her oppressive situation, but toward hastening her own self-destruction.

Relationships Between Women in *Hōrōki*

As her experiences as a café waitress begin to dominate the novel, the possibility of the narrator satisfying her sexual and emotional desires with men seems increasingly remote. Yet there is another series of relationships in *Hōrōki:* the relationships between the protagonist and the other women—fellow factory laborers, clerical workers, and café waitresses—with whom she lives and works. In contrast to the desperate, shallow, and often commercialized relationships between men and women, these relationships are depicted as intimate and supportive, bonds forged not only by shared circumstances, but also by the ritual of personal storytelling.

The relationships between women in *Hōrōki* are both physically and emotionally intimate. A number of intimate scenes between women occur at the public bath: as the women observe one another's bodies, they exchange stories of childhood, relationships with men, abortion, pregnancy, and child-rearing. The women's shared living quarters, typically on the second floor of a café, is another scene of intimacy; for the waitresses, this cramped but private second-floor space serves as a contrast to the space of commercial-erotic exchange on first floor. "When women go to work at a place like this," the narrator writes of the café, "no matter how unfriendly and reticent they may be at first, they'll eventually be caught off guard, and reveal their true selves. Then, as if they've known each other for ten years, they'll soon be closer than sisters. After the customers left, we'd often curl up together like snails."[40]

It is safe to say that these co-workers' communal life provides an emotional haven precisely because it is free of the commercialized or exploitative sexuality that characterizes, for the most part, the women's relationships with men. But for the narrator, at least, the intimacy that she develops with her co-workers is not completely separate from the realm of erotic desire. While the narration hints at an erotic attraction between women at a number of points, perhaps the most striking is the description of the narrator's feelings during a brief stint as a clerical worker in a wholesaler's shop in Osaka. Here, she finds herself sharing lodging with two other women workers at the shop, O-ito and O-kuni:

By eight o'clock, the main doors were already locked, and the nine clerks and shopboys had slipped away one by one. As I gently stretched out my legs on the well-starched futon and looked up at the ceiling, a sad, forlorn feeling began to creep over me. O-ito and O-kuni's two black lacquered pillows were lined up next to the bedding, and O-ito's red kimono slip was thrown over her futon. For a long time, I stared at that red slip as though with the eyes of a man. I could hear the splashing sound as the two women wordlessly took their bath. I felt a desire to be touched by O-ito's beautiful arms, with their fine white down of hair. As if I had turned completely into a man, I fell in love with O-ito in that red slip.

If I were man, I would make love to all the women of the world. . . . The flowerlike scent of silent women is carried to me from afar. Closing my tear-filled eyes, I turned away from the bright lamp.[41]

The narrator's attraction to other women remains an undeveloped and barely articulated theme in *Hōrōki* and *Zoku hōrōki*. Even when such feelings are articulated, the narrator must take recourse to male subjectivity, describing her gaze "as though with the eyes of a man," or fantasizing "if I were a man . . . ." In contrast to the language of heterosexual desire, which seems overdetermined, overlaid with layers of literary and journalistic associations, there seems to be no language or subject-position available for the narrator to articulate female-female desire. Nevertheless, while in the passage above the narrator seems overwhelmed by an aching loneliness, her relationships with women as a whole are her only reliable source for emotional grounding, support, and fulfillment, incomplete though it may be. Indeed, the unquestioning strength of these women's bonds appears to be conditional on any sexual desire that attends these relationships remaining unvoiced and unconsummated.

The Edo-esque and the Independent Woman

Within the "entertainment" realm of commercialized social and sexual activity, the institutions of the café and the dance hall were taken to be central features of Tokyo's new urban culture: conspicuous sites for the performance and representation of "modern life."[42] These institutions, however, did not altogether replace earlier cultural sites associated with erotic "entertainment" and commercial sex. Rather, the new institutions of "modern life," including cafés and dance halls, developed alongside institutions whose physical, social, and linguistic construction had a longer history, extending into the Meiji and Edo periods. Within the urban space depicted in Hayashi's *Hōrōki*, this cultural juxtaposition is epitomized in the sites where the protagonist works as a waitress: "modern" cafés that often border the entrance to a licensed district, or *kuruwa*.

This disposition on the edge of the licensed quarter highlights the cultural ambivalence of the café, and the precariousness of the narrator's position as a waitress. On the one hand, the relationship of the café and the licensed quarter is one of proximity: the waitresses' existence is contiguous with, and in part economically dependent upon, longstanding practices of prostitution. On the other hand, the café waitresses, while working in a male-centered service industry, exert an independence denied to their sisters in the neighboring quarter: the café serves as a harbor, albeit a precarious one, for the self-reliant and anarchic spirit typified by the narrator herself.

The spatial and cultural juxtaposition of the café and the licensed quarter is captured in passages such as the following, from *Zoku hōrōki*:

May Xth

Today Toki-chan said she would teach me how to ride a bike. Once we finished our cleaning, we borrowed the shop's bicycle, and went out onto the wide road in front of the licensed quarters. The street was bathed in the morning light, and the *futon* were all airing out on the railings on the second floor of the brothels. On the photo boards below, the names of the new girls were written on white strips of paper, which flapped in the wind like placards announcing a funeral. With a derisive smile, Toki-chan said the men coming out of the brothels looked liked umbrellas on a rainy day. Fearlessly, she pedaled the bike around the wide road. Both men and women stopped to stare at this woman with her hair tied up in a chignon, riding a bicycle down the brothel-front road.

"So, Yumi,[43] hop on! I'll give you a push."

Filled with a crazy kind of levity, I had fun pretending to be Don Quixote. After two or three times around, I found the pedals responding to my feet, and was firmly in control of the handle bar.[44]

This passage, although merely one of the many vignettes within the diary-entry montage of Hayashi's work, says much about the narrator's claim to Tokyo's urban space—about her assertion of a "modern" freedom denied the working women housed in the nearby quarter. Notably, the prostitutes who work in the brothel are absent from this scene; rather they are represented metonymically by the futon hanging from the second floor windows, and the placards announcing the names of new prostitutes (*hatsumise*). This is in keeping with the predominantly enclosed nature of nineteenth-

and early twentieth-century Japanese prostitution, in which prostitutes working in the licensed quarters were often kept under close watch by their brothel owners and discouraged from appearing on the street or in public places.

By boldly claiming the street in front of the brothel as their space of public play, the protagonist and her companion are asserting their spiritual independence from the cultural system that encloses the other women within the brothel, making their bodies goods to be purchased by their freely mobile male customers. While the café adjoins the licensed quarter geographically and is contiguous with the brothel as a site of commercialized erotic activity, a certain cultural ambiguity also allows it to serve as a harbor for the anarchic impulses of the café waitresses. This ambiguity permits the *Hōrōki/Zoku hōrōki* narrator to assert, in passages such as the one above, new possibilities for women within Tokyo's urban space: to claim for women the priority of the public versus the enclosed, the free versus the bound, and the modern over the traditional.[45]

The café, an institutional representation of "modern life," is thus shown to physically border on the licensed quarters, which carries in its physical, linguistic, and social construction echoes of pre-modern Japanese urban culture. Interestingly, this proximate relationship can be observed on a much larger scale in the protagonist's movements throughout Tokyo. While the chronological and geographic movements within the narration are nonlinear and often confusing, we can discern a general movement over the course of *Hōrōki* from "modern" western Tokyo to "Edo-esque" eastern Tokyo.

As described earlier, the narrator lodges in a Shinjuku flophouse when she first arrives in Tokyo. She works as a street peddler for a time on Dōgenzaka in Shibuya; one of her first jobs as a waitress is again in Shinjuku; and there is a brief interlude when she lives even farther west, on the outskirts of the city in present-day Setagaya Ward. Such western-Tokyo locations were on the newest, expanding edge of the city, being steadily incorporated into the urban network through new train lines, suburban housing projects, and department stores. These neighborhoods were thus associated in the 1920s with the development of Tokyo's new urban culture, or "modern life" (*kindai seikatsu*). Later in the novel, however, the protagonist seems to be working primarily in cafés near Asakusa and Kanda, both in the older, eastern section of Tokyo, with cultural associations reaching back into the Edo period.

Indeed, as *Hōrōki* progresses, there is a steady increase in the number of references to Edo culture, particularly the Edo culture associated with the "floating world" of the licensed quarters, enfolded within Hayashi's montage. These cultural elements of Edo do not carry over automatically into twentieth-century modernity, however, but must be constantly reproduced within the modern system in order to survive.[46] By incorporating the Edo-esque as one of the many conflicting montage elements in her narrative, Hayashi acknowledges its seductive power, as well as its danger, as a possible cultural and social construction within Japan's modern culture.

The Edo-esque element reaches its height in the last chapter of *Hōrōki*, when the protagonist and a co-worker, Toki-chan, rent a room in Shitaya, one of the neighborhoods of eastern Tokyo most associated with Edo *chōnin*, or townsman, culture. Soon after the two women arrive in their new room, they overhear a ballad being sung by a *kouta* instructor across the street. The lyrics of this *kouta* ballad, a musical form that was integral to the culture of the Edo licensed quarters, are incorporated as an element of Hayashi's textual montage:

> Lifting my umbrella against this blizzard—
> The licensed quarter's falling cherry blossoms!
> When this samurai's song has passed
> Spring in Edo, aglow in the purple dusk[47]

Such fragments of the Edo-esque do more than simply serve as local color for the later portions of *Hōrōki* set in eastern Tokyo. By incorporating such fragments within her textual montage, Hayashi acknowledges their cultural power. Yet within their picturesque allure is a set of gender and social constructions that represent a dead end, an intolerable outcome, for the novel's protagonist. The intolerability, as well as the allure, of the Edo-esque is elucidated in the final chapter, which outlines the differing fates of the protagonist and her companion, Toki-chan.

As we learn from the prose diary sections of this final chapter, the protagonist has sold a ring bequeathed by a drunken café customer, and used the money to rent and furnish a room away from the café, to be shared with her co-worker Toki-chan. According to their plans, Toki-chan will continue working as a waitress, while the protagonist will quit waitressing to devote herself to writing full time. Here, the protagonist seems to be seeking a space apart from the chaotic heterosexual relationships that dominated the early chapters of the novel, and from the commercialized sexual situations that come with her job as a café waitress. Indeed, her actions in setting up house with her younger co-worker seem very much like attempts to construct an alternative "family" based on emotional intimacy and economic cooperation between women.

The logistical aspects of this construction of a private living space are emphasized by the inclusion of a shopping list, describing how the two women spent the thirteen yen gained from the sale of the café patron's ring:

Tea serving tray	1 yen
Hibachi brazier	1 yen
Potted plant	35 sen
Rice bowls	20 sen (for two)
Soup bowls	30 sen (for two)
Pickled wasabi	5 sen
Pickled radish	11 sen
Chopsticks	5 sen (five pairs)
Tea set with saucers	1 yen 10 sen
Painted cover	15 sen
Plates	20 sen (two)
Partial month's rent	6 yen
	(9 yen/mo. for three-mat room)
Tongs for hibachi	10 sen
Rice cake grill	12 sen
Aluminum soup ladle	10 sen
Rice paddle	13 sen
Tissue paper	20 sen
Facial cream	28 sen
Saké for the altar	25 sen
"Moving-in noodles" for the downstairs neighbors	30 sen

—1 yen 16 sen change remaining[48]

The narrator thus details the terms of her own economic conversion from dependence to independence: the ring, a manifestation of the semi-sexual service economy of the café, is converted into the living space and goods with which to build a new lifestyle independent of this economy. Their independence, however, is still only a partial one, since Toki-chan is still dependent on the café economy, and comes home one night wearing another ring from a customer, much to the narrator's dismay.

Ironically, while the narrator records the prosaic details of their shopping trip in her literary diary, it is the younger Toki-chan who seems captured by the lyrical element of the Edo-esque to which they are exposed in their Shitaya neighborhood. The next found text incorporated into Hayashi's montage is a ballad sung, not by the teacher across the street, but by Toki herself:

> Gazing upon the thin sheet of snow, I think only
> How futile—how soon it will vanish!
> The willows gently tremble
> In the dawn of spring's heart. . . .[49]

Placed within a few pages of each other, the protagonist's shopping list and the two Edo-esque ballads point toward two opposing fates. These fates are revealed in the final juxtaposition in the novel: the juxtaposition of a letter from Toki, recorded as a found text at the head of the diary entry, and a letter from an editor, Shiroki, which is described at the close:

February Xth

Fumiko-sama.

Please don't get angry, and forgive me. I was bullied by the man who gave me the ring, and I'm now in a house of assignation in Asakusa.
This man has a wife, but he says he'll get rid of her.
Please don't laugh. He's a contractor, and he's forty-two years old.
He bought me a lot of kimono, and when I told him about you, he said he'd send you about forty yen a month.
I'm so glad.

As I read the letter, my eyes flamed up with tears, and my teeth chattered, jangling like pieces of metal.

It didn't have to be this way! When did I ever ask for anything like this? Fool! Was this eighteen-year-old girl so weak?

With my eyes swollen and blinded with tears, I cried out to the absent Toki-chan.

Why don't you tell me where you are? What is this "house of assignation" in Asakusa?

A forty-two-year-old man!

Kimono, kimono.

What do you want with a ring or a kimono? Faithless woman!

This girl, with her lovely, slender form like a wild lily, her soft skin like
a peach blossom, her jet black hair—she was still a virgin.

Why did she have to give her first flower to some good-for-nothing man
from the "floating world"? She who bent her delicate head to me and sang
"in the dawn of spring's heart." She's now the plaything of a forty-two-
year-old man!

"Miss Hayashi! A registered letter!" The woman downstairs called to
me, sounding in better than usual spirits. I picked up the envelope she left
on the stairs.

Twenty-three yen from Shiroki at the Jiji Newspaper inside! It's the
payment for one of my children's stories.

I guess I won't have to starve for a while. My chest swelled with happiness, like I was drunk. But a stream of loneliness also flowed in my heart.

The friend who would share my happiness is in the arms of a forty-two-
year-old man![50]

The protagonist's attempt to set up an alternative women's
domestic space has failed; the intensity of her reaction suggests that
she has lost more than a roommate, but rather a dear friend and
perhaps a lover. Now, the opposing fates of the two women are
clear: the protagonist will make her way as an independent writer,
while her companion has been captured irrevocably by the sexual
service economy. Although this point may not be stated explicitly,
we can conclude from the textual evidence that it is more than a
single man, or the gift of a ring or kimono, which has captured
Toki-chan. Rather it is a whole life-world, which I have termed the
Edo-esque, which has seduced the young café waitress: its currency
is the ring and the kimono, its human representative is the forty-
two-year-old contractor, and its literary elements are the songs that
give a romantic view of the "floating world."

The contrast with the protagonist's fate could not be more clear:
while Toki-chan, bullied into a "house of assignation" (*machiai*) in
Asakusa, has crossed the line from the service economy of the café
into out-and-out prostitution, the protagonist has escaped this service economy altogether, and is able to earn money as a writer, an

independent cultural producer. This final vision of the female protagonist as a financially and spiritually independent writer is very much in tune with the image of the independent modern woman promoted by the feminist journal *Nyonin geijutsu*, in which *Hōrōki* was first serialized. Indeed, the rather heavy-handed symmetry of the two letters received by the protagonist highlights the feminist ideology of this final scene.

Nevertheless, the protagonist's "victory," already soured by her grief over the loss of her companion, is a limited one: her position within the capitalist system has shifted slightly, but this system, seemingly immune from the winds of revolution, still provides the framework for her present and future daily life (*seikatsu*). The protagonist has withdrawn for the time being from the marketplace of heterosexual relationships, and is freed from the degrading experiences of an urban immigrant on the labor market. For these, she has substituted a stake in the literary market—still very much a part of the same capitalist system that routinely commodifies sexuality.

Rather than having to sell her labor, or her "service," or even her body, she can now sell cultural products of her own creation, and thus attempt to define her own position in society. Yet in order to survive, she must match these cultural products to a market; and, we may well ask, what will the literary market ask of her in the future? Over the course of the narration, the reader has observed the protagonist keeping notes of her experience in her diaries, and reading over former diary entries in her spare time. Indeed, the reader has been encouraged to connect this diary within the narration to the "diary" before the reader's eyes. So we can well imagine that the protagonist's future offering to the literary market will be the diaries themselves: the montage of her various roles in the urban labor and sexual markets.

Just as the sexually exploitative world of the Edo-esque has its literary elements, such as the tune sung by Toki-chan, so we can imagine, in the worst case, that the narrator will be called by the literary market to produce from her diaries a "modernist" literature of sexual mores, which will accompany a new but similarly exploitative series of gender constructions known as "modern life."[51] Or, on the contrary, we can imagine that the protagonist, by gaining an author's voice in the public sphere, will be able to influence the construction of this modern life, and help to open new and liberating possibilities within Japanese modernity. The novel's final chapter, while giving us hope that the protagonist will at least be able to keep food on the table, provides no conclusive answer to these questions.

Hayashi's *Hōrōki* and *Zoku hōroki* thus track the protagonist as she performs a bewildering variety of labor roles, and tests various constructions of sexual and emotional relationships with men and women, in a harsh urban environment in which commodification seems to permeate both work and sexuality. Through the use of montage techniques, and through her attentiveness to ideological and linguistic contrasts within the lines of her own poetry and prose, Hayashi explores the relationship between her protagonist's consciousness and the literary and journalistic constructions that shape her world. She thus creates a work uniquely suited to what Hirabayashi Hatsunosuke called the "age of collapsed authority," in which the thoughts and morals of the younger generation are not absorbed from their elders, but pieced together from their own mass-media environment.

By sketching the protagonist on the verge of becoming a professional writer, she completes the circle of this media-subject formation, opening the possibility that her heroine will shape the development of Japanese modernity through her role as a cultural producer. Nevertheless, the pervasiveness of sexual commoditization experienced by the protagonist thus far and the failure of her attempt to construct an alternative domestic space in the final chapter beg the question of the limits of this modernity for a young female protagonist, even in her new role as a professional writer.

6 / ANARCHISM AND IMPERIALISM
Hagiwara Kyōjirō's *Danpen* and Beyond

The City and the Country

As indicated by such spirited and critical literary explorations of modern Tokyo as Hagiwara's *Shikei senkoku* and Hayashi's *Hōrōki*, cultural and political attention to urban concerns intensified in the 1920s, and the decade can be seen as a high point in the prewar development of Japanese urban culture. The economic boom during the First World War had set the stage for this urban renaissance by fostering industrialization and urban migration. The destruction of Tokyo in the Great Kanto Earthquake of 1923, rather than reversing the trend of urbanization, helped focus the nation's energy on its urban life, allowing the city to be reborn with new streets, buildings, and cultural institutions. The expansion of media—including newspaper, magazine, and book publishing, film, radio, and the recording industry—contributed to the development of urban culture and extended the cultural hegemony of the city over the countryside.

By the end of the decade, cultural commentators such as Ōya Sōichi could declare that "today's culture exists nowhere but the city." "Contemporary culture," Ōya wrote in a 1930 essay, "has developed on the basis of the total subjugation of the country by the city." Rural villages, Ōya argues, can no longer constitute a viable alternative to urban culture, but exist only as part of the city, or as "underdeveloped cities."[1]

Nii Itaru, the most prominent journalist and literary critic connected with the anarchist movement in Japan, offered a similar appraisal of urban cultural and political domination in his *Anakizumu geijutsu ron* (*Theory of Anarchist Art*), also published in 1930. In one passage, Nii describes the effects of new media such as popular novels, films, songs, and radio broadcasts in extending the city's influence over the countryside:

The flamboyance of current popular novels (*tsūzoku shōsetsu*) is due, in, short, to their incorporation of urban color. To put it concretely, they insert such elements as department stores, hotels, and every other organ of entertainment that exists in the city (cinema, theater, concerts, bars, cafés, dance halls, strolls along the boulevards, sports), and every type of urbanite found in these locations. And when these works are made into movies, these urban elements, far from being eliminated, appear all the more intensely.

Furthermore, the lyrics of new popular song writers . . . spread the cheap perfume of the cities even further, and radio broadcasts send these urban scents out into the entire country. The "noisification" of the country, which has preceded even so-called "village electrification," will doubtless broadcast ever more urban colors to the countryside, and merge these provincial spaces into urban ones.[2]

By the end of the 1920s, the rapid growth of the cities and their industrial base, together with the ever-expanding scale and scope of the urban-based communications media, seemed to support Ōya and Nii's conclusions about the cultural and political domination of the countryside by the cities. Nevertheless, even in this decade of urban exuberance, the metropole's domination over the country provoked a diverse reaction of critics who decried the cities' corruption and exploitation (*sakushu*) of the country and championed rural social values and political prerogatives, with left-oriented critics drawing on communist and anarchist political critiques, and right-oriented critics drawing on a rich corpus of agrarianist thought stretching from Tokugawa-period nativist scholars to Meiji-era nationalist ideologues. As Japan entered the 1930s, conditions of economic crisis in rural Japan pushed these voices to the fore, helping to promote a surprising comeback for those who advocated for rural concerns, and proving Ōya and Nii's declarations of rural cultural eclipse premature.

The rural crisis of the 1930s might be said to have begun as early as the year 1920, when the bubble of farm commodity prices inflated by wartime demand burst. After a brief recovery in the early 1920s, the rural economy grew steadily worse throughout the late 1920s and early 1930s. The price of rice dropped by over 25 percent between 1927 and 1931, to a level that was only two-fifths of the price during the war boom of 1919. While many farm families relied on sericulture to supplement their income from staple crops, silk prices suffered an even more drastic fall, with the price of raw silk dropping by nearly two-thirds between 1925 and 1931. In the 1930s, repeated crop failures intensified the rural misery brought about by the deflation of agricultural prices; a particularly severe failure in 1933 resulted in famine conditions in parts of rural northern Japan.[3]

These conditions, combined with the increase in absentee land-lordism and growing political consciousness among tenant farmers, prompted a marked increase in tenancy disputes and sometimes violent rural conflict in the early 1930s, further propelling rural issues into the national spotlight. While the most pressing aspects of this rural crisis were economic and political, in interwar Japan economic and political issues were perceived to be closely inter-twined with cultural issues. Thus, in the pivotal year of 1930, the question of the relationship between city and country was an inescapable one for Ōya Sōichi and Nii Itaru, both of whom labored in the hybrid politico-cultural vineyards of "Proletarian Literature."

Nii Itaru's own attitude toward urban versus rural culture was highly ambivalent, like that of many Japanese intellectuals in the interwar period. On the one hand, he praised the stimulating elements of urban culture, including the "artificial beauty" of its architecture, its "speedy tempo, convenience, and amusement value," and its "constructive beauty" (*kōseibi*), formed of the constant "dissolving and reassembling of movement."[4] As an anarchist, however, he was suspicious of the centralization of power (*chūō shukenteki kinō*), which the city also fostered.

In his *Theory of Anarchist Art* quoted above, Nii contrasts the anarchist position, which he represents as basically anti-urban, with that of the Marxists, who he depicts as being group-oriented and predisposed to centralized authority, and who thus naturally take the city and its industrial workers as their power base. Still, he cannot embrace the position of some anarchists who "vainly oppose the city and excessively channel their passions toward the rural villages." Rather, citing the work of architectural theorist Ishihara Kenji, he suggests the promotion of garden cities and satellite cities as a way to preserve the benefits of urban culture while discouraging the centralization of authority.[5]

While Nii was lukewarm about the potential of rural culture and gave relatively short shrift to rural political concerns, other Japanese anarchists embraced the agrarian cause wholeheartedly. Many of the anarchist movement's early gains had been among urban industrial workers, and the intellectual leadership provided by Ōsugi Sakae was fundamentally cosmopolitan in tone. After Ōsugi's assassination in 1923, however, the anarchist political movement was increasingly dominated by "pure anarchists" who pinned their hopes on an uprising of tenant farmers.[6] Meanwhile, something of Ōsugi's mantle as intellectual leader passed to Ishikawa Sanshirō (1876–1956), who, returning from a lengthy period of exile in Europe, rejected both urbanism and Western cultural influence. Ishikawa developed a theory of radical democracy based on village self-rule and the independence and free association of the Japanese peasants, whom he referred to as *domin*, or "people of the earth."[7]

Inspired in part by Ishikawa's political philosophy, Inuta Shigeru (1893–1957) and Yoshie Takamatsu (1880–1940), two aspiring writers with rural backgrounds, spearheaded a literary movement to advocate rural self-determination (*nōmin jiji shugi*), founding the journal *Nōmin (Farmers)* in 1927.[8] Despite Nii Itaru's suggestion that Marxists were temperamentally indisposed to rural culture, members of the Communist "Proletarian Literature" movement responded to the challenge of Inuta and Yoshie's "farmer's literature" with their own forums and works addressing rural concerns.

Nevertheless, the most conspicuous, and ultimately the most influential, advocates for rural Japan were the bureaucrats, military officers, and right-wing ideologues grouped together as *nōhonshugisha*, or agrarian nationalists. While such *nōhonshugisha* as Gondō Seikyō (1868–1937) and Tachibana Kōzaburō (1893–) may have seemed marginal when they first published their theories in the

1920s, they gained considerable notoriety after their ideas were cited as inspiration for two shocking incidents of right-wing violence by rural activists and radical young military officers in 1932: the assassination of two top financial leaders in February and March; and a bloody coup d'état attempt in May.[9]

The increase in right-wing violence in the 1930s, when added to the left-wing agitation of tenancy disputes, was successful in focusing the country's attention on rural issues, and not incidentally, in destabilizing the institutions of parliamentary democracy. The problems facing rural Japan came to the fore in a period of deepening political and economic crisis at home, and rapid military expansion and conflict abroad. As militarist, imperialist, and totalitarian factions within the government grew in power, the new leaders found elements of the agrarian nationalist position to be useful in promoting a conservative, anti-urban, anti-Western, and emperor-centered vision of ethnic-national identity. Thus, while the actual political domination of the country by the city continued, the balance of rhetorical power shifted from the urban "modernism" of the 1920s to a cultural and political ethos that placed rural Japan, or at least a romanticized vision of timeless rural values, at the heart of its concerns.

While Hagiwara Kyōjirō was by any standard a marginal figure in the larger debates over Japanese cultural identity and political orientation, his personal life and poetic career run in a strange parallel to the cultural shift from the "urban" 1920s to the "rural" 1930s. Although the publication of Hagiwara's intensely urban, avant-garde poetry collection *Shikei senkoku* in October of 1925 had a major impact on the Japanese poetry world, it apparently did nothing to improve the poet's desperate financial situation. Only three months after *Shikei senkoku*'s publication, Hagiwara was forced to dissolve his Tokyo household, sending his wife and child back to her home in Ibaragi Prefecture, and returning to his great-aunt's home in rural Gunma Prefecture, just outside the provincial city of Maebashi. After six months at his childhood home, Hagiwara reunited with his wife and child and made a second go of life in Tokyo. However, following two more years in Tokyo, Hagiwara abandoned the metropolis for good, returning with his family to Gunma Prefecture.

The change in Hagiwara's physical environment coincided with a change in his poetic output, which shifted from the avant-garde poetry on urban themes that dominated *Shikei senkoku,* to poems which were less exuberantly experimental in form, and which thematized the everyday life of rural Japan. Hagiwara's political thought also underwent a transformation, eventually intersecting not only with the agrarian anarchist thought of his close acquaintance Ishikawa Sanshirō, but eventually with the agrarian nationalism of Gondō Seikyō. Moreover, his final poems, which seem to endorse both the Imperial institution and Imperialist military and cultural expansion in Asia, provoke troubling questions as to how a poet strongly identified with the anarchist political position could make such an apparent ideological about-face. The poems of his second poetry collection *Danpen* (*Fragments,* 1931), which focus largely on political questions, as well as his subsequent poetry centering on rural concerns, provide crucial clues for understanding Hagiwara's ideological transformation, and may shed light on the broader ideological shifts of his time.

It is important to note that while Hagiwara seemed to have rediscovered the issues of rural poverty and cultural malaise after his return to Gunma Prefecture in 1928, these issues were in fact highlighted in his earliest writings. Although it was his poems on urban themes that would gain him his initial literary notoriety, Hagiwara first took up the agrarian cause just after moving to Tokyo in September of 1922. Even after he had enthusiastically absorbed the work of self-proclaimed futurist poet Hirato Renkichi, Hagiwara somewhat surprisingly began publishing poems depicting the tribulations of rural Japan, and decrying the abandonment of the farm by city-enamored young people (such as himself!). In the first issue of the nominally avant-garde poetry journal *Aka to kuro,* which he co-founded in January 1923, Hagiwara published both a long-winded agrarianist poem and a manifesto-like article entitled "Mura no koto" ("About the Village"):

A village of thirty-two households! A cold village on the edge of the Akashiro Mountains! I was born in such a place, where from spring to fall people stake their livelihood on sericulture. My father was buried in that earth. And my grandmother. Today, all of my father's brothers and sisters, and my own elder brother, and my elder sister, and all younger brothers and sisters take up the hoe as farmers.

Country rubes! Who? Everyone around us is a country rube! Someone called us country rubes? How many boys and girls have been led out of their villages by these words? Bringing chaos to the hard life of the village!

Poetic! Simple. Country rubes! What are you talking about? What's poetic? What's simple? What's a country rube?

The article climaxes with the rhetorical question, "The literature of—To the city! To the city! Is there no literature of—To the village! To the village!? Why?"[10]

Hagiwara's fellow *dōjin* at *Aka to kuro,* however, were evidently unimpressed with his agrarian poetry. In issue four of the magazine, Tsuboi Shigeji articulated the group's misgivings about his poetic style and subject matter:

We were afraid that, in the worst case, that kind of poem would become more and more separated from Hagiwara's daily life, and fall into a kind of sentimentalism. . . . Those of us who knew Hagiwara personally couldn't get over the feeling that there was something unnatural [about the poems]. Even Hagiwara himself seemed to be aware of this.[11]

Indeed, after the third issue of the journal, Hagiwara began to develop the style of poetry found in *Shikei senkoku,* and would not return to the literature of "To the village!" until nearly ten years later.

Hagiwara's torturous experience over the next two decades, which seems in some respects so solitary and idiosyncratic, nevertheless intersects with many of the most pressing issues of early twentieth-century Japanese intellectual history. These issues include not only the balance of power between urban and rural Japan, but the related issues of access to communications media, the relationship between art and politics, the question of intellectuals' relation to the so-called masses, and the history of political opposition movements and their suppression. Hagiwara's second poetry collection, *Danpen* (*Fragments,* 1931), serves as a fulcrum between the two main stages of his career, and provides an intriguing point of entry into the ideological dilemmas of his age.

Tokyo, 1924–1928: Integration and Disintegration

I have previously suggested that the poems of Hagiwara's first poetry collection *Shikei senkoku* merge the self and the city (modern Tokyo) in unusual and complex ways. The urban quality of these poems is one facet of Hagiwara's determination to connect art and daily life—in the language of his 1924 essay, to find the self (*jiga*) in the society-self (*shakaiga*), and the society-self in his own self.[12]

In addition to its direct role as a thematic element in his poetry, the city also played another, equally important role in Hagiwara's poetic and intellectual development. For the city was the ground for his contact with a diverse array of poets, artists, political activists, and ideologues. One important association of writers and intellectuals coalesced at the Café Lebanon in Hongō, where, during the period 1923–1925, Hagiwara had daily contact with writers such as Okamoto Jun, Tsuboi Shigeji, Ono Tōzaburō, Takahashi Shinkichi, Tsuji Jun, and Hayashi Fumiko.

The second important association Hagiwara developed in Tokyo was with the Mavo group of avant-garde visual artists. Hagiwara became a co-editor of the group's eponymous journal for its last three of seven issues, and collaborated with the Mavo artists to produce his poetry collection *Shikei senkoku*, which credits thirteen Mavo-associated artists for the linocut prints and photographic inserts that form an essential part of the collection's layout. The publication of *Damu damu* (*Dum dum*) magazine in 1924, and *MAVO* magazine and *Shikei senkoku* in 1925, marked the height of Hagiwara's integration into a network of artists and poets who were actively transforming a segment of Tokyo's urban culture.

Hagiwara's work in co-producing the *MAVO* magazine placed him among a group of artists who were exploring the nature of the printed text in the context of machine reproduction and mass culture. Although *MAVO* magazine was only produced in small numbers, it represented, as art historian Gennifer Weisenfeld argues, a dialogue between the techniques of hand production and those of mass reproduction. By exploring different techniques of typography, printing, and reproduction of visual images, and incorporating newspapers and other mass-produced print media as collage elements, the Mavo group sought to "champion the artist's role in the construction of mass culture and the strategic deployment of mass communication as well as to emphasize the collaborative and reproducible nature of art in the technological era."[13] Cognizant of a new role for the artist in constructing modern life, Hagiwara himself described *MAVO* magazine as "a training ground for new artists and new engineers."[14]

In his essays in the next several years following his involvement in the *MAVO* magazine project, Hagiwara expanded on this view of the artist as engineer: each artist, he argued, should seek to become familiar with multiple aspects of industrial production, such as printing, welding, glasswork, and so on. Needless to say, this vision of the artist as engineer was by no means unique to Hagiwara: similar views were articulated, with varying inflections, by a great number of artists throughout the 1920s, from the Bauhaus group, to the Russian Constructivists, to Hagiwara's fellows in Mavo.

As he became more deeply involved in the anarchist movement, Hagiwara connected this ideal of the artist as engineer to a political critique of industrial production based on the division of labor. Following a strain of anti-industrialist criticism exemplified in the writings of William Morris, Edward Carpenter, and the early Marx, Hagiwara decried the situation under modern capitalism, in which industrial workers were alienated from the technical and creative processes of production, and had become mere servants to their machines. Not only should artists and intellectuals familiarize themselves with the processes of manual labor, he suggested, but more importantly, manual laborers should themselves become artist/engineers, each with the knowledge, creativity, and power to construct his own life.[15] Hagiwara thus revealed an ambivalent position in regard to machine culture, at times extolling the place of technology in modern life and glorifying the role of the engineer, while at other times execrating modern industry and advocating social reforms with distinctly anti-industrial overtones.[16]

We can surmise, then, that Hagiwara's experience with the Mavo group sharpened his scrutiny on the printing process as a focal point of larger issues of the relationship between art, industrial production, and mass communication. Another concern which Hagiwara shared with the Mavo group was his interest in theater, dance, and performance—arts that the Mavoists explored extensively both within their own group's activities and in concert with other groups of artists. The theatrical mode held a number of attractions for the Mavoists: it enabled them to make their own bodies the expressive basis of their art (and thereby explore the politics of body and gender); and it allowed them to combine elements of several different arts, including set design, scenario writing, and the creation of lighting, sound, and olfactory effects. Moreover, it put them in direct contact with the public, both inside and out of the formal space of the theater, as the Mavo exploration of the theatrical mode extended beyond the theater to various public performances, demonstrations, and provocations.[17]

During the mid-1920s, Hagiwara found a number of ways to infuse the dramatic and the bodily into his work as a poet. While Hagiwara and his Mavo collaborators placed great emphasis on the visual presentation of the poems in his poetry collection *Shikei senkoku*—and on the collection itself as a physical artifact—it is clear from contemporary accounts that the oral/aural, theatrical, and bodily were also important aspects of Hagiwara's poetics. Hagiwara and his associates gave several dramatic public readings of the poems in *Shikei senkoku*. One observer left the following account of a reading at the Tsukiji Little Theater in November 1925:

When I first opened the pages of *Shikei senkoku*, without even catching the meaning I felt like I was walking through the streets of contemporary Tokyo, and I thought to myself that this wasn't a poetry collection to be read, but rather one to look at. Then, at the Poet's Festival at the Tsukiji Little Theater, after all of the young poets had read their works, Hagiwara and Tsuboi Shigeji jumped up on stage ringing gongs, and proceeded to read—or rather, I should say, shout—the poems from *Shikei senkoku*. At that time, I thought that this wasn't a poetry collection to look at, but rather one to be heard. Certainly, it seemed to suggest something new which was to come.[18]

In fact, Hagiwara's involvement with the stage went beyond the oral performance of poetry. From 1925, he began to perform modern dance under the stage name Fujimura Yukio, following on the work of Mavo leader Murayama Tomoyoshi, who had caused a sensation a year earlier by performing semi-nude modern dances influenced by German Expressionist dance. He also helped organize a regional arts festival in Maebashi in May 1926 featuring dance, music, and drama; and he performed with the anarchist theater group Kaihōza at the Tsukiji Little Theater in October 1927.[19]

In an essay of 1926, Hagiwara summarized his aesthetic project with a call for an "auditorium-like, outdoor-like, advertisement-like literature" (*kaijōteki yagaiteki sendenteki bungaku*). In this essay, Hagiwara attempted to articulate his avant-garde aesthetic in the context of what the Marxist writers were referring to as "massification." Contrasting his own art with the socialist-realist aesthetic of the Marxists, he defended the possibility of a "neo-dadaist" art based on individual rebellion to serve a stimulus for social change. The sentiment of the individual, he argued, when expressed in the most grotesque, shocking, and violent way, can constitute a "fearsome existence" which will itself serve as a "mighty propaganda." At the same time, Hagiwara acknowledged that the Dadaistic art of the past was not in itself sufficient to address the need for a new social art, and urged his fellow artists and poets to seek new ways to unite with the proletarian class.[20]

This essay captured a turning point in Hagiwara's poetic: it was his most coherent exposition of the poetics of *Shikei senkoku*, and yet it marked a heightened awareness of the need to address this art to the issue of class struggle in an age of mass communication. While the essay represented an attempt to explore the possibilities of his avant-garde art as a vehicle of social change, in the end Hagiwara moved away from the *Shikei senkoku* aesthetic and toward a combination of more blatantly propagandistic poetry and direct involvement in extra-literary political action.

This shift in Hagiwara's politics and style was foreshadowed by the break-up of the Mavo group in the fall of 1925. In fact, the publication of *Shikei senkoku* in October of that year turned out to be the Mavo group's final collective project. The group's activities had reached both a climax and a breaking point a month earlier at the second Sanka art exhibition, a joint exhibition of works by Mavoists and other anti-establishment artists held at the Jichi Kaikan assembly hall in Ueno. This heavily attended, heavily reviewed exhibition of over one hundred works represented a triumph of the style of constructivist and dadaistic assemblages (*kōseibutsu*) pioneered by the Mavo artists. Yet conflicts between the Mavoists and non-Mavo contributors to the exhibition exacerbated the considerable tensions already present within the Mavo group itself.

The planning and execution of this event were marred by numerous squabbles between more aesthetically and politically moderate artists outside the Mavo group and the members of the radical anarchist wing of Mavo, some of whom had been excluded from the exhibition altogether. Mavo leader and exhibition organizer Murayama Tomo-yoshi was caught between these two factions, and, dismayed by the increasing polarization, announced his withdrawal from Mavo, effectively ending the group's meteoric two years of activity.[21] After this point Murayama became more intensively involved in the theater, and, by the following year, he had relinquished his eclectic Mavo-period resistance to Marxist ideology and socialist-realist aesthetics to join the Marxist "proletarian arts" movement.[22]

The break-up of Mavo was just one aspect of the increasing polarization in the artistic and literary worlds from the mid- to late 1920s. Another rift which was to effect Hagiwara's career was the breakup of the coalition of Marxist and anarchist writers that had formed around the influential "Proletarian Literature" magazine *Bungei sensen*. In November 1926, at the second meeting of a conference of writers connected with the magazine,[23] the anarchist members were purged from the group, and powerful new members from the Marxist faction were added, including Nakano Shigeharu, Hayashi Fusao, and Kamei Katsuichirō.[24] These events coincided with a general surge in activity in the Marxist camp in Japanese politics, including an increase in strikes and labor conflicts, a new emphasis on Marxist orthodoxy under the influence of theoretician Fukumoto Kazuo, and the reestablishment of the formerly dissolved Japan Communist Party in December 1926.

Following this breakdown in the united front between the Marxists and anarchists, the anarchist camp responded by organizing the Bungei kaihōsha (Literature of Liberation Association) and its journal *Bungei kaihō* in January 1927. Although the masthead of *Bungei kaihō* featured a number of writers from such previous magazines as *Aka to kuro* and *Damu damu* (including Hagiwara, Okamoto Jun, Tsuboi Shigeji, and Ono Tōzaburō), this magazine, unlike the previous ones, explicitly defined itself as the literary organ of an organized anarchist political movement, just as the now purely

Marxist *Bungei sensen* was presented as the literary organ of the communist political movement. In keeping with the newly political tone of the journal, the works that Hagiwara contributed to *Bungei kaihō* differed from his previous contributions to *Aka to kuro* and *Damu damu*, and from the style of *Shikei senkoku*. The following verse, published to coincide with the year's May Day observations, illustrates Hagiwara's attempt to create a doctrinaire, propagandistic anarchist literature:

OUR BLACK FLAG, FLAPPING IN THE MAY DAY PARADE

O Black Flag!
Our Black Flag!
Now we are grasping   The Flag of the proletariat!
Black Flag!

In the morning
We pledged to one another   Underneath the Flag!
Our will is a spear!
We will protect this, Black Flag! . . . [25]

Actually, over the course of 1927, Hagiwara's literary output decreased, while he became increasingly active as a political organizer. These activities apparently included forming a worker's study group in the industrial Kōtō district of Tokyo, and an effort to establish contact with different anarcho-syndicalist activists across the Kantō region. Hagiwara and other members of the Bungei kaihōsha also actively participated in the movement to release the American anarchists Nicola Sacco and Bartolomeo Vanzetti, whose death sentence had provoked international protests; he was among a group of prominent anarchists, which included Ishikawa Sanshirō and Nii Itaru, who were arrested during a protest at the American embassy in August 1927.[26] This year marked the height of Hagiwara's involvement with the anarchist movement in Tokyo, but it was also a year in which the weakness and fractiousness of the anarchist movement also became manifest.

As the real organizing power of the anarchists continued to decline in the face of the burgeoning communist movement, an increasingly bitter rift developed between the anarcho-syndicalists, who advocated gradual social change through practical labor activism, and the so-called pure anarchists, who argued that a nationwide revolution must be sudden and total. In December of 1927, Hagiwara's longtime fellow Tsuboi Shigeji was attacked and seriously wounded by a group of young toughs from the pure anarchist faction, after he published an article in *Bungei kaihō* critical of the conduct of the anarchist movement; it was Hagiwara who carried the wounded Tsuboi back to his home. Following this incident, Tsuboi switched allegiance to the Marxist camp, and the Bungei kaihōsha, to which Hagiwara had devoted a year of activity, was dissolved.[27]

Several of the poems of Hagiwara's *Danpen* comment on the fracture and marginalization experienced by those within the anarchist movement. "Fragment 12," like many of the poems from this collection, contains a strong element of self-exhortation. Its opening two lines give a harrowingly direct description of the anarchists' deteriorating position:

FRAGMENT 12

Yesterday's friends have parted, one by one, and become enemies
Steadily, we become minorities, drawing near to the place designated
    by the majority.
To the howling ones, the clamoring ones, the ones in high places
We bid a silent, wordless farewell.

Knowing neither scorn, nor rebuke, nor praise, we move our world
    into tomorrow.
Today, no one here asks for, or listens to, superfluous words.

While urban destitution and concern over his great-aunt left behind at home may have been the most pressing reasons for Hagiwara's return to rural Gunma, it is not difficult to imagine that disappointment in the state of the anarchist movement within the metropolis contributed to his decision to leave. His decision to abandon Tokyo could thus be interpreted as an acknowledgement of the defeat of his efforts to build an urban-based poetics and politics. Yet this decision also afforded Hagiwara the opportunity to reassess the fundamentals of his poetry and his political thought, and to reapply his poetic and political agenda to an entirely new set of living conditions.

Danpen: Fragments of Self-construction and Self-critique

In the years immediately following his return to rural Gunma in September 1928, Hagiwara continued to work as an organizer for the anarchist movement among groups of workers in the Maebashi area, although the extent of his activities is unclear.[28] He also began to publish brief, epigraphic poems entitled "Danpen" (fragments) in various anarchist journals. These poems were gathered together for Hagiwara's second poetry collection, *Danpen*, published in October 1931 by a small Tokyo printing venture dedicated to the production of books related to the anarchist movement.[29]

Like the poems of *Shikei senkoku*, Hagiwara's *Danpen* reflect an aesthetic vision of reciprocality between poetry and life praxis—poetry as both a product of daily life (*seikatsu*) and an element in the construction of the subjective consciousness that will carry out this life. "In order for one true word to be written," Hagiwara states in the collection's afterword, "there must have been ten times that amount of living (*seikatsu*)." Hagiwara compares the poems in *Danpen* to "scraps of paper which, broom in hand, I have swept out of my daily life"; yet he also makes claims for their constructive role, calling them "nails which I have pounded into my own body, in order to construct myself from today to tomorrow."[30]

Despite the continuity in Hagiwara's conception of poetry as an element of life praxis, the poems of *Danpen* are radically different in style from those of *Shikei senkoku*. Gone are the varied poetic and visual devices of the earlier collection, such as the printing of characters in different sizes and orientations, and the incorporation of lines, bars, *fuseji*, alphabetic and numeric symbols, and graphic art. In the preface of *Shikei senkoku*, Hagiwara had written of his desire to move beyond the individual voice in his poetry to incorporate the varied voices and mechanical noises of the city:

My poem listens to the music inside my private box, but it also listens to the screech of the elevated railroad as it mixes with the noise of the city. It listens to the sound of the printing press, to the sound of my pen scribbling beside it, to the cry of a single insect. Joy, laughter, anger, pleas, screams, and blows: with a momentary fall, they explode, they're reborn; born, they dash forth. . . .[31]

In *Danpen*, the "noise of the city" is shorn away, and the poems no longer reverberate with screams, blows, and explosions. Rather, the voice of the poet dominates, (or often the voice of a unified "we," a plural subject formed by the "I" and the "I"'s anarchist comrades). A spare, straightforward, declarative style replaces the cacophony that sought to capture the varied sounds of the city. While few of the poems of *Danpen* directly depict life in rural Japan, commentators such as Itō Shinkichi have seen the stark form of the poems, stripped of all extraneous elements, as reflecting the harsh exigencies of the rural life to which Hagiwara was re-exposed during the period of their composition.[32]

Shikei senkoku, with its stated program to incorporate everything from "the screech of the elevated railroad" to the "cry of a single insect," gestures toward the idea of totality, toward a fantasy of total artistic representation. The poems of *Danpen*, with their repeated invocation of silence and wordlessness (paradoxical, of course, in a verbal medium), point toward an ideal not of totality, but of efficiency. The fantasy of totally efficient action—an ideal that encompasses both Hagiwara's poetics and his politics in this period—is vividly expressed in the second half of "Fragment 36":

> We know that the bullet, never straying from its path, threads the
>   darkness
>   in a straight line
> Smoothly, soundlessly reaching the place it should strike, it bursts.
> At that time, the bullet first demonstrates its existence
> Until then, it was no more than a clump of lead[33]

Although most, if not all, of the poems of *Danpen* have moved a step away from the formulaic propaganda of a poem such as "Our Black Flag, Flapping in the May Day Parade," it is still possible to read the majority of the collection's poems as statements affirming Hagiwara's intense commitment to the anarchist cause. Indeed, this has been the main approach that critics and literary historians have taken to this text. The critic Nii Itaru, who reviewed the collection for the anarchist journal *Kokushoku sensen*, recognized it as "*Danpen*, which we could call Kyōjirō's anarchist poetry collection" ("*Kyōjirō no museifushugi shishū to mo ieru 'Danpen'* "), and wrote, "The reason our comrade Hagiwara Kyōjirō's collection *Danpen* has such a strong flavor is because it sings of the faith and determination an anarchist must possess. It's because it sings of the white-hot passion and silent iron will, expressed only in action. It's because . . . it hurls out scorn at demagoguery and craftiness and ambitions to power."[34]

Nevertheless, while the poems of the collection do in fact sing of all that Nii mentions, there is also an unmistakable countercurrent of poems that perform, not a profession of faith, but a searching act of autocritique. Such poems betray the contradictions and fissures underlying the poet's political conceptions, suggesting that the political consciousness so defiantly declared in the majority of poems faces the danger of disintegration from within. Again, the issues of individual subjectivity, and the relationship of individual to group, are critical to the construction and possible disintegration of Hagiwara's artistic and political conceptions.

The most central subjective parameters in *Danpen* are those of the individual and the closed circle of anarchist comrades. As Hirai Ken notes in his study of the collection, there is a subtle rivalry between those poems narrated from a position of group subjectivity, employing such plural subject markers as "wareware," "warera," "watashitachi," and "oretachi," and those which express individual subjectivity, employing singular pronouns such as "ore" and "boku."[35] Hirai further suggests a broad schema informing the progression of poems in the collection, moving loosely from poems which envision the victory of anarchists as a group; to those which dramatize the fissures and ruptures within the anarchist group, yet still express the will to a group identity (such as "Fragment 12" above); to those in which the individual finally stands alone. "Fragment 10" stands as an example of the attempt to visualize the victory of anarchists as a group, while in "Fragment 35" the group has split into "you" and "I," who must carry on the struggle in isolation:

FRAGMENT 10

The joy of unequivocal victory
The rising joy which rends our breasts
The shouts of men, like blasts from a terrifying organ

The striking shouts of women, as if launched from a spring
The resounding songs
The windpipes of humanity rising up
Grasping their breasts   dancing   tumbling
Tumbling, like balls of joy
In the shooting, exploding, liberating light
      like the rays of morning sun, burning with bright joy and tears
         of emotion
We will bathe in the light, washing our bodies of all the past
We cannot forget this day
We must not forget that this day will come[36]

FRAGMENT 35

You will walk your own path
I won't meet you for a while
But I'm not going to miss you at all
Today, I have no doubts about my friends
Then again, neither do I have great expectations
Because the thoughts in each of our minds are not light or trivial
Because today we can tell the difference between demagogues and
      true friends[37]

Hirai draws mixed conclusions from his study of subjectivity in *Danpen*. On the one hand, from a humanist point of view he deplores the tendency for the will to group subjectivity to smother all traces of individualism and deny individual self-worth, pointing to the danger inherent in the combination of utopianism and violent fantasy in Hagiwara's vision of the subject-group's future victory.[38] Yet neither can he give a positive evaluation to the subject's final emergence as a solitary and independent voice. Rather, he suggests that given the degree of identification of the individual with the group of anarchist comrades expressed earlier, the dissolution of this group represents not the healthy emergence of the individual, but rather the "cracking apart" (*bunretsu*) of the self, which has no positive basis other than in group identity.[39]

In addition to the problem of the individual's identity vis-à-vis the group of anarchist fellows, there remain two more troublesome questions inherent in the poems of *Danpen*: the identification of an enemy, and the relationship between the politically conscious subject (whether singular or plural) and the "masses."[40] To refer to the language of Japanese anarchist Ōsugi Sakae, if modern society is defined by the "reality of subjugation" (*seifuku no jijitsu*), there must be both a class of the subjugated (*hiseifukusha / hiseifuku kaikyū*) and of the oppressors (*seifukusha / seifuku kaikyū*).[41] In order for Hagiwara's ideal of totally efficient political action to be realized, both the subjugated and the oppressors must be clearly identifiable. In other words, the oppressors must be vulnerable to revolutionary action, and the oppressed must be capable of political awakening, or at least the desire to be freed from their subjugation. To cite the metaphor used in "Fragment 36," the anarchist's bullet must directly reach "the place it should strike" and explode (*ataru beki basho ni sumiyaka ni todoite haneru*).

Yet while a number of victims are described in *Danpen*, the identity of the oppressor—the target for the bullet to strike—is never clarified. On the contrary, a poem such as "Fragment 25" raises doubts that the oppressor can be identified at all:

> I knew that there was a gigantic entity which could not be crushed
>   until the end
> Now I'm convinced that it's not something on the outside, but
>   something between myself and ourselves
> We can try to threaten it, drag it around,
> Strike it, scatter it like ashes, but now
> I'm convinced it will not disappear.[42]

If the enemy, a seemingly "gigantic entity" (*kyōdai naru jittai*), is actually in the spaces "between myself and ourselves" (*ware to warera no aida ni aru*), then there is scant hope that even the most efficient bullet can slay this enemy. This single, isolated poetic fragment reveals the doubts that were apparently preying upon Hagiwara's fundamental political conceptions, and strikes a major blow at the positivity that the other poems in the collection are struggling to assert.

Another dilemma in *Danpen* is the relationship of the poet, or the poet's immediate political circle, to the masses of everyday people. In one of his most self-critical poems, Hagiwara appears to look back on his involvement in the theatrical mode as a form of propaganda, and questions the relationship between the consciousness of the "vanguard" on stage and the "masses" to whom they supposedly appealed:

FRAGMENT 51

The flag mounted on a shining spear, waving red on the podium—
        that was a fine sight
The demagogues danced fervently on the stage
The gathered crowds were silent
We heard the foolish applause and cheers pass over our heads
But after the crowds dissipated
We felt the gloom, that we'd touched nothing in their posture or their
        words or their horizons
When the players and the audience go their separate ways
They remain perfect strangers
The legs of those returning to their own harsh lives
The legs striving to overcome, struggling to bear up
Are different from the hairy shanks on stage, playing the play of
        ambition[43]

While Hagiwara may have had doubts about anarchist propaganda even while in Tokyo, this poem suggests a perspectival shift from that of the "vanguard" on stage to that of the "masses" in the audience. This perspectival shift may be at least partly attributable to his having separated from the core of the leftist intelligentsia in Tokyo and moved to rural Gunma, where he was surrounded every day by the "harsh lives" of local farmers and laborers.

As a part of this perspectival shift, there is a tendency in *Danpen* to reinscribe anarchism not as a political agenda that an intellectual vanguard can promote, but as a natural force that opposes subjugation by irrepressible instinct:

FRAGMENT 26

We rejoice in the fact that we are opponents to those in power,
        and we are utterly valueless to them
We are valueless because we don't recognize their values or
        their order
We obstruct where they want to move, we offer them
        no compensation
No matter how they try to trump us with a final card
From the darkness, from the earth, our buds extend

They sprout up, overcoming bricks or concrete or rocks or steel
Because we don't stand on privileges or interests—
That which is alive, lives
This is a principle that needs no theory[44]

While this poem is still narrated from the point of view of a "we," the metaphor of multiple subterranean shoots suggests that the locus of this "we" has moved away from a political vanguard and toward the vital energy of "the masses," which is closely connected to the earth. A more complex exploration of the same idea can be found in "Fragment 17":

For a moment, the few outlets have been stopped by your plugs
But the water will only change its course
It's in the nature of the water's source: its flow cannot be stopped
Squeezing its pressure into the very capillaries of the earth
The rising water can be halted by no one
Moment by moment, the interior naturally collapses
Standing above the water's source, it is we who sink, moment by moment,
    into the earth[45]

Reading this poem as a political allegory, the poem's first line acknowledges the temporary defeat of the anarchist movement by the unspecified interlocutor "you" (*omaetachi*)—presumably, the forces of political repression. However, the irrepressible anti-authoritarian force will move back to its underground source—corresponding, arguably, to "the masses"—where, unobserved, it will grow in both scale and pressure.

The final line reintroduces the "we" (which can be identified with the politically conscious poet and the anarchist vanguard), and offers an ironic twist on the poem's allegory. As the unstoppable pressure builds among the masses, rather than being forced up to a position of prominence, the poetic "we" sinks further into the earth. In a positive light, the "vanguard" may be tactically concealing itself and reconnecting with the "masses" at society's vital source. Yet, in sinking moment by moment into the earth, there is clearly the possibility that the poetic subject (the "vanguard" consciousness) will not be merely submerged, but completely annihilated.

The poems of *Danpen*, then, are attempts to capture moments of self-exhortation and self-construction, or the self-willed girding of the poet's political consciousness. Yet they also trace a course of self-questioning and self-critique, revealing the fissures of doubt and contradiction underlying the poet's political conceptions. Indeed, the very insistence on self-exhortation and self-construction can have the contradictory effect of suggesting an underlying vulnerability:

FRAGMENT 27

> Clamp all sentimentalism and vanity with the brake-gears of your
>   willpower and passion
> Your fast-beating heart, your flesh, palpitating, vibrating with the joy of
>   tomorrow's victory—
> Make this heart as strong and fiery as a boiler!
> When you push yourself to the limit
> Believing in yourself, believing in the world—then you can be born in
>   tomorrow's world
> If not, all your passion and willpower will become remorse, your body
>   filled with abscesses
> Like a bee hive, riddled with the holes of nihilism

While the first five lines would make this poem a rousing call to inner strength and positivity, these lines risk being overshadowed by the strength of the final image, which envisions the poet's body riddled "like a bee hive" "with the holes of nihilism."

Hagiwara's Agrarian Turn

The year following the publication of *Danpen*, Hagiwara's poetic career took a decisive turn with the publication of a new journal, *Kuropotokin o chūshin ni shita geijutsu no kenkyū* (*Art Studies Centering on Kropotkin*). Hagiwara was the sole editor and publisher of this journal, which ran from issue one in June 1932 to issue four in December 1932. This journal featured two new components of Hagiwara's work as a writer: a new style of relatively lengthy poems focused on life in rural Japan; and a four-part study of the Russian anarchist Piotr Kropotkin (1842–1921), who had exerted a long-standing influence on Japanese anarchism and whose complete works in Japanese translation had been published under the supervision of Ishikawa Sanshirō beginning in 1929.

After a decade of conflict among his peers as to the nature of political transformation and the role of art in transforming society, the series of essays on Kropotkin demonstrates Hagiwara's earnest desire to re-engage the fundamentals of anarchist thought and to reassess the value of art and literature in building a future society. While Kropotkin's writings themselves contain no sustained forays into art theory, Hagiwara's essays are attempts to pull together Kropotkin's various isolated statements on artists and writers and to distill from Kropotkin's general social views the confirmation for his own belief that art and literature are a natural expression of people's will to freedom and are thus essential to both revolutionary and post-revolutionary society.[46]

In addition to serving as the self-published forum for Hagiwara's theoretical examinations, *Kuropotokin o chūshin ni shita geijutsu no kenkyū* represented his attempt to overcome his geographic isolation and build a new network of rural poets, analogous to the extensive network of avant-garde poets and artists he had helped to foster in Tokyo. While a few of Hagiwara's fellows in Tokyo, such as Ono Tōzaburō, contributed to the journal, most of the contributors were little-known young poets from rural Gunma Prefecture. Indeed, Hagiwara's network of rural poets extended beyond Gunma, including contributors from Chiba and Shizuoka prefectures, and as far away as Ehime, Akita, and Hokkaido.[47]

Although *Kuropotokin o chūshin ni shita geijutsu no kenkyū* brought together a diverse group of contributors from the Japanese provinces, the actual editing and publication of the journal was a solo effort, in contrast to previous journals in which Hagiwara had participated. Due to lack of financial resources and access to printing facilities, the rough, handmade physical appearance of the final product differed markedly from professionally printed poetry journals produced in the metropolis. In fact, Hagiwara himself cut all the paper for the journal and hand-wrote (or rather hand-carved) each page on a wax stencil; this stencil was then hand-rolled on a so-called "gari-ban" mimeographic press. The initial results were apparently a disappointment: the second issue carried a "want ad" from Hagiwara acknowledging, with a typical mixture of sarcasm and self-deprecating humor, his readers' complaints about the nearly illegible quality of the reproduction, and offering to buy a new, better quality, hand press.[48]

Hagiwara's poems from this period evince a new concern for the working and living conditions in rural Japan. His best-remembered poem of this type is "Mōroku zukin" ("Headscarves"), which he published in the first issue of *Kuropotokin o chūshin ni shita geijutsu no kenkyū*. This poem describes the temporary winter departure of a middle-aged farmer, surrounded by a close-knit community of neighbors who have gathered to see him off. The poem's scenario invokes the practice of *dekasegi* (going out to earn money), in which rural residents would leave home, often during the off-season, to earn money in the city and reduce their burden on the family budget; this practice increased during periods of rural crisis, such as that being experienced in the early 1930s. Indeed, the preface of the poem elaborates, "to call it [the farmer's departure] *dekasegi* would be too optimistic," implying that the farmer's chances of actually accumulating money in the city are slim—the best he can hope for is to reduce by one the number of mouths for his wife to feed.

The long lines and regional dialect employed in the poem make it quite difficult to translate effectively:

———*The 'old man' leaves home. It would be too optimistic to say he's "going out to make money."*———

"Take care now. . ."
"You take care . . ."
Surrounded by the headscarves of the gathered neighbors, the fifty-year-old man changes out of his farming clothes, taking off the quilted gloves which hang on a string from his neck, and pulling his seldom-worn vest out of the closet.

In the yard, resting a moment from their threshing, the neighborhood women whisper, often falling into silence. Their heads, too, are covered with thick dark scarves.

Inside the home, the distressed wife and children gather by the light of the paper doors, by the side of the cold hearth. Telling him to "come home soon," through their sobs.

The 'old man' pokes his sunburnt, bearded face out for a moment to mutter assent, without looking at their faces. He tucks in the back of his kimono, which clings to his farmer's underpants.

"Take care now . . ."
"You take care . . ."
When the 'old man' goes out to the yard, the headscarves of men and women surround him.
"We'll look after them for you"
"We'll keep an eye on them"
With these words, the women pat him on the back, pledging to themselves to take as best care of his family as they can . . .[49]

A number of Hagiwara's commentators and former associates, such as Itō Shinkichi, Akiyama Kiyoshi, and Tsuboi Shigeji, place the poems of this period, including "Mōroku zukin" and "Kikoku nikki" ("Diary of a Homecoming"), among Hagiwara's very best works.[50] Yet it is difficult to view these poems on a formal level as anything but a return to the style of Naturalist prose and so-called People's Poetry against which Hagiwara and his associates at *Aka to kuro* had rebelled ten years before. And while the above commentators have praised the "realism" of Hagiwara's new style, there remains more than a hint of the "sentimentalism" that Tsuboi had identified in Hagiwara's earlier efforts at an agrarian poetry.

The question of the literary merit of these works aside, it is clear that Hagiwara showed a renewed interest during this period in the problems of the farm economy and everyday rural life. This change of thematic focus was shortly accompanied by a shift of ideological orientation as well. Personal associates testify that from about the year 1933 (the year he ceased publication of *Kuropotokin o chūshin ni shita geijutsu no kenkyū*), Hagiwara immersed himself in the writings of Gondō Seikyō, the classical scholar and former advocate of imperial expansion who had become one of the leading ideologues of *nōhonshugi*, or agrarian nationalism.[51]

While this interest in *nōhonshugi* certainly bespeaks a major shift of ideological orientation, the viewpoint advocated by Gondō actually held many similarities to the agrarian anarchist vision of village self-government advanced by figures such as Ishikawa Sanshirō and, to a certain extent, Hagiwara himself. Both ideologies were based on a suspicion of grandiose political systems (including Marxism) and a view of rural moral and social values as the proper basis for a future society; both ideologies articulated a primary goal of village cooperation and self-government. Furthermore, Gondō's writings included vociferous attacks on militarism, monopoly capitalism, and the form of "Prussian-style" nationalism that had shaped the modern Japanese nation-state; these critiques, too, suggested a basic sympathy with anarchist thought.

Despite these similarities, however, Gondō's ideology departed from anarchism in its vision of society as *shashoku*, a term which, according to historian Thomas Havens, referred both to early Japanese society under the Shinto agricultural deities, and to a future restoration of society into "self-governing units beneath a single ruling institution, the imperial throne":[52]

Gondō Seikyō's nationalism stood on the twin pillars of village communalism and local self-rule, both of which were venerable themes in Japanese popular thought. From these images of a harmonious *shashoku* and an autonomous system of local government, supposedly found in Japan's ancient past, he constructed a critique of modern centralized rule, capitalist production, and urban life which both rejected the main trends of modernization and reaffirmed the Japanese nation and *kokutai* [the 'national polity' with the Emperor at its head].[53]

Gondō's agrarianism thus differed from anarchism in several key respects: it discouraged any manifestations of individualism, and it allowed no place for rural class conflict, but instead held that "landlords and tenants were not antagonists but customary members of a historical hierarchy that permitted village solidarity." Furthermore, it stressed the uniqueness of the Japanese people "as an ethnonationality group which possessed the distinctive customs of self-rule and the *shashoku*, based on village agriculture and a deep faith in the gods of Shinto."[54] The most crucial difference of Gondō's thought from anarchism, however, was the central place it afforded the emperor as the benevolent spiritual and temporal ruler of the *shashoku*. Hence for Hagiwara to countenance the views of Gondō Seikyō marked a major step away from the fundamental anarchist opposition to the imperial institution.

Hagiwara's Late Works and the Problem of *Tenkō*

Hagiwara's attraction to the thought of Gondō Seikyō is significant because it provides a possible transition between the poems of

1932–1934 that thematize the problems of rural poverty, and a group of poems among his final works that show unmistakable support for Japanese nationalism and imperial expansion abroad. As early as 1935, Hagiwara published the poem "Achira" ("Over There"), which, four years after the Manchurian Incident and two years before the outbreak of full-scale war with China, described an advance of Japanese forces on the Asian continent:

> In the middle of the peeled-off sun, the disheveled faces of your Father and Mother are staring right at you.
> Saying "You're a soldier of the Imperial Army!"
>
> The deliberately-moving army suddenly advances into the smoke
>
> Again, the cries of "banzai" rise up
>
> New smoke crawls across the horizon
>
> A single horizon swings around in a circle
>
> At its far edge, the giant of the Imperial Nation bares its teeth, raises its arms, and stands tall[55]

After this poem was written in 1935, Hagiwara's output as a writer dropped precipitously, with almost no works being published over the next two years. His health also declined severely during this time; he developed a painful and debilitating stomach ulcer, which he exacerbated by continuing to drink saké to ease his stomach pains. Anemia resulting from this ulcer was to cause his death in November 1938, at the age of 39.

Following the Marco Polo Bridge incident of July 1937 and the so-called China incident marking the beginning of full-scale war between Japan and China, Hagiwara wrote two more poems in apparent support of imperialism: "Hokushi hōmen" ("The North China Front," published January 1938) and "Ajia ni kyojin ari" ("A Giant Is in Asia," published December 1938). The first of these carries, in addition to an evocation of heroic warfare, an idealistic affirmation of Japanese cultural tutelage in China:

[. . .]

This morning I saw a photograph of the children of North China
　　studying Japanese
Look! The children, properly lined up to their desks, are stretching up,
　　raising their hands to answer a question!

Oh Continent! Oh children of North China!
Study your Japanese!
And then, together with us, study the world![56]

While these two poems would have been sufficient to establish
Hagiwara's pro-imperialist stance, it was the poem "Ajia ni kyojin
ari," published in the major poetry journal *Serupan* (*Serpent*) just as
Hagiwara's poetic peers were receiving word of his premature death,
which shocked many of his former comrades with its pro-imperial
rhetoric, and came to symbolize for the anarchist-affiliated poetry
community the problem of Hagiwara's ideological about-face:

A giant of ancient times, from the world of myth
Today flies across the mire of the Asian Continent, with a halberd
　　as his wings.

If he finds a gate of precipitous stones, he will surely open it
If he finds a mighty river, he will surely cross it

Even if the bloodless fields shake and rumble
At the race's destination, across the mountains and fields,
He will crush what must be crushed
He will build what must be built
The giant will realize this great ambition.

Now, in autumn's chilly wind, though the voice of the Ta-pieh
　　Mountains is hushed,
　　　　though the waves of the Yangtze stir,
We know more surely than ever the way of our ancestral vocation

The East, seething, will become a new East
The World will tremble before its philosophy
The pages of History will double
Each one of us, as fresh pages, will cultivate this New World.

Autumn deepens on the Japanese Islands,
The scarlet maple leaves and chrysanthemums abound
　　　　Even if soaked by the ocean spray,
The giant, steadfast, will grasp his halberd, and gaze at the

race's progress
Behold him now: seated at the Orient's source, amid the
mountain mists;
Standing, gazing forth, with the spirit of the Ancestral Gods![57]

What may have shocked Hagiwara's erstwhile anarchist comrades was not so much his affirmation of Japanese military and cultural imperialism, which had already been established in the previous two poems, but the conservative language which Hagiwara employed to express this affirmation—language which speaks of the progress of the Japanese race (*minzoku*), of the "ancestral vocation" (*sogyō*) and "Ancestral Gods" (*ōmi oyagami*), and even invokes, through the image of the chrysanthemum, the emperor himself.

This poem was reportedly the subject of informal discussions at the memorial gathering of about thirty of Hagiwara's friends, family members, and literary associates held in Tokyo. It has remained a touchstone for postwar writings that try to account for Hagiwara's poetic and political trajectory. Of course, Hagiwara was not the only formerly leftist poet or public intellectual to relinquish his former ideology and embrace Japanese imperialism—on the contrary, by the outbreak of the war with America, nearly all leftist writers had either embraced the imperial cause or been forced into silence. The widespread phenomenon of leftist ideological "conversion" has even engendered its own name: *tenkō,* literally, a change of orientation. Yet Hagiwara's case was dramatic because it seemed to occur so suddenly and whole-heartedly, because it occurred relatively early in the wartime period, and because Hagiwara's premature death and his sparse poetic and critical output during his final years left no explanation or theoretical underpinnings for his ideological shift. The postwar analysis of the phenomenon of *tenkō* may shed light on Hagiwara's enigmatic embrace of imperialism, even as his case is acknowledged as distinct.

Sociologist Patricia G. Steinhoff, who has studied the phenomenon extensively, defines *tenkō* as "an act of renouncing an ideological commitment under pressure."[58] The term first came into widespread use in the year 1933, following the defection of two high-level leaders of the Japan Communist Party, Sano Manabu and Nabeyama Sadachika. This defection came after a massive police crackdown on tens of thousands of suspected Communist Party members and sympathizers, and a major public trial of nearly two hundred Party leaders, including Sano and Nabeyama—a crackdown which invoked the legal authority of the Peace Preservation Law of 1925 (*Chian iji hō*), criminalizing allegiance to organizations which advocated abolition of private property or alteration of the *kokutai*.[59] Citing misgivings about Party doctrine and organization, and particularly about the control of the Japan Communist Party by the Comintern in Moscow, Sano and Nabeyama produced a joint statement detailing their *tenkō*, or shift in orientation, and renouncing their Party allegiances; this statement was then circulated by prison officials to nearly 1,800 Party members in custody, who were urged to produce their own disavowals.[60]

The Justice Ministry's policy of eliciting public disavowals of Communist Party allegiance met with astonishing success: within a month after Sano and Nabeyama's statement, 548 others had formerly renounced their Party ties, and two-thirds to three-fourths of all Peace Preservation Law violators had committed *tenkō* within a few years. Soon after this initial wave of defections, a number of writers identified with the Proletarian Literature movement wrote works describing their own experience of *tenkō* and exploring the personal and political issues involved. Among these writers were a number of Hagiwara's former associates, including Murayama Tomoyoshi and Takami Jun.[61]

The widespread phenomenon of *tenkō,* and the general inability of the Japanese left to sustain its resistance to nationalism and imperialism, has proved to be a major issue for modern Japanese intellectual history. The *tenkō* phenomenon has been the subject of numerous postwar analyses, most notably that of the group Shisō no kagaku kenkyūkai, formed under the leadership of social critic Tsurumi Shunsuke. Hagiwara Kyōjirō is one of two figures whose experiences are introduced as *"tenkō* by anarchists" in an article by Akiyama Kiyoshi for this group's authoritative multivolume study *Kyōdō kenkyū: tenkō.*[62]

Hagiwara's case differs significantly from that of the figures mentioned above, however, in that his so-called *tenkō* did not involve the renunciation of ties to an organized political party such as the JCP, and that it did not come after an extended period in prison. If *tenkō* is held to involve the renunciation of "an ideological commitment under pressure," then to determine whether this is an appropriate conceptual rubric for Hagiwara's political transformation, we must address the question of under how much pressure, and under what kinds of pressure, this transformation occurred. In broader terms, how can we account for his abrupt swing from the intense commitment to the anarchist cause proclaimed in so many of the poems of *Danpen*, to the nationalist, imperialist rhetoric of "Ajia ni kyojin ari"?

While Hagiwara was never subjected to lengthy imprisonment, it cannot be said that he was subject to no pressure from government officials to curtail his anarchist activities. Former acquaintances recall Hagiwara's home being watched by detectives of the special higher police, i.e., those assigned to "thought crimes" (*shisōhan*), at various times from Hagiwara's first return to the Maebashi area in 1927 until his death in 1938.[63] This surveillance reached a peak in 1934, as preparations were under way in Maebashi for a grand review of the army, involving the Emperor, his family, advisors, and top military brass. At this time, a detective was assigned to watch Hagiwara around the clock. In fact, the authorities nearly forced him to leave the prefecture during the event, only desisting after the intercession of a pair of local journalists, who found prominent community members willing to act as guarantors (*hoshōnin*) for the poet, and after arrangements were made for him to be permanently employed at a Maebashi book company.[64]

After this episode, Hagiwara was arrested but not charged during a nationwide round-up of anarchists in October 1937, when the Justice Ministry moved to widen its successful application of the Peace Preservation Law to dissident groups outside the Japan Communist Party. At this juncture, the already beleaguered Anarchist Party folded, as well as the Kaihō bunka renmei (Liberation Culture Alliance), the only anarchist organization to which Hagiwara still had ties.[65]

Beyond this direct surveillance and harassment by members of the thought police, Hagiwara also faced the intangible pressure of attempting to sustain, and act upon, his political beliefs in a setting still dominated by the conservatism of rural society. Itō Shinkichi, a young anarchist sympathizer and friend of Hagiwara who also moved back from Tokyo to the Maebashi area in the early 1930s, gives the following description of the situation:

As I mentioned before, at that time [1933–34] the Proletarian Literature movement was rapidly being forced into a very difficult position. Any attempt to resist these conditions and do [political] work in the rural villages would not only be followed closely by police, but would attract unwanted attention from everyone around. Even the slightest movement would attract notice. When "ideology" (*shisō*) moved to the countryside, the eyes of the world were all around, and it was difficult to raise your voice. You could push forward your ideology under great strain, or you could disappear into the daily life (*seikatsu*) of the people all around you. Hagiwara was certainly placed in such a position, and as he burrowed into the life of those around him, his ideology faced the crisis of self-dismemberment. At the very least, his ideas of rural self-government imperceptibly began to change.[66]

While the long-term psychological effects of police repression should not be discounted, the most compelling explanations for Hagiwara's ideological reorientation may be found in his individual isolation and his desire to find a connection to "the daily life of the people all around" him—issues which were already thematized in the poems of *Danpen*. While the specific circumstances of Hagiwara's situation differed from those of the imprisoned Communists' *tenkō*, the underlying issue of interpersonal connection suggests a significant parallel.

In her study of Communist *tenkō*, Steinhoff argues that such reorientations typically were not the result of the struggle between two competing ideologies, but rather "an internal struggle between a commitment to a particular abstract ideology and some other emotional tie which came to be more and more salient to the individual."[67] She identifies four different types of emotional ties which would come to take priority over loyalty to the Communist Party and its ideology: a sense of loyalty to particular persons (thus explaining the tendencies of subordinates within the Communist hierarchy to follow the *tenkō* of their leaders); the priority of family ties; a strong sense of national and racial identity as a Japanese; and a reevaluation among spiritually or artistically inclined prisoners of the priority of individual identity and artistic integrity over abstract political principles—a "spiritual *tenkō*" crisis often precipitated by the fear of death in prison.[68] Prison officials consciously manipulated these emotional issues in their efforts to extract statements of *tenkō* from Communist prisoners, exposing them to the isolation of solitary confinement and the fear of torture, disease, and death, and then using pressure from concerned family members or apostate ex-Communist leaders to induce an ideological change of heart.

While Hagiwara's case does not fit neatly into any ready-made pattern, we can find evidence for each of the issues enumerated by Steinhoff as playing a role in Hagiwara's ideological reorientation during the 1930s. First of all, rather than a personal loyalty to political comrades facilitating Hagiwara's "*tenkō*," it is the feelings of isolation, betrayal, and disgust with factional infighting, amply recorded in *Danpen*, which may have contributed to his move away from his former anarchist comrades and his search for new social and political affiliations. A deepening concern with family and home life can be also found in numerous poems of *Danpen*. In fact, the only contemporary reviewer to read the poems of the *Danpen* period against the grain, not as anarchist propaganda but as a move away from anarchism, pointed to the emergence of "domestic poetry" (*kanaishi*) in Hagiwara's oeuvre, and presciently suggested that this "domestic poetry" would extend in the future to "ethnic poetry" (*minzokushi*) and on to "nationalist poetry" (*kokuminshi*).[69]

While Steinhoff identifies "spiritual *tenkō*" as a particularly salient experience for writers and artists, such a "spiritual *tenkō*" could not be the same for Hagiwara and the Communists, since the aspiration for individual freedom and artistic expression that drove some *tenkō* prisoners away from the Communist Party's policy of subordination of art to politics was already a primary basis for Hagiwara's justification for his affiliation with anarchism over Marxism. Nevertheless, while such interpretations will remain speculative, some commentators have suggested that a kind of spiritual crisis precipitated Hagiwara's embrace of imperialism, pointing to a deepening "nihilism" and awareness of death in such late works as "Tani" (Valley) from 1935.[70]

Hagiwara had parted ways with the already splintering network of anarchist and avant-garde colleagues in Tokyo, and was placed in a situation of relative literary and political isolation in rural Japan; moreover, he was faced with the reality of persistent surveillance and the evisceration of the broader leftist movement. In this context, it would seem that his "*tenkō*," if such we may call it, was the answer to his search for a new basis of connection between the self and society. In place of an identification with a select group of anarchist comrades, Hagiwara attempted to forge an ideological connection to the Japanese race, or *minzoku*. Indeed, he embraced the concept of *minzoku* in its full imperialist articulation as a race with an expansionist historical mission, whose uniqueness was predicated on its relationship to its ancestors, Shinto gods, and sovereign emperor.

As can be seen in his early theoretical statement on "the power of the self" (*jiga no ken'i*), Hagiwara's writing evinced a sympathy with the faith in the primacy of individualism upheld by a wide variety of Japanese intellectuals, from Humanists such as Mushakōji Saneatsu to fellow anarchists such as Ōsugi Sakae, whose ethical, political, and aesthetic embrace of individual rebellion resonated strongly in Hagiwara's work. Indeed, we can detect in many of Hagiwara's poems an attraction to heroic individual action, whether it be the outsized truculence of the "armored coil," the mysterious and powerful agency of the "one man" striding across Hibiya, or the giant in Asia.

However, despite this attraction to the hero, we can also see in Hagiwara's writing a tendency that subverts the ideology of both the rational independent subject that was the basis of Enlightenment thought and of the Romantic individual who will stand apart from society in solitary vision and action. Instead, even his heroic figures typically possess complex, alloyed subjectivities: the "armored coil" is an amalgamation of the poet and the city, man and machine; the "one man" of Hibiya seems to be both a constituent of this locus of Japanese modernity and a threat to it; while the giant in Asia is less an individual than a personification of the Japanese race. Moreover, we can see the individual assume many guises and disguises in Hagiwara's poems: strategically anonymous in Hibiya; multiplied, dispersed, encrypted, and extended across various cybernetic paths of information exchange—poetic, capitalist, and political—in "Advertising Tower"; or pushed underground toward the vital communal source of popular resistance in "Fragment 17" of *Danpen*. In his poems as well as his theoretical writings, Hagiwara consistently sought new ways to understand and imaginatively construct an intersubjective relation between what he termed the "self" and the "society-self." In examining this search, we can observe substantial continuities as well as differences across his experience of "ideological reorientation."

CONCLUSION

Japanese modernist and avant-garde literatures emerged as centrifugal elements at a time of cultural and political consolidation. Against a powerful logic of linguistic standardization undergirded by the ideology of *genbun itchi* and extended by linguistic reforms in the print industry and the establishment of standard speech protocols in the new medium of radio, modernist and avant-garde texts experimented with linguistic heterogeneity in ways that explicitly challenged *genbun itchi*. As the rapidly expanding print, film, and broadcasting organs took shape as "mass media" which sold a "mass culture" product to a wide swath of society conceptualized as "the masses," modernist and avant-garde writers and artists organized themselves into various urban subcultures who alternately criticized and celebrated the products of mass culture while often struggling with ways to engage "the masses" with their own works.

The dynamic of centripetal versus centrifugal cultural power which distinguishes the relationship between avant-garde urban subcultures and the organs of mainstream media played itself out in a different way in the cultural and political tension between the city and the country. Thus, to take the example of Hagiwara Kyōjirō, despite the dramatic difference in context and content between his work for the urban avant-garde journal *Damu damu* and his production of the agrarian anarchist journal *Kuropotokin o chūshin ni shita geijutsu no kenkyū*, there remained a continuity in both of these projects insofar as they defined themselves against the perceived cultural hegemony of the *bundan*, *shidan*, and mainstream journalism. This structure of hegemony and counter-hegemony may partly explain the close association between Japanese avant-garde art and literature and anarchist politics and theory.

It would be a mistake, however, to imagine that the relation between mass culture and modernism was strictly one of opposition. The organs of mass media were quick to seize upon the new themes of "modern" urban life that were thrown into focus by modernist art and literature. Mainstream literary journals, film studios, and advertising agencies also readily incorporated stylistic elements of modernist and avant-garde art and writing, such as those pioneered by the Mavo artists' group, the "Dadaist" and "anarchist" contributors to *Damu damu*, the prose stylists of the Shinkankaku-ha, or such independent-minded young writers as Hayashi Fumiko. Moreover, many of these artists and writers engaged with the organs of mass media quite directly, even while maintaining ties to their modernist and avant-garde subcultures.

In fact, some of the most dramatic interwar successes of the major publishing houses and film studios in mass-marketing and cross-promoting their products came with modernist-influenced works that thematized "modern" urban life. For example, two of the hit movies of 1929 were *Ikeru ningyō* (*A Living Doll*), filmed for Nikkatsu studios by Uchida Tomu and based on a novel (which had already been successfully adapted as a *shingeki* play) by the leftist Shinkankaku-ha writer Kataoka Teppei; and *Tokai kōkyōgaku* (*City Symphony*), directed by Mizoguchi Kenji and based on a novel collectively authored by Kataoka Teppei, Asahara Rokurō, Hayashi Fusao, and Okada Saburō.[1]

Meanwhile, in the same year, the title song to another successful Mizoguchi film, *Tōkyō kōshin kyoku* (*Tokyo March*), was a sensational hit in the field of popular music. The film was based on a story serialized in the popular *Kingu* (*King*) magazine by *bundan* kingpin Kikuchi Kan. The lyrics for the title song, penned by Saijō Yaso, were a kaleidoscopic inventory of words, locations, and fleeting romantic situations associated with Tokyo's "modern life."[2] As a promotional effort, one thousand free copies of the record were distributed to bars and cafés throughout Tokyo, and sales eventually totaled a record-breaking 250,000 disks.[3]

Hayashi Fumiko's *Hōrōki*, her "poetry diary" (*uta nikki*) of modern urban life, was being serialized in *Nyonin geijutsu* at the same time as the above novels, songs, plays, and films were before the public. The commercial success of Hayashi's novel when published as a book a year later reflects the same public attentiveness to issues of urban life—and receptivity to modernist techniques—that greeted Mizoguchi and Uchida's films. As I have argued in Chapters 2 and 3, however, *Hōrōki* was more than another modernistic mass-cultural phenomenon, but was itself a personal-national history of the development of mass culture, and a commentary on the nature of Japanese modernity. In this work, Hayashi explored the relationship between mass culture and the formation of individual subjectivity; similarly, she probed the relationship of metropole to province, creating a protagonist who is constantly moving between these two poles. At this stage in her career, Hayashi can be viewed as an active and creative intermediary between the avant-garde subculture in which she had immersed herself as a poet, and the institutions of mass media into which she would soon be absorbed.

Hagiwara Kyōjirō's temperament was more extreme: having early established an anti-*bundan* stance, he showed little interest in practical collaboration with capitalist "mass culture," unlike some visual artists and designers also affiliated with the Mavo group. Nevertheless, although his poetry never achieved a broad popular success, an *imagination* of the masses and the possibilities of mass media was a key component of Hagiwara's work from the mid-1920s. The poem "Kōkokutō!" from *Shikei senkoku*, which imagined the poem/poet as a text-emitting "advertising tower," attests to Hagiwara's keen awareness of a transformation in the mode of being of artist, artwork, and audience in the new age of mechanical production and reproduction. Likewise, his call for an "auditorium-like, outdoor-like, advertisement-like literature" was an attempt to envision a mass art that was neither capitalist entertainment product nor formulaic Marxist propaganda.

Like Hayashi, Hagiwara was a provincial native operating in an urban cultural milieu, and was keenly aware of the question of the metropole's cultural hegemony over provincial Japan. In contrast to Hayashi, however, who explored the cultural interpenetration of metropole and province in *Hōrōki*, Hagiwara tended to view country and city as irreconcilable cultural rivals, and a commitment to one seemed to contravene a commitment to the other. Thus he abruptly dropped his call for a literature of "to the village!" in 1923 to develop the style of *Shikei senkoku* and solidify his position of leadership in the urban avant-garde; his reversion to the cause of agrarian poetry ten years later was equally absolute.

Despite their differences, Hagiwara and Hayashi's works share a common focus on the dynamics of centripetal and centrifugal cultural power, and a common concern for the relationship between mass culture and individual subjectivity. Furthermore, we can identify in the works of both authors a tension between a desire to assert a strong individual subjectivity and a contravening tendency for the individual to be absorbed or dispersed into various forms of mass subjectivity. Thus, in Hayashi's *Hōrōki*, in the context of an active interwar feminist movement that was seeking to affirm women's positions as speaking subjects, we can detect a narrative tension between a feminist imperative to assert the narrator-protagonist's identity as a writer, with her own voice as a cultural producer, and a contrary impulse to identify the protagonist as a protean avatar of the masses, and to explore the formation of her identities as a consumer.

In Hagiwara's *Shikei senkoku*, we find a similar tension between a desire to assert individual subjectivity as a locus for social rebellion, as per the early political-cultural theory of anarchist Ōsugi Sakae, and a contrary movement toward a more complex, dispersed, and anonymous subjectivity. This latter movement can be read as a response both to the treacherous, politically repressive space of the modern city, full of "endless pitfalls and burials" ("Hibiya"), and to the newly disembodied, mechanical, and dispersed nature of artist and artwork in the age of mass media ("Kōkokutō!"). In Hagiwara's later works, we see both a lingering individualism reinforced by circumstances of social isolation, and a contrary impulse for the individual subject to adhere strongly to various forms of group identity, whether the group of anarchist comrades, the rural masses, or the Japanese race (*minzoku*).

In the previous chapter, I have traced how Hagiwara moved from the style of *Shikei senkoku* to a poetry of anarchist propaganda in the late 1920s, through the poems of *Danpen* (which, although they eschew the headlong avant-gardism of *Shikei senkoku*, still embody a certain pared-down modernism), to the technically conservative agrarian poems of his later years. Hayashi Fumiko also began to distance herself from the radically heterogeneous prose style and the disorienting montage form of *Hōrōki* and to move toward more conventional types of narration. In fact, in a postscript-like final section of the novel's sequel, *Zoku hōrōki*, Hayashi expresses her dissatisfaction with the form and content of *Hōrōki* and her desire to move on to something else.

In this unusual final section, Hayashi strips away a layer of fictionality from the text and addresses the reader directly as Hayashi Fumiko, author of *Hōrōki*. Somewhat awkwardly compelling the reader to draw an equivalence between this authorial voice and the voice of the narrator-protagonist, "Hayashi" comments upon the changes in her life between the period covered in the novel's diary entries and the period since *Hōrōki*'s successful publication. Ironically, rather than clarify her position of authorial subjectivity, this postscript only adds to the proliferation of subjectivity that was symptomatic of the *Hōrōki* text itself. Assuming the voice of the author meditating upon her own identity, she addresses the fact that "Hayashi Fumiko" is now a commodity in circulation in the media:

The name Hayashi Fumiko has begun to bother me a little. Since I am such an indulgent, unsteady, and lonely person. Just once, I'd really like to rid the world of this name for good. Sometimes, walking down the street, I see the words "Hayashi Fumiko" written on posters for magazines. I wonder just who this Hayashi Fumiko could be.[4]

In her authorial voice as Hayashi Fumiko, she describes the confusion of her daily life, or *seikatsu*, and expresses regret over the "adulterated" quality of her work, which she refers to as *kyōzatsubutsu*, an admixture or adulteration. In a striking parallel to Hagiwara's conception of the poet as advertising tower, she writes, "my way of living today is like chopping myself into pieces and throwing myself in every direction, like an advertisement" (*Watashi no seikatsu wa watashi to iu mono o, kōkoku no yō ni kirikizande hōbō e fukitobashite iru yō na mono deshō*).[5] And of her work, she declares, "it is nothing more than an admixture of many things—there is not one pure thing in it."[6] Finally, she expresses her desire to create a work diametrically opposite in character to *Hōrōki*: "quiet contemplation, the purification of materials, the creation of a solitary realm—for many years, I have been yearning for this type of work."[7] While this declaration signals a possible reorientation, it does not mean that the issues and techniques explored in her most aggressively modernist novel *Hōrōki* would become irrelevant to her later career as a writer.

As traced in the preceding chapter, despite his considerable interest in the artistic and social potential of the print medium, Hagiwara became progressively more alienated from the organs of mass media in Tokyo, to the point of hand-producing a mimeographed journal on the quixotic topic of Kropotkin's art theories from his home in rural Gunma Prefecture. Hayashi, by contrast, quickly forged strong ties with major newspapers, journals, and publishing houses after the success of *Hōrōki*.[8] Throughout the next decade, she produced a bewildering number of stories, sketches, essays, travel accounts, and reportage for various media organs. Using a combination of her own book royalties and financial and logistical support from the publishing houses, she embarked on an unceasing series of travels (both international and domestic) and speaking tours: in September 1934, for example, she participated in a special airplane "relay" of popular writers sponsored by the Yomiuri newspaper, a publicity stunt that sent her flying to Aomori, Sapporo (Hokkaido), and Noshiro (Akita Prefecture).[9] From newspaper presses to airplanes, Hayashi had achieved access to the technologies of communication that were the very symbols of global modernity in the interwar period.

Already thus "mobilized" by the organs of mass media, it was not long before Hayashi was collaborating with the combined forces of state and media to produce supportive accounts of the Japanese army's advances in China. In December 1937 through January 1938, she achieved renewed notoriety by riding into Nanking in the back of the *Tōkyō nichi nichi shinbun* (*Tokyo Daily News*) news truck, becoming the first Japanese woman to enter the city after its fall to Japanese troops. (Japanese atrocities, as has frequently been noted, were absent from Hayashi's account).[10] In August of 1938, she was recruited as one of twenty-two writers in the first "Pen Squadron" set up by the Ministry of Information to provide journalistic and literary accounts of life at the battlefront. She received further publicity when, acting independently from the rest of the "Pen Squadron," she was again among the first civilians to enter the city of Hankow behind Japanese troops. Her repeated achievement of *ichiban nori* ("first to ride in") highlights the considerable agency that Hayashi exercised in exploiting the media system and the opportunities of war to advance her own fame as a writer: more than being passively "mobilized," she was also taking the media for a ride.[11]

Upon returning from the China front in October of 1938, she immediately embarked on a nationwide speaking tour to convey her observations of the front, and reworked the material she had submitted for newspapers into a book, *Sensen* (*Battle Front*). An ad balloon, one of the new urban advertising media developed in interwar Japan, raised a giant banner bearing a notice for this book over the skies of Tokyo from the roof of the Asahi Newspaper Company.[12] Thus, reviewing Hayashi's activities of the late 1930s, we see a close symbiotic relationship between writer, media organization, and state, as each used the others to promote its own agenda.

While Hagiwara may have written pro-imperialist poems in his final years in a seemingly desperate attempt to forge a connection with the Japanese masses (redefined as *minzoku*), the irony is that he was already so marginalized, so distanced from the organs of mass media, that his decision to resist or affirm imperialism was largely irrelevant in terms of an impact outside of a limited circle of poets. Hayashi Fumiko, on the other hand, exercised considerable cultural and political power in helping to determine the domestic perception of the unfolding conflict in China.

Although both Hayashi and Hagiwara eventually distanced themselves from the most explicitly modernist and avant-garde elements of their works, it would be inaccurate to conclude from these two experiences that Japanese modernist and avant-garde practices were wiped out in the increasingly conservative political and social environment that accompanied the "fifteen-years war" beginning with the Manchurian Incident of 1931.[13] Rather, Japanese modernism mutated and diversified in a continuing interplay with political authority and resurgent Japanese nationalism, in some cases the subject of government repression and in other instances revealing points of sympathy with nationalist and imperialist public agendas. In the case of poetry, I have already suggested that the work of some writers associated with the *Shi to shiron* represented a reaction against the eclectic avant-gardism and aggressively politicized engagement with daily life found in the early poetic avant-garde. This later, more formally oriented phase of modernist poetry was often dominated by a rhetoric of poetic purity. Nevertheless, several writers who broke with *Shi to shiron* demonstrated ambivalence or outright antagonism toward the rhetoric of poetic purity, and expressed instead an intent to address the "reality" of the political situation in Japan, as suggested by the title of their journal, *Shi to genjitsu* (*Poetry and Reality*, 1930–1931). While the story of Japanese poetic modernism is continued most directly in the diverging activities of the writers formerly associated with *Shi to shiron*, it can also be traced in the new lyricism of the Nihon roman-ha (Japan Romantic School) and Shiki-ha (Four Seasons group). Although these groups were ostensibly founded on a rejection of modernist aesthetics and embrace of a nativist poetics, closer scrutiny of their work reveals a sophisticated incorporation and reinterpretation of modernist poetic strategies.

In the world of prose, literary modernism in the early 1930s is most closely associated with the writers of the Shinkō geijutsu-ha (New Arts School) and the journals *Bungei toshi* (*Literary Metropolis*, 1928–1929) and *Bungaku jidai* (*Literary Age*, 1929–1932).[14] However, from a wider perspective, the urban themes, disruptive formal techniques, and rebellious attitudes of 1920s modernist and avant-garde literature were broadly pursued in the 1930s by the diverse constellation of writers whose work has been identified with the *ero-guro* ("erotic-grotesque") trend in literature and popular culture, including some affiliates of the *Shinkō geijutsu-ha*, writers for the *Shinseinen* (*New Youth*) journal such as Edogawa Rampo and Yumeno Kyūsaku, the second-generation Dadaist Yoshiyuki Eisuke, or the author, editor, and publisher Umehara Hokumei. This diverse constellation of writers further extended the exploration of new forms of media, as well as the cultivation of new reader constituencies, which had galvanized the attention of authors of modernist, popular, and Proletarian Literature alike in the previous decade.

The work of writers associated with the *ero-guro* trend was, unsurprisingly, the target of frequent government censorship in the 1930s and 1940s, and even more obscure Surrealist poets were viewed with suspicion by political authorities, subject to questioning and arrest by the special police during the war years.[15] Such evidence of government suppression, however, should not obscure the interrelationship of Japanese modernism and the nationalism and imperialism that were ascendant in the 1930s and 1940s. Both

Japanese modernism and Japanese imperialism were complex and contradictory movements, and an investigation of their points of antagonism and collusion in Japanese intellectual history has only just begun. In the wartime reportage of Hayashi Fumiko, we see the aesthetics of speed, the exuberant exploitation of new forms of media, and the celebration of an independent and productive female subjectivity, first associated with Japanese modernism, being harnessed in support of Japanese military expansion. In the work of Hagiwara Kyōjirō, we can see a continuity in the simultaneous attraction to heroic individual agency and an exploration of alternative forms of intersubjectivity, initially envisioned as a challenge to public authority, and yet eventually fusing with a nationalist and imperialist vision of the Japanese people and polity. While the ultimate forms of these particular convergences were by no means inevitable, they point to deep-seated confluences between modernist ideas and imperialist ideologies with significant implications for our own ostensibly postcolonial and postmodern era.

APPENDIXES

APPENDIX A
Selected Biographical Sketches

Anzai Fuyue (1898–1965)

Poet. Anzai was born in Nara Prefecture and graduated from Sakai Middle School in Osaka Prefecture. In 1920, he migrated to Dalian (Dairen), Manchuria, with his father, a former educator and government bureaucrat turned businessman. The following year he began work as an employee of the South Manchuria Railway Company (Mantetsu), but after only a few months at work he was hospitalized for a severe infection in his knee, seemingly brought on by the harsh continental climate. As a result, his right leg was amputated. After the amputation, Anzai abandoned his career with Mantetsu and devoted himself to the composition of poetry. In 1924, Anzai cofounded the journal *A* with Kitagawa Fuyuhiko and two other poets, and edited the journal for the next three years from his home in Dalian. In 1928, Anzai and Kitagawa went on to become founding members of *Shi to shiron* (*Poetry and Poetics*), the premier modernist literary journal of the prewar period. Through their poetic and critical contributions to *A* and *Shi to shiron*, Anzai and Kitagawa championed two distinctive literary forms, the *tanshi* or short poem and the *shin sanbunshi*, or new prose poem. Anzai returned to Sakai following his father's death in 1934; he continued to compose poetry through the postwar years. His major poetry collections include *Gunkan Mari* (*The Battleship Mari*, 1929), *Ajia no kanko* (*Dry Lakes of Asia*, 1933), and *Daigaku no rusu* (*Time Off from College*, 1943).

Hagiwara Kyōjirō (1899–1938)

Poet. Hagiwara was born to a farming family on the outskirts of Maebashi, a provincial city in Gunma Prefecture on the edge of the Kantō plain, about one hundred kilometers northwest of Tokyo. The third of six children of Hagiwara Morisaburō and his wife Dai, he was adopted at the age of ten by his great-aunt Kanai Sō, after the death of her only son. He excelled in school and showed an interest in literature, contributing tanka and free verse poetry to local newspapers and youth journals. During his late teens, he made the acquaintance of three established poets of national stature who lived in Maebashi: Kawaji Ryūkō (1888–1959), Yamamura Bochō (1884–1924), and Hagiwara Sakutarō (1886–1942), who would serve as mentors to the young poet. Hagiwara Sakutarō, arguably the most talented and influential practitioner of modern free verse poetry in Japan, was unrelated to Kyōjirō, but nonetheless remained a lifelong friend of the younger poet, and wrote perceptive and enthusiastic reviews of his two poetry collections, *Shikei senkoku* and *Danpen*. Partly under the influence of Yamamura Bochō, Hagiwara briefly showed an interest in Christianity, and served as a Sunday school teacher in 1919; during the same period he studied Russian and read the works of Turgenev and Dostoyevsky.

In October of 1920, Hagiwara attended a meeting of the poets' association Shiwakai to celebrate the publication of the annual *Nihon shishū* (*Anthology of Japanese Poetry*), in which one of his poems was to appear. On this occasion, he first met the futurist poet Hirato Renkichi, and became aware of the incipient avant-garde art and poetry movement in Tokyo. By the following year, he had begun to study anarchist literature as well as works on modern art, and had made the acquaintance of such young artists and poets as Yanase Masamu and Tsuboi Shigeji, who, with Hagiwara, were to play key roles in the anarchist, Proletarian, and avant-garde literary and art movements to come. In September of 1922, Hagiwara finally broke his ties at home and moved to the Hongō section of Tokyo. He was employed by the publishing company Seikōsha to edit the youth-oriented magazines *Shōjo no hana* (*Girl's Flower*) and *Hikō shōnen* (*Young Aviators*).

In January 1923, Hagiwara, Tsuboi, Okamoto Jun, and Kawasaki Chōtarō published the first issue of their new poetry magazine, *Aka to kuro* (*Red and Black*), after receiving seed money from the established Shirakaba-ha (White Birch School) writer Arishima Takeo. *Aka to kuro* was the first Japanese literary journal to adopt an aggressive avant-garde stance, epitomized by the provocative manifesto declaring poetry a bomb and the poet a "black criminal" printed on its cover. Its example helped spur an explosion of similar coterie journals both in and outside of Tokyo, and established its founders as leaders of a new generation of poets. The journal's publication was suspended by the Great Kanto Earthquake of September 1923, and came to a close with a final issue, entitled *Aka to kuro gōgai* (*Red and Black Extra Number*) in June 1924. Although Hagiwara wrote several poems on the theme of the earthquake, he had actually returned to his native Gunma Prefecture, far from the epicenter, when the earthquake occurred.

In the mid-1920s, Hagiwara was a central figure among the writers and anarchists who gathered in the Café Lebanon in Hongō. He also collaborated in producing the journal *Damu damu*, whose one issue (October 1924) was a crystallization of this extended network of avant-garde and anarchist poets. At roughly the same time, Hagiwara became involved with the avant-garde art group Mavo, formed under the leadership of Murayama Tomoyoshi in June 1923. He was co-editor of the *MAVO* journal during the second phase of publication from June to August 1925 (nos. 5–7), and collaborated with the Mavo members to publish his first poetry collection, *Shikei senkoku* (*Death Sentence*), in October 1925. This collection was distinguished by the placement of characters and lines of text in various orientations; by the extensive use of lines, bars, circles, and alphabetic symbols; and by the close integration of text with the linocut prints of Okada Tatsuo and other Mavo artists. The collection was welcomed with much excitement in Japanese poetry circles, and quickly sold out its only two printings. *Shikei senkoku* was published as the Japanese avant-garde artistic ferment was reaching a climax, extending from poetry, prose, and the plastic arts to architecture, film, modern dance, and theater. Hagiwara himself gave a number of avant-garde dance performances in addition to lectures, poetry readings, and other stage appearances.

By the mid-1920s Hagiwara had become intimately involved in the anarchist movement. In January 1927, he helped to found the literary magazine *Bungei kaihō* (*Literature of Liberation*) with a group of writers including former associates Tsuboi and Okamoto. Unlike the previous journals *Aka to kuro* or *Damu damu*, however, *Bungei kaihō* was explicitly defined as the literary organ of an organized anarchist political movement; the poetry Hagiwara wrote for this magazine was markedly more propagandistic than previous work. In the next several years, he contributed poetry and criticism to a number of literary journals associated with the anarchist movement, including *Dora* (*Gong*), *Barikēdo* (*Barricades*), *Kurohata wa susumu* (*The Black Flag Advances*), *Kokushoku sensen* (*Black Front*), and *Gakkō* (*School*). He also became involved in extra-literary anarchist political activity, organizing a workers' study group in the Kōtō district of Tokyo, and participating in the movement protesting the death sentence of American anarchists Nicola Sacco and Bartolomeo Vanzetti. He was among a group of prominent anarchists, including Ishikawa Sanshirō and Nii Itaru, who were arrested during a protest at the American embassy in August 1927.

Hagiwara married Ueda Chiyo in January 1924, and fathered a boy, Kōichi, born in October of the same year; a second boy was born in February 1927 (he would father two more sons and a daughter). Although Hagiwara had achieved prominence in Tokyo's avant-garde subculture, he had quit his editing job with the Seikōsha and was virtually penniless. From January to June 1926 he was forced by financial circumstances to return to his aunt's home in rural Gunma Prefecture and to send his wife and son to live with his in-laws in Ibaragi Prefecture. After another two years in Tokyo, he relinquished his claim to urban life in October 1928, taking his wife and children back with him to Gunma Prefecture, and assisting in the operation of his great-aunt's general store.

Hagiwara's second poetry collection, *Danpen* (*Fragments*), was published in October 1930. In June of the following year, he produced the journal *Kuropotokin o chūshin ni shita geijutsu no kenkyū* (*Art Studies Centering on Kropotkin*), which ran for four issues. This journal featured Hagiwara's title series of essays on the Russian anarchist Piotr Kropotkin, as well as poetry by Hagiwara and regional poets from rural Gunma Prefecture and elsewhere.

During this period, he began to write longer poems on the theme of daily life in rural Japan, many of which reflected the economic crisis that was facing Japanese farmers.

In June of 1934, Hagiwara began working at Kankodō, a book publishing and trading company in Maebashi. His employment at Kankodō was indirectly due to a grand imperial review of the army which was planned to take place in Maebashi: as part of the zealous security preparations for this event, the authorities ordered that all socialists without permanent jobs would have to leave the prefecture; it was only after friends arranged for Hagiwara's employment and lined up character witnesses on his behalf that he was able to avoid extradition.

Hagiwara's final major accomplishment as poet and editor was the publication of the journal *Kosumosu* (*Kosmos*) in November 1935. The thick first issue of this journal featured an impressive line-up of poets and artists, including Hagiwara Sakutarō, Takamura Kōtarō, and Kaneko Mitsuharu contributing poems; Murō Saisei, Yokomitsu Riichi, and Takamura Kōtarō contributing calligraphy; and Munakata Shikō contributing prints; Takahashi Shinkichi, Kusano Shinpei, Kitagawa Fuyuhiko, Okamoto Jun, and Ono Tōzaburō were among those signed as *dōjin*. Regrettably, however, this effort at a revival in Hagiwara's literary activities ended with one issue, and the volume of his poetic output declined severely after this point. His health also declined, and from 1937, a painful stomach ulcer left him partly debilitated.

Hagiwara died from anemia, a complication of his ulcer, in November 1938. The following month, his poem "Ajia ni kyojin ari" ("A Giant Is in Asia"), which appeared to support Japanese imperial expansion in China, was published in the poetry journal *Serupan* (*Serpent*).

Haruyama Yukio (1902–1994)

Poet, nonfiction writer, and editor. Haruyama was born in Nagoya, and dropped out of Nagoya Commercial School at the age of fifteen, henceforth becoming largely self-educated in English, French, and literary studies. He began writing poetry and cofounded *Seikishi* (*Blue Rider*) in Nagoya in 1922, one of the first regional journals active in the interwar modernist movement. He moved to Tokyo in 1924 and began work as an editor for the textbook publisher Kōseikaku in 1928. The same year, he co-founded the influential modernist poetry journal *Shi to shiron* (*Poetry and Poetics,* 1928–1932) and served as its principal editor, also editing its successor journal, *Bungaku* (*Literature,* 1932–1933). In the postwar period, he established himself as an authority in European folklore, social history, and material culture as well as literature, and was active as an essayist and encyclopedia editor. His poetry collections include *Shokubutsu no danmen* (*Cross-Section of a Plant,* 1929) and *Shiruku & Miruku* (*Silk & Milk,* 1932); collections of his literary criticism include *Shi no kenkyū* (*Research on Poetry,* 1931) and *Bungaku hyōron* (*Literary Criticism,* 1934).

Hayashi Fumiko (1903–1951)

Poet and novelist. Hayashi was the illegitimate daughter of Miyata Asatarō, a salesman from Ehime Prefecture, and Hayashi Kiku, from Kagoshima Prefecture. She is said to have been born either in Shimonoseki, a major port on the southwest extreme of Yamaguchi Prefecture, or in the nearby city of Moji, now part of Kita-Kyūshū. At the outbreak of the Russo-Japanese war in 1904, her father founded a pawnshop called the Gunjinya in Shimonoseki; the store was a success, and soon had branches throughout Kyūshū. In 1910, her mother left Miyata's household with Fumiko and Sawai Kisaburō, a clerk at the Gunjinya. The three migrated throughout Kyūshū for the next six years, before settling in the town of Onomichi in Hiroshima Prefecture. Hayashi attended a girls' high school in Onomichi, graduating in 1922; she showed an early interest in literature and contributed poems to local newspapers.

A month after graduating from high school, Hayashi departed Onomichi for Tokyo, joining her boyfriend who was attending Meiji University, and beginning a series of jobs including those of café waitress, factory worker, and nursemaid. She remained in Tokyo after her boyfriend broke off their engagement and returned to Hiroshima Prefecture. After experiencing the Great Kanto Earthquake in September 1923, she temporarily evacuated to

Onomichi. From the following year, she began to publish children's stories and poems, and frequented the Café Lebanon in Hongō, where she met Hagiwara Kyōjirō, Tsuboi Shigeji, Okamoto Jun, Tsuji Jun, Takahashi Shinkichi, and Hirabayashi Taiko. She cofounded the journal *Futari* with Tomotani Shizue, and published her poems in the Proletarian Literature journal *Bungei sensen* (*Literary Front*), the avant-garde journals *MAVO* and *Sekai shijin* (*World Poet*), and the mainstream poetry journal *Nihon shijin* (*Japanese Poet*). She published her first poetry collection, *Aouma o mitari* (*I Saw a Pale Horse*) in 1929. In 1926, she began living with the painter Tezuka Ryokubin, who would become her lifelong companion.

Hayashi serialized her autobiographical novel *Hōrōki* (*Diary of a Vagabond*) in the feminist journal *Nyonin geijutsu* (*Women's Arts*) from October 1928. When published in book form in 1930 *Hōrōki* became a best seller, propelling Hayashi on a career as a successful novelist. She used the proceeds from *Hōrōki* to fulfill a lifelong dream of traveling to Europe, spending the winter and spring of 1931–1932 in Paris and London. After her return, she continued to travel widely through Japan and East Asia. In January 1938 she witnessed the aftermath of the attack on Nanking as a reporter for the *Tōkyō nichi nichi shinbun*. She reported and lectured extensively on the war in China and Southeast Asia throughout the next six years, as both a newspaper reporter and a member of the "Pen Squadron" organized by the Ministry of Information.

In addition to producing an extensive corpus of essays, memoirs, travel writing, and reportage, Hayashi continued to write fiction and occasional poetry until her death in 1951. Outstanding later works include "Fūkin to sakana no machi" ("The Accordion and Fish Town," 1931); "Kaki" ("Oyster," 1935); "Bangiku" ("A Late Chrysanthemum," 1948); "Suisen" ("Narcissus," 1949); "Dauntaun" ("Downtown," 1949); *Ukigumo* (*Drifting Clouds*, 1949–1951); and *Meshi* (*Rice*, 1950–1951).

Hirabayashi Hatsunosuke (1892–1932)

Critic. Hirabayashi was born in Tokyo and graduated from the English department of Waseda University in 1917. He was placed in charge of arts criticism for the *Yamato shinbun* and the prominent intellectual journal *Shinchō* (*New Tide*), writing on diverse topics including literature, film theory, feminism, and socioeconomics. Drawn toward socialist thought, he contributed to *Tane maku hito* (*The Sower*) and became a Communist Party member in 1922. Hirabayashi contributed to the discourse on Japanese modernism in the 1920s, linking modern fashion with mechanization and speed, and holding out hope for modernism as a liberating influence, particularly for women. His criticism encompassed studies of a wide range of literary genres, including detective fiction, women's writing, and Proletarian Literature.

Hirabayashi Taiko (1905–1972)

Novelist. Born in Nagano Prefecture to a rural family which had lost its former prosperity; her mother ran a general store. After graduating from girls' school, she headed for Tokyo, where she held a succession of jobs, including telephone operator and bookstore clerk. Showing an early interest in socialism, she established contact with the prominent Marxist Sakai Toshihiko. She and her lover were imprisoned during the roundup of subversives in the aftermath of the Great Kanto Earthquake. Released on condition they leave Tokyo, they crossed over to Korea and Manchuria. In Manchuria, Hirabayashi gave birth to a girl, who died of malnutrition. One of her first works, "Seryōshitsu nite" ("In the Charity Clinic," 1927), was based on this tragic experience.

Returning to Tokyo in the autumn of 1924, she joined the coalition of anarchist and avant-garde writers who frequented the Café Lebanon in Hongō; she also became a regular contributor to *Bungei sensen*. In 1927, her short story "Azakeru" ("Self-Mockery") won a literary prize from the *Osaka asahi shinbun*, helping to launch her career. From this point, her involvement with the Proletarian Literature movement deepened, and she was recognized as one of its leading figures. Hirabayashi was arrested again in 1937. She contracted tuberculosis in prison, and was granted a release the following year because of her severe medical condition. After a lengthy convalescence, she recovered her health, and reestablished her position as a prominent novelist in the postwar period.

Hirato Renkichi (1893–1922)

Poet and art critic. Hirato was born in Osaka, and dropped out of Jōchi Daigaku; he studied French in night school, and Italian on his own. Hirato found employment as an art critic for the journal *Chūō bijutsu* (*Central Arts*), and began writing poetry under the influence of Italian Futurism. He also showed a keen interest in contemporary Russian art and poetry, translating the poetry of Blok and hosting the visiting Russian Futurist artist David Davidovich Burliuk. In 1921, he passed out leaflets promulgating the "Mouvement Futuriste Japonais" on a street corner in Hibiya, Tokyo—a defining event for the nascent Japanese avant-garde. While he energetically published poetry, manifestoes, and theoretical works over the next year, poverty and ill health took their toll, and he succumbed to tuberculosis in July 1922.

While no collections of his poetry appeared in his lifetime, *Hirato Renkichi shishū*, edited by Kawaji Ryūkō, Hagiwara Kyōjirō, Yamazaki Yasuo, and Kanbara Tai, was published in 1936.

Ishikawa Sanshirō (1876–1956)

Anarchist leader. Ishikawa was born in Saitama Prefecture and moved to Tokyo as a youth, where he graduated from Tōkyō Hōgakuin (present-day Chūō University) in 1901. Following graduation, he worked as a journalist for the *Yorozu chōhō*, and subsequently joined the influential socialist publishing group Heiminsha, where he participated in the movement in opposition to the Russo-Japanese war. He was imprisoned for most of the time between 1906 and 1910. During the so-called winter period in Japanese socialism following the High Treason Incident of 1910, Ishikawa fled to France, where he lived from 1913 to 1921. Upon his return to Japan, Ishikawa advocated a form of anarchism based on the rebellion and self-government of the *domin* or Japanese peasant class. Calling for a rejection of Westernism and a return to the land, he lived as a writer and subsistence farmer on the outskirts of Tokyo.

Kanbara Tai (1898–1997)

Artist and poet. Kanbara was born in Sendai Prefecture and graduated from Chūō University. An enthusiastic exponent of Futurism from an early date, Kanbara's activities were known to Marinetti and other European avant-gardes. He began to publish poetry in 1916, and painted what is widely considered the first abstract oil painting in Japan in 1917. In 1921, he held a solo exhibition and printed the manifesto "Daiichi Kanbara Tai senden sho," one of the first avant-garde manifestoes in Japan; the following year he helped to found the artists' group Action. Later, he was a *dōjin* of the influential poetry journals *Shi to shiron* (*Poetry and Poetics,* founded in 1928) and *Shi-genjitsu* (*Poetry-Reality,* founded in 1930).

Kitagawa Fuyuhiko (1900–1990)

Poet and film critic. Born in Ōtsu, Shiga Prefecture, he spent much of his childhood in Manchuria following his father, an engineer for the South Manchuria Railway Company, through a series of towns and cities along the railway line. He returned to Japan and studied in the Law Department of Tokyo University, graduating from the French Law section in 1925. That same year he began work as an editor and critic for the film journal *Kinema junpō*. He cofounded the poetry journal *A* with Anzai Fuyue and two others in 1924, and went on to become a founding member of the journals *Shi to shiron* (*Poetry and Poetics*) in 1928 and *Shi-genjitsu* (*Poetry-Reality,* in 1930). With Anzai, Kitagawa played an instrumental role in the development of modernist poetry, championing the *tanshi* (short poem) and *shin sanbunshi* (new prose poem). His poetry of the mid and late 1920s was infused with a spirit of social and political criticism, and he joined the Nihon puroretaria sakka dōmei (Japan Proletarian Writers' League) in 1930. Kitagawa was also active as a translator, translating Max Jacob's *Cornet à dés* and André Breton's "Manifeste du surréalisme" (both in the year 1929). In 1942, he was drafted and dispatched to Southeast Asia as a member of the army's press corps (Rikugun hōdō han). He continued his active career as a poet in the postwar period, editing a long second run of the journal *Jikan* (*Time*) from 1950 on. Kitagawa's major prewar poetry collections include *Sanhankikan sōshitsu* (*Loss of the Semi-Circular Canals,* 1925), *Ken'onki to hana* (*Thermometer and Flowers,* 1925), *Sensō* (*War,* 1929), *Kōri* (*Ice,* 1933), and *Iyarashii kami* (*A Hideous God,* 1936).

Kon Tōkō (1898–1977)

Novelist. Kon was born in Yokohama and, after being expelled from middle school, embarked on the bohemian life in Tokyo at the age of sixteen. With Yokomitsu Riichi, Kawabata Yasunari, and others, he was a founding member of the journal *Bungei jidai* (*Literary Age*), and helped to form the nucleus of the Shinkankaku-ha, or New Perception School. In 1925, he broke away from the *Bungei jidai* group and cofounded the journal *Buntō* (*Literary Association*) with Murayama Tomoyoshi and Kaneko Yōbun. After a brief involvement with the Proletarian Literature movement, Kon left the movement to pursue a religious vocation as a monk of the Tendai sect. He continued to write numerous works of fiction and nonfiction in the postwar period.

Kon Wajirō (1888–1973)

Architect and social theorist. Kon was professor of architecture and industrial design at Waseda University. In 1918 he toured the country with Yanagita Kunio to survey the design of farmhouses. After the Great Kanto Earthquake of September 1923, he organized the Baraku sōshokusha (Barracks Decoration Society) with members of the Action artists' group, led by Kanbara Tai. In 1925 he began a series of investigations of popular culture and the practice of everyday life which he called *kōgengaku,* or Modernology.

Murayama Tomoyoshi (1901–1977)

Artist, playwright, set designer, novelist, critic, and leader of the Mavo artists' group. Murayama was born in Tokyo to a middle-class family. As a youth he was drawn to both art and philosophy, painting watercolors and reading the works of Schopenhauer and Nietzsche. He withdrew from the philosophy department of Tokyo University to study Christian history and philosophy in Germany, but was soon pulled away from his studies and into the tumultuous artistic environment of Weimar Berlin. During his stay of less than one year, he became acquainted with the latest works of a great variety of leading European and Russian artists, including poet F. P. Marinetti; artists Alexander Archipenko, Wassily Kandinsky, El Lissitzky, and Kurt Schwitters; dramatists George Kaiser and Ernst Toller; and dancer Niddy Impekoven. Murayama established personal contact with many of the aforementioned artists, and began to exhibit his own artworks in Berlin and elsewhere. In May 1922, he was the Japanese representative to the Congress of International Progressive Artists in Düsseldorf.

Upon his return to Tokyo, he coined the term "Conscious Constructivism" (*ishikiteki kōseishugi*) to describe his artistic program, and made his Japanese debut with a one-man exhibition in May 1923; he co-founded the Mavo artists' group two months later. The scale, scope, and intensity of Murayama's work in the mid-1920s was truly astonishing: in addition to taking a leading position in the Mavo and Sanka artists' groups and producing an innovative and varied series of paintings and assemblages, Murayama extended his creative activities to book design and illustration, architecture, dance, theater, set and costume design, radio drama, criticism, translation, and the writing of plays and short stories. His widely heralded constructivist set for the play *Asa kara yonaka made* (an adoption from Kaiser), staged at the Tsukiji Little Theater in December 1924, further solidified Murayama's reputation as a leader of the contemporary art scene, and inaugurated his long association with the theater.

Murayama's involvement in the literary world included founding the magazine *MAVO* in July 1924 (*MAVO* featured an eclectic mix of visual art, poetry, dramatic scenarios, short stories, manifestoes, and criticism); Murayama was also a *dōjin* of the literary journals *Buntō* and *Bungei shijō*. Following the dissolution of Mavo in the fall of 1925, Murayama became deeply involved in the Proletarian art, literature, and theater movements. He joined the Japan Communist Party in 1931, and was arrested twice during the crackdown on Marxists in the early 1930s. Released from prison after renouncing his ties to the Communist Party, Murayama published *Byakuya* (*White Nights*, 1934), one of the first novels to thematize the problem of *tenkō*. Nevertheless, he renewed his activities as a leftist playwright and producer, founding the drama troupe Shinkyō Gekidan. Murayama was arrested again in 1940, and his troupe was forced to disband. After the war's end, he again took up his work on behalf of socialist theater.

Nii Itaru (1888–1951)

Journalist, literary critic, and politician. Nii was born in Tokushima Prefecture; he graduated in political science from Tokyo University and worked as a reporter for the *Yomiuri shinbun, Ōsaka mainichi shinbun,* and *Tōkyō asahi shinbun.* He then shifted his métier from reporter to literary and social critic; he also became involved in the anarchist movement. Nii was credited by Ōya Sōichi for coining the term *modan gāru* (modern girl), though he denied that this was the case, and textual evidence also suggests otherwise. He contributed critical articles to numerous mainstream publications as well as the early socialist journals *Tane maku hito (The Sower)* and *Bungei sensen (Literary Front);* however, he was among the anarchists purged from the *Bungei sensen* group in 1926. Following this so-called "anarchist-Bolshevik split," Nii polemicized for the anarchist camp, publishing in myriad small anarchist journals and producing his *Theory of Anarchist Art (Anakizumu geijutsu ron)* in 1930. Nii was also active as a translator; his translations include Pearl Buck's *The Good Earth* and Steinbeck's *The Grapes of Wrath.* In the elections immediately following the Second World War, Nii was elected chief *(kuchō)* of Tokyo's Setagaya Ward.

Okada Tatsuo (dates of birth and death unknown)

Artist, Mavo member. Okada is thought to have been born in the present-day Kita-Kyūshū area, but little is known about his life before he debuted as an artist in 1922. He made his way in the Tokyo art world with no formal training, and lived an exceptionally marginal existence even by the standards of 1920s Tokyo bohemia. Soon after the founding of the Mavo artists' group under the leadership of Murayama Tomoyoshi in June 1923, Okada published a caustic article criticizing Murayama and his group. Nevertheless, he quickly reversed his course and joined Mavo, developing his own alternative vision for the group. He was strongly drawn to anarchist thought, and led the youngest and most radical members of the Mavo group to challenge Murayama's dominance. As an artist, Okada was known for his distinctive linocut prints and outlandish public assemblages, such as the *Montō ken idō kippu uriba* (Gate Light and Moving Ticket Selling Machine) constructed for the 1925 Sanka Exhibition.

In 1925, Okada and Hagiwara Kyōjirō formed an alternative organization within the Mavo group called the N.N.K., believed to stand for Nihon Nihirisuto Kyōkai (Japanese Nihilist Association); very little is known about the aims, activities, or composition of this group. He collaborated with Murayama in the illustrations for Murayama's translation of Ernst Toller's poetry collection *Schwalbenbuch* (*Subame no sho* / *Swallow Book*) in April 1925; with Hagiwara in the design and illustration of the poetry collection *Shikei senkoku* (*Death Sentence*) in October 1925; and with Okamoto Jun in the illustration of the poetry collection *Yoru kara asa made* (*From Night to Morning*) in January 1928. In 1928, he founded a magazine devoted to prints, *Keisei hanga*. Okada is rumored to have died in Manchuria after leaving Tokyo in the 1930s.

Okamoto Jun (1901–1978)

Poet. Okamoto was born in Saitama Prefecture, but raised by his grandmother in Kyoto, before leaving for Tokyo in 1920 to attend Chūō University. He soon dropped out of college, however, and began to attend anarchist study meetings; he participated in the formation of the Nihon shakai shugi dōmei (Japan Socialist Alliance) in December 1920. At about the same time, he started to write poetry, and became involved in the nascent avant-garde poetry movement. In January 1923, he helped found the breakthrough avant-garde journal *Aka to kuro* (*Red and Black*) with Hagiwara Kyōjirō, Tsuboi Shigeji, and Kawashima Chōtarō. He was also a *dōjin* of *Aka to kuro*'s ambitious successor project, *Damu damu*, founded in November 1924.

As the united front between Communists and anarchists collapsed, Okamoto remained loyal to the anarchist position, and helped found a series of strongly political anarchist poetry and prose journals, including *Bungei kaihō* (*Literature of Liberation*, 1927),

Mujun (*Contradiction*, 1928), *Dandō* (*Trajectory*, 1930), *Kaihō bunka* (*Culture of Liberation*, 1932), and *Shi kōdō* (*Poetry Action*, 1935). His first poetry collection, *Asa kara yoru e* (*From Night to Morning*) was published in 1926; his second collection, *Batsu atari was ikite iru* (*The Condemned Man Is Alive*, 1933), was suppressed by censors. Okamoto lived in extreme poverty throughout this period, with neither a steady job nor a permanent residence. He was imprisoned for four months during a round-up of socialists in 1935. Finally, in 1936, he left Tokyo for Kyoto, and took work in the planning division of the Makino film studio; he later became a screenwriter for the Shinkō kinema satsueisho. Moving back to Tokyo in the postwar period, he joined the Japan Communist Party and served as a labor leader in the film industry.

Ōsugi Sakae (1885–1923)

The most influential anarchist in prewar Japan. After being expelled from cadet school for insubordination, Ōsugi began to educate himself in natural science and political theory, reading Darwin, Bakunin, Kropotkin, Nietzsche, Stirner, Bergson, and Sorel. Arrested for his role in political agitations numerous times between 1906 and 1910, his imprisonment allowed him to avoid implication in the High Treason Incident of 1910, in which a number of leftist leaders were executed for an alleged plot on the emperor, including the pioneering Japanese anarchist Kōtoku Shūsui (1871–1911). In 1912 Ōsugi co-founded the anarchist journal *Kindai shisō* (*Modern Thought*), which served as a primary vehicle for his thoughts on politics, philosophy, and art. Chief among his early themes were the historical subjugation of the weak to the strong and the expansion/fulfillment of the ego as a means of opposing subjugation.

As his political thought developed, Ōsugi gradually abandoned the emphasis on the individual ego, and concentrated on more practical issues of union organization. He wrote theoretical articles on sexual liberation and free love, but his public image was damaged by the disarray in his own personal life, when he became involved in a love quadrangle involving his first wife, Hori Yasuko, and the feminist leaders Kamichika Ichiko and Itō Noe.

Ōsugi traveled abroad to Shanghai for a meeting of Asian socialists in 1920, and to Europe for a (subsequently aborted) anarchist conference in Germany in 1922; he was arrested in France for traveling with falsified papers and deported to Japan, after a period of internment in La Santé prison. In the chaos following the Great Kanto Earthquake, Ōsugi, Itō Noe, and Ōsugi's nephew were murdered by Military Police Lieutenant Amakasu Masahiko.

Ōura Shūzō (1890–1928)

Artist, designer, and Mavo member. Ōura was born in Tokyo. He worked in the advertising section of the Maruzen Company; his activities included designing window displays and establishing a Maruzen Gallery. He helped to found the Mavo group in 1923, but withdrew the following year, apparently alienated by the increasing political radicalism of the group.

Ōya Sōichi (1900–1970)

Critic. Ōya was born in Osaka and educated at Tokyo Imperial University. He contributed to the major intellectual journals *Chūō kōron* (*Central Review*) and *Kaizō* (*Reconstruction*) in the 1920s and 1930s. His early essays on modernism and 1920s modernity were collected in *Modan sō to modan sō* (*Modern Social Strata and Modern Mores*) in 1929. Although he was initially affiliated with Marxism, his stance became progressively more conservative. Ōya continued to be an influential critic and cultural commentator in the postwar period. His extensive archives of journalistic and popular press materials served as the foundation of the Ōya Sōichi Bunko, one of the most important modern archival collections in Japan.

Takahashi Shinkichi (1901–1987)

Poet. Born in Ehime Prefecture, Takahashi dropped out of secondary school and ran away to Tokyo, where poverty and malnourishment destroyed his health and forced him to return home. At around the age of twenty he had two formative experiences: through the mediation of two newspaper articles, he was made aware of European Dadaism, and on his own initiative, he spent eight months as acolyte in a Buddhist temple. After recuperating from his illness, he returned to Tokyo in 1921, and made the acquaintance of Tsuji Jun, Hirato Renkichi, Hagiwara Kyōjirō, and other poets interested in Dadaism, Futurism, and anarchist thought. His innovative 1923 collection *Dadaisuto Shinkichi no shi* (*Poems of Dadaist Shinkichi*) had a major impact on intellectual circles in Tokyo; together with Hagiwara Kyōjirō's *Shikei senkoku*, it stands as the most significant poetry collection of the early Japanese avant-garde.

In 1927, he embarked on a serious program of Zen Buddhist training, and his engagement with Zen eclipsed his identification with Dadaism. He continued to write poetry informed by his conception of Zen throughout the rest of his lifetime, together with novels, essays, art criticism, and expositions on Buddhism. Significant poetry collections from his later years include *Kirishima* (1942), *Dōtai* (*The Body*, 1956), and *Suzume* (*The Sparrow*, 1966).

Tomotani (Ueda) Shizue (1898–1991)

Poet. Tomotani was born in Osaka, and moved to Tokyo after graduating from a girl's school in Seoul. In 1924 she co-founded the little magazine *Futari* (*Two People*) with Hayashi Fumiko. Henceforth, she continued to write poetry and organize literary journals, drawing close to the Surrealist movement; she married the poet Ueda Tamotsu, and became a *dōjin* of the Surrealist journal *Shinryōdo*. Her first poetry collection, *Gyōten* (*The Dawn*), was published in 1952.

Tsuboi Shigeji (1897–1975)

Poet. Tsuboi was born to a farming family in Kagawa prefecture and attended middle school in Osaka. He entered Waseda University's English department, but dropped out before graduating. Subsequently, he enrolled in the army, but was discharged after two months as a holder of "dangerous thoughts." He began to write poetry at the age of twenty-two, and joined with Hagiwara Kyōjirō, Okamoto Jun, and Kawashima Chōtarō to found the avant-garde poetry journal *Aka to kuro* (*Red and Black*) in 1923. He was a *dōjin* of *Damu damu* in 1924, and was a leader of the anarchist poetry movement during the mid-1920s, helping to found the journal *Bungei kaihō* (*Literature of Liberation*) in 1927. When he published an article critical of Japanese anarchism, however, he was attacked and seriously wounded by a group from the "Pure Anarchist" faction. This incident prompted Tsuboi to break decisively with the anarchists and shift his allegiance to the rival Communist Proletarian literary movement. He became a central committee member of the Proletarian Writers Alliance (Puroretaria sakka dōmei) and helped to edit and publish *Senki* (*Battle Flag*) magazine.

Tsuboi was arrested for his political activism numerous times and was imprisoned for ten months in 1930 and for two years from 1932; he was released after committing *tenkō* (disavowing his allegiance to the Communist Party) in 1934. He continued to publish poetry during the war years, including poetry in support of the war effort. After the war, he renewed his efforts as a social critic, organizer, and writer, and was recognized as a leading leftist poet. His numerous postwar poetry anthologies include *Kajitsu* (*Fruit*, 1946); *Atama no naka no heishi* (*Soldier Inside my Head*, 1956); and *Uma* (*Horse*, 1966).

Tsuji Jun (1884–1944)

Critic, essayist, translator. Tsuji was born in Tokyo's Asakusa Ward; he studied English at the Kokumin eigakkai. In 1902 he began teaching English at various private language schools and public high schools; he combined his teaching activities with translation of Western literature and the publication of autobiographical essays. In 1912 he was dismissed from his teaching position at Ueno Girls' School for having an affair with one of his students, Itō Noe. (Itō later left Tsuji for anarchist Ōsugi Sakae, and became one of the leaders of the Japanese feminist movement). In 1915, he published the first of a series of highly influential translations: *Tensairon*, a translation of Cesare Lombroso's *L'homme de génie* (*The Man of Genius*). A second major translation project was Max Stirner's *Der Einzige und sein Eigenthum* (*The Ego and His Own*), translated as *Jigakyō* in 1921; this work's advocacy of nihilism and extreme individualism had a major impact on Japanese literary and philosophical circles. Tsuji also translated fiction and poetry, including works of Oscar Wilde and Jack London.

The hard-drinking Tsuji led a bohemian and financially precarious life in Tokyo, and had a wide range of acquaintances in the literary world, including Saitō Mokichi (who had been Tsuji's classmate in middle school), Tanizaki Junichirō, Satō Haruo, and Takebayashi Musōan. After a period of Buddhist study and austerities at Mount Hie, he took up playing the *shakuhachi*, an instrument associated with certain forms of Zen practice. In September 1922, he published one of the earliest interpretations of European Dada for a Japanese audience, "Dada no hanashi"; the following year he edited Takahashi Shinkichi's first poetry collection, *Dadaisuto Shinkichi no shi*. Tsuji's personal philosophy of nihilism, anarchism, and individualism, together with his peripatetic lifestyle and extensive knowledge of Western aestheticist and decadent literature, form the basis of his collections of essays and criticism, such as *Furō mango* (1922) and *Desupera* (1924). He traveled to France under the sponsorship of the *Yomiuri shinbun* in 1928.

Returning to Japan the following year, he expressed his deep misgivings about the state of Japanese capitalism and militarism in the essay "Dō sureba ii no ka?" ("What Shall We Do?"). In 1932 he underwent the first of a series of hospitalizations for mental illness. Increasingly alienated from contemporary Japanese society, he began to wander the country begging and playing the *shakuhachi* in the guise of a *komusō*, or member of a mendicant Buddhist sect (largely comprised, in the Edo period, of *rōnin* or masterless samurai) who were distinguished by their *shakuhachi* and basket-like hats. He died of malnutrition in 1944.

Yanase Masamu (1900–1945)

Artist, Mavo member, socialist activist. Yanase was born in Matsuyama Prefecture and grew up in the provincial city of Moji, before moving to Tokyo in 1914. A self-taught artist and superb draftsman, he was employed by the *Yomiuri shinbun* in 1919. In the early 1920s, he divided his artistic activity between socially conscious graphic art and a personal interpretation of Futurist painting. From the mid-1920s, however, Yanase gave up oil painting to concentrate on stage design and graphic art, contributing political cartoons, illustrations, and cover designs to the Proletarian literary journals *Tane maku hito* (*The Sower*), *Bungei sensen* (*Literary Front*), and *Senki* (*Battle Flag*). He was briefly imprisoned and tortured during the Great Kanto Earthquake, and imprisoned for a longer period in 1932–1933. In 1940 he published a photo essay on China and occupied Manchuria in the journal *Chūō kōron* (*Central Review*). He was killed during the Allied firebombings of Tokyo.

Yi Sang (1910–1937)

Poet, essayist, novelist, architect, and graphic artist. After graduating from Korea's foremost polytechnic institute, Yi Sang obtained a position as architectural engineer for the department of public works in Japan's colonial administration. He struggled with tuberculosis and related health problems, however, and resigned his post in 1933, henceforth operating a series of cafés in Seoul, all of which were financial failures. In 1929, his cover design for the journal *Chōsen to kenchiku* (*Korea and Architecture*) won first prize in a design competition sponsored by the journal, and one of his paintings was selected for a national exhibition in 1931. From 1931 through 1932, he published a number of innovative poems in Japanese in *Chōsen to kenchiku*. In 1934, his Korean-language poems in the series *Ogamdo* (*Crow's-Eye Views*) were published in the newspaper *Chosŏn ilbo* (*Korea Daily News*); while they succeeded in drawing the literary world's attention to his work, the poems were so unconventional that the newspaper was forced to discontinue the series due to reader objections. Following this major literary debut, Yi Sang published several highly regarded essays and fictional prose works, including "Nalgae" ("Wings," 1936) and "Pongbyŏlgi," ("Record of a Consummation," 1936), and the posthumously published "Hwanshigi" ("Phantom Illusion," 1938) and "Shilhwa" ("Lost Flowers," 1939). Yi Sang abruptly dismantled his life in Seoul and traveled to Tokyo in the autumn of 1936. He was arrested in February the following year as a *"futei senjin"* or "disorderly Korean." His health deteriorated rapidly in prison, and he died in a Tokyo hospital soon after his release.

Yokomitsu Riichi (1898–1947)

Novelist. In 1924, Yokomitsu and Kawabata Yasunari led a group of young writers away from Kikuchi Kan's mainstream literary journal *Bungei shunjū* (*Literary Seasons*) to found the journal *Bungei jidai* (*Literary Age*). This group of writers, who were experimenting with antirealist, subjectivist, and modernist writing styles, were dubbed the Shinkankaku-ha, or New Perception School, by critic Chiba Kameo. Yokomitsu co-opted the term and became the group's chief theoretician. His style continued to evolve throughout the next twenty years; he produced a series of influential short stories, novels, and critical essays, including *Hanazono no shisō* (*Thoughts of a Flower Garden*, 1927); *Kikai* (*Machine*, 1930); *Shanhai* (*Shanghai*, 1928–1931); *Junsui shōsetsu ron* (*Theory of the Pure Novel*, 1935); and *Ryoshū* (*Sorrow in Traveling*, 1937–1946). While his early works thematize issues of perception, mechanization, and reification, his late works, which are sometimes identified with a "return to Japan," focus more directly on the problematic relationship between Eastern and Western cultures.

APPENDIX B

Selected Works of Hagiwara Kyōjirō

Translated by William O. Gardner

1. "A New Training Ground for Artists" ("Atarashii geijutsuka no tanrenba"). Published in the *Yomiuri shinbun*, June 29, 1925.

2. "Preface" ("Jo") to the poetry collection *Death Sentence* (*Shikei senkoku*) by Hagiwara Kyōjirō. Published October 1925.

3. Selected poems from *Death Sentence* (*Shikei senkoku*), published October 1925.

4. Selected poems from *Fragments* (*Danpen*), published October 1931.

5. Selected later works, 1932–1938.

Note: The linocuts which accompany the poems "Morning ● Noon ● Night ● Robot" and "Advertising Tower!" are by Okada Tatsuo and Yanagawa Kaito. *Shikei senkoku*, reprinted edition (Tokyo: Nihon Kindai Bungaku-kan, 1972) 119, 139.

A New Training Ground for Artists: On the Revival of "Mavo"

Hagiwara Kyōjirō

SUMMER! Trees along the boulevards, leafing out under the renewing stimulus of oxygen. Undulating street corners with their vivid overlapping hues. The diffusion of enamel; the invigorating steel of the bridges, the scent of gasoline on construction sites! Horns and speeding tires! Clothes in lively white movement. The sun gaping with brilliant energy. Sparks flying out from the electric poles. Pure, cool drinking water. Sweet-smelling fruit. The animal, energetic scent of skin! Sweat! Taste! Department stores.

In summer, the expressions of the fluid, multicolored city coordinate their movements and begin to take shape. Youthful vigor. Sportsmanlike training. Hygienic beauty. Summer has its mechanical order, yet its true nature is fearless, adventuresome curiosity.

Our sensibility and overflowing life-spirit seek the all-inclusiveness of summer. We part ways with the literati of the past, with their privilege to waste away their lives, with their ennui and passivity and silences and sentimental hysteria. No longer will we tolerate that deformed mode of existence called the artist.

The fast tempo of our society. Our revolving lives. Machinelike speed. Luminescent ebullience, heat, lateral movement, vertical movement. The multileveled, three-dimensional form that spreads out from the many facets of our daily life, rivaling the greatest artworks, effecting a fusion of craft and nature unimagined even by artists. We mustn't overlook the importance of this daily life.

On this foundation, *MAVO*, edited by Murayama Tomoyoshi, Okada Tatsuo, and myself, has been published by Chōryūsha. *MAVO* is an engineer who puts into practice the intercourse and commonality of all things: architecture, movies, sports, machines, literature, science, industry, manufacture, etc. The works have an individuality worthy of this engineer—if they have productive value, all the better. Yet it doesn't matter if, on the contrary, they are Dadaistic. And if they could be the "one great entity" which would construct and synthesize our daily lives in the most effective, economical way possible, giving birth to a new form of economic capitalism. . . .

We have departed from our canvases, from books to a new movement! From music to jazz! The spirit that leaps to all things! We take as our movement that which conforms in body and spirit to the newest class. Our art leaps in every direction: thought, philosophy, science—giving birth to a new art that will accompany our expanded daily lives.

MAVO is a training ground for new artists, and new engineers.

Preface to *Death Sentence*

Hagiwara Kyōjirō

●

A warning about my poetry ● ●

Those who consider my poems decadent—such is a myopia fit for ridicule!

My poetry collection is a rejection of so-called decadence—so much so, I want to call it a "Beastly, Human Love Poem Collection." I possess the will to pierce through all of the phenomena that are pushing modern civilization into a state of decadence. On the day that dissects itself, on the day that mixes malicious rage and scorn: I say, beware of our own "bourgeois sadism"! (and this doesn't refer to the capitalist as opposed to the laborer).

●

She who belches forth racket, rumbling, noise, and ugliness against my poetry: an arrow to her inane heart!

Desire is our unassailable banner, our clear motto. A massacre of the impotence of every tame academy!

"If only it's vulgar, if only it's low". . . no longer can we permit these words. Scorn! Crush! The new values pledge only this. It's only the spirit of a domesticated watchdog that is barking! As a defensive movement against the arts and values that they themselves ignored:

●

The flock of sheep who only feel safe if they make something holy! When they make something holy, they only deceive themselves! The cowardice of those who try to set up values! You yourself build a prison and lock yourself up; you can't sleep soundly unless you live within a fixed form. Neurotic!

Idolater!

The heart of poets who feel they have no right to create verse unless they can give a complete answer to the question "what is poetry"! (The cleverness of those who hide their own fear under the compulsion to make a statement.)

Those who, in order to improve their poems, delve into research on poetics—they do this to calm themselves, and to avoid their anxiety about other things. Surely this is the best way to make themselves look good in front of other people! Monkeys!

But real poems aren't created as a banner for poets to fight under, saying, "Poetry is like this! Write poetry this way!" Rather poetry is only created when it doesn't battle under this kind of phony banner.

●

But let me say one word in advance about the flood of poetry whose necessity is mine alone. For the sake of the past, which saw the passage of my First Movement—

My poem listens to the music inside my private box, but it also listens to the screech of the elevated railroad as it mixes with the noise of the city. It listens to the sound of the printing press, to the sound of my pen scribbling beside it, to the cry of a single insect. Joy, laughter, anger, pleas, screams, and blows: with a momentary fall, they explode, they're reborn; born, they dash forth. Glaring yellow smoke compresses the swelling excreting heart.

Don't tire yourself carrying each phrase, each line, as if it was the heavy weight of prose! Renounce the duty of carefully transferring it to the next line! Make each line its own master! Roughen it with your own wild laughter! Roughen it once more with your screams! Bring on a strong, strong sensation!

If such proves impossible, then, while the line isn't completely exposed, make it a line that spins into the next phrase at a breakneck pace! Its unexploded spirit will surely mutate, spinning forward, trailing its hiss of smoke.

Ceaseless new reality! Ceaseless battle! Ceaseless change: this is the way that leads to highest excitement and rapture, until it approaches madness!

And so, what is beauty for us? Take tranquil and classic beauty, and mix it with religious harmony and dignity and beastliness and maidenliness and rags and bedbugs and noblewomen and automobiles, and still it won't be the type of beauty we seek.

Where does our beauty, our desire wander?

Write from the left, write from the right, write up and down, read it from every direction, throw in characters large and small, insert pictures, throw yourself into it as long as you can, until you're sick of it, and still you won't attain the beauty we seek. Where does our beauty, our desire wander?

Our poetry is not the whole! It's only a part. The whole is

infinite. The part only continues its accelerating revolutions. From the part, we have to discover the meaning of the whole. Even so, ultimately we cannot arrive at completion. Only in incompletion can we find the endless, intense shape. Go on through the fearful rumbling tunnel! In the momentary outbreak of destruction, revenge, burial, and birth, our shape climbs the raging current!

It's being just as we want, just as we feel. It's the strength, the energy to move, to run forward. It's the objectlessness that tries to reach the ultimate object. It's the giant steamroller that forges ahead, crushing the life of the present and past, accelerating over hypocrisy and hunger, riding over its own empty shell.

But positively! It is the firm will alone that cheers us, transcending judgment of good and evil, transcending every political authority, until it reaches crime and sin. Already we know of the building of a great tower of spirit. Already we know the shape that grows taller and taller, layer after layer. Again we can see that which topples with a deafening roar. In its shadow, the pale fight, the searing marvel, panic, joy. In an instant rapidly heating up, cooling down, lengthening, shortening: the entangling, swirling spray, leap, fall! Even a flower we perceive as a pale sheet of tin. A painful voice, letting out even one word against contempt and prohibition and stifling oppression. I know—the shared spirit that runs through all of this! Through our companions! Through the crowds! Through the age! Discover, in this—the uproar of our poetry! The seething! The multilayered solidity! The great clamor of that which progresses! Anti-art! (True art!) Humanity!

Discover also our gloomy idleness! Know our lives, our energy that bursts forth, disintegrates, stagnates, and comes to a temporary halt! Absolute nothing! Nihil! Our mischief! Our calm! Emptiness that expands until it encompasses nostalgia for the spirit of the ancients! Longing for classic beauty! Truth!

Every revolution, turning until it approaches the harsh unlimited nothingness—rich, minute, acute, expanding, contracting, radiating. Revolving! When this revolution ends, my own life will expire. When I leave the orbit of this revolution, my corpse will be laid down.

Freedom! Freedom! Away with every slave! Away with your own presumptuous, weak conscience—a conscience naught but a memory of the shameful past, bringing on no hopes for the future . . .

●

But now I have only the will to advance! I have only forward momentum! To the friends of my poetry, this alone I would bid you understand. In my first stage, I have thrown the bomb of my entire art in the movement toward conscious destruction. Know now my preparations to move to the second stage. Henceforth, my poetry will commence its drive ever more fiercely toward destruction and creation. And then, the era when our intelligentsia will reach its end and fall. . . .

From *Shikei Senkoku* (*Death Sentence*, 1925)

● Armored Coil

Amid the leaping bustle of the modern city
I see a giant mechanical armored coil
Spouting out moody smoke
A charmless and dull-witted fellow

He gives out a military shout
Ignorant of the flavors, colors, and delicate textures
That give the city its high taste
He spouts out strong yellow smoke
Soiling the city, getting angry
Oppressing the fearful heart

He follows neither the bullet nor the heart of the crowd
Possessing the reddest, most barbarian heart
Tenaciously, indifferently
Resisting the throng's commercial world
A powerful, powerful emergence, towards chaos

Ah! That charmless fellow, shrugging his broad shoulders
At fine, oversensitive Female Civilization
Neither joy nor sadness
Appears on his ugly face

Still, as if about to cry,
The flutter of his obstinate heart!
His passion!
His strength!
His destruction!
His creation!
His strong, true motion!
The fight against Civilization!

Ah! Behold! Now, I am
A giant mechanical armored coil!
Amid the leaping bustle of the modern city

Love Has Ended

On our mother's breast   countless scratches, stained with blood!
Or red bruises from fists!
The scars from thrown stones! Scars from the gnawing of teeth!
Ah, these painful red scars
Are all wounds endured for the life of her beloved children!

These unforgettable breasts are no longer for us to suck
Like the desolation of an abandoned house
Ah   love has already ended!

And so now   we kick once more her breast!
For the sake of the new century's loves!
For the sake of the new world's youth!
Ah   we take as our principle
To destroy the relics of our old fathers!

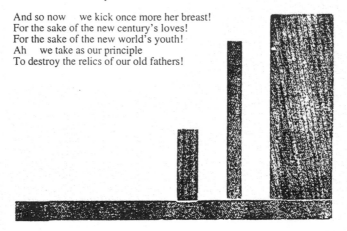

Goose in the Attic

The goose is a long-time bachelor salaryman!

Every night   from the attic, towards the
            Distant--------------------yellow heart, the goose is
        Honking   chattering   chirping
            ------Tonight, it seems, he will wrap
                A certain amount of money inside the letter
His lover is a girl with a poor yellow heart

------Rats are tearing apart the newspaper pasted on the walls
Someone in the darkness is kissing a ferocious kiss
In the corner of the room, recalling a long monologue, a boy is standing
------The darkness clarifies every heart

Below the stairs, I'm
            "Talking in my home-town accent"

------Someone might be born in this house tonight
------No, someone might die!

The goose had folded his old suit
The hard bed is waiting for his slender body

*Note: *Kamo* (wild duck) is slang for a mark, dupe, or sucker.

Hibiya

Intense rectangles
    Chains and gunfire and intrigue
    Troops and gold and honors and fame
Higher higher higher higher higher   soaring higher
The very center of the city---------------Hibiya

A refracted space
    Endless pitfalls and burials
    The graveyard of the new intellectual employees
Higher higher higher higher higher even higher even higher
    The dark spaces between high buildings
    Slaughter and exploitation and mauling

Higher higher higher higher higher higher higher
  higher higher higher higher higher higher higher
Hibiya

He goes through------------
He goes through------------
    Pushing everything forward
He holds his own key in his hands
      A nihilistic laugh
      The stimulating dance of currency
He goes through-------------
One
One more one more----------cemetery--------------towards the eternal burial
The final toast and dance
The center and summit
Higher higher higher higher higher higher a tower soaring ever higher

He goes through   one man
He goes through   one man
Hibiya

Untitled

A woman and a boy
  In the square
    It's autumn
They're playing with firecrackers
I was starving
I crawled up the slope
    With a steely eye
And cool nerves

Damn!
  Around the corner
Turned an ash-colored car
As fast as a criminal

I turned
My nerves   like a spiral
Making my small eyes-----harder
My body forward   as if bending down

Pressing down on my heart

Go! At once
To the third location
The intersection

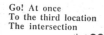

----------------------------that ●●●●●
----------------------------that ●●●●●●●
Chasing
        the cloud of yellow dust

Starving stomach
        That suddenly painful malice
Advance!
Ten times   A hundred times
                faster than   drastic
The explosion's   rush
The streets where laughter and tears have dried
Run! Stinking of gunpowder
    Run   Run   Run   Rage of instinctual flight
              ------that × × × × × ×
            ------that × × × × × × × × × ×

Self-carving

Fruitless labor stretches on like the artery of a bull!
The flag of revolution clings to my rib-bones
Like a withered flower!
That emaciated dog is sniffing for my bones!
My pale handshake is colder than death!
The night's prey is all that touches me!
My friends, flapping their wings to Hell!
The black target!
I love my cold pistol and cold-blooded intention!

Calm and wordless autumn

The past has collapsed!
I have only one goal!
Cracking the whip of destiny
At the summit of boredom and obscurity
A pierced throat, and the blood runs down!

I have only one goal!
Angry will and angry blood!
Calm and wordless autumn!
The graveyard, even quieter, has endless void and earth
It's waiting for the day our corpses are lain down!

Death cares not whether master or slave

Days and nights of fear
--------Crickets and rain   A melancholy autumn
A sleepless, hungry autumn
Pursued by frightful shadows

Feebly trembling
My love extinguished
After the shock is gone, its clump
Circles listlessly in my breast
Which has already expunged letters and philosophy

The rain flows down
          The cricket keeps chirping
My soul hurts like a red welt
Blood begets blood-------------revenge begets revenge
Night begets night--------------death begets death

Life can only be saved by the sword
Death cares not whether master or slave
My only goal
Is to fire my shot

On the day of the earthquake

Those called by death don't know

In a crack of the discouraged road
A head, rolling down, grins
The torn flesh, separated, grins
A burst heart,
Twisted, is still

Lick the bitter dried-up blood
Comrades!
-------Living, living.......................
Open your arms
　　　Sink your teeth into the head
And place a kiss

Choking on blood and dust, dried-up
Strongly,
　　I
Let out a wail
Onto that flesh
-----------I pour blood
-----------I wash it with blood!
On top of the crumbled streets
Our thoughts, his and mine,
Turn pale, and ignite

To whom shall we dedicate
The tumbled head,
The white bones, remaining from the fire,
The remaining life?
Lick the blood and blood,
Comrades!

Human Fault-line
Embracing each other, they were buried alive

Darkness ∿∿∿∿＜＜＜＜
Weariness is a skeleton buried underground!
Beneath the massacre of piled-up bricks and tiles!
Gas ● ● ●
Gravity pushed down by a concrete building!
Beneath the lead pipes-------countless moving faces!
The lantern sways!
A human fault-line!
A horse, fallen in the pitch-black mud!
A man, crawling out of the last train!
A laborer with bandaged arm, stumbling out of the hospital!
High voltage wires!
Gas!
Breathing gas!
The machines have stopped-------the factory turns pale!
Wires-------my eyes, lips, chest, and legs!
Desire?!-------I'd rather kiss a pig!
You think there's anyone who instead of ● ●
Does the job with roses and lilies?!
Love isn't a card-game to predict the present!
Gas ● ● iron ● fatigue-------mixed inside the brain!
-------A woman with huge eyeballs comes falling down!
Kuku ● kuku ● kuku ●
Kii ● kii ● kiki ● kiki ● kafaela!
The laughter is caught in the cloudy sky's telephone wires!
The spark is disrupted!
 X X X X X
 ● ● ● ● ●
Fizz spluttle splatter leaking leaking leaking
Morning-------after the "exhausted night" has passed
A single trail of white smoke!
Sick man ● murderer ● corpse ● pistol
Weariness is trampled beneath the earth's crust!

A Love Letter

One second
A film of massacre is projected on the wave of hats
● ● ● It's cut off by the shout of the crowd- -
Cries!
Countless **alphabet** faces
---------- *"What'll I do? I don't have the money to get home!"*
A packed elevator
An underground room encased in lead pipes ● ● **"Dried Fish and Whisky"**
Turning like a globe----------the exposed man's eyeball
"Kill me with the napkin!"
"Marvelous! ● ● ● *Come on!"*
"Even insensitive men have loves and beliefs."
"You're not so dull after all."
"I hear one love letter costs over 150 million yen."
Footstep● Ay!   Bee!

"You're such a wretch!"
Stairs----------*"Goodbye!"*
"Tomorrow!"
Doh● doh ● doh ● ● ● G
Medicine vial ● ● ● ● diary++++**knife**
Hair   Thermometer reads 40 degrees
Pale face with sign attached
Blood is spit into the handkerchief!
A starved rat lies under the curtain's shadow!
The water-main pipe!
Smoke dissipating in darkness!
Bibi   bibi
Booooom!
Cliff
----------*"My lover's coming back on the express train this morning."*
● ● ● On a corner of the attic-----
Feeble rays of the morning sun
A closed window

Morning•Noon•Night•Robot

▲▲▲The rose has bloomed!
〰〰〰Scoop out the eyes!
Give birth to the white-robed **robot**!
═════A long **tunnel**!
In the lab, his intelligence failed to become a biscuit!

● Put on the blue hat!
A **robot** blindfolded with a **belt**
On! Off! Walk! On! Off! Walk!

■ Stick the antennae into the poem!
I can hear the radio!
I sew up the body needles with needles and thread
It's become a sagging yellow Yankee bag
Almost ready
I'm going to fire this body as a bullet!
Fire!

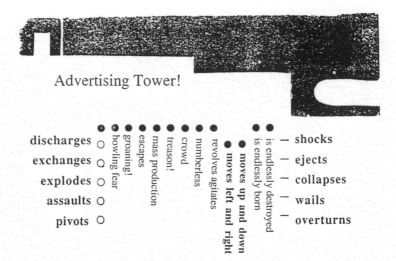

The languid brains sing a song
I'm listening to the noise of the water
Everything is the ocean's sunless black abyss!
With no beginning and no end!
Each thing comes and passes!
Life? Who has a clue?! The face of a hobby-horse!
Ah, Pierrot!
I can believe in neither freedom, nor God, nor mankind!
Only, I find the utmost fissure in the Dadaists!
You want to find a meaning?! Go ahead!
All is but a series of affectations!
I'm tired of this continual boredom!
The melancholy gospel washes over bones on the ocean floor!
Why?! Must I keep on living?!
Now, I don't believe we'll return to the earth or the sky!
Even my passion is listless!
I desire neither growth nor individuality!
Even cinema and pigments are dark!
Sadness, joy, and sentiment fossilize!
I'm a wood-block, an ornament!
I only rattle along!

A noise-making comforter!
Why must I keep on living?!
I'm a dead man!
I'm a moving thing!
The only thing that touches me is death!

He laughs!	He drives the carriage!	She gives thanks to God!
He cries!	He is cold and gray!	She turns to bones!
He walks!	He saw her!	She walks the path of thorns!
He rejoices!	He is a cosmopolitan!	She withers with fatigue!
He sleeps!	He also spies!	She keeps it a secret!
He eats!	He holds the ticket!	She is a fine wine!
He rages!	He smokes a cigar!	She is the shade of death!
He runs!	He is a gambler!	She is delicate!
He sinks!	He set up a seat!	She has no husband!
He births!	He chatters happily!	She drips with blood!
He fattens!	He swells and walks!	She commits a sin!
He steals!	He tied up the woman!	She embraces him!
He comes!	He refuses the interview!	She believes steadfastly!
He goes!	He makes it into a game!	She is naked!
He rips!	He is just as we asked!	She has a premonition!
He collapses!	He shoots at everything!	She plucks his beard!
He rides!	He is an assessin!	She trembles her breast!
He bends!	He was birthed by explosion!	She drops her shoulders!
He leaks!	He was piled up!	She goes to the rear!
He falls!	He laughs at folly!	She is a great miracle!
He dies!	He is a realist!	She slides along!
He echoes!	He is a wish!	She wipes her face!
He embraces!	He is a demand!	She has painful eyes!
He receives!	He is assertion!	She has black legs!
He pains!	He is negation!	She is dust!
He chirps!	He is affirmation!	She is a distant rose!

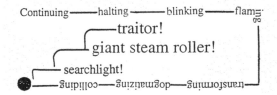

Continuing——halting——blinking——flame

traitor!

giant steam roller!

searchlight!

colliding——dogmatizing——transforming

In the road, on the streets, on the rooftops, in the rooms,

the warehouses, the cafes, I-----------------●

-------I live like a pig!
-------I live like a spy!
-------I live like an informer!
-------I live like a butcher!
-------I live like an emperor!
-------I'm listening to the pale gloomy cartridge tear apart!
-------I'm watching the changes and ornaments of the life outside myself!

Advertising tower
A huge gamble
A forest of chimneys, pouring out black smoke

-----------------------Several bodily cavities and a bumpy face and several round sticks and

yellow and hair and *springs* and a *compass* and tendons
and a *tapeworm* and socks and a calling card!

A dirty *shirt* with several *buttons* coming off and *pants* that look like I just changed--

--that instrument called me!

Ah ha ha ha ha-----ha ha   ha

From *Danpen* (*Fragments,* 1931)

FRAGMENT 2

The flag waves in the breeze
Amid a powerful unprecedented silence,
The flag waves in the breeze
Amid the unprecedented silence, the flag, raised, advances!

FRAGMENT 3

My wife, carrying a baby on your back, setting off for the streets
    with a pack of leaflets!
The rich are singing their victory song, their song of horrible
    black slaughter
We hear the report of the bullets, concealing their passion
My wife!
This morning, in the red of the poppies, my eyes absorb the
    pathos of love.

FRAGMENT 5

In the sky, there are scraps of heart
Sticking there, like black stars
Is there anyone who forgets him?
        who silently met death at the sky's towering guillotine
                      (to a comrade of old)

FRAGMENT 10

The joy of unequivocal victory
The rising joy that rends our breasts
The shouts of men, like blasts from a terrifying organ
The striking shouts of women, as if launched from a spring
The resounding songs
The windpipes of humanity rising up
Grasping their breasts   dancing   tumbling
Tumbling, like balls of joy
In the shooting, exploding, liberating light

like the rays of morning sun, burning with bright joy
and tears of emotion
We will bathe in the light, washing our bodies of all the past
We cannot forget this day
We must not forget that this day will come

FRAGMENT 12

Yesterday's friends have parted, one by one, and become enemies
Steadily, we become minorities, drawing near to the place
    designated by the majority.
To the howling ones, the clamoring ones, the ones in high places
We bid a silent, wordless farewell.

Knowing neither scorn, nor rebuke, nor praise, we move our
    world into tomorrow.
Today, no one here asks for, or listens to, superfluous words.

FRAGMENT 17

For a moment, the few outlets have been stopped by your plugs
But the water will only change its course
It's in the nature of the water's source: its flow cannot be stopped
Squeezing its pressure into the very capillaries of the earth
The rising water can be halted by no one
Moment by moment, the interior naturally collapses
Standing above the water's source, it is we who sink, moment
by moment, into the earth

FRAGMENT 25

I knew that there was a gigantic entity which could not be
    crushed until the end
Now I'm convinced that it's not something on the outside, but
    something between myself
        and ourselves
We can try to threaten it, drag it around,
Strike it, scatter it like ashes, but now
I'm convinced it will not disappear.

FRAGMENT 26

We rejoice in the fact that we are opponents to those in power,
　　　and we are utterly valueless to them
We are valueless because we don't recognize their values or
　　their order
We obstruct where they want to move, we offer them
　　no compensation
No matter how they try to trump us with a final card
From the darkness, from the earth, our buds extend
They sprout up, overcoming bricks or concrete or rocks or steel
Because we don't stand on privileges or interests
That which is alive, lives
This is a principle that needs no theory

FRAGMENT 27

Clamp all sentimentalism and vanity with the brake-gears of
　　your willpower and passion
Your fast-beating heart, your flesh, palpitating, vibrating with
　　the joy of tomorrow's victory—
Make this heart as strong and fiery as a boiler!
When you push yourself to the limit
Believing in yourself, believing in the world—then you can be
　　born in tomorrow's world
If not, all your passion and willpower will become remorse,
　　your body filled with abscesses
Like a bee hive, riddled with the holes of nihilism

FRAGMENT 35

You will walk your own path
I won't meet you for a while
But I'm not going to miss you at all
Today, I have no doubts about my friends
Then again, neither do I have great expectations
Because the thoughts in each of our minds are not light or
　　or trivial
Because today we can tell the difference between demagogues
　　and true friends

FRAGMENT 51

The flag mounted on a shining spear, waving red on the
    podium—that was a fine sight
The demagogues danced fervently on the stage
The gathered crowds were silent
We heard the foolish applause and cheers pass over our heads
But after the crowds dissipated
We felt the gloom, that we'd touched nothing in their posture
    or their words or their horizons
When the players and the audience go their separate ways
They remain perfect strangers
The legs of those returning to their own harsh lives
The legs striving to overcome, struggling to bear up
Are different from the hairy shanks on stage, playing the play
    of ambition

FRAGMENT 59

When you were born, I was in the next room
Listening to your mother's pains, feverishly writing a manuscript
Because, you see, in those days I didn't have a red cent
I set off to mail the manuscript
Trying to still my quaking heart, I went to borrow money
    from friends in Ueno
Through the woods in the park, dim in the arc-shaped lights
I walked on, singing in a buoyant voice
Unconsciously, I was singing
Even after I realized I it, I kept on singing
You see, I was so happy
My friends gave me money, and some diapers and towels
They saw me off at the door, watching me intently
Seeing their faces I smiled,
I went straight out and bought some fruit with the money
And took it home to your mother.
But, now that you're born
We don't visit the place your father was born
We don't visit the place your mother was born

You see, the people in both those places hate us
We don't have any contact with them
But what does that matter?
You can start out from where you are now
You don't be afraid of anything
Until the day I die, I'll wave for you
The flag of the brave and righteous battle.

Selected Later Works

MŌROKU ZUKIN (HEADSCARVES)

————*The "old man" leaves home. It would be too optimistic to say he's "going out to make money."*————

"Take care now . . ."
"You take care . . ."
Surrounded by the headscarves of the gathered neighbors, the fifty-year-old man changes out of his farming clothes, taking off the quilted gloves which hang on a string from his neck, and pulling his seldom-worn vest out of the closet.

In the yard, resting a moment from their threshing, the neighborhood women whisper, often falling into silence. Their heads, too, are covered with thick dark scarves.

Inside the home, the distressed wife and children gather by the light of the paper doors, by the side of the cold hearth. Telling him "come home soon," through their sobs.

The "old man" pokes his sunburnt, bearded face out for a moment to mutter assent, without looking at their faces. He tucks in the back of his kimono, which clings to his farmer's underpants.

"Take care now . . ."
"You take care . . ."
When the "old man" goes out to the yard, the headscarves of men and women surround him.

"We'll look after them for you"
"We'll keep an eye on them"
With these words, the women pat him on the back, pledging to themselves to take the best care of his family as they can.

Stiff, with only his bearded face nodding, the "old man" looks as though he's put on a heavy yoke.

He leads a horse with a long fine mane out of the barn. The horse chews on a final clump of hay. Its long tail blows in the wind.

Crossing the fields, the men and women see the "old man" off, as far as the first hill. As he turns the corner of the hill, the "old man"'s husky voice burrows into their heads.

"Be good to the wife and young'uns for me."

When winter comes, the headscarves and tight-sleeved coats go out to collect brushwood, draping a quilt over their shoul-ders to stave off the freezing four o'clock darkness. How did the echo of his voice resonate in those shoulders? How did his voice pass through to their thick, cracked hands? How did his voice reverberate in their hardened palms, tying up the ropes at night? Like a whirlwind, the headscarves pursued the "old man."

mōroku zukin (headscarf)—A thick cotton scarf or muffler, dyed indigo or black. In the place where I was born, this was the only garment the farmers had to protect themselves against the cold of winter. On snowy days, they didn't use an umbrella to keep off the snow, but let the snow pile up on their headscarves, leading their horses down the road. [Author's note.]

VALLEY

Somewhere at the bottom of this deep valley, pure water filters up from an unseen spring, bringing forth a lush coat of grass and trees. In the spring, the valley is draped with flowers and the birds lay their eggs; in the autumn, the turning leaves create a beautiful view. In the last ten years or so, at least one or two people have descended into the valley. Oddly, those who descended did not climb back up the cliffs. Some say there must be monstrous birds and beasts in the thick undergrowth. I've been bringing my sadness and self-reproach to throw into this deep, fathomless valley. And I've sniffed an indescribable scent carried back up on the breeze. Nevertheless, not a single bit of refuse built up on the valley floor. In the end, I too wanted to be one who descends into this valley, never to return.

A GIANT IS IN ASIA

A giant of ancient times, from the world of myth
Today flies across the mire of the Asian Continent, with a
    halberd as his wings.

If he finds a gate of precipitous stones, he will surely open it
If he finds a mighty river, he will surely cross it

Even if the bloodless fields shake and rumble
At the race's destination, across the mountains and fields,
He will crush what must be crushed
He will build what must be built
The giant will realize this great ambition.

Now, in autumn's chilly wind, though the voice of the Ta-pieh
    Mountains is hushed,
        though the waves of the Yangtze stir,
We know more surely than ever the way of our
    ancestral vocation

The East, seething, will become a new East
The World will tremble before its philosophy
The pages of History will double
Each one of us, as fresh pages, will cultivate this New World.

Autumn deepens on the Japanese Islands,
The scarlet maple leaves and chrysanthemums abound
        Even if soaked by the ocean spray,
The giant, steadfast, will grasp his halberd, and gaze at the
    race's progress
Behold him now: seated at the Orient's source, amid the
    mountain mists;
Standing, gazing forth, with the spirit of the Ancestral Gods!

REFERENCE MATTER

NOTES

Introduction

1. Yamaki Toshio, *Nihon kōkokushi* (Tokyo: Nihon keizai shinbunsha, 1992), 10.

2. Nagamine Shigetoshi, *Modan toshi no dokusho kūkan* (Tokyo: Nihon editā sukūru shuppanbu, 2001), 8–10.

3. On the modification of architectural styles to include window displays, see Hatsuda Tōru, *Modan toshi no kūkan hakubutsugaku—Tokyo* (Tokyo: Shōkokusha, 1995), 95–99. On the work of Ōura Shūzō, a member of the Mavo artists' group, in designing window displays for Maruzen, see Gennifer Weisenfeld, *Mavo: Japanese Artists and the Avant-Garde, 1905–1931* (Berkeley: University of California Press, 2002), 208–13.

4. On the Asakusa Rokku lighting display, see Yamaki, 106; on the proliferation of large shop signage and product advertisements on commercial buildings, as well as government attempts to regulate them, see Nagamine, 7-9; on the development of neon signage and architectural decoration, as well as the rapid growth of cafés, which, according to police statistics, numbered over 6,000 establishments in Tokyo by 1929, see Hatsuda, 128–34.

5. *Chindonya* bands, a type of ensemble devoted to street advertising, typically combined Japanese instruments, such as drums, gongs, and shamisen, with Western instruments such as the clarinet and cornet. Developing out of previous forms of street entertainment and promotion, they flourished around the turn of the century and remained a colorful but diminishing element of popular street culture into the postwar era.

6. Landmarks in the modern development of the advertising industry include the formation of the Dentsū advertising agency (now the largest in the world) in 1901, the establishment of the Mitsukoshi Department Store design department in 1909, the formation of the Society for the Study of Advertising in 1914, the inauguration of the leading monthly advertising design journal *Kōkokukai* (Advertising world), in 1926, and the first advertising poster exhibition organized by the designers' collective *Shichininkai* (Group of Seven), also in 1926. Yamaki, 107–40; James Fraser, Steven Heller, and Seymour Chwast, *Japanese Modern: Graphic Design Between the Wars* (San Francisco: Chronicle Books, 1996), 1–29. For a chronology of advertising innovations including the Kirin automobile brigade and various airborne advertising strategies, see Yamaki, 484–88.

7. The article was published in vol. 8 of the monumental 24-volume book set *Gendai shōgyō bijutsu zenshū* [*Complete Modern Commercial Arts*]; quoted in Hatsuda, 187.

8. Major governmental campaigns of the 1920s included the Campaign to Encourage Diligence and Thrift (1924–26) and the Moral Suasion Mobilization Campaign (1929–30). See Sheldon Garon, *Molding Japanese Minds: The State in Everyday Life* (Princeton, N.J.: Princeton University Press, 1997), 10–15. On the changing tides of the advertising industry in the prewar and wartime periods, see Kawahata Naomichi, "Konton to shita sen kyūhyaku sanjū shichi nen: bijutsu to shōgyō bijutsu no ryōiki o megutte" (1937, a Year of Confusion: Centering on the Fields of Art and Commercial Art), in *Modanizumu/Nashonarizumu: 1930 nendai nihon no geijutsu*, ed. Omuka Toshiharu (Tokyo: Serika shobō, 2003), 132–54; Miriam Silverberg, "Advertising Every Body: Images from the Japanese Modern Years," in *Choreographing History*, ed. Susan Leigh Foster (Bloomington: Indiana University Press, 1995), 29–148.

9. Untitled sketch, *MAVO*, no. 5 (June 1925), 31. This work and a related poem are discussed in further detail in Chapter 3.

10. *Shinpan hōrōki* (Tokyo: Shinchōsha, 1979), 291.

11. On the Great Kanto Earthquake, see Noel F. Busch, *Two Minutes to Noon* (New York: Simon and Schuster, 1962); Edward Seidensticker, *Low City, High City, Tokyo from Edo to the Earthquake: How the Shogun's Ancient Capital Became a Great Modern City, 1867–1923* (New York: Knopf, 1983); Edward Seidensticker, *Tokyo Rising: The City Since the Great Earthquake* (Cambridge, Mass.: Harvard University Press, 1991); and Andrew Gordon, *Labor and Imperial Democracy in Prewar Japan* (Berkeley: University of California Press, 1991), 176–83. On the reactions of writers and artists to the event, see Uranishi Kazuhiko, "Kantō daishinsai to bungaku" (The Great Kanto Earthquake and literature), *Kokubungaku: Kaishaku to kyōzai*

no kenkyū 34.4 (March 1991 extra); special issue *Kantō shinsai to bungaku* in *Shakai bungaku* 8 (July 1994); Takematsu Yoshiaki, "Metsubō suru teitō: bungakushijō no kantō daishinsai" (The capital destroyed: the Great Kanto Earthquake in literary history), in *Haikyō no kanōsei: Gendai nihon bungaku no tanjō*, ed. Ikeda Hiroshi (Tokyo: Inpakuto shuppankai, 1997), 172–82; Gennifer Weisenfeld, "Omoiegakareru sanka: Kantō daishinsaigo no shutō o meguru gakatachi" (A catastrophe memorialized: painters in the capital following the Great Kanto Earthquake), in *'Mobo-Moga 1910–1935'* *ten*, ed. Mizusawa Tsutomu et al. (Kamakura: Kanagawa kenritsu gendai bijutsukan, 1998), 235–39.

12. For English-language studies on Taishō Democracy, see George O. Totten, ed., *Democracy in Prewar Japan: Groundwork or Facade* (New Haven, Conn.: Yale University Press, 1965); and Bernard S. Silberman and H. D. Harootunian, eds., *Japan in Crisis: Essays on Taishō Democracy* (Princeton, N.J.: Princeton University Press, 1974).

13. A number of these intellectual positions, including those of Hirabayashi Hatsunosuke and the modernologist Kon Wajirō, have been explicated in Harry D. Harootunian's recent book *Overcome by Modernity: History, Culture, and Community in Interwar Japan* (Princeton, N.J.: Princeton University Press, 2000). Other recent studies that explore the *modan*/modern consciousness in interwar Japan include Sharon A. Minichielo, ed., *Japan's Competing Modernities: Issues in Culture and Democracy, 1900–1930* (Honolulu: University of Hawaii Press, 1998); and Elise K. Tipton and John Clark, eds., *Being Modern in Japan: Culture and Society from the 1910's to the 1930's* (Honolulu: University of Hawaii Press, 2000). Two pioneering Japanese studies on the cultural history of the interwar period are Minami Hiroshi, ed., *Taishō bunka* (Tokyo: Keisō shobō, 1965); and Minami Hiroshi, ed., *Shōwa bunka: 1925–1945* (Tokyo: Keisō shobō, 1987).

14. Amid the extensive literature on the problem of subjectivity in modern Japanese literature, a few landmarks are Maruyama Masao, "From Carnal Literature to Carnal Politics," in *Thought and Behavior in Modern Japanese Politics,* ed. Ivan Morris (London: Oxford University Press, 1969); Masao Miyoshi, *Accomplices of Silence: The Modern Japanese Novel* (Berkeley: University of California Press, 1974); Karatani Kōjin, *Origins of Modern Japanese Literature,* trans. Brett de Bary (Durham: Duke University Press, 1993); James A. Fujii, *Complicit Fictions: The Subject in Modern Japanese Prose Narrative* (Berkeley: University of California Press, 1993); and Tomi Suzuki, *Narrating the Self: Fictions of Japanese Modernity* (Stanford: Stanford University Press, 1996). In *The Dilemma of the Modern in Japanese Fiction* (New Haven, Conn.: Yale University Press, 1995), Dennis C. Washburn also

examines the issue of subjectivity, while testing the concept of the modern against a variety of pre- and post-Meiji texts, arguing for a "modernist" consciousness on the part of Japanese writers in a historical frame that is considerably broader than the time span I will explore in this study.

15. "Higyakusha no geijutsu" (The art of masochism), *MAVO* 6 (July 1925): 6.

16. See, for example, the special feature on "Kōsokudō jidai" (The high-speed society), in *Shinchō*, 25.3 (March 1928): 20–55. See also Nii Itaru, *Anakizumu geijutsu ron* (Tokyo: Yamani shobō, 1991 [1930]), 71–90; and Wada Hirofumi, *Tekusuto no kōtsūgaku* (Kyoto: Shirojisha, 1992), 70–107.

17. Miriam Silverberg suggests that the term *seikatsu* did not refer to all modalities of everyday life but was specifically "associated with a radically transformed material culture or rationalized lifestyle accompanying new forms of leisure activities"; see "The Café Waitress Serving Modern Japan," in *Mirror of Modernity: Invented Traditions of Modern Japan*, ed. Stephen Vlastos (Berkeley: University of California Press, 1998), 208.

18. "Atarashii geijutsuka no tanrenba: *MAVO* fukkatsu saigen ni saishite" (A training-ground for new artists: on the revival of *MAVO*), *Yomiuri shinbun*, June 29, 1925, *Hagiwara Kyōjirō zenshū*, vol. 2 (Tokyo: Seichisha, 1980), 343.

19. Takeuchi Yoshimi, "Kindai to wa nani ka," in *Takeuchi Yoshimi zenshū* (Tokyo: Chikuma shobō, 1980), 4: 129–32.

20. Ibid., 134.

21. Naoki Sakai, "Modernity and Its Critique: The Problem of Universalism and Particularism," in *Postmodernism and Japan*, ed. Masao Miyoshi and H. D. Harootunian (Durham: Duke University Press, 1989), 116.

22. Peter Duus, *The Abacus and the Sword: The Japanese Penetration of Korea 1895–1910* (Berkeley: University of California Press, 1995).

23. Dipesh Chakrabarty, "Postcoloniality and the Artifice of History: Who Speaks for 'Indian' Pasts?" *Representations* 37 (Winter 1992), 5.

24. Dennis Keene, *Yokomitsu Ri'ichi: Modernist* (New York: Columbia University Press, 1980), 68–69.

25. Ibid., 62.

26. Ibid., 69.

Chapter 1

1. On the divisive allegiances between modernism and Proletarian Literature among the writers of the feminist journal *Nyonin geijutsu* (as well as the problematics of "popular literature"), see Ogata Akiko, *Nyonin*

geijutsu no sekai: Hasegawa Shigure to sono shūhen (Tokyo: Domesu shuppan, 1980). Non-feminist women's journals also proliferated in the 1920s, and the category of "women's literature" emerged during this decade. See Maeda Ai, *Maeda Ai chōsakushū*, vol. 2, *Kindai dokusha no seiritsu* (Tokyo: Chikuma shobō, 1989), 151–98; and Joan E. Ericson, *Be a Woman: Hayashi Fumiko and Modern Japanese Women's Literature* (Honolulu: University of Hawaii Press, 1997).

2. To cite one example, a literary sketch of the "newspaper headquarter streets" (*Tōkyō asahi shinbun*'s headquarters in Sukiyabashi) was one of "Eighteen Views of Show Tokyo" in a special feature of the *Bungei shunjū* magazine, together with such other representative modern sites as a Ginza café street, the subway, a dance hall, a department store, and the *maru biru* building. Tokunaga Sunao, "Shinbunsha gai," *Bungei shunjū ōru yomimono gō* (July 1930), 278–79. For an examination of newspapers as a symbol of modernity in this period, see also Wada Hirofumi 99–106.

3. It should be noted that the *genbun itchi* movement encompassed diverse experiments and written forms, and not all of these forms were purported to be direct representations of colloquial speech. Nevertheless, by the early Taishō period, a standard modern writing style had emerged out of the *genbun itchi* movement, as seen, for example, in the works by the writers of the Shirakaba school. The first polemicists for what came to be known as "colloquial free verse" (*kōgojiyūshi*) also used the term *genbun itchi* to describe this form of verse. (Examples of such polemics include Morikawa Kison's "Genbun itchi shi" and Hatori Yoshika's "Genbun itchi no shi," both from 1907. Kawaji Ryūkō's *Hakidame* from 1907 and Sōma Gyofū's *Yaseinu* from 1908 are considered important early examples of the "colloquial free verse" mode.) While the "colloquial free verse" came to dominate the Tokyo *shidan* in the Taishō period, its preeminence did not go unchallenged: veteran poet Kitahara Hakushū in particular attacked this mode as unpoetic, criticizing "colloquial free verse" in general and the "People's Poets" in particular in the September and October 1922 issues of the journal *Shi to ongaku* (*Poetry and Music*). *Nihon gendai bungaku daijiten, jinmei jikō hen*, ed. Miyoshi Yukio et al. (Tokyo: Meiji shoin, 1994), 403.

4. For a study on the *bundan* in the interwar period, see Edward Thomas Mack II, "The Value of Literature: Cultural Authority in Interwar Japan" (Ph.D. Diss., Harvard University, 2002).

5. As Mack observes, in addition to literary journals such as *Bungei shunjū*, the *sōgō zasshi* or general-interest magazines *Chūō kōron* and *Kaizō* held important positions in the literary world, and their editors assumed roles as key arbiters of the *bundan*. These magazines included articles on diverse topics including politics, economics, and society, as

well as publishing works of literature and literary criticism. Mack 64–69, 154–56.

6. On the history of the Shiwakai and its relationship to the emerging avant-garde, see Kikuchi Yasuo, *Gendaishi no taidōki: aoi kaidan o noboru shijintachi* (Tokyo: Genbunsha, 1967), 55–70.

7. I borrow this term from Edward Seidensticker's two-volume study of Tokyo's history and culture, *Low City, High City: Tokyo from Edo to the Earthquake* (New York: Alfred A. Knopf, 1983) and *Tokyo Rising: The City Since the Great Earthquake* (Cambridge, Mass.: Harvard University Press, 1991).

8. *Nihon shuppan hyakunenshi nenpyō* (Tokyo: Nihon shoseki shuppan kyōkai, 1968), 371–72.

9. On the impact of the Great Kantō Earthquake on the publishing industry, see Mack, 93–146.

10. Miterai Tatsuo, "Taishō, Shōwa zenki," *Nihon shinbun hyakunenshi* (Tokyo: Nihon shinbun renmei, 1962), 326–28.

11. Arase Yutaka, "Mass Communication Between the Two World Wars," *Developing Economies* 5.4 (December 1967): 760.

12. *Nihon shuppan hyakunenshi nenpyō*, 376.

13. Fujitake Akira, "The Formation and Development of Mass Culture," *Developing Economies* 5.4 (December 1967): 775–76.

14. Ibid., 396.

15. Advertisement in the *Asahi Newspaper*, October 18, 1926. Quoted in *Maeda Ai chōsakushū*, vol. 2, 205.

16. Komori Yōichi, personal interview, August 20, 1998.

17. For the history of the film industry in the first decades of the twentieth century, see Komatsu Hiroshi, "Some Characteristics of Japanese Cinema Before World War I," in Arthur Noletti, Jr., and David Desser, eds., *Reframing Japanese Cinema: Authorship, Genre, History* (Bloomington: Indiana University Press, 1992), 229–58; Joanne Bernardi, *Writing in Light: The Silent Scenario and the Japanese Pure Film Movement* (Detroit: Wayne State University Press, 2001); and Aaron Andrew Gerow, *Writing a Pure Cinema: Articulations of Early Japanese Film* (Ph.D. Diss., University of Iowa, 1996).

18. *Shōwa kokusei sōran*, vol. 3, ed. Tōyō keizai shinpōsha (Tokyo: Tōyō keizai shinpōsha, 1991), 398.

19. See Monica Elsner, Thomas Müller, and Peter M. Spangenberg, "The Early History of German Television: The Slow Development of a Fast Medium," *Materialities of Communication*, ed. Hans Ulrich Gumbrecht and K. Ludwig Pfeiffer (Stanford: Stanford University Press, 1994), 107–46. For an early introduction of both the "talkie" and television technology in

Japan, see Mori Iwao, "Geijutsu no saisentan: kikai ni yoru hyōgen jidai" ("The Vanguard of Art: The Age of Expression through Machines"), in the first issue of the modernist literary journal *Bungaku jidai* (May 1929): 140–48.

20. Harris I. Martin, "Popular Music and Social Change in Prewar Japan," *Japan Interpreter* 7.3–4 (Summer–Autumn 1972): 342–43.

21. In 1928, the number of radio receivers exceeded the one-half million mark, and broadcasting expanded beyond the major cities to a nationwide network.

22. Martin, 334. Fujitake 776–78. For further information on radio censorship, see Gregory J. Kasza, *The State and the Mass Media in Japan, 1918–1945* (Berkeley: University of California Press, 1988), 72–101.

23. From the NHK's "Hōsō yōgo no chōsa ni kan suru ippan hōshin," quoted in *Nihongo no rekishi*, ed. Doi Tadao (Tokyo: Shibundō, 1957), 234.

24. For a brief introduction to the problem of the "masses" in interwar Japanese culture, see Eugene Soviak, "Tsushida Kyōson and the Sociology of the Masses," in *Culture and Identity: Japanese Intellectuals During the Interwar Years*, ed. J. Thomas Rimer (Princeton, N.J.: Princeton University Press, 1990), 83–98.

25. See, for example, Ōyama Ikuo's essay "Gaitō no gunshū: seijiteki seiryoku to shite no minshū undō" ("The Crowd in the Streets: On the Political Power of the Democracy Movement"), originally published in *Shin shōsetsu* magazine on January 12, 1916. Reprinted in *Taishō daizasshi* (Tokyo: Ryūdō shuppan, 1978), 80–88.

26. *Shinchō nihon bungaku jiten* (Tokyo: Shinchōsha, 1988), 742–43.

27. For an analysis of the urban Japanese readership of the 1920s and the various spaces and institutions that mediated reading, see Nagamine Shigetoshi, *Modan toshi no dokusho kūkan* (Tokyo: Nihon editāsukūru shuppanbu, 2001).

28. The Proletarian Literature movement had been a common front between anarchists, syndicalists, Bolsheviks, and other socialists; however, this cooperation ended when anarchists and other non-Marxists were purged from the Japan Proletarian Literary Federation in 1926. After further schisms, the Proletarian Literature movement was reorganized in 1928, with its most powerful faction emerging as the Zen nihon musansha geijutsu renmei (All-Japan Federation of Proletarian Arts, or NAPF), with its journal *Senki* (*Battle Flag*). See Yoshio Iwamoto, "Aspects of the Proletarian Literary Movement in Japan," in *Japan in Crisis: Essays on Taishō Democracy*, ed. Bernard S. Silberman and H. D. Harootunian (Princeton, N.J.: Princeton University Press, 1974), 156–82.

29. Sano Kasami, "Bungei no taishūka" ("The Massification of Literature"), *Bungei sensen* (July 1925), 1–2. See Kurihara Yukio, "Taishū-ka to Puroretaria Bungaku" ("Massification and Proletarian Literature"), '*Taishū' no tōjo: hīrōtachi to dokusha no 20–30 nendai*, ed. Ikeda Hiroshi (Tokyo: Inpakuto shuppankai, 1998), 205–17; and *Maeda Ai chōsakushū*, vol. 2, 199–216.

30. "Kaijōteki yagaiteki sendenteki bungaku no ichikōsatsu" ("A Thought on Stadium-like, Outdoor-like, Advertising-like Literature"), *Bungei hihyō* 2.2 (February 1926), *HKZS*, vol. 2, 392–98.

31. *Bungei shijō* 1.1 (November 1925): 1. In the second issue, coterie members Umehara Hokumei and Kaneko Yōbun were joined by Iwata Seiji and Mavo leader Murayama Tomoyoshi. The cover of *Bungei shijō* featured characters in various unconventional orientations and decorative use of mathematical and other graphic symbols in a style pioneered by the poets and artist-designers associated with the journals *Aka to kuro* and *MAVO* (even the advertisements in *Bungei shijō* feature this style!). Mavo members Murayama Tomoyoshi and Yanase Masamu contributed cover art as well as articles to *Bungei shijō* and were active throughout the 1920s as book designers.

32. Ibid., 1.

33. The trial of Kikuchi Kan appears in *Bungei shijō* 1.1 (November 1925): 48–50; the auction of manuscripts is featured in collages of newspaper coverage on the covers of issues 1.2 and 2.1 (December 1925 and January 1926); see also Murayama Tomoyoshi, "*Bungei shijō* no koro," supplement to the reprinted edition of *Bungei shijō*, ed. Senuma Shigeki (Tokyo: Nihon kindai bungakukan, 1976), 5–6.

34. Editorial trends in *Bungei shijō*, associated with its editors Kaneko and Umehara respectively, included support for Proletarian Literature within a pluralist context and an exploration of taboo or provocative sexual topics. Kaneko had been a key member of the coterie producing *Tane maku hito* (*The Sower*), the first Proletarian Literature journal in Japan. Umehara was an important figure in the trend toward the exploration of sexuality and sexual deviance in popular culture later identified as *ero-guro* (Erotic-Grotesque), in his role as editor of *Bungei shijō* and later journals such as *Hentai shiryō* (*Documents Related to Sexual Perversion*) and *Gurotesuku* (*Grotesque*), as well as his role in publishing translations of foreign sexual and erotic literature.

35. Translated in Tomi Suzuki's *Narrating the Self: Fictions of Japanese Modernity* (Stanford: Stanford University Press, 1996), 177–78. The original essay by Yokomitsu Riichi, "Bungei jihyō" ("A Review of the Literary Scene"), appeared in the December 1928 issue of *Bungei shunjū*.

Yokomitsu Riichi zenshū, vol. 11 (Tokyo: Kawade shobō, 1956), 307–14. Seiji Lippit discusses Yokomitsu's theories of literature and the significance of the rejection of *genbun itchi* for modernist literature in Japan in his study *Topographies of Japanese Modernism* (New York: Columbia University Press, 2002), 17, 28–31.

36. This movement "to the streets" was the intention explicitly stated and enacted by Hagiwara, Murayama, and other avant-garde writers and artists during the 1920s. However, it should be noted that many of the semi-public spaces associated with the production and reception of European art and literature, such as the bookstore, the café, the studio, the theater, and the gallery, were relatively new institutions and themselves associated with the modern transformation of daily life (*kindai seikatsu*). Thus, in a complex situation discussed further in this chapter, the institutions of bourgeois art production and reception were being critiqued by the Japanese avant-garde at the same moment they were being developed.

37. See Suzuki Sadami, *Modan toshi no hyōgen: jiko, gensō, josei* (Kyoto: Shirojisha, 1992), 45–69.

38. For a history of the Nantendō, see Terashima Tamao, *Nantendō: Matsuoka Toraōmaro no Taishō, Shōwa* (Tokyo: Kōseisha, 1999).

39. On the housing conditions in Hongō, see Tsuboi Shigeji, *Gekiryū no sakana: Tsuboi Shigeji jiden.* Collected in *Tsuboi Shigeji zenshū,* vol. 5 (Tokyo: Seijisha, 1989), 109.

40. Kon Tōkō, *Hanayaka na shikeiha* (Tokyo: Shinchōsha, 1972), 42. Literary and autobiographical representations of the Café Lebanon abound: see also Hayashi Fumiko, *Hōrōki* (Tokyo: Shinchōbunko, 1979); Okamoto Jun, *Shijin no unmei: Okamoto Jun jiden* (Tokyo: Rippū shobō, 1974); Ono Tōzaburō, *Kimyō na hondana: Shi ni tsuite no jidenteki kōsatsu,* collected in *Ono Tōzaburō chōsakushū,* vol. 3 (Tokyo: Chikuma shobō, 1991); Hirabayashi Taiko, *Hinata aoi,* collected in *Hirabayashi Taiko zenshū* (Tokyo: Shio shuppansha, 1979); and Tsuboi Shigeji, *Gekiryū no sakana: Tsuboi Shigeji jiden,* collected in *Tsuboi Shigeji zenshū,* vol. 5 (Tokyo: Seijisha, 1989).

41. Translated as *Jigakyō* in 1921.

42. Itō Shinkichi, *Reppu no naka ni tachite: Hagiwara Sakutarō to Hagiwara Kyōjirō* (Tokyo: Seichisha, 1981), 108–14; Wada Hirobumi, "Zen'ei geijutsu no nettowāku: Hagiwara Kyōjirō 'Shikei senkoku' no kontekusuto," in *Haikyō no kanōsei: Gendai bungaku no tanjō,* Ikeda Hiroshi et al., eds. (Tokyo: Inpakuto shuppankai, 1997), 78–93.

43. "Zenkoku dōjin zasshi," *Bungei shijō* 2.6 and 2.7 (June and July 1926).

44. A dum dum is a type of "soft-noted bullet designed to expand upon impact" (*American Heritage Dictionary, Third Edition*).

45. Miryam Sas discusses Tomotani Shizue's poetry in her dissertation, "Cultural Memory and Literary Movements: Dada and Surrealism in Japan" (Yale University, 1995), 197–211. Tomotani later married the Surrealist poet Ueda Tamotsu and changed her name to Ueda Shizue.

46. Hayashi Fumiko, *Hōrōki* [reprinted edition] (Tokyo: Nihon kindai bungakukan, 1973), 96–98. Hashizume refers to anarchist/Dadaist poet and critic Hashizume Ken, a *dōjin* of the *Dum dum* journal. All translations are my own unless otherwise noted. An alternative translation of *Hōrōki* (part one) is available in Joan A. Ericson, *Be a Woman: Hayashi Fumiko and Modern Japanese Women's Literature* (Honolulu: University of Hawaii Press, 1997), 123–214.

47. *Don* poetry almost certainly refers to the work associated with the minor avant-garde poet Don Zakkii (Miyakozaki Tomoo). Don Zakkii advocated his own school of poetry, *Don sōgōshugi*, and edited the journal *Sekai shijin* (*World Poet*), to which Hayashi Fumiko contributed; his 1925 poetry collection *Hakuchi no yume* was banned by state censors. Ericson mistakenly translates this passage as "an exhibit of John Donne's poetry" (157).

48. Tsuboi, 110. Kawaura Sanshirō, "Nenpyō" ("Biographical Timeline"), in Itō Shinkichi and Kawaura Sanshirō, eds., *Hagiwara Kyōjirō no sekai* (Maebashi: Kankodō, 1987), 232.

49. Omuka Toshiharu, *Taishōki shinkō bijutsu undō no kenkyū* (Tokyo: Sukaidoa, 1995), 486–90.

50. The serialization of Itō Chikusui's "Shuppan jōshiki jiten: amachua shuppanka no tame ni" began in the second issue of *Bungei shijō* (December 1925).

51. Astradur Eysteinsson, *The Concept of Modernism* (Ithaca: Cornell University Press, 1990), 2.

52. An important exception can be found in the criticism of Hirabayashi Hatsunosuke, who frequently employed the terms *gendai-ha, modan-ha,* and *modanizumu* to refer to Japanese writers in such essays as "Modan-ha haigeki" ("Denouncing the Modern School") from 1929 and "Geijutsu-ha, puroretarua-ha oyobi kindai-ha" ("The Arts School, Proletarian School, and Modern School") from 1930. *Hirabayashi Hatsunosuke bungei hyōron zenshū* (Tokyo: Bunseidō shoten, 1975), 239–52, 304–7. Critic Senuma Shigeki offered a perceptive and comprehensive view of modernist trends in his work *Gendai bungaku* (*Contemporary Literature*) of 1933, which employs the term *Moderunisumu bungaku* to describe various Japanese literary

developments following the establishment of the Shinkankaku-ha in 1924. Senuma Shigeki, *Gendai bungaku* (Tokyo: Mokuseisha shoin, 1933).

53. A somewhat larger umbrella term did emerge in the late 1920s: many of the prose writers now commonly referred to as "modernist" were grouped together by the contemporary critical and publishing apparatuses as the Shinkō geijutsu-ha (New Arts School). This appellation referred primarily to writers associated with the journals *Bungei toshi* (*Literary Metropolis*, 1928–1929) and *Bungaku jidai* (*Literary Age*, 1929–1932).

54. Matei Calinescu, *Five Faces of Modernity: Modernism, Avant-Garde, Decadence, Kitsch, Postmodernism* (Durham: Duke University Press, 1987), 95.

55. "Mavo no sengen" ["Mavo Manifesto"] (July 1923), supplement to the reprinted edition of *MAVO*, ed. Odagiri Susumu (Tokyo: Nihon kindai bungakukan, 1991).

56. Calinescu, 68.

57. The theatrical project *Gekijō no sanka*, in which the artists of the Mavo group collaborated, provides an example of the disruption of narrative temporality and the simultaneous occurrence of seemingly unrelated events in avant-garde theater. For a concise survey of Japanese interwar avant-garde activity in art, literature, and drama, focusing on Dadaistic theatrical performances, see Toshiharu Omuka, "Tada = Dada: (Devotedly Dada) for the Stage: The Japanese Dada Movement, 1920–1925," in *The Eastern Dada Orbit: Russia, Georgia, Ukraine, Central Europe, and Japan*, ed. Stephen C. Foster (New York: G. K. Hall, 1998), 223–310.

58. Motoe Kunio, "Hakai to Sōzō no ishi: 'Konsutorukuchion,'" in *Nihon no kindai bijutsu: zen'ei geijutsu no jikken*, ed. Yurugi Yasuhiro (Tokyo: Taigestu shoten, 1993), 82–83. Murayama's "Konsutorukuchion" is presently in the collection of the Tokyo National Museum of Modern Art.

59. In her book *Languages of Revolt*, Inez Hedges has proposed the ideas of frame-making and frame-breaking as a way of understanding Dada and Surrealist art, literature, and film, basing her analysis in part on the cognitive frame theory of Marvin Minsky (34–78). She takes up these terms again in her book on film, *Breaking the Frame*. Inez Hedges, *Languages of Revolt: Dada and Surrealist Literature and Film* (Durham, N.C.: Duke University Press, 1983); *Breaking the Frame: Film Language and the Experience of Limits* (Bloomington: Indiana University Press, 1991).

60. "Hyōgen geijutsu yori seikatsu geijutsu e" ("From Expressionist Art to the Art of Daily Life"), *Atelier* 2.7 (July 1925), quoted and translated in Weisenfeld, *Mavo*, 103.

61. Peter Bürger, *Theory of the Avant-Garde* (Minneapolis: University of Minnesota Press, 1984), 22.

62. These accounts vary in the details: I have followed Omuka Toshiharu's synthesis in *Taishōki shinkō bijutsu undō no kenkyū*, 481–84.

63. Ide Magoroku, *Nejikugi no gotoku: gakka Yanase Masamu no kiseki* (Tokyo: Iwanami shoten, 1996), 198–207.

64. Okada Tatsuo, "Insatsujutsu no rittaiteki danmen" ("A Three-dimensional Section of Printing Techniques") *Shikei senkoku*, reprinted edition (Tokyo: Nihon kindai bungakukan, 1972), postscript 4.

65. *Nihon shuppan hyakunenshi nenpyō* (Nihon shoseki shuppan kyōkai, 1968), 375.

66. See Jay Rubin, *Injurious to Public Morals: Writers and the Meiji State* (Seattle: University of Washington Press, 1984), 29–31, for a definition of *fuseji*, and throughout for examples of *fuseji* and other forms of state and self-censorship, as well as for cases of resistance to censorship by prominent writers.

67. Maud Lavin, "Photomontage, Mass Culture, and Modernity," in *Montage and Modern Life, 1919–1942,* ed. Matthew Teitelbaum (Cambridge, Mass.: The MIT Press, 1992), 56.

68. Although employing the earlier-mentioned term *sentan* here, he uses a different set of Chinese characters for this term, literally "leading edge" rather than "sharpened edge" as used in the Mavo manifesto. *Ōya Sōichi zenshū*, vol. 2 (Tokyo: Sōyōsha, 1981), 5.

69. An essay originally published in *Shinchō* (February 1930), quoted in Barbara Hamill, "Nihonteki modanizumu no shisō: Hirabayashi Hatsunosuke o chūshin to shite" ("Japanese Philosophies of Modernism: Focusing on Hirabayashi Hatsunosuke"), in *Nihon modanizumu no kenkyū,* ed. Minami Hiroshi (Tokyo: Burēn shuppan, 1982), 102.

70. Miriam Silverberg notes that the parallel term *modan bōi* (modern boy) was less clearly defined and much less frequently employed than *modan gāru*. "The Modern Girl as Militant," in *Recreating Japanese Women, 1600–1945,* ed. Gail Bernstein (Berkeley: University of California Press, 1991), 239–66. For further discussion of the "modern girl," see Barbara Sato, *The New Japanese Woman: Modernity, Media, and Women in Interwar Japan* (Durham, N.C.: Duke University Press, 2003), 45–77.

71. *Ōya Sōichi zenshū*, vol. 2, 10–17.

72. The spatial/temporal distinction between collage and montage is offered in Andrew M. Clearfield, *These Fragments I Have Shored: Collage and Montage in Early Modernist Poetry* (Ann Arbor, Mich.: UMI Research Press, 1984), 10–13.

73. *The Question Concerning Technology and Other Essays,* trans. William Lovitt (New York: Harper and Row, 1977), 115–54.

Chapter 2

1. For two of the most sophisticated and influential of such studies, see Masao Miyoshi, *Accomplices of Silence: The Modern Japanese Novel* (Berkeley: University of California Press, 1974); and Karatani Kōjin, *Origins of Modern Japanese Literature* (Durham, N.C.: Duke University Press, 1993).

2. Toshiko Ellis, "Questioning Modernism and Postmodernism in Japanese Literature," in *Japanese Encounters with Postmodernity,* ed. Johann P. Arnason and Yoshio Sugimoto (London and New York: Kegan Paul International, 1995), 142.

3. Dennis Washburn, *The Dilemma of the Modern in Japanese Fiction* (New Haven: Yale University Press, 1995), 78–79.

4. *Shintaishi shō (A Selection of New-Style Verse,* 1882) and Mori Ōgai's *Omokage (Vestiges,* 1889) are two landmarks in the early Japanese translation of European poetry.

5. See Donald Keene, *Dawn to the West: Japanese Literature in the Modern Era,* Vol. 2, *Poetry, Drama, Criticism* (New York: Henry Holt and Company, 1984), 194–204.

6. Toyama Masakazu, Yatabe Ryōkichi, and Inoue Tesujirō, *Shintaishi shō,* facsimile edition (Tokyo: Nihon kindai bungakukan, 1972). On the relationship between the development of modern poetry and the nationalist, phonocentric ideology of *genbun itchi,* see two critical studies by Suga Hidemi: *Shiteki modanitei no keifu* (Tokyo: Shichōsha, 1990), 10–62; and *Nihon kindai bungaku no 'tanjō': Genbun itchi undō to nashonarizumu* (Tokyo Ōta shuppan, 1995), 15–56, 209–48.

7. The year of publication of Kawaji Ryūkō's poetry collection *Hakidame,* as well as Morikawa Kison's essay "Genbun itchi shi" and Hatori Yoshika's "Genbun itchi no shi."

8. Examples of important textual introductions of European art by these authors include Kanbara's *Miraha kenkyū (Studies in Futurism,* 1925) and Murayama's *Genzai no geijutsu to mirai no geijutsu (The Art of Today and the Art of the Future,* 1924).

9. Information on modernist and avant-garde movements in Europe appeared in a variety of media, including literary journals, art journals, and the popular press. For example, Marinetti's first Futurist manifesto, "Manifeste de Futurisme," originally published in the Parisian newspaper *Le Figaro* in 1909, had already appeared in four different Japanese translations by 1924, beginning with Mori Ōgai's translation for the literary journal *Subaru* in

1909, and receiving three additional translations in art journals and books of art criticism. Chiba Sen'ichi, *Gendai bungaku no hikakubungakuteki kenkyū* (Tokyo: Yagi shoten, 1978), 62–64. Dadaism was introduced in 1920 in a series of articles in the *Yorozu chōhō* newspaper, which are said to have inspired Takahashi Shinkichi's interest in the Dadaist movement. Makoto Ueda, *Modern Japanese Poets and the Nature of Literature* (Stanford: Stanford University Press, 1983), 335–79. See Chiba for several informative articles on the transmission of European modernism and avant-garde literature to Japan; for an overview in English of the development of modernism in Japan, see Hirata 131–48.

10. On Takahashi's views on Zen and Dada, see Ko Won, *Buddhist Elements in Dada* (New York: New York University Press, 1977).

11. In his study *Shōwa seishinshi*, Oketani Hideaki offers an analysis of Hirotsu Kazuo's novel *Shōwa shonen no interi sakka* (*An Intellectual Writer in the Early Shōwa Years*, 1930) as one example of the tendency for America and the Soviet Union to be contrasted as two possible sites of affiliation for Japanese intellectuals. Oketani Hideaki, *Shōwa seishinshi* (Tokyo: Bungei shunjū, 1992), 168–73. Another set of examples can be found in a special feature on "America and Russia as [Two] Wombs of New Art and Culture" in the first issue of the modernist journal *Bungaku jidai*, including Chiba Kameo's "Kikai seijuku jidai no geijutsu to hankō ishiki bungaku" ("The Arts of the Mature Machine Age and the Literature of Resistance") and Nii Itaru's "Yuibutsu bungaku no nitaiyō to sono botai" ("Two Forms of Materialist Literature and their Wombs") *Bungaku jidai* 1.1 (May 1929), 12–16, 17–21.

12. The image of America in Japan was complex and contradictory. In addition to the association of America with hypercapitalism, Taylorist efficiency, and a decadent Hollywood consumer culture, the nature and significance of American political values received broad public scrutiny in the 1920s, with Wilsonian democratic idealism on the one hand, and American racism as expressed in the exclusionary Immigration Act of 1924 on the other, offering two focal points of debate.

13. This rhetorical distancing from the Soviet model preceded Murayama's later embrace of a more positive view of the role of technology and constructivism in Japan, which eventually led to a distancing from anarchism and eventual alignment with Soviet-oriented Communist orthodoxy and the Socialist Realist style.

14. For discussion of Murayama's theory of "conscious constructivism" and the shifts in his artistic philosophy, see Weisenfeld, *Mavo: Japanese Artists and the Avant-Garde, 1905–1931*, 42–46, 158–63.

15. Murayama Tomoyoshi, "Kōsei-ha ni kan suru ikkōsatsu: keisei geijutsu no han'i ni okeru," *Atorie* 2.8 (August 1925), 57.

16. Ibid., 58.

17. The term Hagiwara uses to describe the letters is *keishō,* "shape" or "figure." In Japanese *keishō* is combined with *moji,* "character," as a term for a hieroglyph or pictograph (or more commonly, the two Chinese characters that comprise the word *keishō* are inverted as part of the term *shōkei moji,* "hieroglyph" or "pictograph"). Thus Hagiwara's poem involves a re-imagining of the ostensibly phonetic roman alphabet as a hieroglyphic or pictographic system.

18. Hagiwara, *Shikei senkoku,* 158–59. Further compounding the play of linguistic registers in this poem, Hagiwara uses hiragana to transcribe the word *aruhabetto* (alphabet) here, rather than the more standard katakana.

19. See discussion of Hagiwara's artistic theories in Chapter 3.

20. Hirata, 185.

21. Hirato Renkichi, "Nihon miraiha sengen undō (Mouvement Futuriste Japonais)," reprinted in Kikuchi Yasuo, *Gendaishi no taidōki: aoi kaidan o noboru shijintachi* (Tokyo: Genbunsha, 1967), 154. Hirata's statements on poetic language closely echo Marinetti's "Technical Manifesto of Futurist Literature" of 1912. See Chiba Sen'ichi, 121.

22. Andō Yasuhiko, "Chō to bakudan," in *Gendaishi monogatari,* ed. Fundō Junsaku and Yoshida Hirō (Tokyo: Yūhikaku, 1978), 6–8.

23. Ivan Parker Hall, *Mori Arinori* (Cambridge, Mass.: Harvard University Press, 1973), 188–95.

24. The "scriptures" of Christianity and Marxism were, of course, translated into Japanese.

25. "Pictographic" and "ideographic" are placed in quotes because both Egyptian and Chinese writing systems have significant phonetic elements.

26. The quotation from Jean Pierre Abel-Rémusat is found in Robert Kern, *Orientalism, Modernism, and the American Poem* (Cambridge, U.K.: Cambridge University Press, 1996), 1. Earlier examples of the Western fascination with hieroglyphic and pictographic characters include various seventeenth-century theories that Chinese or Egyptian represented the Primitive Language given by God to Adam. The fascination with Egyptian hieroglyphs was revived among nineteenth-century intellectuals following Jean-François Champollion's deciphering of the Rosetta stone in the 1820s, in ways that both challenged and reinforced the mysticism of seventeenth-century linguistic theorists. See John T. Irwin, *American Hieroglyphics: The Symbol of Egyptian Hieroglyphics in the American Renaissance* (New Haven, Conn.: Yale University Press, 1980). On the subject of Chinese writing and Anglo-American modernism, see also Laszlok Géfin, *Ideogram: History of*

a Poetic Method (Austin: University of Texas Press, 1982). For one example of the modernist fascination with ideogrammatic writing outside of the Anglo-American context, see Michel Truffet, *Edition critique et commentée de Cent Phrases Pour Éventails de Paul Claudel* (Paris: Annales littéraires de L'Université de Besançon, 1985). Claudel's poetry collection of 1927, which combines Chinese calligraphy with experiments in roman-alphabet lettering, has been translated into English by Andrew Harvey and Iain Watson as *A Hundred Movements for a Fan* (London: Quartet Books, 1992).

27. Translated by John Solt in *Shredding the Tapestry of Meaning: The Poetry and Poetics of Kitasono Katsue (1902–1978)* (Cambridge, Mass.: Harvard University Asia Center, 1999), 57.

28. The question of poetry's relationship to "reality," particularly the political reality of Japan circa 1930, was a focus of debate and an eventual schism within the *Shi to shiron* group. See Hirata, 139–48.

29. A section of the poem series "ALBUM" from the 1929 poetry collection *Shokubutsu no danmen* (*Cross-section of a Plant*). Anthologized in *Nihon no shiika 25: Kitagawa Fuyuhiko, Anzai Fuyue, Kitasono Katsue, Haruyama Yukio, Takenaka Iku*, ed. Takanashi Shigeru (Tokyo: Chūō kōronsha, 1975), 283.

30. Miryam Sas, *Fault Lines: Cultural Memory and Japanese Surrealism* (Stanford: Stanford University Press, 1999), 35.

31. See Hirata, 167–98.

32. The port city of Dalian (Dairen in Japanese) was at the southernmost end of a corridor of land ceded to Japan by Russia in the Treaty of Portsmouth of 1905, and administered by the South Manchuria Railway Company until the establishment of the Japanese puppet state of Manchukuo in 1932. See Ramon H. Myers, "Japanese Imperialism in Manchuria: The South Manchuria Railway Company, 1906-1933," *The Japanese Informal Empire in China, 1895–1937,* ed. Peter Duus et al. (Princeton, N.J.: Princeton University Press, 1989), 101-132.

33. On the impact of Japanese haiku and tanka on early twentieth-century French poetry, see William L. Schwartz, "L'Influence de la poésie Japonaise sur la poésie Française contemporaine," *Revue de Littérature Comparée* 6 (1926): 654-72; Vera Linhartová, "Avant-Propos: La Poésie Européenne a L'heure Japonaise, 1905–1924," in *Dada et Surréalisme au Japon* (Paris: Publications Orientalistes de France, 1987), 9–26.

34. Quoted in Sakurai Katsue, *Kitagawa Fuyuhiko no sekai* (Tokyo: Hōbunkan, 1984), 133.

35. Hagiwara, "Jo," *Shikei senkoku* [numbered 1–11 in separate pagination from the main text]. See appendix for translation.

36. Ibid., 136.

37. The original poem was printed on one page, with a line framing the entire poem, and Anzai's name in small characters below the title; between the two lines of the poem was a space of roughly ten lines. *A* 2.3 (March 1925) [unpaginated].

38. Kawamoto Kōji, *The Poetics of Japanese Verse: Imagery, Structure, Meter*, translated by Stephen Collington, Kevin Collins, and Gustav Heldt (Tokyo: University of Tokyo Press, 2000), 73–79.

39. Anzai Fuyue, *Anzai Fuyue zenshishū* (Tokyo: Shichōsha, 1966), 47. The final version of the poem was published in Anzai's 1929 poetry collection *Gunkan Mari* (*The Battleship Mari*). A selection of Anzai's poems have been translated in Dennis Keene's *The Modern Japanese Prose Poem: An Anthology of Six Poets* (Princeton, N.J.: Princeton University Press, 1980).

40. Although the poem's title seems to point to the haiku practice of referencing a season, in fact haiku do not generally have titles, so the title serves as a distancing element as well. Anzai published a variant of this poem in haiku form, although this haiku is generally held to be less successful than his *tanshi*. See Ellis Toshiko, "Nihon Modanizumu no saiteigi: 1930 nendai sekai no bunmyaku no naka de" ("A Reappraisal of Japanese Modernism: Within the Context of the World of the 1930s"), in *Modanizumu kenkyū* (Tokyo: Shinchōsha, 1994), 561.

41. The two kanji for "Tartar" (韃靼) share the "leather" radical 革, thus associating this toponym with a nomadic herding existence viewed as alien or barbaric from the vantage point of rice-cultivating peoples such as Han Chinese and Japanese. For a study of toponyms related to northeast China, see Mark C. Elliott, "The Limits of Tartary: Manchuria in Imperial and National Geographies," *Journal of Asian Studies* 59.3 (August 2000), 603–646.

42. For an analysis of the poem that builds upon previous readings while placing Anzai's work within the historical development of Japanese modernism, see Toshiko Ellis, "Nihon Modanizumu no saiteigi," 559–561.

43. In 1920 at the age of twenty-two, Anzai Katsu moved to Dalian with his father, a former educator and government bureaucrat turned businessman. The next year he secured a position at the South Manchuria Railway Company, but soon after assuming his position he was hospitalized for a severe infection in his knee, for which his right leg was amputated. After the amputation, Anzai abandoned his career with the South Manchuria Railway Company and devoted himself to the composition of poetry, frequently employing the pen name of Anzai Fuyue; he remained in Manchuria until the death of his father in 1934. For biographical

information on Anzai, see Myochin Noboru, *Hyōden Anzai Fuyue* (Tokyo: Ōfusha, 1974).

44. Joshua A. Fogel, *The Literature of Travel in the Japanese Rediscovery of China, 1862–1945* (Stanford: Stanford University Press, 1996), 66–125.

45. Anzai, 129–30.

46. Anzai, 131.

47. Anzai, 114.

48. For a discussion of Japanese orientalism and imperialism, see Stefan Tanaka, *Japan's Orient: Rendering Pasts into History* (Berkeley: University of California Press, 1993). Anzai's citations of orientalist discourses can be compared with the many forms of European orientalism described in Edward W. Said's pioneering study *Orientalism* (New York: Vintage Books, 1979 [originally published by Random House, 1978]).

49. See Fogel, *The Literature of Travel in the Japanese Rediscovery of China, 1862–1945*. For translations and analysis of some representative literary accounts of Japanese colonial territories and "informal empire," see Joshua A. Fogel, ed., "Japanese Travelogues of China in the 1920s: The Accounts of Akutagawa Ryūnosuke and Tanizaki Junichirō," *Chinese Studies in History* 30.4 (Summer 1997), 3–103; Natsume Sōseki, *Rediscovering Natsume Sōseki, celebrating the centenary of Sōseki's arrival in England 1900–1902: with the first English translation of Travels in Manchuria and Korea*, trans. Inger Sigrun Brodey and Ikuo Tsunematsu (Folkestone: Global Oriental, 2000); Yosano Akiko, *Travels in Manchuria and Mongolia: A Feminist Poet from Japan Encounters Prewar China*, trans. Joshua A. Fogel (New York: Columbia University Press, 2001); Atsuko Sakaki, "Japanese Perceptions of China: The Sinophilic Fiction of Tanizaki Jun'ichirō," *Harvard Journal of Asiatic Studies* 59.1 (June 1999), 187–218; Faye Yuan Kleeman, *Under an Imperial Sun: Japanese Colonial Literature of Taiwan and the South* (Honolulu: University of Hawai'i Press, 2003).

50. Shu-mei Shih, *The Lure of the Modern: Writing Modernism in Semicolonial China, 1917–1937* (Berkeley: University of California Press, 2001), 21–30.

51. My use of the term "informal empire" is derived from Peter Duus, Ramon H. Myers, and Mark R. Peattie's study *The Japanese Informal Empire in China, 1895–1937* (Princeton, N.J.: Princeton University Press, 1989).

52. Jesuit cartographers in the seventeenth century transliterated the Latin word "Asia" into Chinese characters, choosing for the first syllable a character whose meaning is literally "secondary," as in the compound *aryū*, "second rate" or "imitative." This character was probably chosen for the journal title not only for these etymological associations, but also for

the character's distinctively symmetrical and angular shape, as well as its pronunciation as a clear monosyllable "ah" sound. See Higuchi Satoru, *Shōwashi no hassei: 'Sanshu no shiki' o mitasu mono* (Tokyo: Shinchōsha, 1990), 153.

53. For a more detailed analysis of Kitagawa and Anzai's poetry in regard to the concepts of "Asia" and "orientalism," see William O. Gardner, "Colonialism and the Avant-garde: Kitagawa Fuyuhiko's Manchurian Railroad," *Stanford Humanities Review* 7.1 (1999): 12–21; and William O. Gardner, "Anzai Fuyue's Empire of Signs: Japanese Poetry in Manchuria," *Acts of Writing: Language and Identities in Japanese Literature. Proceedings of the Association for Japanese Literary Studies*, vol. 3. For important Japanese-language studies of these issues, see Higuchi, *Shōwashi no hassei*; Kawamura Minato, *Ikyō no kindai bungaku: 'Manshū' to kindai nihon* (Tokyo: Iwanami shoten, 1990); Kawamura Minato, *'Yoidorebune' no seishun: mō hitotsu no senchū, sengo* (Tokyo: Inpakuto shuppankai, 2000); and Nakagawa Shigemi, "Anzai Fuyue ron," in *Toshi modanizumu no honryū: 'Shi to shiron' no rusupuri nūbō (L'esprit Nouveau)*, ed. Sawa Masahiro and Wada Hirofumi (Tokyo: Shōeidō, 1996).

54. In addition to the sources on Yi Sang cited below, see the extensive treatment of this topic in Shu-Mei Shih's *The Lure of the Modern: Writing Modernism in Semicolonial China, 1917–1937*.

55. I should make clear from the beginning of this section my own limitations in not having access to a large body of scholarship on Yi Sang, together with Yi Sang's Korean-language works in the original, due to my inability to read Korean. I have consulted as widely as possible the growing body of criticism and translations on Yi Sang in English, together with scholarship in Japanese and Yi Sang's original works in Japanese. References to these works in English and Japanese appear in the notes below.

56. On Yi Sang's relationship to Japanese modernism, see Saegusa Toshikatsu, "Ri San no modanizumu: sono seiritsu to genkai," *Chōsen gakuhō* 141 (October 1991): 119, 173n18; Walter K. Lew, "Jean Cocteau in the Looking Glass: A Homotextual Reading of Yi Sang's Mirror Poems," *Muae* 1 (1995): 225–26. For a general English-language bibliography and introduction to Yi Sang's work, see Walter K. Lew, "Yi Sang," in *The Columbia Companion to Modern East Asian Literature*, ed. Joshua S. Mostow (New York: Columbia University Press, 2003), 657–63.

57. See Henry H. Em, "Yi Sang's *Wings* Read as an Anti-Colonial Allegory," *Muae* 1 (1995): 105–11; Kim U-Chang, "The Situation of the Writers Under Japanese Colonialism," *Korea Journal* (May 1976), 4–15. I would like to thank Professor John Treat for introducing me to these articles and to Yi Sang's work.

58. In his article "An Eccentric Reversible Reaction: Yi Sang's Experimental Poetry in the 1930s and Its Meaning to Contemporary Design," *Visible Language* 33.3: 196–235, Min-Soo Kim offers an intriguing analysis of Yi Sang's poetry, focusing on its appropriation of post-Newtonian scientific concepts, particularly quantum physics and Einstein's theory of relativity.

59. Yi Sang, *Yi Sang si chongjakchip* (Seoul: Kabin ch'ulp'an sa, 1978), 219.

60. Ibid. 253–55. This poem is especially difficult to translate because of its use of the word *hito* (translated here as "you"). *Hito* has numerous possible equivalents, including "person," "people," "other people (outsiders)," "he," "she," "they," "you," or "my beloved." At times it seems that Yi Sang is addressing "people" in general, while at others he could be addressing his beloved (or, *hito* could be a double of the poet—see the discussion of mirror images below).

61. From "Poem No. II" from "Crow's-Eye View," translated by Walter K. Lew, *Korean Culture* 13.4 (Winter 1992): 36.

62. The poem "Sen ni kan suru oboegaki 6" ("Notes Concerning Lines 6") contains the aphoristic line, "Temporality (according to the vulgar way of thinking, historicity)." *Yi Sang si chongjakchip*, 256.

63. This historical situation is alluded to most clearly in a line from the poem "Abnormal Reversible Reaction": "Doesn't develop and doesn't develop and / this is resentment." Ibid., 228. The pervasive Hegelian idea of the nation-state as the subject of history was succinctly stated by Korean historian Sin Ch'aeho, who wrote in 1908: "Without the nation there is no history." Carter J. Eckert, "Epilogue: Exorcising Hegel's Ghosts: Toward a Postnationalist Historiography of Korea," in *Colonial Modernity in Korea*, Gi-Wook Shin and Michael Robinson, eds. (Cambridge, Mass.: Harvard University Asia Center, 1999), 367.

64. "Poem No. I" begins "13 Children Rush down a Street./(A dead end alley is Suitable.)//The 1st Child says it's frightening./The 2nd Child says it's frightening/The 3rd Child says it's frightening" and continues in the same vein through the series of 13 children. Translated by Walter K. Lew, "Crow's-Eye View," 36. In his translation of this poem, Walter K. Lew does not include spaces between words, in order to convey the effect of the original Korean. I have inserted spaces for legibility here.

65. Choi Won-shik, "Seoul, Tokyo, New York: Modern Korean Literature Seen Through Yi Sang's 'Lost Flowers,'" *Korea Journal* 39.4 (Winter 1999): 131.

66. *Yi Sang si chongjakchip*, 246.

67. In Japanese, "sūji no gobi no katsuyō ni yoru sūji no shōmetsu." From "Sen ni kan suru oboegaku 6" ("Notes Concerning Lines 6"), ibid., 258.

68. Ibid., 227. It is worth noting that the characters, 異常, pronounced "ijō" in Japanese are pronounced "yi sang" in Korean, are thus homophonous with the poet's pen name. This is one of the several instances of Korean/Japanese wordplay in Yi Sang's oeuvre. See Lim Chong-kuk, "Yi Sang: Yo no gyakusa ni ikita hito" ("Personal Introduction: Lee Sang"), trans. Pae Kang-Hwan, *Koria hyōron* 294 (December 1986): 49–52.

69. In his essay "1930 nen Tōkyō-Shanhai-Keijō," ("Tokyo, Shanghai, Keijō, 1930"), Sano Masato writes, "In his Japanese-language poems, Yi Sang does not use Japanese in a Japanese-like (*nihongo rashiku*) way, but gives the impression of using the language abusively, abstracting it like the signs of logic or mathematics." *Nihon bungaku kenkyū ronbun shūsei 38: Yokomitsu Riichi*, ed. Taguchi Ritsuo (Tokyo: Wakagusa shobō, 1999), 87.

70. In the essay "Tōkyō de shinda otoko: Modanisto I San no shi" ("A Man Who Died in Tokyo: The Poetry of Modernist Yi Sang"), collected in *'Yoidorebune' no seishun: mō hitotsu no senchū, sengo* (Tokyo: Inpakuto shuppankai, 2000), 177–78. Sano Masato makes a similar observations in his essays "1930 nen Tōkyō-Shanhai-Keijō," 87, and "Kankoku modanizumu no isō: I San Shi to Anzai Fuyue o megutte," *Shōwa bungaku kenkyū* 25 (September 1992): 39.

71. Significantly, many of these kanji compounds passed from the Japanese language into modern Chinese and Korean languages. The predominance of these technical terms, which passed from Japanese to Korean in part under the influence of Japanese imperialism, is one of the factors that is said to make conversion of Yi Sang's poetry from Japanese to Korean and vice versa especially straightforward and fluid, as has been argued by Japanese commentators such as Kawamoto Minato and Kurokawa Sō. Kawamoto, "Tōkyō de shinda otoko," 173–76; Kurokawa Sō, "Kaisetsu: Hata no nai bungaku," in *Gaichi no nihongo bungaku sen 3: Chōsen*, ed. Kurokawa Sō (Tokyo: Shinjuku shobō, 1996), 340–41. On the related phenomenon of the passage of kanji neologisms from Japan to China, see Lydia H. Liu, *Translingual Practice: Literature, National Culture, and Translated Modernity: China, 1900–1937* (Stanford: Stanford University Press, 1995).

72. Furthermore, it is worth noting that "cosmopolitanism" itself could have different political valences for Japanese and Korean intellectuals. In the latter case, "cosmopolitanism" could offer a model of subjectivity transcending the colonizer/colonized binarism; alternatively, Korean

intellectuals would be in a position to question the universalist or idealist "cosmopolitanism" of certain Japanese intellectuals as a camouflage of Japanese imperialism.

73. Kawamura Minato discusses Yi Sang's Japanese and Korean poems as "mirror images" of each other in "Tōkyō de shinda otoko" 166–67, 173–78. Also, it is worth noting the case of the poem "A Problem Concerning the Patient's Condition," which Yi Sang published first in Japanese and later "translated" into Korean as part of the "Crow's-Eye Views" series. This poem consists of a seemingly meaningless grid of numerals framed by the text, "A problem concerning the patient's condition / diagnosis 0:1 / 10.26.1931 / As above Physician-in-Charge Yi Sang." Intriguingly, while the numeric grid was in conventional orientation when the poem was published in Japanese, the poet reversed the numerals into "mirror writing" when the poem was published in Korean. The translation above is from Walter K. Lew's translation of the Korean version, in Yi Sang, "Crow's-Eye View," 37. The Japanese version appears in *Yi Sang si chongjakchip*, 265.

74. On the cultural movement and language reform, see Michael Edson Robinson, *Cultural Nationalism in Colonial Korea, 1920–1925* (Seattle: University of Washington Press, 1988), 88–92.

75. Carter J. Eckert, Ki-baik Lee, Young Ick Lew, Michael Robinson, and Edward W. Wagner, *Korea Old and New: A History* (Seoul: Ilchokak Publishers, for the Korea Institute, Harvard University, 1990), 222–30.

76. Gi Wook Shin and Michael Robinson. "Introduction: Rethinking Colonial Korea," in *Colonial Modernity in Korea* (Cambridge, Mass.: Harvard University Asia Center, 1999), 10.

77. Henry H. Em describes the nationalist context of reception for Yi Sang's work and explores the challenge it offers to Enlightenment rationality, which was both propagated in Korea as part of Western/Japanese hegemony and paradoxically constituted a key aspect of Korean anti-imperialist resistance. He concludes, "The utterances of Yi Sang's emasculated 'I' [in the novel *Wings*] defy the pedagogic impulse of nationalist discourse, and yet succeeds in subverting (momentarily) the syntactic and semantic structure of Enlightenment thought" (78). Henry H. Em, "Nationalist Discourse in Modern Korea: Minjok as a Democratic Imaginary" (Ph.D. diss., University of Chicago, 1995), 69–78.

78. Anzai, 173–74.

79. "Crow's-Eye View," 39, 40.

80. See "Jean Cocteau in the Looking Glass," 121–25, for this comment and a discussion of previous critical approaches to Yi Sang's mirror imagery.

81. *Yi Sang si chongjakchip*, 253.

82. Yi Sang, "Tong'gyŏng" ("Tokyo"), translated by Michael D. Shin, *Muae* 1 (1995): 96–101.

83. Walter K. Lew, Introduction to "Crow's-Eye View," *Korean Culture* 13.4 (Winter 1992): 34–35. For biography and context of Yi Sang's work, see also the chapter "Border Writing: Yi Sang and Colonial Korea," in M. J. Rhee, *The Doomed Empire: Japan in Colonial Korea* (Aldershot, Eng., and Brookfield, Vt.: Ashgate, 1997), 134–51.

Chapter 3

1. "Tōrai shidan e no keikoku" ("A warning to the poetry establishment"), originally published in *Bundan*, August 1924. *Hagiwara Kyōjirō zenshū*, vol. 2, 354.

2. For one historical overview of the varied approaches to the question of the "self" within the European philosophical and literary traditions, see Charles Taylor, *Sources of the Self: The Making of Modern Identity* (Cambridge, Mass.: Harvard University Press, 1989).

3. In 1919, at the age of twenty, Hagiwara attended classes on the bible at a church in Maebashi, studied the works of Japanese Christian Uchimura Kanzō, and taught Sunday School classes. Kawaura, "Nenpyō," 228. On the notion of "inner life," see Janet A. Walker, *The Japanese Novel of the Meiji Period and the Ideal of Individualism* (Princeton: Princeton University Press, 1979) 62–92.

4. Harootunian terms this the "inward migration" of Japanese intellectuals away from politics and toward a focus on inner life in his article "Between Politics and Culture: Authority and the Ambiguities of Intellectual Choice in Imperial Japan," which focuses on the writers Kitamura Tōkoku (1868–1894) and Takayama Chogyū (1871–1902). Collected in *Japan in Crisis: Essays on Taishō Democracy*, ed. Bernard S. Silberman and H. D. Harootunian (Princeton: Princeton University Press, 1974) 110–55. The literary critic Nakamura Mitsuo has examined the shift within Japanese Naturalism from a socially oriented to a more individually focused literature in his influential *Fūzoku shōsetsu ron* of 1950, which helped to establish the orthodox literary interpretation of the I-novel and its geneology (collected in *Nakamura Mitsuo zenshū*, vol. 7 (Tokyo: Chikuma shobō, 1972), 525–648.

5. From Mushakōji's March 1911 essay in the *Shirakaba* journal, "Jibun no fude de suru shigoto" ("Work Done with My Own Pen"), as translated by Tomi Suzuki in *Narrating the Self*, 52. Within the Shirakaba coterie itself, Arishima Takeo distanced himself from the idealist humanism of

Mushakōji and placed his faith in social transformation wrought by the working class, while despairing of his own role as a bourgeois intellectual in such a transformation. See Arima Tatsuo, *The Failure of Freedom: A Portrait of Modern Japanese Intellectuals* (Cambridge, Mass.: Harvard University Press, 1969) 128–51. It might be noted that Arishima, with his profound sympathies toward socialism and anarchism, provided seed money to support the coterie journal *Aka to kuro*, founded by the radical young poets Okamoto Jun, Tsuboi Shigeji, Kawasaki Chōtarō, and Hagiwara Kyōjirō.

6. Thomas A. Stanley, *Ōsugi Sakae: Anarchist in Taishō Japan: The Creativity of the Ego* (Cambridge, Mass.: Harvard East Asian Monographs, 1982), 167.

7. Gennifer Weisenfeld discusses the importance of the idea of individualism for the Mavo group of artists, with reference to Ōsugi's political philosophy, in "Mavo's Conscious Constructivism: Art, Individualism, and Daily Life in Interwar Japan," *Art Journal* 55.3 (Fall 1996): 64–73.

8. *Ōsugi Sakae hyōronshū* (Tokyo: Iwanami Shoten, 1996), 15–81. While Ōsugi maintained a dramatic, rebellious personal life until his death in 1923, his political philosophy later shifted toward a more pragmatic form of anarcho-syndicalism.

9. Ōsugi, 65.

10. Ōsugi, 57, 65–66.

11. Stanley cites Piotr Kropotkin, Georges Sorel, Henri Bergson, Friedrich Nietzsche, and Max Stirner as providing the intellectual foundations for Ōsugi's philosophy. *Anarchist in Taishō Japan*, 59–63.

12. "Kantogen" ("Opening words"), *Damu damu* 1 (November 1924): 1.

13. "Hanranki no geijutsu" ("Art in the Age of the Flood"), *Damu damu* 1 (November 1924): 33–35.

14. See Appendix A for a translation of the preface to *Shikei senkoku*, and Appendix B for a translation of selected poems from the collection.

15. Reviews by Hagiwara Sakutarō, Minami Kōjirō, and Takahashi Shinkichi appeared in *Nihon shijin* 6.4 (April 1926). Kanbara Tai's review appeared on November 21 and 22, 1925, in the *Yomiuri shinbun*. While the collection has maintained an underground reputation as a monument of interwar avant-garde poetry, its long-term impact on the Japanese literary scene was diminished by the shift toward socialist-realist, surrealist, and neo-Romantic modes of poetry. Hagiwara's own retreat from the cultural spotlight and early abandonment of *Shikei senkoku* may have also contributed to this literary-historical eclipse: after the collection's first edition quickly sold out, Hagiwara declared that the second printing would

be the last, saying that he "wanted to cast these poems away from myself."
Hagiwara Kyōjirō zenshū, vol. 2, 232.

16. "Shishū reigen," *Shikei senkoku*, 1–2. This is the second of two prefaces, "Jo" and "Shishū reigen."

17. "Jo," *Shikei senkoku*, 7.

18. Takahashi Shūichirō, *Hakai to gensō: Hagiwara Kyōjirō shiron* (Tokyo: Kasama shoin, 1978), 61–62.

19. This conception of the artwork as part of the construction of consciousness bears a close relation to Mavo leader Murayama Tomoyoshi's theory of "conscious construction" (*ishikiteki kōseishugi/Bewusste Konstruktionismus*), which was informed by the philosophy and art theory of Hegel, Nietzsche, and Kandinsky. While Murayama never fully articulated this theory in the prewar period, it seems to have involved both a "conscious" manifestation of the constructedness of the artwork (as Weisenfeld glosses the theory), and a willful, dialectical process of constructing artistic consciousness, performed by "consciously setting up contradictions against your own subjective standards" (as Murayama retrospectively defined the theory in his autobiography). Weisenfeld states that this theory, in spite of its vagueness, became an "emblematic theory of the [Mavo] group's collective work." Regardless of the close relationship between Murayama and Hagiwara's theories of art, Hagiwara periodically mocked the idea of "conscious construction," and pointedly called *Shikei senkoku* a work of "conscious destruction" (*ishikiteki hakai*). Weisenfeld, *Murayama, Mavo, and Modernity*, 190–200; Murayama Tomoyoshi, "Sugiyuku hyōgenha: Ishikiteki kōseishugi e no joronteki dōnyū," *Chūō bijutsu* 9.4 (April 1923): 27–30; and *Engekiteki jijōden* (Tokyo: Tōhō shuppansha, 1971), 150; Hagiwara Kyōjirō, "Jo," *Shikei senkoku*, 10.

20. The relationship between masochism and the arts is explored in Murayama Tomoyoshi's essay/manifesto "Higyakusha no geijutsu" ("Art of the Masochist") *MAVO* 6 (July 1925), 5–6.

21. *Hagiwara Kyōjirō zenshū*, vol. 1, 290.

22. "Between Politics and Culture," 145–46.

23. *Hagiwara Kyōjirō zenshū*, vol. 2, 359.

24. Gregory Bateson, "The Cybernetics of 'Self': A Theory of Alcoholism" (1971), collected in *Steps to an Ecology of the Mind* (Chicago: University of Chicago Press, 1972, 2000), 319, 331.

25. Amo Hisayoshi, "'Shikei senkoku' shoron," *Shiron* 11 (December 1987), 77–78.

26. Nevertheless, it would be preferable to disengage an analysis of Hagiwara's poetry from such mimetic notions as "city portrait" or "self-

portrait": a rejection of the mimetic is one of the bases for Hagiwara's use of the term "construction."

27. *Hirato Renkichi shishū* [reprinted edition] (Tokyo: Nihon kindai bungakukan, 1991), 173.

28. Ibid., 173.

29. Ibid., 175.

30. Hagiwara's primary obligation at home was caring for his great aunt. As a young lyric poet, Hagiwara Kyōjirō was blessed with two mentors from his native Gunma Prefecture: Hagiwara Sakutarō and Yamamura Bochō. Hagiwara Sakutarō, who was not related to Kyōjirō, is widely considered the poet who brought modern free verse to full maturity in Japan. Yamamura Bochō's highly experimental poetry collection *Seisanryōhari* (*Sacred Prisms*, 1915) is considered a forerunner to Japanese Futurism and Surrealism.

31. This poem first appeared in the *Tokyo nichi nichi shinbun* in March 1921. *Shikei senkoku*, 2–3.

32. The female gendering and subsequent dismissal of *Passéist* elements of urban culture is consistent with the strategies of Marinetti's Futurism, which in its first manifesto advocates "scorn for woman." F. T. Marinetti, "The Founding and Manifesto of Futurism," in *Let's Murder the Moonshine: Selected Writings*, ed. and trans. by R. W. Flint (Los Angeles: Sun and Moon Press, 1991), 50. The second portion of Hagiwara's term, "civilization" (*bunmei*), would have carried a dated or even discredited ring by the time of this poem's composition, being associated with Meiji-period efforts toward the wholesale importation of European Enlightenment material and political culture. On the transition from *bunmei* to *bunka* as an idea of modern culture, see Minami Hiroshi et al., *Taishō bunka* (Tokyo: Keisō shobō, 1965), 35–63.

33. *Shikei senkoku*, 2–3.

34. Ibid., 3.

35. *Shikei senkoku*, 94–95.

36. According to Wada Hirofumi, buildings in pre-war Tokyo were not permitted to rise above seven or eight stories. *Tekusto no kōtsūgaku* , 40–47.

37. Unno Hiroshi, *Modan toshi Tōkyō* (Tokyo: Chūō kōronsha, 1988), 98. Isoda Kōichi gives another reading of Hagiwara's poem, and of the Hibiya district as a multilayered cultural signifier, in *Rokumeikan no keifu* (Tokyo: Bungei shunjū, 1983), 205–34.

38. Isoda, *Rokumeikan no keifu*, 208–11.

39. See Shumpei Okamoto, "The Emperor and the Crowd: The Historical Significance of the Hibiya Riot," *Conflict in Modern Japanese His-*

tory: The Neglected Tradition, ed. Tetsuo Najita and J. Victor Koschmann (Princeton: Princeton University Press, 1982), 258–75.

40. Isoda Kōichi, *Rokumeikan no keifu* 212.

41. Komata Yūsuke, "Hagiwara Kyōjirō—'Shikei senkoku' ron." *Chūō daigaku bungakubu kiyō* (April 1989), 145–46. According to Komata, the poem was dated August 1923; it was originally printed in the October 1925 issue of *Nihon Shijin*.

42. *Modan toshi Tōkyō*, 99.

43. From "Jikoku" ("Self-carving") and "Shi wa dorei to shujin ni mukanshin de aru" ("Death Cares Not Whether Master or Slave"). *Shikei senkoku*, 102, 101.

44. Ibid., 103.

45. Ibid., 105.

46. Komatsu Ryūji, *Nihon anakizumu undōshi* (Tokyo: Aoki shoten, 1972), 186–91.

47. Komata Yūsuke points out this possible connection with the title of Hagiwara's collection, citing the headlines of the extra edition of the *Tōkyō nichi nichi shinbun* (November 13) and the *Ōsaka mainichi shinbun* (November 14). *Zen'eishi no jidai: Tōkyō no 1920 nendai* (Tokyo: Sōseisha, 1992), 69–70. During his trial, Nanba cited reprisal for the Amakasu and Kameido incidents and the anti-Korean lynchings as his motive.

48. Unno Hiroshi, 113; Komata Yūsuke, *Zen'eishi no jidai*, 75. Savinkov was also known by the pen name Ropshin; his autobiographical novel (1909) was translated as *Aozametaru uma* in 1919. Ono Tōzaburō published "Nihirisuto Rōpushin," a study of Savinkov's work, in *Damu damu* magazine (November 1924), 24–32. As Mori Eiichi suggests, *Aozametaru uma* was also a likely source for the title of Hayashi Fumiko's first poetry collection, *Aouma o mitari* (I Saw a Pale Horse, 1929). Mori Eiichi, *Hayashi Fumiko no keisei: sono sei to hyōgen* (Tokyo: Yūseidō, 1992), 17. Even before Ropshin's work, Russian terrorist activity was well known in Japan. The activities of Russian nihilists, who assassinated Tsar Alexander II in 1882, were introduced in the Meiji political novels and translation-adaptations such as Kawashima Tadanosuke's *Strange Tales of the Subjugation if the Nihilists* (1882) and Matsui Shōyō's *Strange Tales of the Nihilists* (1904). See Akamatsu Katsumaro, "The Russian Influence on the Early Japanese Social Movement," in *The Russian Impact on Japan: Literature and Social Thought*, translated and edited by Peter Berton, Paul F. Langer, and George O. Totten (Los Angeles: University of Southern California Press, 1981), 88–90.

49. *Aka to kuro* 1 (January 1923), cover.

50. The idea of reading Nanba Daisuke as the "one man" of Hibiya, despite its apparent anachronism, is explored by all three commentators

294 O Notes to Pages 103-7

on this poem, Unno, Isoda, and Komata. Komata also discusses the relationship between "Hibiya" (the poem) and the other poems in the Hibiya section.

51. Weisenfeld, *Mavo*, 80.

52. Omuka, *Taishōki shinkō bijutsu undō no kenkyū*, 491–514; Weisenfeld, *Mavo*, 77–95. For information on Kon Wajirō, who also founded the discipline of "Modernology," see Miriam Silverberg, "Constructing the Japanese Ethnography of Modernity," *The Journal of Asian Studies* (February 1992), 30–54.

53. Apparently, Hagiwara was acquainted from an early point with Mavo members Sumiya Iwane and Toda Tatsuo, who were also from the Maebashi, Gunma Prefecture area. Weisenfeld, *Mavo*, 97–98; Toda Tatsuo, *Watakushi no kakochō* (Tokyo: Kōbunsha, 1972), 158–63.

54. "Barakkugai ni tai suru geijutsuteki kōsatsu" ("An Art Review of the Barrack Streets"), originally published in the *Chūō shinbun*. *Hagiwara Kyōjirō zenshū*, vol. 2, 345.

55. Omuka Toshiharu, "'Mavo' oboegaki: MV o megutte," ("A note on 'Mavo': concerning MV") *Musashino bijutsu* 76 (1989), 8–13. Weisenfeld, *Mavo*, 95–98.

56. *MAVO* ran through August 1925 for a total of seven issues. Non-Mavoist contributors to the final two issues included Yoshiyuki Eisuke, Tsuji Jun, and Hirabayashi Taiko.

57. *MAVO* 5 (June 1925): 5.

58. *Hagiwara Kyōjirō zenshū*, vol. 2, 380.

59. Weisenfeld, *Mavo*, 181–82.

60. Murayama Tomoyoshi, *Kōseiha kenkyū* (Tokyo: Chūō Bijutsusha, 1926), 68.

61. Ibid., 67–69.

62. Hirabayashi Hatsunosuke, "Bungaku oyobi geijutsu no gijutsuteki kakumei" ("The Technological Revolution in Literature and Art"), *Geijutsu no kakumei to kakumei no geijutsu*, Kurihara Yukio, ed. (Tokyo: Shakai hyōronsha, 1990), 88. Originally published in *Shinchō*, January 1928.

63. Ibid., 86.

64. Some of the material for the following discussion of Hagiwara's sketch and poem "Kōkokutō" was presented in William O. Gardner, "Shi to shin media: Hagiwara Kyōjirō no 'Kōkokutō' o chūshin ni shita 1920 nendai no avan gyarudo ronkō" ("Poetry and New Media: An Essay on the 1920's Avant-garde, Focusing on Hagiwara Kyōjirō's 'Advertising Tower'"), *Tōkyō daigaku hikaku bungaku bunka kenkyū* 16 (February 1999).

65. As a combination of the intense interest in (and anxiety over) the

body and machine culture, mixtures of man and machine achieved considerable cultural prominence in the 1920's: Marinetti's play *Poupées Électriques* (1909) was translated by Kanbara Tai in 1921; Karel Capek's satirical play *R.U.R.* (1921), which introduced the word robot to the world, was performed by the Tsukiji Little Theater in 1924; Fritz Lang's 1927 film *Metropolis* was shown in Japan in 1929. See Appendix B for a translation of Hagiwara Kyōjirō's poem "Asa●hiru●yoru●robot" ["Morning● noon●night●robot"], from *Shikei senkoku.*

66. Christina Lodder, *Russian Constructivism* (New Haven: Yale University Press, 1983), 163–69.

67. Nikolai Punin, "Tatlin's Tower" (1920), *The Tradition of Constructivism*, ed. Stephen Bann (New York: Da Capo Press, 1974), 15–17.

68. On Mavo's theatricalization of urban space, see Weisenfeld, *Mavo*, 231–32. On the contradictions in Mavo's engagement with consumer culture and simultaneous critique of capitalism, see *Mavo*, 165–215; and Shimazaki Osuke, "'Zōkeiteki henreki' josetsu: mavo shutsugen zengo no mokugekiteki kaisō" ("'Plastic' Itinerary: An Eyewitness Account of the Advent of Mavo"), *Nihon dezain shoshi* (Tokyo: Daviddosha, 1970), 56–59.

69. *Shikei senkoku,* 134–39.

70. I place the poet's name in quotation marks here to emphasize that "Hagiwara" can only be a construction of the reader, as suggested by the collection's preface.

71. This line is the closest Hagiwara comes to a direct mention of the Emperor System. The word employed here, *teiōsha*, does not, however, refer directly or exclusively to the Japanese emperor, or *tennō.*

72. Walter Benjamin, "The Work of Art in the Age of Mechanical Reproduction," in *Illuminations,* ed. Hannah Arendt, trans. Harry Zohn (New York: Schocken Books, 1969), 217–52.

73. It should be noted that questions of voice and orality in modern poetry are complicated by the debates over "free verse" versus the employment of poetic meter (or syllabics); both sides of this debate could lay claim to a model of "orality," one based on colloquial speech and one on poetic rhythm. In his important study *Koe no shukusai*, Tsuboi Hideto traces the importance to modern Japanese poetics of the concept of "voice," in its various manifestations from the rise of the "People's Poets" to the postwar period. He suggests that Japanese modernism offered a brief shift away from orally centered models of poetry to one based on the possibilities of the written word and print media. Most intriguingly, he suggests that the ideological shift toward a nationalist poetry in the wartime period was accompanied by a revival of a poetics of the voice, which was mediated by the new medium of radio, specifically in the national broadcasts of patriotic

and pro-war poetry in the years 1940–1945. Tsuboi Hideto, *Koe no shuku-sai* (Nagoya: Nagoya daigaku shuppankai, 1997).

74. Abe Yoshio points out that these lines could continue indefinitely with the same structural pattern in his essay, "Nihon no modanizumu" ("Japanese Modernism"), *Uta to shi no keifu,* ed. Kawamoto Kōji (Tokyo: Chūō kōronsha, 1994), 333.

75. Since a single kanji character can represent more than one syllable, there is not necessarily a one-to-one correspondence between the number of syllables and the number of characters in a poetic line consisting of a mix of kanji characters and syllabic hiragana characters, such as found in this section of "Kōkokutō!"

76. The concept of the cyborg emerged from American cybernetics and biological research in the postwar period, and thus, unlike the robot, was unknown to Hagiwara and his contemporaries. For the first print explication of the cyborg, see Manfred E. Clynes and Nathan S. Kline, "Cyborgs and Space," *Astronautics,* September 1960. Reprinted in *The Cyborg Handbook,* ed. Chris Hables Gray (New York and London: Routledge, 1995), 30–31.

77. Benjamin, "The Work of Art," 242.

78. Gregory J. Kasza describes the Peace Preservation Law as "the most lethal weapon used [by the state] against the left" during the prewar period. *The State and the Mass Media in Japan, 1918–1945* (Berkeley: University of California Press, 1988), 41. See also Richard H. Mitchell, *Thought Control in Prewar Japan* (Ithaca: Cornell University Press, 1976), 56–68.

79. *Rokumeikan no keifu,* 220.

Chapter 4

1. The first chapter of *Hōrōki,* entitled "Hōrōki izen" when collected as a novel, was first published in the journal *Kaizō* (October 1929) under the title "Kyūshū tankōgai hōrōki" ("Diary of a Vagabond: A Kyushu Mining Town"). Thus the chapter differs from the rest of *Hōrōki* not only in setting and literary style, but in its original venue of publication. Serialization in *Nyonin geijutsu* of the chapters collected in *Hōrōki* continued from October 1928 until July 1930; three chapters collected in *Zoku hōrōki* were also published in *Nyonin geijutsu* from August to October 1930. See Imagawa Hideko, " 'Hōrōki': seisei to sono sekai" ("The creation of *Hōrōki* and its world"), *Hōrōki arubamu,* ed. Imagawa Hideko (Tokyo: Haga shoten, 1996), 68–69.

2. According to Ericson, *Hōrōki* sold 600,000 copies in its first two years, including editions of the novel combined with its sequel. Ericson also cites evidence suggesting that the novel continued to be "the best

known and most popular modern work by a woman" in Japan, even into the 1980s. Joan E. Ericson, *Be a Woman: Hayashi Fumiko and Modern Japanese Women's Literature* (Honolulu: University of Hawaii Press, 1997), 57.

3. *Hōrōki* thus carries a complex textual history. This history is further complicated by the fact that the author made a number of revisions to the text of *Hōrōki* even after it was published as a novel. The most significant of these revisions came in 1939, when Shinchōsha published a *ketteiban*, or "definitive edition" of the text. Most subsequent editions of the text, including the readily available *Shinchō bunko* edition (which combines *Hōrōki* and its two sequels), follow the *ketteiban*, which differs markedly from the first published edition. While the 1939 revisions turned *Hōrōki* into a more polished and easily readable novel, a good deal of the original's vitality and stylistic audacity were lost. Although I consult both versions of the text, I have chosen to base my translations and analysis on the first edition, both for its chronological primacy, and for its more aggressive literary style, which clarifies *Hōrōki*'s status as a modernist work. For an analysis of the differences between the first edition and the *ketteiban*, see Imagawa Hideko, 65–76; Mori Eiichi, "'Hōrōki' ron: sono kisōteki kenkyū" ("A Study of *Hōrōki*:: Fundamental Investigation"), *Kanazawa daigaku kyōiku gakubu kiyō: jinmon kagaku, shakai kagaku hen* 33 (February 1984): 101–8; Ericson, 69–71.

4. Hayashi Fumiko, *Shinpan hōrōki* (Tokyo: Shinchōsha, 1979), 295.

5. Ericson, 92.

6. Watanabe Kazutami, "Mō hitotsu no toshi shōsetsu: Hayashi Fumiko 'Hōrōki' o megutte" ("One more urban novel: concerning Hayashi Fumiko's Hōrōki"), in Odagiri Susumu, ed., *Shōwa bungaku ronkō: Machi to mura to* (Tokyo: Yagi shoten, 1990), 3–20; Unno Hiroshi, *Modan toshi Tōkyō* (Tokyo: Chūō kōronsha, 1988), 197–223.

7. Seiji M. Lippit, *Topographies of Japanese Modernism* (New York: Columbia University Press, 2002), 17.

8. Ibid., 163.

9. M. M. Bakhtin, *The Dialogic Imagination: Four Essays*, ed. Michael Holquist, trans. Caryl Emerson and Michael Holquist (Austin: University of Texas Press, 1981), 262, 270–71.

10. Ibid., 270–71.

11. A strong interest in cinematic montage, and more generally in cinema and film-writing, is seen throughout Japanese modernism. The enthusiastic critical reception for Alexander Volkov's *Kean* (1924), the first of several French Impressionist films to be screened in Japan, helped to establish an influential new idiom of film criticism that valorized the use of montage and emphasized the qualities of speed, rhythmicality, and

musicality. This critical vocabulary was echoed in the literary criticism and manifestos of Japanese modernists, such as Kawabata Yasunari's "Shin-shin sakka no shin keikō kaisetsu" (*Bungei jidai*, January 1925). An interest in montage was also shared by Japanese modernist poets, such as Iijima Tadashi and Kitagawa Fuyuhiko, two writers who doubled as film critics and poets, who were both founding members of the important modernist journal *Shi to shiron* (*Poetry and Poetics*, founded 1928). Several modernist poets, including Kitagawa, Iijima, and Takenaka Iku, experimented with the *cinépoème*, a hybrid of poetry and film scenario. On the introduction of French Impressionist film criticism and its cultural significance, see Yamamoto Kikuo, *Nihon eiga ni okeru gaikoku eiga no eikyō: hikaku eigashi kenkyū* (Tokyo: Waseda daigaku shuppanbu, 1983), 144–66.

The related artistic practices of photomontage, collage, and assemblage were explored extensively by the Mavo group of avant-garde artists in the mid-1920s, with whom Hayashi had contact through her acquaintances at the Café Lebanon (Hayashi published poems in the fifth and sixth issues of the *MAVO* journal).

My use of the term "montage" with regard to Hayashi Fumiko's writing has two interrelated aspects: the first is temporal, referring to Hayashi's fragmentation and permutation of the narrative diegesis, contributing to an effect of speed and frequent disorientation; and the second is material, referring to the incorporation of disparate elements into the text, including poetry, songs, lists, etc., as well as contrastive prose styles and language types.

12. Hayashi Fumiko, *Hōrōki*, reprinted edition (Tokyo: Nihon kindai bungakukan, 1973), 21–37. See Lippit, 182–84, 187, for additional commentary on this section of Hayashi's text.

13. Extensive discussion of montage in film journals and a few surviving films give an overview of the different types of montage employed by Japanese filmmakers during this decade. Itō Daisuke was acclaimed for his bravura use of highly rhythmic, accelerated montage in action-filled period films. The montage of Kinugasa Teinosuke was inspired in part by the French impressionist filmmakers, and employed rhythmic principles and psychological association, as demonstrated by his two surviving avant-garde films from this decade, *Kurutta ippeiji* (*A Page of Madness*, 1926) and *Jūjiro* (*Crossways*, 1928). Mizoguchi Kenji's montage of this period reportedly relied heavily on disjunction and juxtaposition, and was compared by contemporary critics to Soviet montage practices. Hollywood continuity editing was also widely studied by Japanese filmmakers and offered another, less disruptive model of montage. The prose of Hayashi's *Hōrōki*, in contrast to Hollywood continuity filmmaking, consists of many discrete

sections, often temporally disconnected. While strictly literary precedents for narrative ellipsis certainly exist—particularly in the Japanese tradition—I would argue that the aggressive, kaleidoscopic disjunctiveness of Hayashi's text, as well as its close attention to optics and movement, points to its remediation of the film medium. It should be noted that one of Mizoguchi's narrative films of this period was also entitled "city symphony," or in Japanese *Tokai kōkyōgaku* (1929). On this lost film, see Iwamoto Kenji, "Tokai kōkyōgaku: Mizoguchi Kenji to akai senpū," *Nihon eiga to modanizumu 1920–1930* (Tokyo: Riburopōto, 1991), 150–53. For a recent study of the many historical, technological, and thematic links between trains and cinema, see Lynne Kirby, *Parallel Tracks: The Railroad and Silent Cinema* (Duke University Press, 1997).

14. Hayashi Fumiko was born out of wedlock in 1903 and spent her childhood following her parents, itinerant peddlers and shop-owners, throughout the port cities, factory towns, and mining centers of Kyushu—an experience also reflected in the semi-autobiographical *Hōrōki*. Her home life was chaotic, and she experienced varying degrees of poverty in early childhood, but by adolescence her family's fortunes had stabilized to the extent that she was able to attend a girls' secondary school, a privilege still rare for a child of Hayashi's humble background. Hayashi demonstrated literary ambitions in secondary school, and soon after her graduation in 1922 she moved to Tokyo, where she supported herself through a wide variety of jobs and began to write stories and poetry. For English-language discussion of Hayashi's life and its relationship to her works, see Susanna Fessler, *Wandering Heart: The Work and Method of Hayashi Fumiko* (Albany: State University of New York Press, 1998).

15. On the literary relationship between Hayashi and Tokuda Shūsei, see Mori Eiichi, *Shūsei kara Fumiko e* (Kanazawa: Noto insatsu, 1990).

16. On *Nyonin geijutsu* (*Women's Arts*), see Ogata Akiko, '*Nyonin geijutsu' no hitobito* (Tokyo: Domesu shuppan, 1981) and '*Nyonin geijutsu' no sekai: Hasegawa Shigure to sono shūhen* (Tokyo: Domesu shuppan, 1980).

17. Quotation from "Watashi no chiheisen" (1931), translated as "My Horizon" by Susanna Fessler, in *Wandering Heart*, 159–62.

18. Kon's project consisted of surveys of urban architectural forms (e.g., awnings, signs, lanterns and gutters); material culture (e.g., items found in the possession of university students); fashion (such as clothes worn by men and women on the Ginza); and spatial practices (the distribution of cherry-viewing picnics and suicides in Inokashira Park). Kon associated with a number of members of the artistic avant-garde in the 1920s, including Kanbara Tai and members of the Action group, with whom he co-founded the Barracks Decoration Society in the aftermath of the Great

Kanto Earthquake, and the set designer Yoshida Kenkichi, who was his chief collaborator in the modernology studies. Before beginning his ethnographic studies of modern urban life, Kon collaborated with Yanagita Kunio in a survey of farmhouses and living conditions in rural Japan, which were collected in the volume *Nihon no minka* in 1922. See Miriam Silverberg, "Constructing the Japanese Ethnography of Modernity," *Journal of Asian Studies* 51.1 (February 1992): 30–54; Kon Wajirō, *Kōgengaku nyūmon*, ed. Fujimori Terunobu (Tokyo: Chikuma Shobō, 1987).

19. Yanagita Kunio, *Meiji Taishōshi: sesōhen* (Tokyo: Kōdansha, 1976).

20. Watanabe Kazutami, 3–20; Unno Hiroshi, 197–223.

21. Raymond Williams, "The Metropolis and the Emergence of Modernism," in Edward Timms and David Kelley, eds., *Unreal City: Urban Experience in Modern European Literature and Art* (Manchester: Manchester University Press, 1985), 13.

22. Ibid., 21.

23. In the year 1901, there were only 70 secondary schools nationwide for female students, with a total of 17,540 students. By 1913, the number of schools had increased dramatically to 330 schools with 83,287 students, and by 1922, the year of Hayashi Fumiko's secondary school graduation, it had nearly doubled again to 618 schools with over 200,000 students. Murakami Nobuhiko, *Taishō joseishi, jō* (Tokyo: Rironsha, 1982), 33–43.

24. Ibid., 22.

25. Benedict Anderson, *Imagined Communities: Reflections on the Origin and Spread of Nationalism* (New York: Verso, 1983, 1991).

26. Williams, 23.

27. Ibid., 20–21.

28. Komori Yōichi, personal interview, Tokyo, 11 May 1998. A shared metropolitan-provincial experience of "simultaneity" is one of the elements securing the formation of modern nation-states, according to Benedict Anderson's *Imagined Communities*. Most studies of modernism, however, emphasize the experience of "simultaneity" (*dōjisei, dōjidaisei*) as a privileged experience of urban culture, ignoring the ways in which the provinces are also implicated in this phenomenon.

29. Hayashi, *Hōrōki* (1973), 3. Hayashi struck the phrase "I am a crossbreed, a mongrel" from the later versions of the text. She also changed the words "Shimonoseki in Bakan" to "Shimonoseki in Yamaguchi Prefecture."

30. *Zasshu* (crossbreed) and *chabo* (mongrel) were politically charged terms in imperialist Japan. As Eiji Oguma outlines in his study *A Genealogy of 'Japanese' Self-Images*, debates over the mixed-race versus pure-blooded origins of the Japanese people continued throughout the Meiji, Taisho,

and Showa periods; and extended into questions of assimilationist versus eugenicist policies toward colonial subjects, including Ainu, Koreans, and Taiwanese. See Eiji Oguma, *A Genealogy of 'Japanese' Self-Images*, trans. David Askew (Melbourne: Trans Pacific Press, 2002).

I have found no explanations of why Hayashi eliminated the *zasshu/chabo* line from her text. One could speculate on the changed political climate, including the increased public emphasis on purity of blood and the influence of eugenic theory, when she produced her *ketteiban*, or "definitive edition" of the text in 1939; direct censorship is one possibility, though I have found no evidence for this. As discussed in the introduction to this chapter, Hayashi appeared to distance herself from the hybrid formal qualities of the work, and, by extension, the hybridity of the authorial persona projected in it, as early as October 1930, on the publication of *Zoku hōrōki*.

31. *Hirabayashi Taiko zenshū*, vol. 10 (Tokyo: Shio shuppansha, 1979), 17.

32. Although Hirabayashi's passage does not use this term, one word that was often used to describe the vagrant underclass in prewar Japan was *runpen*, from the Marxist term "lumpen proletariat." In fact the word *runpen* was often used to describe (or denigrate) both Hayashi and her works. Furthermore, as Joan Ericson notes, *Hōrōki* can be related to a developing genre of *runpen-mono*, or "lumpen stories," reportage, literature, film, and song, including Ryūtanji Yū's novel *Hōrō jidai* (1928), and films spanning from Murata Minoru's *Rojō no reikon* (1921) to Mizoguchi Kenji's *Shikamo karera wa iku* (1931). Ericson, 63–69. The vogue of this term, extending from academic discourse to popular culture, reminds us that in addition to the wide-reaching notion of *taishū* or "the masses" discussed below, more restrictive types of class-based social analysis were also central features of prewar Japan's self-understanding. Nevertheless, since the question of *Hōrōki* as *runpen* literature has already been explored by Ericson and others, I have focused on other aspects of Hayashi's novel in relation to contemporary discourse.

33. Currently, Nōgata is the standard pronunciation of this place name. In the original edition of *Hōrōki*, however, the characters of this name are given the *furigana* reading Nōkata, and so I am following this reading.

34. Shogakkan's *Nihon kokugo daijiten* (vol. 4, p. 312) cites a usage of the word *kairyōfuku* in Kosugi Tengai's novel *Hayari uta* from 1902. The word appears as early as 1873 in the title of a book of patterns for Western-style dress, *Kairyōfuku saihō shoshinden*. See Shōwa joshi daigaku hifukugaku kenkyūshitsu, *Kindai nihon fukusōshi* (Tokyo: Kindai bunka kenkyūsho, 1971), 44–45. For general information on the shift toward new

machine-woven textiles and new forms of dress, see *Kindai nihon fukusōshi*, 8–12, 91–93, 201–2. An interesting if somewhat idiosyncratic account of these changes, focusing on the diffusion of cotton goods and the adoption of brighter dyes, can be found in Yanagita Kunio's *Meiji Taishōshi: sesōhen* [originally published 1930] (Tokyo: Kōdansha, 1976), 22–50. The significance of textiles and the textile trade to *Hōrōki* was brought to my attention by Komori Yōichi in a series of advising sessions in Tokyo from April through July 1988.

35. Hayashi, *Hōrōki* (1973), 5. In later editions, Hayashi changed "improvement clothes" to "muslin improvement clothes," presumably to clarify this somewhat archaic term.

36. Ibid., 6.

37. See Kawakatsu Heita, *Nihon bunmei to kindai seiyō: 'sakkoku' saikō* (Tokyo: NHK Books, 1991), 62–94; Peter Duus, "Zaikabō: Japanese Cotton Mills in China, 1895–1937," in Michael Smitka, *The Textile Industry and the Rise of the Japanese Economy* (New York: Garland Publishing, 1998); Shōwa joshi daigaku hifukugaku kenkyūshitsu, 91–93, 201–2.

38. *Historical Statistics of Japan*, vol. 1, ed. Japan Statistical Association (Tokyo: Japan Statistical Association, 1987), 96, 274–75.

39. Horiuchi Keizo and Inoue Takeshi, eds., *Nihon shōkashū* (Tokyo: Iwanami shoten, 1958), 132.

40. Hayashi, *Hōrōki* (1973), 7–8.

41. Ude no Kisaburō was the hero of Kawatake Mokuami's kabuki play *Koko ga Edo koude no tatehiki*. *Hototogisu*, serialized by Tokutomi Rōka in 1898–99, was given its most famous performance as a *shinpa* play by Tokyo's Hongōza in 1908. *Nasanu naka*, by Yanagawa Shunyō, was serialized as a novel from 1912 to 1913; *Uzumaki*, by Watanabe Katei, was serialized from 1913 to 1914; both of these novels also became standards in the *shinpa* repertoire.

42. Hayashi, *Hōrōki* (1973), 9–10.

43. For biographical information on Matsui Sumako, see Phyllis Birnbaum, *Modern Girls, Shining Stars, The Skies of Tokyo: 5 Japanese Women* (New York: Columbia University Press, 1999), 1–52.

44. Kisō Tetsu, *Uta no furusato kikō* (Tokyo: Nihon hōsō shuppan kyōkai, 1986), 152–57; Harris I. Martin, "Popular Music and Social Change in Prewar Japan," *The Japan Interpreter* 7.3–4 (Summer–Autumn 1972): 335–38.

45. Tanaka Jun'ichirō, *Nihon eiga hattatsushi*, vol. 1 (Tokyo: Chūō Kōron, 1957), 207–9.

46. Harris I. Martin argues, "The new forms of popular music which evolved during the Taishō and early Shōwa years were more than mere

reflections of their times. They appear to have been among the earliest elements in twentieth-century life that contributed to the transformation of traditional Japanese society into one of mass consumption and mass culture." "Popular Music and Social Change in Prewar Japan," 335.

47. *Hōrōki* (1973), 14–15.

48. Soeda Tomomichi, *Enka no Meiji Taishō shi* (Tokyo: Tōsui shobō, 1982), 106–8; Komota Nobuo et al., *Nihon ryūkōka shi* (Tokyo: Shakai shisōsha, 1970), 25–26.

49. *Hōrōki* (1973), 78.

50. On the employment choices for rural women in Meiji Japan, see "Alternatives: The Loom and the Brothel," in E. Patricia Tsurumi, *Factory Girls: Women in the Thread Mills of Japan* (Princeton, N.J.: Princeton University Press, 1990), 174–90.

51. See Margit Nagy, "Middle-Class Working Women During the Interwar Years," in Gail Lee Bernstein, ed., *Recreating Japanese Women, 1600–1945* (Berkeley: University of California Press, 1991), 199–216. For an excellent in-depth analysis of *Hōrōki* and the women's labor market, see Kanai Keiko, "Hisagime no shuki: 'Hōrōki' o megutte" ("The notebooks of a peddler-woman: on *Hōrōki*"), *Bungaku* 5.2 (April 1994): 16–126.

52. Soeda, 269. The song was published in 1920.

53. Irrespective of the upbeat, forward-looking perspective of Soeda's lyrics, and the aggressive montage-based modernism of Hayashi's text, the structure of both "Shokugyō fujin no uta" and *Hōrōki* is also indebted to the premodern rhetoric of *mono-zukushi*, or exhaustive listing, found in Edo-period lyrical and dramatic texts such as Chikamatsu's *joruri*, and in a more extensive sense, in the exhaustive series of stations in life occupied by the protagonist of Saikaku's *Koshoku ichidai onna* (*The Life of an Amorous Woman*, 1686), to which *Hōrōki* bears a particularly strong resemblance.

54. Ericson, 63–69.

55. According to the statistics cited by Kurosawa Ariko, about 14 percent of female Tokyo residents were working in 1920; 85 percent of these women were making less than 30 yen per month, while the cost of living for a single tenant in Tokyo was estimated to be 40 yen per month (although this estimate may be somewhat high). In a survey of the reasons for women working, 76.57 percent replied "to supplement the family budget," while only 9.83 percent answered "to support myself independently." Kurosawa Ariko, "Shukkyō suru shōjotachi: 1910–20 nendai, Yoshiya Nobuko, Kaneko Misuzu, Ozaki Midori, Hirabayashi Taiko, Hayashi Fumiko hoka," in Ikeda Hiroshi, ed., *Taishū no tōjō: hīrōtachi no 20–30 nendai* (Tokyo: Inpakuto shuppankai, 1998), 91.

56. *Hōrōki* (1973), 71.

57. See Kurihara, 205–17; *Maeda Ai chōsakushū*, vol. 2, 199–216.

58. For example, when the narrator declares in the opening paragraphs that "the open road became my home town," her words echo the famous opening passage of Matsuo Basho's *Oku no hosomichi* (*Narrow Road to the Deep North*, 1702), in which the poet invokes the lives of the wandering souls who "make travel their dwelling" (*tabi o sumika to su*).

When published in the journal *Nyonin geijutsu*, the novel's installments carried the subtitle *uta nikki* ("poetic diary"), suggesting its self-conscious ties to literary diaries such as *Sarashina nikki*, as well as classical *uta monogatari* such as *Ise monogatari*. On the classical "lineages of a woman's diary," see Ericson, 59–63.

59. J. L. Anderson, "Spoken Silents in the Japanese Cinema; or, Talking to Pictures: Essaying the Katsuben, Contexturalizing the Texts," in Arthur Nolletti, Jr., and David Desser, eds., *Reframing Japanese Cinema: Authorship, Genre, History* (Bloomington: Indiana University Press, 1992), 259–310.

60. The chapter "Hitori tabi" begins with the lines: "Asakusa is great. Asakusa's a great place to go any time. Amid the fast-paced lights, I'm a swirling, wandering Katyusha." *Hōrōki* (1972), 172. Asakusa set-pieces, each including the refrain "Asakusa is a great place" (*Asakusa wa ii tokoro da*), are also featured in *Hōrōki*'s sequels, *Zoku hōrōki* and '*Hōrōki*' *daisanbu*. Hayashi, *Shinpan hōrōki*, 280–83, 318–19.

61. Yoshimi Shunya, *Toshi no doramatourugii: Tōkyō, sakariba no shakaishi* (Tokyo: Kōbundō, 1987), 209–13.

62. In addition to *Hōrōki*, a number of important modernist works were set wholly or partially in Asakusa—most notably, Kawabata Yasunari's novel *Asakusa kurenai dan* (1930). The Mavo artists' group also chose Asakusa as the site of their first public exhibition, rather than more traditional gallery sites such as Hibiya, Ginza, or Ueno. On this exhibition, see Ide Magoroku, *Nejikugi no gotoku: gakka Yanase Masamu no kiseki* (Tokyo: Iwanami shoten, 1996), 183–94. For a reading of Kawabata's *Asakusa kurenai dan*, see Lippit, 119–57.

63. Eighteen readings and radio-play versions were broadcast on NHK and other radio networks between 1957 and 1967; *Hōrōki* was also broadcast as a television drama three times in the early 1960s. Shinjuku rekishi hakubutsukan, ed., *Hayashi Fumiko: Shinjuku ni ikita hito* (Tokyo: Shinjuku rekishi hakubutsukan, 1991), 82–85, 87. Nakagawa Shigemi, "Hayashi Fumiko to sono jidai: Naruse Mikio sakuhin kara," *Shōwa bungaku kenkyū* 18 (February 1989): 86–87.

64. *Gendai nihon josei jinmei roku*, ed. Nishigai asoshietsu (Tokyo: Nichigai asoshietsu, 1996), 1135. The original Geijutsuza disbanded in

1918 after Shimamura Hōgetsu's death and Matsui Sumako's subsequent suicide. The group was reconstituted from 1924 to 1945 under the leadership of Mizutani Chikushi, and a third incarnation of the Geijutsuza was founded by Mizutani Yaeko in the postwar period.

Chapter 5

1. One recent example of a media image of the prewar Japanese modern girl would be the NHK serial drama *Aguri* (1997), a fictionalized profile of Yoshiyuki Aguri, who created one of the first modern beauty parlors in Japan (Aguri was the wife of modernist writer Yoshiyuki Eisuke and mother of postwar writer Yoshiyuki Junnosuke).

Prewar visual images of the "modern girl" were highlighted in the art exhibition "Mobo-Moga 1910–1935 ten," held at the Kanagawa Prefectural Museum of Art (Kamakura: May–June 1998) and the New South Wales State Museum of Art (Sydney: July–August 1998). While the exhibition's title gave equal space to "modern boys" (*mobo*) and "modern girls" (*moga*), images of the "modern girl" in the exhibition were many, while works by female artists were few.

2. Barbara Hamill, "Nihonteki modanizumu no shisō: Hirabayashi Hatsunosuke o chūshin to shite" ("Japanese Philosophies of Modernism: Focusing on Hirabayashi Hatsunosuke"), *Nihon modanizumu no kenkyū*, ed. Minami Hiroshi (Tokyo: Burēn shuppan, 1982), 102. The 1920s thus represented a brief moment in which women were held to represent "culture" while men represented "nature." In Japan this brief inversion of tropes was overturned once again in the late 1930s, when government propaganda insisted on the "natural" role of women as childbearers and embodiments of Japanese tradition. See Yoshiko Miyake, "Doubling Expectations: Motherhood and Women's Factory Work Under State Management in Japan in the 1930s and 1940s," in *Recreating Japanese Women 1600–1945*, ed. Gail Bernstein (Berkeley: University of California Press, 1991), 267–95.

3. *Ōya Sōichi zenshū*, vol. 2 (Tokyo: Sōyōsha, 1981), 5. In this passage, as well as the one below, Ōya plays on the multiple denotations of "antenna" as the sense organ (*shokushu, shokkaku*) of an insect, and as the reception and transmission device (*antena*) of a radio; both of these images are congruous with the Japanese word *sentan*, which suggests the sharp tip of an object. Although I am translating *sentan* as "vanguard," it should be noted that another word, *zen'ei*, served as the standard contemporary translation for "vanguard," primarily in the Marxist context. Subsequently, *zen'ei geijutsu* has become the standard translation for "avant-garde art";

note, however, that the word *sentan,* rather than *zen'ei,* appeared in the first Mavo manifesto, quoted in Chapter 1.

4. Ibid., 18.

5. Ibid., 22–23.

6. Ibid., 10–17.

7. Miriam Silverberg, "The Modern Girl as Militant," *Recreating Japanese Women, 1600–1945,* ed. Gail Bernstein (Berkeley: University of California Press, 1991), 249. On this point, Silverberg cites Barbara Hamill's essay "Josei: Modanizumu to kenri ishiki" ("Women: Modernism and Rights Consciousness"), *Nihon modanizumu no kenkyū,* ed. Minami Hiroshi (Tokyo: Burēn shuppan, 1982), 210.

8. Silverberg "Modern Girl," 240, 266. Silverberg quotes the Shinkankaku-ha writer Kataoka Teppei on the phantasmal indeterminability of the modern girl: "When we say the Modern Girl exists in our era we are not in particular referring to individuals named Miss So-and-so-*ko* or Mrs. Such-and-such-*e.* Rather, we are talking about the fact that somehow, from the midst of the lives of all sorts of women of our era, we can feel the air of a new era, different from that of yesterday. That's right; where can you folks clearly say that there is a typical modern girl?" Silverberg, "Modern Girl," 250. Quoted from Kataoka Teppei, "Modan gāru no kenkyū," September 9, 1926.

9. Silverberg, "Modern Girl," 260.

10. *Hirabayashi Hatsunosuke bungei hyōron zenshū,* vol. 2 (Tokyo: Bunseidō shoten, 1975), 388. While Hirabayashi emphasizes that the roots and effects of the "age of collapsed authority" are much wider than the historical accident of the Great Kanto Earthquake, he does toy with the idea that "the modern girl appeared for the same reason as the barrack architecture after the earthquake."

Compared with the "traditional" buildings they sometimes replaced, the "barracks," or temporary replacement structures, had a Western-style, functionalist appearance. In addition, young Japanese artists were often mobilized to decorate the buildings. These artists typically employed bright colors and eye-catching designs; some were influenced by Futurist, Expressionist, and Constructivist art and architecture. Hirabayashi's comparison is an interesting one, since the clothes, makeup, and hairstyles sported by Japanese "modern girls" were also considered more functional than Japanese styles on a structural level, and yet were often more colorful or gaudy on the level of surface decoration.

11. Ibid., 385.

12. Ibid., 385, 386.

13. Ibid., 386.

14. See p. 303, note 55.

15. See Silverberg, "Modern Girl," 255–59.

16. Ibid., 242–43.

17. Ueda Yasuo, "Josei zasshi ga mita modanizumu" ("Modernism as Viewed by Women's Magazines"), *Nihon modanizumu no kenkyū*, ed. Minami Hiroshi (Tokyo: Burēn shuppan, 1982), 126; Suzuki Sadami, *Modan toshi no hyōgen: jiko, gensō, josei* (Kyoto: Shirojisha, 1992), 20, 171–72. While the protagonist of *Hōrōki* pursues her romantic and sexual relationships seemingly without concern for the possibility of pregnancy, the problems of childbirth (intramarital and otherwise) and abortion are thematized through the stories of the other café waitresses with whom the protagonist works, which are often shared during the women's baths. See especially the chapter "Aki ga kitanda" (the first chapter of *Hōrōki* to be serialized), *Hōrōki* (1973), 140–56.

18. Kuriyagawa (1880–1923) was a prominent critic and scholar of English literature. His collection of essays *Kindai no ren'ai kan* (*Modern Views on Love*) was published in 1921.

19. Takamure Itsue, "Musan kaikyū no ren'ai shisō" ("The Philosophy of Love of the Proletarian Class"), *Bungei sensen* 2.3 (July 1925): 30–32. These views were expounded in detail in Takamure's book *Ren'ai no sōsei*, published in 1926; see E. Patricia Tsurumi, "Visions of Women and the New Society in Conflict: Yamakawa Kikue Versus Takamure Itsue," in *Japan's Competing Modernities: Issues in Culture and Democracy 1900–1930*, ed. Sharon A. Minichiello (Honolulu: University of Hawaii Press, 1998), 335–57.

20. The "Women's Demands" Yamakawa drafted for a proletarian conference in 1925 included the abolition of the family headship system, equality of educational and employment opportunities, equal pay to men and women for equal work, a universal minimum wage, paid maternity leave and postnatal care for female workers, and the abolition of prostitution. Tsurumi, "Visions of Women," 351.

21. See, for example, Hayashi Fusao, "Puroretaria ren'ai gaku: oboegaki fū ni" ("A Study of Proletarian Love: Random Notes"), *Chūō kōron* 45.1 (January 1930): 199–206.

22. The story was one of three published by Kollontai in the collection *Lyubov' pchel trudovykh* (*Love of the Worker Bees*, 1923); it was retranslated by Matsuo Shirō from the English and published by Sekaisha in November 1927. The other two stories from *Love of the Worker Bees* were translated by Hayashi Fusao and published as *Ren'ai no michi* in April 1928. Hayashi Fusao and others translated five of Kollontai's essays on sexuality, morality, the family, work, and class struggle as *Ren'ai to shindōtoku*, published in

September 1928. Akiyama Yōko, "'Akai koi' no shōgeki: korontai no juyō to gokai" ("The Shock of *Red Love*: The Reception and Misunderstanding of Kollontai"), in *Taishū no tōjo: Hīrō to dokusha no 20–30 nendai*, ed. Ikeda Hiroshi (Tokyo: Inpakuto shuppankai, 1998), 98–116.

On Kollontai's fiction, see Barbara Evans Clements, *Bolshevik Feminist: The Life of Aleksandra Kollontai* (Bloomington: Indiana University Press, 1979), 225–305. For English translations of Kollontai's essays, see Alexandra Kollontai, *Selected Writings of Alexandra Kollontai*, translated by Alix Holt (Westport, Conn.: Lawrence Hill and Company, 1978).

23. Hirabayashi Taiko, "Korontai joshi no 'Akai koi' ni tsuite" ("Concerning Mme. Kollontai's *Red Love*"), *Bungei sensen* 5.1 (January 1928): 190.

24. On the reception of *Akai koi,* see Suzuki Sadami, 174–75, as well as Akiyama Yōko's article above.

25. From an advertisement in the *Tōkyō asahi shinbun,* April 19, 1927. Quoted in Akiyama Yōko, 98.

26. Although relatively few Soviet films were allowed to be screened in Japan, translations of Soviet film theory and descriptions of Soviet works steadily filtered into the country. Japanese directors responded with their own experiments with montage techniques; one important example (unfortunately now lost) was Mizoguchi Kenji's *Tokai kōkyōgaku,* or *City Symphony,* which, according to contemporary accounts, successfully employed an aggressive style of montage to articulate a critique of contemporary Japanese society. Kinugasa Teinosuke's *Kurutta ippeiji,* or *A Page of Madness,* is one of the few examples of avant-garde Japanese film montage which survives from this period. See Iwamoto Kenji, "'Tokai kōkyōgaku': Mizoguchi Kenji to akai senpū" ("*City Symphony*: Mizoguchi Kenji and the Red Whirlwind"), in *Nihon eiga to modanizumu*, ed. Iwamoto Kenji (Tokyo: Libroport, 1991), 152.

27. Hayashi's work in this period displays an uncanny sense of timing and topicality. For example, her poem "Jokō no utaeru," or "The Factory Girl's Song," appeared in the same issue of the Proletarian journal *Bungei sensen* that offered on its back cover a full-page advertisement for Hosoi Wakizō's seminal historical survey of labor conditions for women in Japanese spinning mills, *Jokō aishi. Bungei sensen* 2.4 (August 1925).

28. *Hōrōki* (1973), 156.

29. *Hōrōki* (1973), 75. In later versions of the text, Hayashi substituted "watashi" for "onna" in this passage. *Shinpan hōrōki,* 49.

30. For one analysis of café waitresses' position in the labor market, see Hori Makoto, "Gendai jokyūron," *Chūō kōron* 46.7 (July 1931): 191–96.

31. In her recent article, "The Café Waitress Serving Modern Japan," Miriam Silverberg writes, "The term *seikatsu* was associated with a radically transformed material culture or rationalized lifestyle accompanying new forms of leisure activity, and the café, along with the cinema, was the site most often associated with experiences characteristic of the new age, which was defined by a series of 'vanguard' gestures that had ostensibly broken away from any traditional framework." "The Café Waitress," 208.

32. Miriam Silverberg argues for a contextualization of the café waitress as follows: "While we can say that the *jokyū* was a form of sex worker who provided erotically charged services (usually remunerated only by tips) and that she was not a prostitute because she did not engage in sexual intercourse, we are also obliged to associate her both diachronically and synchronically with other women paid to be erotic." Ibid., 211.

33. From Furuya Tsunatake, *'Seishun no denki': Hayashi Fumiko* (1967), quoted in Mori Eiichi, "Hōrōki ron," 99–100.

34. *Hōrōki* (1973), 140.

35. *Hōrōki* (1973), 164. Female criminality, linked with the phenomenon of juvenile delinquency (*furyōshōnenshōjo*), was another significant aspect of the journalistic representation of Japanese modernity. (A parody of this discourse, in which the protagonist seeks aid from a Viscountess who has expressed interest in "rescuing delinquent boys and girls," appears in *Hōrōki* [1973], 120–23.) The narrator's idea of becoming a "female mounted bandit" (*onna bazoku*), however, seems linked to the metropole's imagination of romantic outlaws on the margins of Japan's sphere of colonialist influence in Manchuria. Examples of the "mounted bandit" image in Japanese popular culture include Arimoto Hōsui's adventure novel *Bazoku no ko* (*Child of the Mounted Bandits*, 1915), and Ikeda Fuyō's *Bazoku no uta* (*Song of the Mounted Bandits*, serialized in the magazine *Nihon shōnen* from 1925). A popular song (authorship unknown) entitled "Bazoku no uta" ("Song of the Mounted Bandits") also appeared around 1922. See Umehara Teikō, "'Bazoku no uta' no keifu: taishū bungaku no gaishi ni yosete," ("The Genealogy of 'Song of the Mounted Bandits': Towards an Unofficial History of Popular Literature"), in *Taishū no tōjo: Hīro to dokusha no 20–30 nendai*, ed. Ikeda Hiroshi (Tokyo: Inpakuto shuppankai, 1998), 170–94.

36. Ibid., 163.

37. *Shinpan hōrōki* (1979), 237–39.

38. This was the theme song for the movie *Jokyū* (*Café Waitress*) released in 1930, the same year as the publication of *Hōrōki* and *Zoku hōrōki*; the movie was based on Hirotsu Kazuo's novel by the same name, which was serialized in the magazine *Fujin kōron* from August 1930.

39. Kata Kōji, *Uta no shōwashi* (Tokyo: Jiji tsūshinsha, 1975), 24. While the resemblance of Hayashi's poem with this song might suggest that she is referring to it directly, her poem was originally published as part of the collection *Aouma o mitari* in 1929; thus any direct influence would have to be from Hayashi's poem to Saijō's lyrics. Rather than suggest such a direct relationship, however, I would argue that both Hayashi's poem and Saijō's lyrics are drawing on a shared body of stereotypes and cultural/linguistic constructions.

40. *Hōrōki* (1973), 161. In later editions, either to clarify the meaning or to rid it of its sexual ambiguity, Hayashi changed the last sentence to "we'd often curl up together like snails in a circle and talk."

41. *Hōrōki* (1973), 199.

42. The very idea of a field of "entertainment" or "recreation" (*goraku*) tying together various types of social, cultural, and erotic activities within the larger framework of a commercial exchange economy, was itself a newly emergent aspect of the discourse on modernity in the 1920s. See Miriam Silverberg, "Constructing the Japanese Ethnography of Modernity"; and Jeffrey E. Hanes, "Media Culture in Taishō Osaka," in *Japan's Competing Modernities: Issues in Culture and Democracy 1900–1930*, ed. Sharon A. Minichiello (Honolulu: University of Hawaii Press, 1998).

43. Yumi is a professional pseudonym taken by the protagonist, elsewhere known as Fumiko.

44. Hayashi Fumiko, *Shinpan hōrōki* (1979), 237. This passage is also cited in Unno Hiroshi's *Modan toshi Tōkyō*, 221–22. Unno's essay was one of the first to call renewed attention to Hayashi's work as a modernist urban novel; his essay also gestures toward the political significance of a woman's claim to Tokyo's urban space—a point I discuss further below.

45. Hayashi's novels can thus be reappraised through the work of recent feminist critics, who have noted the importance of free access to urban public space to social and cultural theories of modernity, such as the theory of the *flâneur* developed in the critical essays of Baudelaire and the theoretical works of Walter Benjamin. Janet Wolff, for example, has examined the exclusion of women in the nineteenth-century European public sphere, and offered a criticism of their closely related subsequent exclusion from nineteenth- and twentieth-century theories of modernity. Susan Buck-Morss, in a more thorough reading of the work of Baudelaire and Benjamin, has further explored the gender asymmetry of the *flâneur* type, pointing out that in nineteenth-century Paris, the *flâneur* "was simply the name of a man who loitered, but all women who loitered risked being seen as whores, as the term 'street-walker' or 'tramp' applied to women makes clear" (119).

While the cultural situation of nineteenth- and twentieth-century Japan differs markedly from that of Europe, particularly in regard to the predominantly enclosed, rather than public, nature of prostitution, the importance of women's claim to the public sphere in relation to the discourse of modernity is common to both locations. Indeed, Hayashi's work serves as a powerful example of a feminist-modernist effort to claim Tokyo's urban space as a woman. Hayashi's feminist-modernist claim to represent Tokyo's urban space as a writer (a claim to the public sphere of literature) is mirrored by her protagonist's claim to work and play in Tokyo's urban space (a claim to the physical public sphere) within the narrative.

See Janet Wolff, "The Invisible Flâneuse: Women and the Literature of Modernity," in *Feminine Sentences: Essays on Women and Culture* (Cambridge, UK: Polity Press, 1990), 43–50. Susan Buck-Morss, "The Flâneur, the Sandwichman and the Whore: The Politics of Loitering," *New German Critique* 39 (Fall 1986): 99–140.

For the classical studies of modernity and *flânerie*, see Charles Baudelaire, "The Painter of Modern Life," in *Selected Writings on Art and Literature*, translated by P. E. Charvet (New York: Penguin Books, 1972); Walter Benjamin, "The Paris of the Second Empire in Baudelaire," in *Charles Baudelaire: A Lyric Poet in the Era of High Capitalism*, translated by Harry Zohn (New York: Verso, 1983).

46. Indeed, in the realm of literature, one can trace a number of waves of reproduction of the Edo-esque, including one which crested in the late Meiji and early Taishō (spearheaded by anti-naturalist writers), and another which was building as Hayashi wrote *Hōrōki* in the early Shōwa. For a political reading of one aesthetician's use of Edo-esque to build a "modernist" (anti-rationalist) national aesthetics in the early Shōwa, see Leslie Pincus, *Authenticating Culture in Imperial Japan: Kuki Shūzō and the Rise of National Aesthetics* (Berkeley: University of California Press, 1996).

47. This *kouta* can be found under the title "Kasa sashite" in the *Nihon onkyoku zenshū: kouta utasawa hauta zenshū* (Tokyo: Seibundō, 1927), 41–42. *Hōrōki* (1975), 244.

48. *Hōrōki* (1975), 245–47.

49. I have been unable to identify this song among compilations of *kouta* or prewar popular songs, but it is likely either another *kouta* text, or a contemporary popular song which consciously evokes the Edo-esque. While this song, unlike the previous *kouta*, does not mention the *kuruwa*, or licensed quarters, by name, it does evoke them metonymously by the

mention of willow trees, which have a long literary association with the licensed quarters and prostitution. *Hōrōki* (1975), 249.

50. *Hōrōki* (1975), 257–60.

51. In fact, a new group of writers, the so-called "Shinkō geijutsu-ha" of the late 1920s and early 1930s, did emerge to apply the techniques of modernism to the subject matter of contemporary urban sexual mores (*fūzoku*). This group of writers was associated with such magazines as *Bungei toshi* (1928), *Gendai seikatsu* (1929), and *Shinkō geijutsu-ha kurabu* (1930). For an overview of post-Shinkankaku-ha developments in interwar Japanese modernism, see Itō Sei, "Modanizumu" ("Modernism"), *Nihon bungaku kōza*, vol. 6 (Kawade shobō, 1952), 95–106.

Chapter 6

1. *Ōya Sōichi zenshū*, vol. 2, 202.

2. Nii Itaru, *Anakizumu geijutsu ron* (Tokyo: Yumani shobō, 1991), 56–57. Originally published in 1930.

3. Thomas R. H. Havens, *Farm and Nation in Modern Japan: Agrarian Nationalism, 1870–1940* (Princeton: Princeton University Press, 1974), 135–38.

4. Nii Itaru, *Anakizumu geijutsu ron*, 62–63.

5. Ibid., 64–65. In particular, Nii cites Ishihara Kenji's *Toshi kenchiku zōkei riron e no kōsatsu.*

6. See John Crump, *Hatta Shūzō and Pure Anarchism in Interwar Japan* (New York: St. Martin's Press, 1993). Crump summarizes "pure anarchist" leader Hatta Shūzō's view of agriculturally based revolution as follows: "What was required [for revolution] was a process of self liberation carried out by the 'propertyless masses' (*musan taishū*). For Hatta, these 'propertyless masses' encompassed a far wider range of people than the wage-earning working class and at their core stood the tenant farmers" (64).

7. "By *domin* I mean people living an independent life close to the earth. Neither submitting to nor exploiting others, they stand on the great earth on their own two feet, managing their affairs through free cooperation." Ishikawa Sanshirō, *Kinsei domin tetsugaku* (1932), quoted in Ōsawa Masamichi, "Kaisetsu: domin shakai undōshi no kokoromi" ("Commentary: The Experiment of a History of Peasants' Social Movements"), in *Domin no shisō: taishū no naka no anakizumu*, ed. Ōsawa Masamichi (Tokyo: Shakai hyōronsha, 1990), 275.

8. See Inuta Shigeru, *Nihon nōmin bungaku shi*, expanded edition, ed. Odagiri Hideo (Tokyo: Nōsan gyoson bunka kyōkai, 1977).

9. Havens 163, 178–80, 242–47.

10. *Aka to kuro* 1 (January 1923): 18.

11. Tsuboi Shigeji, "Dōjin zakki" ("Editors' Random Notes"), *Aka to kuro* 4 (April 1923): 15.

12. "Tōrai shidan e no keikoku" ("A Warning to the Poetry Establishment"), *Hagiwara Kyōjirō zenshū*, vol. 2, 354–61. See discussion of this essay in the first section of Chapter 2.

13. Weisenfeld, *Mavo*, 180–81.

14. *Hagiwara Kyōjirō zenshū*, vol. 2, 380.

15. For the fullest expression of these ideas, see the essays "Warera no jiyūjiji no michi hitotsu de aru" ("There Is One Path to Our Freedom and Self-Government") and "Geijutsu no shakaiteki gijutsuka" ("The Social Engineering of Art") from June and July 1928. *Hagiwara Kyōjirō zenshū*, vol. 3, 145–63.

16. In a review (May 1926) of Mavo leader Murayama Tomoyoshi's major study of European and Russian Constructivism, *Kōseiha kenkyū*, Hagiwara wrote, "You [Murayama] say that the Constructivists have shaken hands with industrialism. But wasn't industrialism itself the womb of capitalism? Perhaps the industrialism that you speak of is different from the one I'm thinking of. But we should be cautious of the Constructivists, before we become an ally of the industry that gave birth to capitalism." "Kōseiha kenkyū no chūshin e" ("To the Author of Studies of Constructivism"), *Hagiwara Kyōjirō zenshū*, vol. 2, 411–12.

Both Hagiwara and Murayama's positions regarding Futurism, Dada, Constructivism, industrialization, and class struggle evolved and shifted over time. In the mid-1920s, both of them expressed opposition to capitalism as well as suspicion of Marxist ideology; both saw a need for a period of destructive "neo-dada" as a means of destabilizing Japanese capitalism and authoritarianism. Nevertheless, despite these basic similarities, the relationship between Murayama and Hagiwara was more often distinguished by rivalry rather than cooperation. See the interview in Itō Shinkichi, ed., *Gekidōki no shi to shijin* (Tokyo: Gekidōki no shi to shijin kankō kai, 1993), 120–23, for Murayama's recollections of the tensions between himself and Hagiwara, and for his impressions of Hagiwara's *Shikei senkoku*.

17. A number of the Mavoists' theatrical performances were produced in association with a wider group of progressive artists known as Sanka; their chief theatrical collaboration was entitled *Gekijō no sanka*. Murayama and other Mavo artists also were active in creating set design for the Tsukiji Little Theater and other venues. See Weisenfeld, *Murayama, Mavo, and Modernity*, 336–90; Omuka, *Taishōki shinkō bijutsu undō no kenkyū*, 594–624.

18. Remarks by the senior poet Kawai Suimei on the "Poet's Festival" (Shijinsai) performance at Tsukiji Little Theater (Tsukiji shōgekijō) on November 7, 1925. Quoted in Tsuboi Hideto, 38.

19. Kawaura Sanshirō, "Nenpyō" ("Biographical Timeline"), *Hagiwara Kyōjirō zenshū*, vol. 3, 499–501. According to a protégé's account of a dance performance in Maebashi in May 1926, Hagiwara "stripped down to his underpants and covered his body with silver and gold powder, attaching silver bands to his wrists and ankles; he then performed a conscious-constructivist dance expressing the joy of liberation, which was enthusiastically received." Tōmiya Katsuo, "Watashi to Kyōjirō" ("Kyōjirō and Myself"), in *Bochō, Takuji, Kyōjirō*, ed. Seki Shunji et al. (Tokyo: Miyama bunko, 1978), 227.

20. *Hagiwara Kyōjirō zenshū*, 392–98.

21. On the second Sanka exhibition, see Weisenfeld, *Murayama, Mavo, and Modernity*, 169–80; Omuka, *Taishōki shinkō bijutsu undō no kenkyū*, 681–706. On the break-up of Mavo, see Weisenfeld, 178–86; Omuka, 544–46.

22. The shifting of the tide from the eclectic dadaist-constructionist work pioneered by the Mavo group to the socialist-realist style that dominated the late 1920s was punctuated by the Shin roshia bijutsuten, an exhibit of Soviet art in 1927, featuring socialist-realist rather than Constructivist works. See Abe Yoshio, *Modorunite no kiseki* (Tokyo: Iwanami shoten, 1993), 126–27.

23. The Nihon puroretaria bungei renmei (Japan Proletarian Literary Alliance). After the purge of anarchists at the second conference, the group's name was changed to at the Nihon puroretaria geijutsu renmei (Japan Proletarian Arts Alliance). As far as my sources indicate, Hagiwara was never a member of the Nihon puroretaria bungei renmei, although he had occasionally contributed to *Bungei sensen* magazine.

24. See *Tsuboi Shigeji zenshū*, vol. 5, 129–30; Okamoto Jun, *Shijin no unmei*, 176–77.

25. "Mēdē no retsu ni hirugaeru waga kurohata," originally published in *Bungei kaihō* 1.5 (May 1927), *Hagiwara Kyōjirō zenshū*, vol. 1, 347.

26. Kawaura Sanshirō, "Nenpyō," *Hagiwara Kyōjirō zenshū*, vol. 3, 500–501; Akiyama Kiyoshi, "Anakisuto: Iwasa Sakutarō, Hagiwara Kyōjirō," 455.

27. For details on this incident, see the chapter "Bōryoku no wakare" ("A Violent Parting") from Tsuboi's autobiography. *Tsuboi Shigeji zenshū*, vol. 5, 130–34.

28. The timeline prepared by Kawaura Sanshirō records Hagiwara's efforts to promote the anarchist cause among spinning mills in the

Maebashi area. *Hagiwara Kyōjirō zenshū*, vol. 3, 503. Itō Shinkichi recalls Hagiwara carrying anarchist leaflets from Tokyo to Maebashi, visiting printing workshops in the north Maebashi area, and attending clandestine meetings near Maebashi Park; he casts doubt, however, that the scale of these efforts ever exceeded that of "the ideological movement of a few people" (*kazu sukunai hitotachi no shisō undō*). *Gyakuryū no naka no uta: shiteki anakizumu no kaisō* (Tokyo: Shichiyōsha, 1964), 61.

29. The publishing house was Keibunsha, founded by Kamiya Noboru and Takeuchi Teruyo, who raised funds from anarchist sympathizers to buy a press and type. See Takahashi Shūichirō, 111–13; Kamiya Noboru, "Shishū 'Danpen' ga dekiru made" ("Until the Poetry Collection 'Danpen' Was Completed"), in *Hagiwara Kyōjirō no sekai*, ed. Itō Shinkichi and Kawaura Sanshirō (Maebashi: Kankodō, 1987) 92–95.

30. *Hagiwara Kyōjirō zenshū*, vol. 1, 290.

31. *Shikei senkoku*, 4–5.

32. Itō Shinkichi, "Nōteki mebyuusu no wa" ("An Agrarian Moebius Strip"), in *Hagiwara Kyōjirō no sekai*, ed. Itō Shinkichi and Kawaura Sanshirō (Maebashi: Kankodō, 1987), 166.

33. *Hagiwara Kyōjirō zenshū*, vol. 1, 268. See citation and discussion of this poem in Takahashi Shūichirō, 118–19.

34. Nii Itaru, "Kyōjirō to Shōhei no shi: 'Danpen' to 'Mekura to tenba' to ni tsuite" ("The poetry of Kyōjiro and Shōhei: on 'Danpen' and 'Mekura to tenba'), *Kokushoku sensen* 2.1 (January 1932), 14–15.

35. Hirai Ken, "Hagiwara Kyōjirō 'Danpen' ron," *Nihon bungaku kenkyū* 46.2 (September 1994): 49–57.

36. *Hagiwara Kyōjirō zenshū*, vol. 1, 246.

37. Ibid., 267.

38. Hirai, 52.

39. Ibid., 57–62.

40. Both of these questions are explored extensively in Takahashi Shūichirō's *Hakai to gensō: Hagiwara Kyōjirō shiron*.

41. Ōsugi, 49–57.

42. *Hagiwara Kyōjirō zenshū*, vol. 1, 257–58.

43. Ibid., 282.

44. Ibid., 258.

45. Ibid., 253–54.

46. Hagiwara Kyōjirō zenshū, vol. 3, 307–30.

47. Akiyama Kiyoshi, "Anakisuto: Iwasa Sakutarō, Hagiwara Kyōjirō," 458.

48. "Tōshaki o kaitai!," *Kuropotokin o chūshin ni shita geijutsu no kenkyū* 2 (August 1932): 32.

49. *Hagiwara Kyōjirō zenshū*, vol. 1, 463–64. The *zenshū* text is based on the version of the poem that Hagiwara published in the magazine *Bungaku hyōron* in March 1934; it differs slightly from the original version published in *Kuropotokin o chūshin ni shita geijutsu no kenkyū*.

50. Akiyama Kiyoshi, *Aru anakizumu no keifu: Taishō-Shōwa no anakisuto shijintachi* (Tokyo: Tōjusha, 1973), 283–311; Itō Shinkichi, "Nōteki mebyuusu no wa," 140–69; Tsuboi Shigeji, "Hagiwara Kyōjirō danpen" (A Fragment on Hagiwara Kyōjirō"), *Tsuboi Shigeji zenshū*, vol. 3, 86–89.

51. Gondō was a scholar of the Chinese classics as well as an expert on the *Nan'ensho*, a text (now discredited) that was said to be the record of a seventh-century Confucianist tutor to the emperor Tenji. From 1902 to 1910, prior to writing his works of agrarianist political theory, Gondō had been a key member of the Amur River Society, which agitated for the annexation of Korea and the expansion of Japanese influence in China and Manchuria. Havens, 164–76.

52. Ibid., 195.

53. Ibid., 228.

54. Ibid., 228–29, 231.

55. *Hagiwara Kyōjirō zenshū*, vol. 1, 498–99.

56. Ibid., 517–18.

57. Ibid., 519–20.

58. Patricia G. Steinhoff, "Tenkō and Thought Control," in *Japan and the World: Essays on Japanese History and Politics in Honor of Ishida Takeshi*, ed. Gail Lee Bernstein and Haruhiro Fukui (London: Macmillan Press, 1988), 78.

59. In the years 1928–1934, the Peace Preservation Law was invoked in the arrest of over 57,000 suspected Communists, although a far smaller number were actually indicted, suggesting the law was used for the purpose of harassment as well as prosecution. Ibid., 79–80.

60. Ibid., 82–84. Sano later elaborated his rejection of Comintern direction of the Japanese Party, using the slogan "socialism in one country." See Germaine A. Hoston, "Tenkō: Marxism & the Nationalism Question in Prewar Japan," *Polity* 16.1 (Fall 1983): 96–118.

61. See Donald Keene, "Tenkō Literature: The Writings of Ex-Communists," in *Dawn to the West: Japanese Literature of the Modern Era*, vol. 1 (New York: Holt, Rinehart, and Winston, 1984), 846–905.

Incidentally, Hayashi Fumiko was also arrested in 1933 for contributing money to the Communist Party, an allegation which centered on the evidence of her subscription to a Party newspaper. As Ericson notes, however, her involvement with the Party was so slight, and her subsequent support of the war effort was so strong, that the question of Hayashi's *"tenkō"* has never become an issue for literary or intellectual historians. Ericson, *Be a Woman*, 80.

62. Akiyama Kiyoshi, "Anakisuto: Iwasa Sakutarō, Hagiwara Kyōjirō," 435–67.

63. Yokochi Shōjirō, "Hagiwara Kyōjirō," in *Hagiwara Kyōjirō no sekai*, ed. Itō Shinkichi and Kawaura Sanshirō (Maebashi: Kankodō, 1987), 88; Kobayashi Teiji, "Hagiwara Kyōjirō no shi no zengo" ("Before and After Hagiwara Kyōjirō's Death"), in *Hagiwara Kyōjirō no sekai*, 112–13; Tōmiya Katsuo, "Kyōjirō no bannen" ("Kyōjirō's Last Years"), in *Hagiwara Kyōjirō no sekai*, 172–73.

64. Tōmiya Katsuo, "Kyōjirō no bannen," 172–73.

65. Akiyama Kiyoshi, "Anakisuto: Iwasa Sakutarō, Hagiwara Kyōjirō," 464.

66. Itō Shinkichi, *Gyakuryū no naka no uta*, 60–61.

67. Steinhoff, "Tenkō and Thought Control," 87.

68. Ibid., 88–91. Steinhoff discusses each of these categories in more detail in her earlier doctoral thesis, *Tenkō: Ideology and Societal Integration in Prewar Japan* (Ph.D. Dissertation: Harvard University, 1969). The writers whose works she cites in support of her final category of "spiritual *tenkō*" include Shimaki Kensaku, Kamei Katsuichirō, Shiina Rinzō, and Hayashi Fusao (187–213).

69. Yamada Akira, "Hagiwara Kyōjirō!," *Shishin* 6.8 (August 1930): 68.

70. See Appendix B for a translation of this poem. For the arguments connecting "Tani" to Hagiwara's *"tenkō,"* see Tsuboi Shigeji, "Hagiwara Kyōjirō danpen," 86–89; Tsuboi Shigeji, "'Tani' o chūshin ni," in *Hagiwara Kyōjirō no sekai*, ed. Itō Shinkichi and Kawaura Sanshirō (Maebashi: Kankodō, 1987), 10–14; Itō Shinkichi, "Nōteki mebyuusu no wa," 167–69.

Conclusion

1. Iwamoto, 150–53.

2. "Tokyo March" featured numerous *gairaigo*, or imported words, including *jazu* (jazz), *rikyūru* (liquor), *dansā* (dancer), and *shinema* (cinema). The lyrics imagistically evoked the fleeting romance of the city, singing of such things as "a rose picked up during rush hour," and "the moon rising over the department stores" of Shinjuku.

3. Martin, 342; Hamada Yūsuke, "Rekōdo jidai no taishū kayō: 'Tōkyō kōshinkyoku' no chii" ("Popular Song in the Age of Records: The Place of 'Tokyo March'"), in *Utau sakkatachi*, ed. Noyama Kashō (Tokyo: Shibundō, 1998) 224–25.

4. *Shinpan hōrōki* (Tokyo: Shinchōsha, 1979), 291.

5. Ibid., 291.

6. Ibid., 295.

7. Ibid., 298.

8. The circumstances of Hayashi's career after the publication of *Hōrōki* are discussed in detail in Ericson, *Be a Woman*, and Fessler, *Wandering Heart*. The purpose of the following brief remarks on her activities of the 1930s is to put them in comparative perspective with Hagiwara's activities in the same period, and to consider their significance as a part of the trajectory of Japanese modernism and modernity.

9. Imagawa Hideko, "Nenpu" ("Biographical Timeline"), in *Hayashi Fumiko zenshū*, vol. 16 (Tokyo: Bunseidō, 1977), 296. In addition to traveling repeatedly throughout Japan, Hayashi journeyed to Taiwan, China, Manchuria, and across Siberia to Paris and London, all within a few years of publishing her first novel. For an analysis of the depiction of the Japanese empire in Hayashi's major postwar novel *Ukigumo* (*Drifting Clouds*, 1949), see Kleeman, 54–66.

10. Ericson, *Be a Woman*, 80–81. See also Keene, 909–10, 955.

11. On the complex issues of gender, personal agency, state, and media surrounding Hayashi's war reportage, see Nakagawa Shigemi, "Hayashi Fumiko: Onna wa sensō o tatakau ka" ("Hayashi Fumiko: Do Women Fight Wars?"), in *Nanpōchōyōsakka: sensō to bungaku*, ed. Kamiya Tadataka and Kimura Kazuaki (Tokyo: Sekai shisōsha, 1996), 242–53.

12. Ibid., 247.

13. I am grateful to both of the anonymous readers for Harvard University Asia Center in encouraging me to reconsider this issue.

14. Writers associated with the *Shikō geijutsu-ha* include Ryūtanji Yū, Kuno Toyohiko, Ibuse Masuji, and Abe Tomoji.

15. Poet Takiguchi Shūzō was jailed for nine months in 1941 for "leading avant-garde activities with revolutionary, communist, and leftist tendencies" (Sas, 204); see Sas, *Fault Lines*, 21, 204.

BIBLIOGRAPHY

Abe, Yoshio. *Moderunite no kiseki.* Tokyo: Iwanami shoten, 1993.
———. "Nihon no modanizumu" ("Japanese Modernism"). *Uta to shi no keifu.* Ed. Kawamoto Kōji. Tokyo: Chūō kōronsha, 1994.
Adorno, Theodor W. *Aesthetic Theory.* Ed. Gretel Adorno and Rolf Tiedemann; trans. Robert Hullot-Kentor. Minneapolis: University of Minnesota Press, 1997.
Aka to kuro. January 1923–June 1924. Facsimile edition. Tokyo: Tōji shobō, 1963.
Akamatsu, Katsumaro. "The Russian Influence on the Early Japanese Social Movement." *The Russian Impact on Japan: Literature and Social Thought.* Trans. and ed. Peter Berton, Paul F. Langer, and George O. Totten. Los Angeles: University of Southern California Press, 1981.
Akiyama, Kiyoshi. "Anakisuto: Iwasa Sakutarō, Hagiwara Kyōjirō" ("Anarchists: Iwasa Sakutarō, Hagiwara Kyōjirō"). *Kyōdō kenkyū: Tenkō.* Tokyo: Shisō no kagaku kenkyūkai, 1960.
———. *Aru anakizumu no keifu: Taishō-Shōwa no anakisuto shijintachi.* Tokyo: Tōjusha, 1973.
Akiyama, Yōko. "'Akai koi' no shōgeki: korontai no juyō to gokai" ("The Shock of *Red Love*: The Reception and Misunderstanding of Kollontay"). *Taishū no tōjō: Hīrō to dokusha no 20–30 nendai.* Ed. Ikeda Hiroshi. Tokyo: Inpakuto shuppankai, 1998.
Amo, Hisayoshi. "'Shikei senkoku' shoron" ("A Short Essay on *Shikei senkoku*"). *Shiron* 11 (December 1987): 74–81.
Anderson, Benedict. *Imagined Communities: Reflections on the Origin and Spread of Nationalism.* New York: Verso, 1991.

Anderson, J. L. "Spoken Silents in the Japanese Cinema; or, Talking to Pictures: Essaying the *Katsuben*, Contexturalizing the Texts." *Reframing Japanese Cinema: Authorship, Genre, History.* Ed. Arthur Nolletti, Jr., and David Desser. Bloomington: Indiana University Press, 1992.

Andō, Yasuhiko. "Chō to bakudan." *Gendaishi monogatari.* Ed. Fundō Junsaku and Yoshida Hirō. Tokyo: Yūhikaku, 1978.

Anzai, Fuyue. *Anzai Fuyue zenshishū.* Tokyo: Shichōsha, 1966.

———. "Shippi suru gaikei to bunmei" ("Townscape and Civilization Ranged in File"). *A* 2.3 (March 1925) [unpaginated]. Reprinted edition. Beppu: Beppu Daigaku bungakubu kokubungakuka kenkyūshitsu, 1981.

Arase, Yutaka. "Mass Communication Between the Two World Wars." *The Developing Economies* 5.4 (December 1967): 748–66.

Arima, Tatsuo. *The Failure of Freedom: A Portrait of Modern Japanese Intellectuals.* Cambridge, Mass.: Harvard University Press, 1969.

Bakhtin, M. M., *The Dialogic Imagination: Four Essays.* Ed. Michael Holquist. Trans. Caryl Emerson and Michael Holquist. Austin: University of Texas Press, 1981.

Bateson, Gregory. *Steps to an Ecology of the Mind.* Chicago: University of Chicago Press, 1972, 2000.

Baudelaire, Charles. *Selected Writings on Art and Literature.* Trans. P. E. Charvet. New York: Penguin, 1972.

Benjamin, Walter. *Charles Baudelaire: A Lyric Poet in the Era of High Capitalism.* Trans. Harry Zohn. New York: Verso, 1973.

———. *Illuminations.* Ed. Hannah Arendt. Trans. Harry Zohn. New York: Schocken Books, 1969.

Bernardi, Joanne. *Writing in Light: The Silent Scenario and the Japanese Pure Film Movement.* Detroit: Wayne State University Press, 2001.

Birnbaum, Phyllis. *Modern Girls, Shining Stars, The Skies of Tokyo: 5 Japanese Women.* New York: Columbia University Press, 1999.

Brown, Janice. *I Saw a Pale Horse and Selected Poems from Diary of a Vagabond.* Ithaca, N.Y.: East Asia Program, Cornell University, 1997.

Buci-Glucksmann, Christine. *Baroque Reason: The Aesthetics of Modernity.* Trans. Patrick Camiller. London: Sage Publications, 1994.

Buck-Morss, Susan. "The Flâneur, the Sandwichman and the Whore: The Politics of Loitering." *New German Critique* 39 (Fall 1986): 99–140.

Bungei shijo (November 1925–May 1927). Facsimile edition. Tokyo: Nihon kindai bungakukan, 1976.

Bürger, Peter. *Theory of the Avant-Garde.* Minneapolis: University of Minnesota Press, 1984.

Busch, Noel F. *Two Minutes to Noon*. New York: Simon and Schuster, 1962.

Calinescu, Matei. *Five Faces of Modernity: Modernism, Avant-Garde, Decadence, Kitsch, Postmodernism*. Durham, N.C.: Duke University Press, 1987.

Chakrabarty, Dipesh. "Postcoloniality and the Artifice of History: Who Speaks for 'Indian' Pasts?" *Representations* 37 (Winter 1992): 1–26.

Chiba, Kameo. "Kikai seijuku jidai no geijutsu to hankō ishiki bungaku" ("The Arts of the Mature Machine Age and the Literature of Resistance"). *Bungei jidai* 1.1 (May 1929): 12–16.

Chiba, Sen'ichi. *Gendai bungaku no hikakubungakuteki kenkyū*. Tokyo: Yagi shoten, 1978.

Choi Won-shik. "Seoul, Tokyo, New York: Modern Korean Literature Seen Through Yi Sang's 'Lost Flowers.'" *Korea Journal* 39.4 (Winter 1999): 118–43.

Claudel, Paul. *A Hundred Movements for a Fan*. Trans. Andrew Harvey and Iain Watson. London: Quartet Books, 1992.

Clearfield, Andrew M. *These Fragments I Have Shored: Collage and Montage in Early Modernist Poetry*. Ann Arbor, Mich.: UMI Research Press, 1984.

Clements, Barbara Evans. *Bolshevik Feminist: The Life of Aleksandra Kollontai*. Bloomington: Indiana University Press, 1979.

Crump, John. *Hatta Shūzō and Pure Anarchism in Interwar Japan*. New York: St. Martin's Press, 1993.

Damu damu (*Dum dum*). November 1924. Tokyo: Nantendō Shobō.

de Certeau, Michel. *The Practice of Everyday Life*. Trans. Steven Rendall. Berkeley: University of California Press, 1984.

Doi, Tadao, ed. *Nihongo no rekishi*. Tokyo: Shibundō, 1957.

Duus, Peter. "Zaikabō: Japanese Cotton Mills in China, 1895–1937." *The Textile Industry and the Rise of the Japanese Economy*. Ed. Michael Smitka. New York: Garland Publishing, 1998.

Duus, Peter, Ramon H. Myers, and Mark R. Peattie, eds. *The Japanese Informal Empire in China, 1895–1937*. Princeton, N.J.: Princeton University Press, 1989.

Eckert, Carter J. "Epilogue: Exorcising Hegel's Ghosts: Towards a Postnationalist Historiography of Korea." *Colonial Modernity in Korea*. Ed. Gi-Wook Shin and Michael Robinson. Cambridge, Mass.: Harvard University Asia Center, 1999.

Eckert, Carter J., Ki-baik Lee, Young Ick Lew, Michael Robinson, and Edward W. Wagner. *Korea Old and New: A History.* Seoul: Ilchokak Publishers, for the Korea Institute, Harvard University, 1990.

Elliott, Mark C. "The Limits of Tartary: Manchuria in Imperial and National Geographies." *The Journal of Asian Studies* 59.3 (August 2000): 603–46.

Ellis, Toshiko. "Nihon Modanizumu no saiteigi: 1930 nendai sekai no bunmyaku no naka de" ("A Reappraisal of Japanese Modernism: Within the Context of the World of the 1930s"). *Modanizumu kenkyū.* Tokyo: Shinchōsha, 1994.

———. "Questioning Modernism and Postmodernism in Japanese Literature." *Japanese Encounters with Postmodernity.* Ed. Johnann P. Arnason and Yoshio Sugimoto. London and New York: Kegan Paul International, 1995.

Em, Henry H. *Nationalist Discourse in Modern Korea: Minjok as a Democratic Imaginary.* Ph.D. Dissertation, University of Chicago, 1995.

———. "Yi Sang's *Wings* Read as an Anti-Colonial Allegory." *Muae* 1 (1995): 104–11.

Ericson, Joan Elaine. *Be a Woman: Hayashi Fumiko and Modern Japanese Women's Literature.* Honolulu: University of Hawaii Press, 1997.

———. *Hayashi Fumiko and Japanese Women's Literature.* Ph.D. Dissertation, Columbia University, 1993.

Eysteinsson, Astradur. *The Concept of Modernism.* Ithaca: Cornell University Press, 1990.

Fessler, Susanna. *Hayashi Fumiko: The Writer and Her Works.* Ph.D. Dissertation, Yale University, 1994.

———. *Wandering Heart: The Work and Method of Hayashi Fumiko.* Albany: State University of New York Press, 1998.

Fogel, Joshua A. *The Literature of Travel in the Japanese Rediscovery of China, 1862–1945.* Stanford, Calif.: Stanford University Press, 1996.

Fogel, Joshua A., ed. "Japanese Travelogues of China in the 1920s: The Accounts of Akatagawa Ryūnosuke and Tanizaki Junichirō." *Chinese Studies in History* 30.4 (Summer 1997): 3–103.

Fraser, James, Steven Heller, and Seymour Chwast. *Japanese Modern: Graphic Design Between the Wars.* San Francisco: Chronicle Books, 1996.

Fujii, James A. *Complicit Fictions: The Subject in Modern Japanese Prose Narrative.* Berkeley: University of California Press, 1993.

Fujitake, Akira. "The Formation and Development of Mass Culture." *The Developing Economies* 5.4 (December 1967): 767–82.

Gardner, William O. "Anzai Fuyue's Empire of Signs: Japanese Poetry in Manchuria." *Acts of Writing: Language and Identities in Japanese Literature.* Proceedings of the Association for Japanese Literary Studies, Vol. 2 (Summer 2001): 187–200.

―――. "Shi to shin media: Hagiwara Kyōjirō no 'Kōkokutō' o chūshin ni shita 1920 nendai no avan gyarudo ronkō" ("Poetry and New Media: An Essay on the 1920s Avant-Garde, Focusing on Hagiwara Kyōjirō's 'Advertising Tower'"). *Tōkyō daigaku hikaku bungaku bunka kenkyū* 16 (February 1999): 28–41.

Géfin, Laszlok. *Ideogram: History of a Poetic Method.* Austin: University of Texas Press, 1982.

Gerow, Aaron Andrew. *Writing a Pure Cinema: Articulations of Early Japanese Film.* Ph.D. Dissertation, University of Iowa, 1996.

Gordon, Andrew. *Labor and Imperial Democracy in Prewar Japan.* Berkeley: University of California Press, 1991.

Gumbrecht, Hans Ulrich. *In 1926: Living on the Edge of Time.* Cambridge, Mass.: Harvard University Press, 1997.

Hagiwara, Kyōjirō. *Hagiwara Kyōjirō zenshū.* Tokyo: Seichisha, 1980.

―――. *Shikei senkoku.* Reprinted edition. Tokyo: Nihon kindai bungakukan, 1972.

Hagiwara, Sakutarō. "Reppu no naka ni tachite" ("Standing in the Gale"). *Nihon shijin* 6.4 (April 1926): 31–35.

Hall, Ivan Parker. *Mori Arinori.* Cambridge, Mass.: Harvard University Press, 1973.

Hamada, Yūsuke. "Rekōdo jidai no taishū kayō: 'Tōkyō kōshinkyoku' no chii" ("Popular Song in the Age of Records: The Place of 'Tokyo March'"). *Utau sakkatachi.* Ed. Noyama Kashō. Tokyo: Shibundō, 1998.

Hamill, Barbara. "Nihonteki modanizumu no shisō: Hirabayashi Hatsunosuke o chūshin to shite" ("Japanese Philosophies of Modernism: Focusing on Hirabayashi Hatsunosuke"). *Nihon modanizumu no kenkyū.* Ed. Minami Hiroshi. Tokyo: Burēn shuppan, 1982.

Hanes, Jeffery E. "Media Culture in Taishō Osaka." *Japan's Competing Modernities: Issues in Culture and Democracy 1900–1930.* Ed. Sharon A. Minichiello. Honolulu: University of Hawaii Press, 1998.

Harootunian, Harry D. *Overcome by Modernity: History, Culture, and Community in Interwar Japan.* Princeton, N.J.: Princeton University Press, 2000.

Hatsuda, Tōru. *Modan toshi no kūkan hakubutsugaku—Tokyo.* Tokyo: Shōkokusha, 1995.

Havens, Thomas R. H. *Farm and Nation in Modern Japan: Agrarian Nationalism, 1870–1940*. Princeton, N.J.: Princeton University Press, 1974.

Hayashi, Fumiko. *Hayashi Fumiko shishū*. Tokyo: Shinchōsha, 1984.

———. *Hayashi Fumiko zenshū*. Tokyo: Bunseidō, 1977.

———. *Hōrōki*. Reprinted edition. Tokyo: Nihon kindai bungakukan, 1973.

———. *Shinpan hōrōki*. Tokyo: Shinchōsha, 1979.

Hayashi, Fusao. "Puroretaria ren'ai gaku: oboegaki fū ni" ("A Study of Proletarian Love: Random Notes"). *Chūō kōron* 45.1 (January 1930): 199–214.

Hayashi, Masao. "Kantōgen" ("Opening words"). *Damu damu* 1 (November 1924): 1.

Hedges, Inez. *Breaking the Frame: Film Language and the Experience of Limits*. Bloomington: Indiana University Press, 1991.

———. *Languages of Revolt: Dada and Surrealist Literature and Film*. Durham, N.C.: Duke University Press, 1983.

Heidegger, Martin. *The Question Concerning Technology and Other Essays*. Trans. William Lovitt. New York: Harper and Row, 1977.

Higuchi, Satoru. *Shōwashi no hassei: 'Sanshu no shiki' o mitasu mono*. Tokyo: Shinchōsha, 1990.

Hirabayashi, Hatsunosuke. "Bungaku oyobi geijutsu no gijutsuteki kakumei" ("The Technological Revolution in Literature and Art"). *Geijutsu no kakumei to kakumei no geijutsu*. Ed. Kurihara Yukio. Tokyo: Shakai hyōronsha, 1990.

———. *Hirabayashi Hatsunosuke bungei hyōron zenshū*. Tokyo: Bunseidō shoten, 1975.

Hirabayashi, Taiko. *Hirabayashi Taiko zenshū*. Tokyo: Shio shuppansha, 1979.

———. "Korontai joshi no 'Akai koi' ni tsuite" ("Concerning Mme. Kollontay's *Red Love*"). *Bungei sensen* 5.1 (January 1928): 190–91.

Hirai, Ken. "Hagiwara Kyōjirō 'Danpen' ron" ("An Essay on Hagiwara Kyōjirō's 'Danpen'"). *Nihon bungaku kenkyū* 46.2 (September 1994): 49–62.

Hirata, Hosea. *The Poetry and Poetics of Nishiwaki Junzaburō: Modernism in Translation*. Princeton, N.J.: Princeton University Press, 1993.

Hirato, Renkichi. *Hirato Renkichi shishū*. Reprint edition. Tokyo: Nihon kindai bungakukan, 1991.

Hori, Makoto. "Gendai jokyūron" ("An Essay on Contemporary Café Waitresses"). *Chūō kōron* 46.7 (July 1931): 191–96.

Horiuchi, Keizo, and Inoue Takeshi, eds. *Nihon shōkashū.* Tokyo: Iwanami shoten, 1958.

Hoston, Germaine A. "Tenkō: Marxism and the Nationalism Question in Prewar Japan," *Polity* 16.1 (Fall 1983): 96–118.

Huyssen, Andreas. *After the Great Divide: Modernism, Mass Culture, Postmodernism.* Bloomington: Indiana University Press, 1986.

Ide, Magoroku. *Nejikugi no gotoku: gakka Yanase Masamu no kiseki.* Tokyo: Iwanami shoten, 1996.

Imagawa, Hideko. "'Hōrōki': seisei to sono sekai" ("The creation of *Hōrōki* and Its world"). *Hōrōki arubamu.* Ed. Imagawa Hideko. Tokyo: Haga shoten, 1996.

———. "Nenpu" ("Biographical Timeline"). *Hayashi Fumiko zenshū,* vol. 16. Tokyo: Bunseidō, 1977.

Inuta, Shigeru. *Nihon nōmin bungaku shi.* Expanded edition. Ed. Odagiri Hideo. Tokyo: Nōsan gyoson bunka kyōkai, 1977.

Isoda, Kōichi. *Rokumeikan no keifu: Gendai nihon bungei shishi.* Tokyo: Bungei shujū, 1983.

———. *Shisō to shite no Tōkyō: Gendai bungakushiron nōto.* Tokyo: Kōdansha, 1990.

Itō, Sei. "Modanizumu" ("Modernism"). *Nihon bungaku kōza,* vol. 6. Kawade shobō, 1952.

Itō, Shinkichi. *Gyakuryū no naka no uta: shiteki anakizumu no kaisō.* Tokyo: Shichiyōsha, 1964.

———. "Nōteki mebyūsu no wa" ("An Agrarian Moebius Strip"). Ed. Itō Shinkichi and Kawaura Sanshirō. *Hagiwara Kyōjirō no sekai.* Maebashi: Kankodō, 1987.

———. *Reppu no naka ni tachite: Hagiwara Sakutarō to Hagiwara Kyōjirō.* Tokyo: Seichisha, 1981.

Itō, Shinkichi, ed. *Gekidōki no shi to shijin.* Tokyo: Gekidōki no shi to shijin kankō kai, 1993.

Itō, Shinkichi, and Kawaura, Sanshiro, eds. *Hagiwara Kyōjirō no sekai.* Maebashi: Kankodō, 1987.

Ivy, Marilyn. "Formations of Mass Culture." *Postwar Japan as History.* Ed. Andrew Gordon. Berkeley: University of California Press, 1993.

Iwamoto, Kenji. "'Tokai kōkyōgaku': Mizoguchi Kenji to akai senpū" ("*City Symphony*: Mizoguchi Kenji and the Red Whirlwind"). *Nihon eiga to modanizumu.* Ed. Iwamoto Kenji. Tokyo: Libroport, 1991.

Kamiya, Noboru. "Shishū 'Danpen' ga dekiru made" ("Until the Poetry Collection *Danpen* Was Completed"). *Hagiwara Kyōjirō no sekai.* Ed. Itō Shinkichi and Kawaura Sanshirō. Maebashi: Kankodō, 1987.

Kanai, Keiko. "Hisagime no shuki: 'Hōrōki' o megutte" ("The Notebooks of a Peddler-woman: On *Hōrōki*"). *Bungaku* 5.2 (April 1994): 116–26.

Kanbara, Tai. "'Shikei senkoku' o yomu" ("Reading 'Shikei senkoku'"). *Yomiuri shinbun*, November 21, 22, 1925.

Kantō shinsai to bungaku. Special issue. *Shakai bungaku* 8 (July 1994).

Karatani, Kōjin. *Origins of Modern Japanese Literature.* Trans. Brett de Bary. Durham, N.C.: Duke University Press, 1993.

Kasza, Gregory J. *The State and the Mass Media in Japan, 1918–1945.* Berkeley: University of California Press, 1988.

Kata, Kōji. *Uta no Shōwashi.* Tokyo: Jiji tsūshinsha, 1975.

Kawahata, Naomichi. "Konton to shita sen kyūhyaku sanjū shichi (1937) nen: bijutsu to shōgyō bijutsu no ryōiki o megutte" ("1937, a Year of Confusion: Centering on the Fields of Art and Commercial Art"). *Modanizumu/Nashonarizumu: 1930 nendai nihon no geijutsu.* Ed. Omuka Toshiharu. Tokyo: Serika shobō, 2003.

Kawakatsu, Heita. *Nihon bunmei to kindai seiyō: 'sakkoku' saikō.* Tokyo: NHK Books, 1991.

Kawamoto, Kōji. *The Poetics of Japanese Verse: Imagery, Structure, Meter.* Trans. Stephen Collington, Kevin Collins, and Gustav Heldt. Tokyo: University of Tokyo Press, 2000.

Kawamura, Minato. *Ikyō no kindai bungaku: 'Manshū' to kindai nihon.* Tokyo: Iwanami shoten, 1990.

———. *'Yoidorebune' no seishun: mō hitotsu no senchū, sengo.* Tokyo: Inpakuto shuppankai, 2000.

Kawaura, Sanshirō. "'Kitsune no su' kara 'Shikei senkoku' made" ("From 'Fox's Den' to 'Death Sentence'"). *Bochō-Takuji Kyōjirō.* Ed. Seki Shunji et al. Tokyo: Miyama Bunko, 1978.

———. "Nenpyō" ("Biographical Timeline"). *Hagiwara Kyōjirō zenshū.* Tokyo: Seichisha, 1980.

———. "Nenpyō" ("Biographical Timeline"). *Hagiwara Kyōjirō no sekai.* Ed. Itō Shinkichi and Kawaura Sanshirō. Maebashi: Kankodō, 1987.

Keene, Dennis. *The Modern Japanese Prose Poem: An Anthology of Six Poets.* Princeton, N.J.: Princeton University Press, 1980.

———. *Yokomitsu Ri'ichi: Modernist.* New York: Columbia University Press, 1980.

Keene, Donald. *Dawn to the West: Japanese Literature of the Modern Era.* Two volumes. New York: Holt, Rinehart and Winston, 1984.

Kern, Robert. *Orientalism, Modernism, and the American Poem.* Cambridge, UK: Cambridge University Press, 1996.

Kikuchi, Yasuo. *Gendaishi no taidōki: aoi kaidan o noboru shijintachi.* Tokyo: Genbunsha, 1967.

Kim, Min-Soo. "An Eccentric Reversible Reaction: Yi Sang's Experimental Poetry in the 1930s and Its Meaning to Contemporary Design." *Visible Language* 33.3: 196–235.

Kim, U-Chang. "The Situation of the Writers Under Japanese Colonialism." *Korea Journal* (May 1976): 4–15.

Kisō, Tetsu. *Uta no furusato kikō.* Tokyo: Nihon hōsō shuppan kyōkai, 1986.

Kleeman, Faye Yuan. *Under an Imperial Sun: Japanese Colonial Literature of Taiwan and the South.* Honolulu: University of Hawai'i Press, 2003.

Kobayashi, Teiji. "Hagiwara Kyōjirō no shi no zengo" ("Before and After Hagiwara Kyōjirō's Death"). *Hagiwara Kyōjirō no sekai.* Ed. Itō Shinkichi and Kawaura Sanshirō. Maebashi: Kankodō, 1987.

Kollontai, Alexandra. *Selected Writings of Alexandra Kollontai.* Trans. Alix Holt. Westport, Conn.: Lawrence Hill and Company, 1978.

Komata, Yūsuke. "Hagiwara Kyōjirō—'Shikei senkoku' ron" (An essay on Hagiwara Kyōjirō's 'Shikei senkoku'"). *Chūō daigaku bungakubu kiyō* (April 1989): 83–147.

———. *Zeneishi no jidai: Tōkyō no 1920 nendai.* Tokyo: Sōseisha, 1992.

Komatsu, Hiroshi. "Some Characteristics of Japanese Cinema Before World War I." *Reframing Japanese Cinema: Authorship, Genre, History.* Ed. Arthur Nolletti, Jr., and David Desser. Bloomington: Indiana University Press, 1992.

Komatsu, Ryūji. *Nihon anakizumu undōshi.* Tokyo: Aoki shoten, 1972.

Komota, Nobuo, et al. *Nihon ryūkōka shi.* Tokyo: Shakai shisōsha, 1970.

Kon, Tōkō. *Hanayaka na shikeiha.* Tokyo: Shinchōsha, 1972.

Kon, Wajirō. *Kōgengaku nyūmon.* Ed. Fujimori Terunobu. Tokyo: Chikuma shobō, 1987.

Kōno, Ichiro, and Rikutaro Fukuda, eds. and trans. *An Anthology of Modern Japanese Poetry.* Tokyo: Kenkyusha, 1957.

Kurihara, Yukio. "Taishūka to Puroretaria Bungaku" ("Massification and Proletarian Literature"). *Taishū no tōjo: hīrōtachi to dokusha no 20–30 nendai.* Ed. Ikeda Hiroshi. Tokyo: Inpakuto shuppankai, 1998.

Kurokawa, Sō. "Kaisetsu: Hata no nai bungaku." *Gaichi no nihongo bungaku sen 3: Chōsen.* Ed. Kurokawa Sō. Tokyo: Shinjuku shobō, 1996.

Kuropotokin o chūshin ni shita geijutsu no kenkyū. Facsimile edition. Tokyo: Senki Fukkokuban Gyōkai, 1978.

Kurosawa, Ariko. "Shukkyō suru shōjotachi: 1910–20 nendai, Yoshiya Nobuko, Kaneko Misuzu, Ozaki Midori, Hirabayashi Taiko, Hayashi Fumiko hoka" ("The Girls Who Left Their Hometowns: The 1910s–1920s, Yoshiya Nobuko, Kaneko Misuzu, Ozaki Midori, Hirabayashi Taiko, Hayashi Fumiko and others"). *Taishū no tōjo: hīrōtachi no*

20–30 nendai. Ed. Ikeda Hiroshi. Tokyo: Inpakuto shuppankai, 1998.

Kusabe, Kazuko. "Miyamoto Yuriko to Hayashi Fumiko no buntai: sono sanbunsei to jojōsei" ("The Literary Style of Miyamoto Yuriko and Hayashi Fumiko: Their Lyrical and Prose-like Qualities"). *Kindai joryū bungaku: Nihon bungaku kenkyū sōsho*. Tokyo: Yūseidō, 1983.

Lavin, Maud. "Photomontage, Mass Culture, and Modernity." *Montage and Modern Life: 1919–1942*. Ed. Matthew Teitelbaum. Cambridge, Mass.: The MIT Press, 1992.

Lew, Walter K. "Introduction to 'Crow's-Eye View.'" *Korean Culture* 13.4 (Winter 1992).

———. "Jean Cocteau in the Looking Glass: A Homotextual Reading of Yi Sang's Mirror Poems," *Muae* 1 (1995): 118–49.

———. "Yi Sang." *The Columbia Companion to Modern East Asian Literature*. Ed. Joshua S. Mostow. New York: Columbia University Press, 2003.

Lim, Chong-kuk. "I Sangu: Yo no gyakusa ni ikita hito." ("Personal Introduction: Lee Sang.") Trans. Pae Kang-Hwan. *Koria hyōron* 294 (December 1986): 49–58.

Linhartová, Vera. *Dada et Surréalisme au Japon*. Paris: Publications Orientalistes de France, 1987.

Lippit, Seiji M. *Topographies of Japanese Modernism*. New York: Columbia University Press, 2002.

Liu, Lydia H. *Translingual Practice: Literature, National Culture, and Translated Modernity: China, 1900–1937*. Stanford, Calif.: Stanford University Press, 1995.

Lodder, Christina. *Russian Constructivism*. New Haven, Conn.: Yale University Press, 1983.

Lower, Lucy. *Poetry and Poetics: From Modern to Contemporary in Japanese Poetry*. Ph.D. Dissertation, Harvard University, 1987.

Mack, Edward Thomas II. *The Value of Literature: Cultural Authority in Interwar Japan*. Ph.D. Dissertation, Harvard University, 2002.

Maeda, Ai. *Maeda Ai chōsakushū*. Tokyo: Chikuma shobō, 1989.

Marinetti, F. T. *Let's Murder the Moonshine: Selected Writings*. Ed. R. W. Flint. Trans. R. S. Flint and Arthur A. Coppotelli. Los Angeles: Sun and Moon Press, 1991.

Martin, Harris I. "Popular Music and Social Change in Prewar Japan." *The Japan Interpreter* 7.3–4 (Summer–Autumn 1972): 332–52.

Maruyama, Masao. "From Carnal Literature to Carnal Politics." *Thought and Behavior in Modern Japanese Politics*. Ed. Ivan Morris. London: Oxford University Press, 1969.

MAVO. July 1924–August 1925. Facsimile edition. Tokyo: Nihon kindai Bungakukan, 1991.

Minami, Hiroshi, et al. *Shōwa bunka: 1925–1945.* Tokyo: Keisō shobō, 1987.

———. *Taishō bunka.* Tokyo: Keisō shobō, 1965.

Minami, Kōjirō. "'Shikei senkoku' no chōsha" ("The author of *Shikei senkoku*"). *Nihon shijin* 6.1 (January 1926): 84–86.

Mitchell, Richard H. *Thought Control in Prewar Japan.* Ithaca: Cornell University Press, 1976.

Miterai, Tatsuo. "Taishō, Shōwa zenki" ("Taishō and early Shōwa"). *Nihon shinbun hyakunenshi.* Tokyo: Nihon shinbun renmei, 1962.

Miyake, Yoshiko. "Doubling Expectations: Motherhood and Women's Factory Work Under State Management in Japan in the 1930s and 1940s." *Recreating Japanese Women, 1600–1945.* Ed. Gail Bernstein. Berkeley: University of California Press, 1991.

Miyoshi, Masao. *Accomplices of Silence: The Modern Japanese Novel.* Berkeley: University of California Press, 1974.

Mori, Eiichi. *Hayashi Fumiko no keisei: sono sei to hyōgen.* Tokyo: Yūseidō, 1992.

———. "'Hōrōki ron: sono kisōteki kenkyū" ("A Study of *Hōrōki*: Fundamental Investigation"). *Kanazawa daigaku kyōiku gakubu kiyō: jinmon kagaku, shakai kagaku hen* 33 (February 1984).

———. *Shūsei kara Fumiko e.* Kanazawa: Noto insatsu, 1990.

Mori, Iwao. "Geijutsu no saisentan: kikai ni yoru hyōgen jidai" ("The Vangard of Art: The Age of Expression Through Machines"). *Bungaku jidai* 1.1 (May 1929): 140–48.

Motoe, Kunio. "Hakai to Sōzō no ishi: 'Konsutorukuchion.'" *Nihon no kindai bijutsu: zen'ei geijutsu no jikken.* Ed. Yurugi Yasuhiro. Tokyo: Taigestu shoten, 1993.

Murakami, Nobuhiko. *Taishō joseishi, jō.* Tokyo: Rironsha, 1982.

Murayama, Tomoyoshi. "*Bungei shijō* no koro" ("Around the time of *Bungei shijō*"). Supplement to the reprinted edition of *Bungei shijō*, ed. Senuma Shigeki. Tokyo: Nihon kindai bungakukan, 1976.

———. *Engekiteki jijōden.* Tokyo: Tōhō shuppansha, 1971.

———. "Higyakusha no geijutsu" ("Art of the Masochist"). *MAVO* 6 (July 1925).

———. *Kōseiha kenkyū.* Tokyo: Chūō bijutsusha, 1926.

———. "Kōseiha ni kan suru ikkōsatsu" ("An Observation About Constructivism"). *Atorie* 2.8 (August 1925): 45–58.

———. "Sugiyuku hyōgenha: Ishikiteki kōseishugi e no joronteki dōnyū" ("The Passing of Expressionism: A Preliminary Introduction to Conscious Constructivism"). *Chūō bijutsu* 9.4 (April 1923): 1–30.

Myers, Ramon H. "Japanese Imperialism in Manchuria: The South Manchuria Railway Company, 1906–1933." *The Japanese Informal Empire in China, 1895–1937.* Ed. Peter Duus et al. Princeton: Princeton University Press, 1989.

Myochin, Noboru. *Hyōden Anzai Fuyue.* Tokyo: Ōfusha, 1974.

Nagamine, Shigetoshi. *Modan toshi no dokusho kūkan.* Tokyo: Nihon editā sukūru shuppanbu, 2001.

Nagy, Margit. "Middle-Class Working Women During the Interwar Years." *Recreating Japanese Women, 1600–1945.* Ed. Gail Lee Bernstein. Berkeley: University of California Press, 1991.

Nakagawa, Shigemi. "Anzai Fuyue ron." *Toshi modanizumu no honryū: 'Shi to shiron' no rusupuri nūbō (L'esprit Nouveau).* Ed. Sawa Masahiro and Wada Hirofumi. Tokyo: Shōeidō, 1996.

————. "Hayashi Fumiko: onna wa sensō o tatakau ka" ("Hayashi Fumiko: Do Women Fight Wars?"). *Nanpōchōyōsakka: sensō to bungaku.* Ed. Kamiya Tadataka and Kimura Kazuaki. Tokyo: Sekai shisōsha, 1996.

————. "Hayashi Fumiko to sono jidai: Naruse Mikio sakuhin kara" ("Hayashi Fumiko and Her Age: From the Works of Naruse Mikio"). *Shōwa bungaku kenkyū* 18 (February 1989): 78–92.

Nakamura, Mitsuo. *Fūzoku shōsetsu ron.* Tokyo: Shinchō bunko, 1958 [originally published 1950].

Natsume, Sōseki. *Rediscovering Natsume Sōseki, celebrating the centenary of Soseki's arrival in England 1900–1902: with the first English translation of Travels in Manchuria and Korea.* Trans. Inger Sigrun Brodey and Ikuo Tsunematsu. Folkestone: Global Oriental, 2000.

Nihon shuppan hyakunenshi nenpyō. Tokyo: Nihon shoseki shuppan kyōkai, 1968.

Nii, Itaru. *Anakizumu geijutsu ron.* Tokyo: Yumani shobō, 1991.

————. "Kyōjiro to Shōhei no shi: 'Danpen' to 'Mekura to tenba' to ni tsuite" ("The poetry of Kyōjiro and Shōhei: on 'Danpen' and 'Mekura to tenba'"). *Kokushoku sensen* 2.1 (January 1932): 14–15.

————. "Yuibutsu bungaku no nitaiyō to sono botai" ("Two Forms of Materialist Literature and Their Wombs"). *Bungaku jidai* 1.1 (May 1929): 17–21.

Nyonin geijutsu. July 1928–June 1932. Facsimile edition. Tokyo: Funi shuppan, 1987.

Ogata, Akiko. *Nyonin geijutsu no sekai: Hasegawa Shigure to sono shūhen.* Tokyo: Domesu shuppan, 1980.

Oguma, Eiji. *A Genealogy of 'Japanese' Self-Images.* Trans. David Askew. Melbourne: Trans Pacific Press, 2002.

Okada, Tatsuo. "Insatsujutsu no rittaiteki danmen" ("A Three-Dimensional Section of Printing Techniques"). *Shikei senkoku.* Reprint edition. Tokyo: Nihon kindai bungakukan, 1972.

Okamoto, Jun. "Hanranki no geijutsu" ("Art in the Age of the Flood"). *Damu damu* 1 (November 1924): 33–37.

———. *Shijin no unmei: Okamoto Jun jiden.* Tokyo: Rippū shobō, 1974.

Okamoto, Shumpei. "The Emperor and the Crowd: The Historical Significance of the Hibiya Riot." *Conflict in Modern Japanese History: The Neglected Tradition.* Ed. Tetsuo Najita and J. Victor Koschmann. Princeton, N.J.: Princeton University Press, 1982.

Oketani, Hideaki. *Shōwa seishinshi.* Tokyo: Bungei shunjū, 1992.

Omuka, Toshiharu. "'Mavo' oboegaki: MV o megutte." *Musashino bijutsu* 76 (1989): 8–13.

———. "Tada = Dada: (Devotedly Dada) for the Stage: The Japanese Dada Movement 1920–1925." *The Eastern Dada Orbit: Russia, Georgia, Ukraine, Central Europe, and Japan.* Stephen C. Foster, general editor. New York: G. K. Hall, 1998.

———. *Taishōki shinkō bijutsu undō no kenkyū.* Tokyo: Sukaidoa, 1995.

Ono, Tōzaburō."Nihirisuto Rōpushin" ("Nihilist Ropshin"). *Damu damu* 1.1 (November 1924).

Ōsawa, Masamichi. "Kaisetsu: domin shakai undōshi no kokoromi" ("Commentary: The Experiment of a History of Peasants' Social Movements"). *Domin no shisō: taishū no naka no anakizumu.* Ed. Ōsawa Masamichi. Tokyo: Shakai hyōronsha, 1990.

Ōsugi, Sakae. *Ōsugi Sakae hyōronshū.* Tokyo: Iwanami shoten, 1996.

Ōya, Sōichi. *Ōya Sōichi zenshū.* Tokyo: Sōyōsha, 1981.

Ōyama, Ikuo. "Gaitō no gunshū: seijiteki seiryoku to shite no minshū undō" ("The Crowd in the Streets: On the Political Power of the Democracy Movement"). *Taishō daizasshi.* Tokyo: Ryūdō shuppan, 1978.

Pincus, Leslie. *Authenticating Culture in Imperial Japan: Kuki Shūzō and the Rise of National Aesthetics.* Berkeley: University of California Press, 1996.

Poggioli, Renato. *The Theory of the Avant-Garde.* Trans. Gerald Fitzgerald. Cambridge, Mass.: Belknap Press, 1968.

Punin, Nikolai. "Tatlin's Tower." *The Tradition of Constructivism.* Ed. Stephen Bann. New York: Da Capo Press, 1974.

Rhee, M. J. *The Doomed Empire: Japan in Colonial Korea.* Aldershot, Eng., and Brookfield, Vt.: Ashgate, 1997.

Robinson, Michael Edson. *Cultural Nationalism in Colonial Korea, 1920–1925.* Seattle: University of Washington Press, 1988.

Rubin, Jay. *Injurious to Public Morals: Writers and the Meiji State.* Seattle: University of Washington Press, 1984.

Said, Edward W. *Orientalism.* New York: Vintage Books, 1979 (originally published by Random House, 1978).

Sakai, Naoki. "Modernity and Its Critique: The Problem of Universalism and Particularism." *Postmodernism and Japan.* Ed. Masao Miyoshi and H. D. Harootunian. Durham, N.C.: Duke University Press, 1989.

Sakaki, Atsuko. "Japanese Perceptions of China: The Sinophilic Fiction of Tanizaki Jun'ichirō." *Harvard Journal of Asiatic Studies* 59.1 (June 1999) : 187–218.

Sakurai, Katsue. *Kitagawa Fuyuhiko no sekai.* Tokyo: Hōbunkan, 1984.

Sano, Kasami. "Bungei no taishūka" ("The Massification of Literature"). *Bungei sensen* 2.3 (July 1925): 1–2.

Sano, Masato. "Kankoku modanizumu no isō: I San shi to Anzai Fuyue o megutte" ("The Phase of Korean Modernism: Centering on Yi Sang and Anzai Fuyue"). *Shōwa bungaku kenkyū* 25 (September 1992): 31– 43.

———. "1930 nen Tōkyō-Shanhai-Keijō" ("Tokyo, Shanghai, Keijo, 1930"). *Nihon bungaku kenkyū ronbun shūsei 38: Yokomitsu Riichi.* Ed. Taguchi Ristuo. Tokyo: Wakagusa shobō, 1999.

Sas, Miryam. *Cultural Memory and Literary Movements: Dada and Surrealism in Japan.* Ph.D. Dissertation, Yale University, 1995.

———. *Fault Lines: Cultural Memory and Japanese Surrealism.* Stanford, Calif.: Stanford University Press, 1999.

Sato, Barbara. *The New Japanese Woman: Modernity, Media, and Women in Interwar Japan.* Durham, N.C.: Duke University Press, 2003.

Schwartz, William L. "L'Influence de la poésie Japonaise sur la poésie Française contemporaine." *Revue de Littérature Comparée* 6 (1926): 654–72.

Seidensticker, Edward. *Low City, High City: Tokyo from Edo to the Earthquake.* New York: Alfred A. Knopf, 1983.

———. *Tokyo Rising: The City Since the Great Earthquake.* Cambridge, Mass.: Harvard University Press, 1991.

Senuma, Shigeki. *Gendai bungaku.* Tokyo: Mokuseisha shoin, 1933.

Shih, Shu-Mei. *The Lure of the Modern: Writing Modernism in Semicolonial China, 1917–1937.* Berkeley: University of California Press, 2001.

Shimazaki, Osuke. "'Zōkeiteki henreki' josetsu: mavo shutsugen zengo no mokugekiteki kaisō" ("'Plastic' Itinerary: An Eyewitness Account of the Advent of Mavo"). *Nihon dezain shoshi.* Tokyo: Daviddosha, 1970.

Shin, Gi Wook, and Michael Robinson. "Introduction: Rethinking Colonial Korea." *Colonial Modernity in Korea.* Cambridge, Mass.: Harvard University Asia Center, 1999.

Shinchō nihon bungaku jiten. Tokyo: Shinchōsha, 1988.

Shinjuku rekishi hakubutsukan, ed. *Hayashi Fumiko: Shinjuku ni ikita hito.* Tokyo: Shinjuku rekishi hakubutsukan, 1991.

Shōwa joshi daigaku hifukugaku kenkyūshitsu. *Kindai nihon fukusōshi.* Tokyo: Kindai bunka kenkyūsho, 1971.

Shōwa kokusei sōran. Ed. Tōyō keizai shinpōsha. Tokyo: Tōyō keizai shinpōsha, 1991.

Silberman, Bernard S., and H. D. Harootunian, eds. *Japan in Crisis: Essays on Taishō Democracy.* Princeton, N.J.: Princeton University Press, 1974.

Silverberg, Miriam. "Advertising Every Body: Images from the Japanese Modern Years." *Choreographing History.* Ed. Susan Leigh Foster. Bloomington: Indiana University Press, 1995.

———. *Changing Song: The Marxist Manifestos of Nakano Shigeharu.* Princeton: Princeton University Press, 1990.

———. "The Cafe Waitress Serving Modern Japan." *Mirror of Modernity: Invented Traditions of Modern Japan* Ed. Stephen Vlastos. Berkeley: University of California Press, 1998.

———. "Constructing the Japanese Enthnography of Modernity." *The Journal of Asian Studies* 51.1 (February 1992): 30–54.

———. "The Modern Girl as Militant." *Recreating Japanese Women, 1600–1945.* Ed. Gail Bernstein. Berkeley: University of California Press, 1991.

Soeda, Tomomichi. *Enka no Meiji Taishō shi.* Tokyo: Tōsui shobō, 1982.

Solt, John Peter. *Shredding the Tapestry of Meaning: The Poetry and Poetics of Kitasono Katsue (1902–1978).* Ph.D. Dissertation, Harvard University, 1989.

Soviak, Eugene. "Tsushida Kyōson and the Sociology of the Masses." *Culture and Identity: Japanese Intellectuals During the Interwar Years.* Ed. J. Thomas Rimer. Princeton, N.J.: Princeton University Press, 1990.

Stanley, Thomas A. *Ōsugi Sakae: Anarchist in Taishō Japan: The Creativity of the Ego.* Cambridge, Mass.: Harvard East Asian Monographs, 1982.

———. "Tōkyō Earthquake of 1923." *Kodansha Encyclopedia of Japan,* vol. 8. Tokyo: Kodansha, 1983.

Steinhoff, Patricia G. "Tenkō and Thought Control." *Japan and the World: Essays on Japanese History and Politics in Honor of Ishida Takeshi.* Ed. Gail Lee Bernstein and Haruhiro Fukui. London: Macmillan Press, 1988.

———. 1969. *Tenkō: Ideology and Societal Integration in Prewar Japan.* Ph.D. Dissertation, Harvard University.

Suga, Hidemi. *Nihon kindai bungaku no 'tanjō': genbun itchi undō to nashonarizumu.* Tokyo: Ōta shuppan, 1995.

———. *Shiteki modanitei no keifu.* Tokyo: Shichōsha, 1990.

Suzuki, Sadami. *Modan toshi no hyōgen: jiko, gensō, josei.* Kyoto: Shirojisha, 1992.

Suzuki, Tomi. *Narrating the Self: Fictions of Japanese Modernity.* Stanford, Calif.: Stanford University Press, 1996.

Takahashi, Shinkichi. "'Shikei senkoku' no hihyō" ("A Review of *Shikei senkoku*"). *Nihon shijin* 6.1 (January 1926): 86–88.

Takahashi, Shūichirō. *Hakai to gensō: Hagiwara Kyōjirō shiron.* Tokyo: Kasama shoin, 1978.

Takami, Jun. *Shōwa bungaku seisui shi.* Collected in *Takami Jun zenshū,* vol. 15. Tokyo: Keisō shobō, 1972.

Takamure, Itsue. "Musan kaikyū no renai shisō" ("The Proletariat's Philosophy of Love"). *Bungei sensen* 2.3 (July 1925): 30–32.

Takematsu, Yoshiaki. "Metsubō suru teito: bungakushijō no kantō daishinsai" ("The Capital Destroyed: The Great Kanto Earthquake in Literary History"). *Haikyō no kanōsei: Gendai bungaku no tanjō.* Ed. Kurihara Yukio. Tokyo: Inpakuto shuppankai, 1997.

Takeuchi, Yoshimi. *Takeuchi Yoshimi zenshū.* Tokyo: Chikuma shobō, 1980.

Tanaka, Jun'ichirō. *Nihon eiga hattatsushi,* vol. 1. Tokyo: Chūō kōronsha, 1957.

Tanaka, Stefan. *Japan's Orient: Rendering Pasts into History.* Berkeley: University of California Press, 1993.

Taylor, Charles. *Sources of the Self: The Making of Modern Identity.* Cambridge, Mass.: Harvard University Press, 1989.

Terashima, Tamao. *Nantendō: Matsuoka Toraōmaro no Taishō, Shōwa.* Tokyo: Kōseisha, 1999.

Toda, Tatsuo. *Watakushi no kakochō.* Tokyo: Kōbunsha, 1972.

Tokunaga, Sunao. "Shinbunsha gai" ("Newspaper Company Street"). *Bungei shunju ōru yomimono gō* (July 1930): 278–79.

Tōmiya, Katsuo. "Kyōjirō no bannen" ("Kyōjirō's Last Years"). *Hagiwara Kyōjirō no sekai.* Ed. Itō Shinkichi and Kawaura Sanshirō. Maebashi: Kankodō, 1987.

———. "Watashi to Kyōjirō" ("Kyōjirō and Myself"). *Bochō, Takuji, Kyōjirō.* Ed. Seki Shunji et al. Tokyo: Miyama bunkō, 1978.

Totten, George O., ed. *Democracy in Prewar Japan: Groundwork or Facade.* New Haven, Conn.: Yale University Press, 1965.

Toyama, Masakazu, Yatabe Ryōkichi, and Inoue Tesujirō. *Shintaishi shō.* Facsimile edition. Tokyo: Nihon kindai bungakukan, 1972.

Truffet, Michel. *Edition critique et commentée de Cent Phrases Pour Éventails de Paul Claudel.* Paris: Annales littéraires de L'Université de Besançon, 1985.

Tsuboi, Hideto. *Koe no shukusai.* Nagoya: Nagoya daigaku shuppankai, 1997.

Tsuboi, Shigeji. "Dōnin Zakki" ("Editors' Random Notes"). *Aka to kuro* 4 (April 1923).

———. "Mumyō jidai no Hayashi Fumiko" ("Hayashi Fumiko Before Her Fame"). *Hayashi Fumiko shishū.* Tokyo: Shinchōsha, 1984.

———. "'Tani' o chūshin ni" ("Focusing on 'Valley'"). *Hagiwara Kyōjirō no sekai.* Ed. Itō Shinkichi and Kawaura Sanshirō. Maebashi: Kankodō, 1987.

———. *Tsuboi Shigeji zenshū.* Tokyo: Seijisha, 1989.

Tsurumi, E. Patricia. *Factory Girls: Women in the Thread Mills of Meiji Japan.* Princeton, N.J.: Princeton University Press, 1990.

———. "Visions of Women and the New Society in Conflict: Yamakawa Kikue Versus Takamure Itsue." *Japan's Competing Modernities: Issues in Culture and Democracy, 1900–1930.* Ed. Sharon A. Minichiello. Honolulu: University of Hawai'i Press, 1998.

Ueda, Makoto. *Modern Japanese Poets and the Nature of Literature.* Stanford, Calif.: Stanford University Press, 1983.

Ueda, Yasuo. "Josei zasshi ga mita modanizumu" ("Modernism as Viewed by Women's Magazines"). *Nihon modanizumu no kenkyū.* Ed. Minami Hiroshi. Tokyo: Burēn shuppan, 1982.

Umehara, Teikō, "Bazoku no uta: taishū bungaku no gaishi ni yosete" ("The Geneology of Song of the Mounted Bandits: Towards an Unofficial History of Popular Literature"). *Taishū no tōjo: Hīro to dokusha no 20-30 nendai.* Ed. Ikeda Hiroshi. Tokyo: Inpakuto shuppankai, 1998.

Unno, Hiroshi. *Modan toshi Tōkyō.* Tokyo: Chūō kōronsha, 1988.

Uranishi, Kazuhiko. "Kantō daishinsai to bungaku" ("The Great Kantō Earthquake and Literature"). *Kokubungaku: Kaishaku to kyōzai no kenkyū* 34.4 (March 1991 extra): 94–100.

Wada, Hirofumi. *Tekisuto no kōtsūgaku: eizō no modan toshi.* Kyoto: Shirojisha, 1992.

———. "Zen'ei geijutsu no nettowaaku: Hagiwara Kyōjirō 'Shikei senkoku' no kontekusuto." *Haikyō no kanōsei: Gendai bungaku no tanjō.* Ed. Ikeda Hiroshi et al. Tokyo: Inpakuto shuppankai, 1997.

Walker, Janet A. *The Japanese Novel of the Meiji Period and the Ideal of Individualism.* Princeton, N.J.: Princeton University Press, 1979.

Washburn, Dennis C. *The Dilemma of the Modern in Japanese Fiction.* New Haven and London: Yale University Press, 1995.

Watanabe, Kazutami. "Mō hitotsu no toshi shosetsu: Hayashi Fumiko 'Hōrōki' o megutte" ("One More Urban Novel: Concerning *Hōrōki*"). *Shōwa bungaku ronkō: Machi to mura to.* Ed. Odagiri Susumu. Tokyo: Yagi shoten, 1990.

Weisenfeld, Gennifer. *Mavo: Japanese Artists and the Avant-garde, 1905–1931.* Berkeley: University of California Press, 2002.

————. "Mavo's Concious Constructivism: Art, Individualism, and Daily Life in Interwar Japan." *Art Journal* 55.3 (Fall 1996): 64–73.

————. *Murayama, Mavo, and Modernity: Constructions of the Modern in Taisho Avant-garde Art.* Ph.D. Dissertation, Princeton University 1997.

————. "Omoiegakareru sanka: Kantō daishinsaigo no shutō o meguru gakatachi" ("A Catastrophe Memorialized: Painters in the Capital Following the Great Kantō Earthquake"). *'Mobo-Moga 1910–1935' ten.* Ed. Mizusawa Tsutomu et al. Kamakura: Kanagawa kenritsu gendai bijutsukan, 1998.

Williams, Raymond. "The Metropolis and the Emergence of Modernism." *Unreal City: Urban Experience in Modern European Literature and Art.* Ed. Edward Timms and David Kelley. Manchester: Manchester University Press, 1985.

Wolff, Janet. *Feminine Sentences: Essays on Women and Culture.* Cambridge, Eng.: Polity Press, 1990.

Won, Ko. *Buddhist Elements in Dada.* New York: New York University Press, 1977.

Yamada, Akira. "Hagiwara Kyōjirō!" *Shishin* 6.8 (August 1930): 65–68.

Yamamoto, Kikuo. *Nihon eiga ni okeru gaikoku eiga no eikyō: hikaku eigashi kenkyū.* Tokyo: Waseda daigaku shuppanbu, 1983.

Yanagita, Kunio. *Meiji Taishōshi: sesōhen.* Tokyo: Kōdansha, 1976.

Yi, Sang. "Crow's-Eye View." Trans. Walter K. Lew. *Korean Culture* 13.4 (Winter 1992): 33–40.

————. "Tong'gyŏng" ("Tokyo"). Trans. Michael D. Shin. *Muae* 1 (1995): 96–101.

————. *Yi Sang si chongjakchip.* Seoul: Kabin ch'ulp'an sa, 1978.

Yokochi, Shōjirō. "Hagiwara Kyōjirō." *Hagiwara Kyōjirō no sekai.* Ed. Itō Shinkichi and Kawaura Sanshirō. Maebashi: Kankodō, 1987.

Yokomitsu, Riichi. *Yokomitsu Riichi zenshū.* Tokyo: Kawade shobō, 1956.

Yosano, Akiko. *Travels in Manchuria and Mongolia: A Feminist Poet from Japan Encounters Prewar China.* Trans. Joshua A. Fogel. New York: Columbia University Press, 2001.

Yoshimi, Shunya. *Toshi no doramatourugī: Tōkyō, sakariba no shakaishi.* Tokyo: Kōbundō, 1987.

INDEX

Harvard East Asian Monographs
(* out-of-print)

156. George J. Tanabe, Jr., *Myōe the Dreamkeeper: Fantasy and Knowledge in Kamakura Buddhism*

157. William Wayne Farris, *Heavenly Warriors: The Evolution of Japan's Military, 500–1300*

158. Yu-ming Shaw, *An American Missionary in China: John Leighton Stuart and Chinese-American Relations*

159. James B. Palais, *Politics and Policy in Traditional Korea*

*160. Douglas Reynolds, *China, 1898–1912: The Xinzheng Revolution and Japan*

161. Roger R. Thompson, *China's Local Councils in the Age of Constitutional Reform, 1898–1911*

162. William Johnston, *The Modern Epidemic: History of Tuberculosis in Japan*

163. Constantine Nomikos Vaporis, *Breaking Barriers: Travel and the State in Early Modern Japan*

164. Irmela Hijiya-Kirschnereit, *Rituals of Self-Revelation: Shishōsetsu as Literary Genre and Socio-Cultural Phenomenon*

165. James C. Baxter, *The Meiji Unification Through the Lens of Ishikawa Prefecture*

166. Thomas R. H. Havens, *Architects of Affluence: The Tsutsumi Family and the Seibu-Saison Enterprises in Twentieth-Century Japan*

167. Anthony Hood Chambers, *The Secret Window: Ideal Worlds in Tanizaki's Fiction*

168. Steven J. Ericson, *The Sound of the Whistle: Railroads and the State in Meiji Japan*

169. Andrew Edmund Goble, *Kenmu: Go-Daigo's Revolution*

170. Denise Potrzeba Lett, *In Pursuit of Status: The Making of South Korea's "New" Urban Middle Class*

171. Mimi Hall Yiengpruksawan, *Hiraizumi: Buddhist Art and Regional Politics in Twelfth-Century Japan*

172. Charles Shirō Inouye, *The Similitude of Blossoms: A Critical Biography of Izumi Kyōka (1873–1939), Japanese Novelist and Playwright*

173. Aviad E. Raz, *Riding the Black Ship: Japan and Tokyo Disneyland*

174. Deborah J. Milly, *Poverty, Equality, and Growth: The Politics of Economic Need in Postwar Japan*

175. See Heng Teow, *Japan's Cultural Policy Toward China, 1918–1931: A Comparative Perspective*

176. Michael A. Fuller, *An Introduction to Literary Chinese*

177. Frederick R. Dickinson, *War and National Reinvention: Japan in the Great War, 1914–1919*

178. John Solt, *Shredding the Tapestry of Meaning: The Poetry and Poetics of Kitasono Katue (1902–1978)*

179. Edward Pratt, *Japan's Protoindustrial Elite: The Economic Foundations of the Gōnō*

180. Atsuko Sakaki, *Recontextualizing Texts: Narrative Performance in Modern Japanese Fiction*

181. Soon-Won Park, *Colonial Industrialization and Labor in Korea: The Onoda Cement Factory*

182. JaHyun Kim Haboush and Martina Deuchler, *Culture and the State in Late Chosŏn Korea*

183. John W. Chaffee, *Branches of Heaven: A History of the Imperial Clan of Sung China*

184. Gi-Wook Shin and Michael Robinson, eds., *Colonial Modernity in Korea*

185. Nam-lin Hur, *Prayer and Play in Late Tokugawa Japan: Asakusa Sensōji and Edo Society*

186. Kristin Stapleton, *Civilizing Chengdu: Chinese Urban Reform, 1895–1937*

187. Hyung Il Pai, *Constructing "Korean" Origins: A Critical Review of Archaeology, Historiography, and Racial Myth in Korean State-Formation Theories*

188. Brian D. Ruppert, *Jewel in the Ashes: Buddha Relics and Power in Early Medieval Japan*

189. Susan Daruvala, *Zhou Zuoren and an Alternative Chinese Response to Modernity*

*190. James Z. Lee, *The Political Economy of a Frontier: Southwest China, 1250–1850*

191. Kerry Smith, *A Time of Crisis: Japan, the Great Depression, and Rural Revitalization*

192. Michael Lewis, *Becoming Apart: National Power and Local Politics in Toyama, 1868–1945*

193. William C. Kirby, Man-houng Lin, James Chin Shih, and David A. Pietz, eds., *State and Economy in Republican China: A Handbook for Scholars*

194. Timothy S. George, *Minamata: Pollution and the Struggle for Democracy in Postwar Japan*

195. Billy K. L. So, *Prosperity, Region, and Institutions in Maritime China: The South Fukien Pattern, 946–1368*

196. Yoshihisa Tak Matsusaka, *The Making of Japanese Manchuria, 1904–1932*

197. Maram Epstein, *Competing Discourses: Orthodoxy, Authenticity, and Engendered Meanings in Late Imperial Chinese Fiction*

198. Curtis J. Milhaupt, J. Mark Ramseyer, and Michael K. Young, eds. and comps., *Japanese Law in Context: Readings in Society, the Economy, and Politics*

199. Haruo Iguchi, *Unfinished Business: Ayukawa Yoshisuke and U.S.-Japan Relations, 1937–1952*

200. Scott Pearce, Audrey Spiro, and Patricia Ebrey, *Culture and Power in the Reconstitution of the Chinese Realm, 200–600*

201. Terry Kawashima, *Writing Margins: The Textual Construction of Gender in Heian and Kamakura Japan*

202. Martin W. Huang, *Desire and Fictional Narrative in Late Imperial China*

203. Robert S. Ross and Jiang Changbin, eds., *Re-examining the Cold War: U.S.-China Diplomacy, 1954–1973*

204. Guanhua Wang, *In Search of Justice: The 1905–1906 Chinese Anti-American Boycott*

205. David Schaberg, *A Patterned Past: Form and Thought in Early Chinese Historiography*

206. Christine Yano, *Tears of Longing: Nostalgia and the Nation in Japanese Popular Song*

207. Milena Doleželová-Velingerová and Oldřich Král, with Graham Sanders, eds., *The Appropriation of Cultural Capital: China's May Fourth Project*

208. Robert N. Huey, *The Making of 'Shinkokinshū'*

209. Lee Butler, *Emperor and Aristocracy in Japan, 1467–1680: Resilience and Renewal*

210. Suzanne Ogden, *Inklings of Democracy in China*

211. Kenneth J. Ruoff, *The People's Emperor: Democracy and the Japanese Monarchy, 1945–1995*

212. Haun Saussy, *Great Walls of Discourse and Other Adventures in Cultural China*

213. Aviad E. Raz, *Emotions at Work: Normative Control, Organizations, and Culture in Japan and America*

214. Rebecca E. Karl and Peter Zarrow, eds., *Rethinking the 1898 Reform Period: Political and Cultural Change in Late Qing China*

215. Kevin O'Rourke, *The Book of Korean Shijo*

216. Ezra F. Vogel, ed., *The Golden Age of the U.S.-China-Japan Triangle, 1972–1989*

217. Thomas A Wilson, ed., *On Sacred Grounds: Culture, Society, Politics, and the Formation of the Cult of Confucius*

218. Donald S. Sutton, *Steps of Perfection: Exorcistic Performers and Chinese Religion in Twentieth-Century Taiwan*

219. Daqing Yang, *Technology of Empire: Telecommunications and Japanese Expansionism, 1895–1945*

220. Qianshen Bai, *Fu Shan's World: The Transformation of Chinese Calligraphy in the Seventeenth Century*

221. Paul Jakov Smith and Richard von Glahn, eds., *The Song-Yuan-Ming Transition in Chinese History*

222. Rania Huntington, *Alien Kind: Foxes and Late Imperial Chinese Narrative*